SOURCES
Notable Selections
in *Social Psychology*

Edited by

TERRY F. PETTIJOHN
Ohio State University

McGraw-Hill / Dushkin

A DIVISION OF THE McGRAW-HILL COMPANIES

Manufactured in the United States of America

Third Edition

10   9   8   7   6   5   4   3   2   1

Library of Congress Cataloging-in-Publication Data
  Main entry under title:
    Sources: notable selections in social psychology/edited by Terry F. Pettijohn.—3rd ed.
    Includes bibliographical references and index.
    1. Social psychology. I. Pettijohn, Terry F., *comp.*

                                                                    302
0-07-242258-0   ISSN: 1094-7639

Printed on Recycled Paper

About the Editor

TERRY F. PETTIJOHN is a professor of psychology at the Ohio State University at Marion, where he has been teaching psychology for over two decades. As an undergraduate, he attended Alma College and Michigan State University, where he earned his B.S. in 1970. He attended Bowling Green State University for graduate studies, obtaining his M.A. in 1972 and receiving his Ph.D. in psychology in 1974. He is the author of *Psychology: A ConnecText,* 4th ed., published in 1999 by Dushkin/McGraw-Hill, as well as the accompanying teaching and testing materials. He has also written many other teaching publications for psychology courses. He served as editor of *MicroPsych Computer Network Newsletter,* and he currently serves on the Advisory Board for McGraw-Hill/Dushkin's *Annual Editions: Psychology.* In addition to social psychology, he regularly teaches introductory psychology, experimental psychology, learning and memory, motivation, adjustment, and psychobiology. He has been recognized for his teaching efforts, including being a recipient of the University Distinguished Teaching Award three times. His current research interests include the study of social emotion, memory, and animal social behavior. He is a member of the American Psychological Society, the Psychonomic Society, the Animal Behavior Society, the Society for Computers in Psychology, and the American Psychological Association, where he is affiliated with the Society for Teachers of Psychology.

Preface

*I*t is hard to imagine a day in which our lives are not influenced by other people, directly or indirectly. We form impressions of other people, make decisions about the motives of our friends and acquaintances, and evaluate the attractiveness of individuals we meet. Through our experiences and interactions we form and modify our attitudes. We help people in need, are active in groups, and do things requested by others. We fall in love and sometimes have conflicts with others. These examples form the core of social psychology, the study of how an individual's behavior, thoughts, and feelings are influenced by others.

All of these situations come to life in *Sources: Notable Selections in Social Psychology*, 3rd ed., which brings together 42 selections of enduring intellectual value—classic articles, book excerpts, and research studies—that have shaped the study of social psychology and our contemporary understanding of it. This book provides the opportunity for readers to encounter firsthand many of the greatest thinkers in social psychology. It includes carefully edited selections from the works of some of the most distinguished psychological researchers and theorists, past and present.

The field of social psychology is not yet a century old. Like other areas of psychology, it has experienced an explosion of theories and research findings and has become extremely diverse. Although most social psychology textbooks cover the important topics in social psychology, they are not able to go into the depth required for complete understanding of the discipline. Textbooks summarize results of research studies, but the richness of the original sources is not available. The selections in this book provide the original sources for some of the landmark studies in the social psychology discipline. They allow students to obtain a "behind the scenes" look at how the leaders in social psychology think, feel, conduct research, and develop theories.

Many instructors want students to develop critical thinking skills in their courses. One excellent opportunity is to provide original articles and chapters written by the prominent social psychologists who carved out social psychology as we currently know it. Some of these writers are of historical significance, while others are on the cutting edge of research and knowledge today. Through reading what these psychologists have to say, students can truly appreciate what social psychology is and where it is going.

Students will come to appreciate the joys and difficulties of conducting research in social psychology. A number of the selections demonstrate how deception and debriefing can be used effectively in research settings. Students will also learn about hypothesis testing in social psychological research, and they will gain a better understanding of the conclusions presented in their textbooks.

Sources: Notable Selections in Social Psychology, 3rd ed., represents over 75 years of social psychological thought and application. The actual dates of publication range from 1924 to 1999. An effort has been made to portray social psychology as a dynamic and changing discipline. Obviously, new research has modified our understanding of various concepts. An original article might present some information that has been discredited since it was first published; however, the article is still important in a historical context. In many cases, the original work has stood the test of time. Reading these original sources provides a glimpse into the making of social psychology.

Glancing over the table of contents should convince you that many of the people most frequently cited in social psychology textbooks are included in *Sources: Notable Selections in Social Psychology*, 3rd ed. These widely recognized social psychologists have made major contributions to the field and are well-respected researchers and writers. Care has been taken to provide excerpts from sources that are representative of each person included. Of course, not everyone who made major contributions to social psychology was able to be included in the final table of contents. However, I believe that the rich diversity of social psychology is captured by the final selections.

REVISION PROCEDURE.   The challenge of revising this book was carefully considered. In the first two editions, I paid great attention to finding classic works that could best communicate the excitement of social psychology. Readability was the top priority, and each selection was carefully edited so that the essence of the original work could be readily understood. These goals also guided the development of the third edition.

I wanted to ensure that this new edition continued to be truly representative of the breadth of social psychology, both in terms of the distinguished people and of the important issues. I began by reviewing hundreds of sources that were not included in the first two editions as well as the most historical and contemporary influential articles. The second edition was reviewed by current users, and their evaluations of each selection were extremely valuable in making decisions about which ones to replace. I also asked my students to provide feedback. I believe that with the advice of many people I was able to significantly strengthen the book by including some of the best work of the past century.

New to the third edition are 12 selections from some of the most distinguished researchers, theorists, and writers in social psychology. Great care was taken to include gender and cultural diversity issues as they relate to the discipline. A number of the new selections take a sociocultural view of social psychological topics. Because of reviewer feedback, many of the new additions present the results of original research studies. In many ways, the most difficult task was deleting articles, many of which are extremely interesting and important.

Some of the selections in this book provide theories that have shaped the discipline of social psychology. Some discuss crucial issues that have confronted social psychologists during the past century. Together, they comprise a snapshot of social psychology as it currently exists, including the important landmarks of its history.

ORGANIZATION OF THE BOOK.   The selections are organized topically around the major areas of study within social psychology. Part 1 includes selections on Introducing Social Psychology; Part 2, Social Cognitive Processes; Part 3, Attitudes; Part 4, Social Interaction and Relationships; Part 5, Social Influence and Group Processes; Part 6, Helping and Aggression; and Part 7, Applications of Social Psychology. The selections are further organized into 14 chapters that parallel most introductory social psychology textbooks and therefore provide opportunities for students to read the original sources of topics as they are covered throughout the course. However, each selection is independent and can be assigned in any order that is convenient to the instructor.

SUGGESTIONS FOR READING EACH SELECTION.   As you read these original writings, it is important to keep in mind that ideas and standards have changed over the last century. In particular, ethical concerns and language usage need to be mentioned here. Currently, there exist very strict ethical guidelines for conducting psychological research. Today researchers must submit proposals to committees that ensure that ethical standards are met. Some of the studies carried out in the past would not be approved now. As you read these selections, consider the contribution of the research to social psychology and whether or not the benefits in extending knowledge outweigh the potential harm to the subjects who participated in the actual research studies.

Many early experiments in social psychology involved deception. In many cases the deception was crucial to the study because subjects might have behaved differently if the true purpose were revealed. As you read the selections that include deception, identify how deception was used and what steps were taken to debrief subjects. Can you identify alternative procedures in any of these studies? Remember that today there are very strict ethical guidelines and that many of the early studies would have to be altered if they were to be conducted today. Today informed consent and debriefing are standard procedures in social psychological research.

Each selection is representative of the time in which it was written. As psychologists have become more sensitive to ethical considerations over the years, they have also become more sensitive to the language used in writing. Some early writers were not very tactful when discussing gender or ethnic issues. Many of the older articles use the masculine pronoun *he* when referring to both men and women. You should view the selection in the context of when it was written and focus on the psychological issues rather than the semantic ones. These classic studies have had a major impact on the development of social psychology as a discipline and should be read from that perspective.

Some studies in social psychology have been criticized for using only college students as subjects. How generalizable are the results of research conducted on college students compared with the general population? Note, however, that some of the studies in this book did not use college students. For example, Hazan and Shaver (selection 9.3) printed a survey in a local newspaper, Milgram (selection 10.1) used adults who answered an ad in a newspaper, Baron (selection 12.2) interviewed people in a shopping mall, and Bandura, Ross, and Ross (selection 13.1) observed children displaying aggressive behavior.

Each selection is preceded by an introductory headnote designed to help you to get the most from reading it. Each headnote establishes the relevance of the selection, provides useful biographical information about the author, and includes a brief background discussion of the topic. I have also provided suggestions for understanding statistical tests and thought questions designed to guide your critical thinking. It is important to take the time to read the headnote before beginning the selection itself.

As you read these selections, you will experience firsthand the ideas of some of the most important and influential social psychologists. Remember that in most cases they are writing not to students but to other professionals in their field. This means that some of the selections will be more challenging to read, but it also means that you will gain a rare behind-the-scenes experience of how social psychologists think and write.

Try to take an active approach when reading each selection. For example, when reading an experiment, you should ferret out the research hypothesis, identify the independent and dependent variables, and analyze the research methodology. Does the experiment raise ethical concerns? Do the conclusions stem from the results? Can you spot any extraneous variables or suggest any alternative explanations? When reading a theoretical or summary article, you should organize the main themes, identify the conclusions, and question the applications to everyday social situations.

As you read a selection, try to picture the setting in which it was written. Note the date of publication and the institutional location of the author. If it is a research article, note the participants who served in the research. Many of the articles you will read were mainly concerned with American participants. Could the results be generalized to other cultures? How might a multicultural perspective affect the study? You might refer back to your textbook to determine how the selection fits into the overall literature. Was it written early or late in the author's career? Are there conflicting theories or research findings?

Let me make a couple of additional suggestions to help you get the most out of each selection. First, as mentioned above, be sure to read the headnote to gain background information on the topic and on the author. Recognize that some of these selections are easy to read and understand, whereas others are more complicated and involve challenging language, theories, or statistical concepts. You will be able to gain an understanding of the issues discussed in each selection. Try to focus on the main ideas and important details and not get bogged down with all of the minor supporting information. Remember that research journal articles include an introduction to the problem, a description of the research methods, a presentation of the results, and a discussion of the significance of the results. Book chapters often discuss and summarize research and theories and, thus, are written in a more informal style. When you finish reading a selection, reread the headnote to make sure that you focused on the important concepts. Finally, you should take notes on the writing and reflect upon the importance of the selection to social psychology.

SOCIAL PSYCHOLOGY RESOURCES ON THE INTERNET. Each part in *Sources* is preceded by an *On the Internet* page. On these pages, I have provided several Internet links that should be of interest to you as you investigate the topics presented in the book. There are many resources available on the Internet to help you learn about social psychology. In addition to the ones included for each part, here are three general social psychology sites that contain information and additional links to other resources:

Social Psychology Network—This comprehensive site, maintained by Scott Plous of Wesleyan University, contains numerous links and information on all areas of social psychology. Resources include links to social psychology topics, Ph.D. programs, lists of individual social psychologists, journals, and social textbooks.

`http://www.socialpsychology.org`

Social Psychology Archives: Jumping Off Place for Social Psychologists— This site, maintained by Karsten Schwarz of the University of Zurich, contains numerous links to references, social psychology sites, and information useful in social psychology. It features more worldwide links than most sites.

`http://swix.ch/clan/ks/CPSP1.htm`

Home page for APA Division 8, Society for Personality and Social Psychology   This site provides information on careers in social psychology as well as links to other organizations, information about research in personality and social psychology, and information about the organization itself.

`http://www.spsp.org`

A WORD TO THE INSTRUCTOR. An *Instructor's Manual With Test Questions* (multiple-choice and essay) is available for instructors using *Sources: Notable Selections in Social Psychology*, 3rd ed., in the classroom.

ACKNOWLEDGMENTS. I was extremely excited when I was first approached with the idea for including social psychology in the Sources series. For a long time I had wanted to be able to introduce my students to original writings in social psychology. I am thrilled to be able to share with students the excitement of learning directly from some of the most influential figures in social psychology.

This project is very much a joint effort. Although my name as editor is the only one on the cover, I had lots of help from many people. Whenever I had a question about the readability or relevance of a selection, my students provided comments and suggestions. I thank the many students who used the first two editions and took the time to provide evaluative feedback. Molly Beaver, Heather Copeland, Shelly Douce, Laura Haycox, Kathyrn May, Peggy Reeves, Tonya Samsel, Elizabeth Stahl, Brenda Thompson, and Curtis Tuggle have been very supportive. I especially appreciate the efforts of the Marion Library staff and head librarian Betsy Blankenship, who provided outstanding library research for this edition.

I sincerely want to thank the reviewers of the last edition:

Robin A. Anderson
St. Ambrose University

Casimir Danielski
St. Michael's College

Robert Egbert
Southern Adventist University

Glenn Geher
Western Oregon University

Jana Spain
High Point University

They provided many suggestions on potential sources and specific direction for the third edition.

All of the support people at McGraw-Hill/Dushkin were extremely helpful at each step of the way. My parents, Don and Ella Jean, provided suggestions for important topics in everyday life. My wife, Bernie, and my family—Terry and his wife, Shelley; Karen and her husband, Kenny; and Tommy—were supportive as I worked on this project. My son Terry, an assistant professor of social psychology at Mercyhurst College, was especially helpful in providing feedback on the readability and relevance of the selections.

Sources: Notable Selections in Social Psychology, 3rd ed., is designed particularly to meet the needs of those instructors who want to convey to students the richness of the social psychological perspective through original writings. I have worked hard to produce a valuable resource for the social psychology course and would very much appreciate any comments or suggestions that you might have on the book. Although I feel that these selections represent some of the most significant studies in social psychology, not everyone will agree with all of the particular selections. I promise to carefully consider all of your suggestions as the book goes through the revision process (my e-mail address is Pettijohn.1@osu.edu). I hope you find this collection useful in the classroom.

Terry F. Pettijohn
Ohio State University

Contents

PART ONE

Introducing Social Psychology

On the Internet . . .

Sites appropriate to Part One

This site contains a description of the *Journal of Personality and Social Psychology*, a table of contents with abstracts from the current issue, and a list of the tables of contents from previous issues. Looking over the current table of contents should provide you with an overview of recent topics of interest to social psychologists.

```
http://www.apa.org/journals/psp.html
```

This American Psychological Association site provides the full text of ethical principles for all psychologists. Topics include competence, integrity, professional and scientific responsibility, respect for people's rights and dignity, concern for others' welfare, and social responsibility.

```
http://www.apa.org/ethics/code.html
```

CHAPTER 1 The Social Psychological Approach

1.1 FLOYD HENRY ALLPORT

Social Psychology as a Science of Individual Behavior and Consciousness

As the discipline of psychology developed in the early part of the twentieth century, its various subfields began to form. Of the three major textbooks that helped to define social psychology—based on sociology, instinct, and psychology—Floyd Henry Allport's psychology text has been the most influential. Unlike some early social psychologists, he emphasized theory and experimentation on individual subjects. Although the area of social psychology continues to develop, this focus on individual behavior has remained constant.

Allport (1890–1978) earned his Ph.D. at Harvard University in 1919. He was a professor of psychology at Syracuse University, where he directed the country's first doctoral program in social psychology. Allport was the older brother of Gordon Allport, who was also influential in the field of social psychology.

This selection is from chapter 1, "Social Psychology as a Science of Individual Behavior and Consciousness," of Allport's book *Social Psychology*

(Houghton Mifflin, 1924). It is a landmark publication in the history of social psychology, as it clearly defines the field in terms of social influences on individual behavior and consciousness. Notice the emphasis on the individual person in a social context. How does this definition of social psychology differ from the one commonly used today? How would you define the field of social psychology?

Key Concept: early definition of social psychology

APA Citation: Allport, F. H. (1924). *Social psychology.* Boston: Houghton Mifflin. [Chapter 1, Social psychology as a science of individual behavior and consciousness]

T he Province of Social Psychology.   Behavior in general may be regarded as the interplay of stimulation and reaction between the individual and his environment. Social behavior comprises the stimulations and reactions arising between an individual and the *social* portion of his environment; that is, between the individual and his fellows. Examples of such behavior would be the reactions to language, gestures, and other movements of our fellow men, in contrast with our reactions toward non-social objects, such as plants, minerals, tools, and inclement weather. The significance of social behavior is exactly the same as that of non-social, namely, the correction of the individual's biological maladjustment to his environment. In and through others many of our most urgent wants are fulfilled; and our behavior toward them is based on the same fundamental needs as our reactions toward all objects, social or non-social.[1] It is the satisfaction of these needs and the adaptation of the individual to his whole environment which constitute the guiding principles of his interactions with his fellow men.

Social Psychology as a Science of the Individual. The Group Fallacy.   Impressed by the closely knit and reciprocal nature of social behavior, some writers have been led to postulate a kind of 'collective mind' or 'group consciousness' as separate from the minds of the individuals of whom the group is composed. No fallacy is more subtle and misleading than this. It has appeared in the literature under numerous guises; but has everywhere left the reader in a state of mystical confusion. Several forms of this theory will be examined presently. The standpoint of this book may be concisely stated as follows. There is no psychology of groups which is not essentially and entirely a psychology of individuals. Social psychology must not be placed in contradistinction to the psychology of the individual; *it is a part of the psychology of the individual,* whose behavior it studies in relation to that sector of his environment comprised by his fellows. His biological needs are the ends toward which his social behavior is a developed means. Within his organism are provided all the mechanisms by which social behavior is explained. There is likewise no consciousness except that belonging to individuals. Psychology in all its branches is a science of the individual. To extend its principles to larger units is to destroy their meaning. . . .

The individual, then, is the true organism, as he is the psychological unit of society. The group merely furnishes him with a social environment in which he may react. And organized society is essentially a set of rules for guiding his reactions so that they do not trespass upon the life processes of his fellow organisms.

Social Psychology and Sociology.   Behavior, consciousness, and organic life belong strictly to individuals; but there is surely occasion for speaking of the group as a whole so long as we do not regard it as an organism or a mental entity. The study of groups is, in fact, the province of the special science of *sociology*. While the social psychologist studies the individual in the group, the sociologist deals with the group as a whole. He discusses its formation, solidarity, continuity, and change. Psychological data, such as innate reactions and habitual and emotional tendencies of individuals, are explanatory principles upon which sociology builds in interpreting the life of groups. Other sciences also contribute to the same end. Certain sociologists speak of these universal human reactions as "social forces." For example, hatred of a common enemy may be designated as a social force in a country at war. The social psychologist's task is in this case the explanation of the causes and conditions of hatred in the individual, and the part played by his behavior in arousing this emotion in others. The sociologist is interested rather in the widespread effects of this reaction in unifying the group and producing concerted responses of great power in struggles between opposing groups.

Psychology in general, and social psychology in particular, are thus foundation sciences of sociology. Social psychology has in fact grown up largely through the labors of the sociologists. It is a mistake, however, to suppose, as some have done, that it is a branch of sociology rather than of psychology. Professor Ellwood, for example, prefers for social psychology the designation 'psychological sociology.' This seems to the present writer to minimize unjustly the claims of the psychologist. It is surely a legitimate interest to consider social behavior and consciousness merely as a phase of the psychology of the individual, in relation to a certain portion of his environment, without being concerned about the formation or character of groups resulting from these reactions. In spite of the good offices and interests of the sociologists the two sciences must remain separate branches of inquiry.

Behavior and Consciousness in Social Psychology.   The influence of one individual upon another is always a matter of behavior. One person stimulates and the other reacts: in this process we have the essence of social psychology. The means, however, by which one person stimulates another is always some outward sign or action; *it is never consciousness*. Both the stimulating and the reacting behavior may be at times *accompanied by* a social type of consciousness in the respective individuals; but there is, so far as we know, no immediate action of the consciousness of one individual upon the consciousness or behavior of another.[2] An attempt is current in certain quarters to limit the conception of society and the field of social psychology to types of social interaction where consciousness of others and of social relations exists. From the standpoint of the present work this limitation is both non-essential and narrow. Conscious-ness, as we have just intimated, exerts no influence, and therefore explains nothing in mutual reactions of human beings. In social psychology, as in non-social branches of the science, its rôle is descriptive rather than explanatory. Even in the most socialized and conscious of groups there are no forces hold-ing the group together, and no means of arriving at community of thought or organized life except through the interstimulation of one individual by the be-havior of another. It is, moreover, not a *'mental'* interstimulation, if by this term is meant a type of stimulation different from the physiological, for no type of stimulation other than physiological exists. It would seem more suitable, there-fore, to admit to the field we are considering all forms of animal life in which we find definite social behavior; that is, reactions of individuals to one another. The question whether social consciousness accompanies such social behavior in the lower forms of life, though of speculative interest, may be waived as non-essential in our present definition of social psychology. . . .

A Working Definition of Social Psychology. . . . Defining a science is of value only for the purpose of concentrating attention upon a group of allied problems. With this practical rather than dogmatic aim in view, the following definition of our field is proposed: *Social psychology is the science which studies the behavior of the individual in so far as his behavior stimulates other individuals, or is itself a reaction to their behavior; and which describes the consciousness of the individual in so far as it is a consciousness of social objects and social reactions.* More briefly stated, social psychology is the study of the social behavior and the social consciousness of the individual.

NOTES

1. An interesting point of difference, however, exists in the social as distinguished from other environmental relations. In the social sphere the environment not only stimu-lates the individual, but is stimulated *by* him. Other persons not only cause us to react; they also react in turn to stimulations produced by us. A circular character is thus present in social behavior which is wanting in the simpler non-social adjustments.
2. The hypothesis of telepathy is not sufficiently established to be admitted as a possi-bility in the present issue.

1.2 SANDRA D. NICKS, JAMES H. KORN, AND TINA MAINIERI

The Rise and Fall of Deception in Social Psychology and Personality Research, 1921 to 1994

Research is essential to the development of any discipline. Because of the focus of social psychology, researchers sometimes use deception in their studies. Deception involves withholding information about a study from participants until after their participation in the research is completed. Some researchers argue that if participants know the true purpose of a study, they might purposely alter their behavior, thus producing false data. However, it is generally agreed that there are costs involved when deception is employed. Intentional deception raises ethical issues in social psychological research.

Sandra D. Nicks earned her Ph.D. in experimental social psychology from St. Louis University. She taught at Oglethorpe University prior to accepting her current position at Christian Brothers University in Memphis, Tennessee. James H. Korn (b. 1938) received his Ph.D. in 1965 from Carnegie Mellon University, where he taught until 1974, when he accepted his current position at St. Louis University. Tina Mainieri was a professor at Claremont Graduate School when this paper was published.

This selection is from "The Rise and Fall of Deception in Social Psychology and Personality Research, 1921 to 1994," which was published in *Ethics & Behavior* in 1997. For this paper, Nicks, Korn, and Mainieri reviewed sample volumes of the major journals in personality and social psychology to determine the frequency of the use of deception in research studies. As you read this selection, try to understand the factors that have contributed to the rise and fall of deception in research over the years. How does deception affect the results of research studies? Do you think some research could have been done without the use of deception? Will computer simulation reduce social psychologists' need for deception in the future?

Key Concept: deception in research studies

APA Citation: Nicks, S. D., Korn, J. H., & Mainieri, T. (1997). The rise and fall of deception in social psychology and personality research, 1921 to 1994. *Ethics and Behavior, 7,* 69–77.

The frequency of the use of deception in American psychological research was studied by reviewing articles from journals in personality and social psychology from 1921 to 1994. Deception was used rarely during the developmental years of social psychology into the 1930s, then grew gradually and irregularly until the 1950s. Between the 1950s and 1970s the use of deception increased significantly. This increase is attributed to changes in experimental methods, the popularity of realistic impact experiments, and the influence of cognitive dissonance theory. Since 1980 there appears to have been a decrease in the use of deception as compared to previous decades which is related to changes in theory, methods, ethical standards, and federal regulation of research.

The practice of deceiving research participants has become part of the standard methodology in psychological research, particularly in social psychology. If we accept the *Handbook of Social Psychology* (Lindzey, 1954) as the storehouse of knowledge and standards of research practice in this field, we see that deception in research was not discussed as an issue in the first edition in 1954. In 1968, however, the second edition of the handbook contained a chapter on experimentation written as a guide for researchers that contained explicit instructions on the use of deception (Aronson & Carlsmith, 1968). A revised version of this discussion appeared in the third edition (Aronson, Brewer, & Carlsmith, 1985)....

METHOD

We defined deception as an explicit misstatement of fact: stating a false purpose for an experiment, giving incorrect information about stimulus material, providing false feedback to participants about their or someone else's performance, or the use of confederates. We found that, in general, instances of the use of deception can be determined reliably, but that it is more difficult to classify particular kinds of deception. For that reason our analysis concerns only the combined frequency of all types of deception.

The purpose of the first phase of our research was to determine when deception began to be used. The first author read the method sections of all articles that reported empirical studies with human participants in JASP [Journal of Abnormal and Social Psychology] from its beginning in 1921 through 1948 and counted the number of articles in which deception was used. Later, the second author repeated this search for JASP articles from 1921 through 1933 to confirm that we had found all instances of the use of deception in the early years of this journal. This resulted in the discovery of one additional article that reported the use of deception. As an additional check on reliability the second author also searched all articles in JASP for 1935, 1940, and 1945. We agreed on the classification for 88 of 89 articles....

In the second phase of this research, which covered the period from 1948 through 1994, six different raters reviewed articles. All raters used a standard scoring sheet on which they had recorded information from each article containing deception. In addition to the complete reference for the article, the critical information was a verbatim quotation that indicated how deception was used. Before gathering data each rater was required to demonstrate their understanding of the project by first correctly scoring a sample of articles. Early in this phase of our research we conducted occasional reliability checks that resulted in consistently high (over 95%) agreement on whether the article reported the use of deception. After 1950, when the format of journal articles had become standardized, it was much easier to determine whether deceptive methods had been used. The language concerning the use of deception almost always was specific; for example, "Subjects were misinformed..." or "were led to believe...," or it was stated explicitly that a confederate was used.

Raters reviewed sample volumes of JASP, its successor, JPSP [Journal of Personality and Social Psychology], the *Journal of Personality* (JP), and the *Journal of Experimental Social Psychology* (JESP). We selected these journals as being representative of mainstream research in personality and social psychology. We began with JASP in 1948 because that was the date used in the earliest previous survey (Seeman, 1969) and then used 2 to 6 year intervals....

DISCUSSION

This study concerned the growth of the use of deception in social psychological and personality research primarily as represented by the major journals in these fields. We realize that our sample does not include all of the literature of social psychology at any time in the history of this field, but we conclude that the pattern that we found is representative of general research practices.

That pattern has three phases: (a) the development of experimental laboratory methods from the 1920s through the 1950s, when deception in research grew slowly and irregularly; (b) a period from the 1950s through the 1970s characterized by theory development and the popularity of realistic impact experiments; and (c) the 1980s, when changes in theory, method, and ethical standards were related to what appears to be a decline in the use of deception in research as compared with earlier decades.

During the early decades of its development as a discipline, social psychology consisted of a scattered array of topics and issues, with no distinguishing theories to bind the field. Although Gordon Allport (1935) stated that attitudes should be the central topic of social psychology, most work in the area of attitudes concerned their measurement (Smith, 1983) rather than their manipulation in the laboratory. Similarly, measurement had been the focus in the field of personality through the 1930s (Craik, 1986).

Most research in social psychology and personality during this period did not involve manipulation of independent variables. Instead, psychologists were concerned with recording social behavior through naturalistic observation and field studies, as well as with measurement of attitudes and opinions (Craik, 1986; Jones, 1985). Many studies labeled as experimental did not include such features as control groups or random assignment, although materials might be presented to participants in a laboratory setting. With infrequent manipulation of independent variables, the use of deceptive techniques in research was less likely than in later years when certain variables could only be manipulated by deceiving participants.

Kurt Lewin had the greatest impact on theory and method in social psychology, and it was his students in the 1930s and 1940s who began to carry out realistic laboratory experiments that used extensive deception. Lewin came to the United States in 1933, and the research program that he established contained the beginnings of the use of confederates, cover stories, and staged situations. In that same year, Saul Rosenzweig (1933) published an analysis of the experimental situation in which he specifically suggested the use of deception. Following publication of that paper, more studies began to appear that reported using deception, although the practice still was not common.

After World War Two the randomized experiment became the method of choice in experimental psychology and analysis of variance became the favored statistical technique (Rucci & Tweney, 1980). Social psychological studies that incorporated experimental manipulation increased from 30% in 1949 to 83% in 1959 (Christie, 1965). The use of deceptive techniques was an effective way for social psychologists to control many of the problematic extraneous variables that were involved in studying significant human problems. This approach to research design required the careful definition and manipulation of experimental variables, and in social psychology that often required considerable creativity.

Our data show that in 1968 over half of the articles in JPSP used some form of deception. In the same year a new edition of the *Handbook of Social Psychology* (Aronson & Carlsmith, 1968) appeared and included a chapter on experimentation that was presented as a guide that would help graduate students and others learn how to do laboratory research. The authors described the deception experiment as an important way of creating experimental realism, which they said was an essential component of social psychological research. This chapter made it clear not only that deception was an accepted research technique, but that it was an effective way to study important social problems (the relevance issue of the 1960s) and that those who used it effectively were admired for their creativity.

The use of deception in its more dramatic forms led to an extended debate concerning its ethical implications. This debate began with Diana Baumrind's critique of [Stanley] Milgram's study of obedience (Baumrind, 1964). There were strong arguments that deception is harmful to participants, the profession, and to society (e.g., Kelman, 1967). Others saw most deception as innocuous and argued that many important questions would be unanswered without its use (e.g., Christensen, 1988). The ethics of deception continues to be of interest (Fisher & Fyrberg, 1994).

Attempts to regulate ethical research practices increased during the 1970s. In 1973 the American Psychological Association revised their ethical principles to place greater constraints on the use of deception (American Psychological Association, 1973). The investigator was now charged with the responsibility of insuring that the use of deception was justified by the study's prospective value, to consider alternative procedures, and, if deception was used, to debrief participants as soon as possible. Deception was not prohibited, however, as long as the investigator considered these issues.

Also during the 1970s, federal regulation of research with humans began to have a more direct impact on psychologists. In 1971, social and behavioral research specifically were included in the federal policy on protection of human subjects. In 1974, regulations on grants administration stated that all research with humans must be reviewed by institutional boards, not only research that placed participants at risk (Faden & Beauchamp, 1986). However, the impact of these regulations and the American Psychological Association ethical standards on the use of deception was not seen immediately and did not seem to have an effect until the 1980s.

After 1979 there appears to have been a gradual decline in the use of deception from the levels of the 1960s and 1970s. We also found a decrease in the percentage of studies using deception in JPSP and JP, and the percentage was lower in 1987 than in 1983 for all three journals that we surveyed. Similar to Sieber et al. (1995), we found increases for these same journals in 1989 and 1994. However, these increases were small for JPSP and JP and did not show the use of deception to have returned to the frequency of the 1970s. The data for JESP was more variable than for the other two journals, showing a slight increase in 1979 from 1973, a reduction in 1987, an increase in 1989 and then another reduction in 1994. From these results it appears that the use of deception has decreased from the levels seen in the 1960s and 1970s, with some variability in the last two decades. This apparent decline in the use of deception in social psychology research since the 1970s is related to changes in theory and research practices, as well as the impact of imposing more rigid ethical standards.

One major change in theory between 1979 and 1994 was from the dominance of cognitive dissonance theory to that of attribution theories. Bagby, Parker, and Bury (1990) found that citations to [Leon] Festinger in social psychological journals increased through the 1960s, peaked around 1972, and then gradually declined. In contrast, the rate of citations to [Fritz] Heider had peaked around 1975 with more than double the citations of Festinger and has only slightly declined since that period.

Jones (1985) discussed reasons for this shift in interest. First, it was easier to do attribution research that relied more on paper and pencil questionnaires than on elaborate scenarios with casts of confederates. Second, ethical standards changed accompanied by "the increasing pervasiveness of institutional monitoring of research practices" (p. 58). Partly because of the risk of rejection by institutional review boards, investigators became less willing to design experiments in which participants undergo manipulations that are psychologically uncomfortable.

Following the 1970s changes also were occurring in the types of methods used, with less emphasis being placed on randomized laboratory experiments and an increase in nonexperimental methods such as surveys and field studies (Adair et al., 1985; Vitelli, 1988; West, Newsom, & Fenaughty, 1992). We examined the articles for 2 years of JPSP and found an increase in the use of nonexperimental studies from 12% in 1973 to 23% in 1983.

In summary, we see that a combination of factors included the use of deception in research. Social psychologists developed a laboratory culture in which experimental realism and the impact experiment were valued. The leading theorists provided examples for acceptability in research methods, in terms of what was publishable and what was ethical. Deception also was fostered by the dominance of the randomized experimental design, which required manipulation of independent variables. Deceptive research practices were limited, however, by the codifying of ethical standards in psychology and federal requirements for external review. As new theories and topics became popular in the 1980s, there was a reduction in the extent to which dramatic staged situations were used, and there probably has been some decline in the use of all types of deception. Perhaps, as this century comes to an end, the realism in research will be confined to the virtual reality of the computer screen.

REFERENCES

Adair, J. G., Dushenko, T. W., & Lindsay, R. C. L. (1985). Ethical regulations and their impact on research practice. *American Psychologist, 40,* 59–72.

Allport, G. W. (1935). Attitudes. In C. Murchison (Ed.), *Handbook of social psychology* (pp. 798–844). Worchester, MA: Clark University Press.

American Psychological Association. (1973). *Ethical principles in the conduct of research with human participants.* Washington, DC: Author.

Aronson, E., Brewer, M., & Carlsmith, J. M. (1985). Experimentation in social psychology. In G. Lindzey & E. Aronson (Eds.), *The handbook of social psychology* (3rd ed., Vol. 1, pp. 441–486). New York: Random House.

Aronson, E., & Carlsmith, J. M. (1968). Experimentation in social psychology. In G. Lindzey & E. Aronson (Eds.), *The handbook of social psychology* (2nd ed., Vol. 2, pp. 1–79). Reading, MA: Addison-Wesley.

Bagby, R. M., Parker, J. D. A., & Bury, A. S. (1990). A comparative citation analysis of attribution theory and the theory of cognitive dissonance. *Personality and Social Psychology Bulletin, 16,* 274–283.

Baumrind, D. (1964). Some thoughts on ethics of research: After reading Milgram's "Behavioral study of obedience." *American Psychologist, 19,* 421–423.

Christensen, L. (1988). Deception in psychological research: When is its use justified? *Personality and Social Psychology Bulletin, 14,* 664–675.

Christie, R. (1965). Some implications of research trends in social psychology. In O. Klineberg & R. Christie (Eds.), *Perspectives in social psychology* (pp. 141–152). New York: Holt, Rinehart, & Winston.

Craik, K. H. (1986). Personality research methods: An historical perspective. *Journal of Personality, 54,* 18–51.

Faden, R. R., & Beauchamp, T. L. (1986). *A history and theory of informed consent.* New York: Oxford University Press.

Fisher, C. B., & Fyrberg, D. (1994). Participant partners: College students weigh the costs and benefits of deceptive research. *American Psychologist, 49,* 417–427.

Jones, E. E. (1985). Major developments in social psychology during the last past five decades. In G. Lindzey & E. Aronson (Eds.), *Handbook of social psychology* (3rd. ed., Vol. 1, pp. 47–108). New York: Random House.

Kelman, H. (1967). Human use of human subjects: The problem of deception in social psychology. *Psychological Bulletin, 67,* 1–11.

Lindzey, G. (Ed.). (1954). *A handbook of social psychology* (Vols. 1–2). Cambridge, MA: Addison-Wesley.

Rosenzweig, S. (1933). The experimental situation as a psychological problem. *Psychological Review, 40,* 337–354.

Rucci, A. F., & Tweney, R. D. (1980). Analysis of variance and the "second discipline" of scientific psychology: A historical account. *Psychological Bulletin, 87,* 166–184.

Seeman, J. (1969). Deception in psychological research. *American Psychologist, 24,* 1025–1028.

Sieber, J. E., Iannuzzo, R., & Rodriguez, B. (1995). Deception methods in psychology: Have they changed in 23 years? *Ethics and Behavior, 5,* 67–85.

Smith, M. B. (1983). The shaping of American social psychology: A personal perspective from the periphery. *Personality and Social Psychology Bulletin, 9,* 165–180.

Vitelli, R. (1988). The crisis issue assessed: An empirical analysis. *Basic and Applied Social Psychology, 9,* 301–309.

West, S. G., Newsom, J. T., & Fenaughty, A. M. (1992). Publication trends in JPSP: Stability and change in topics, methods, and theories across two decades. *Personality and Social Psychology Bulletin, 18,* 473–484.

A Glance Back at a Quarter Century of Social Psychology

Social psychology, like all disciplines, evolves over time as new findings expand knowledge of the subject matter. It is important for students of social psychology to learn about how the discipline has changed so they can better understand current research conclusions. As illustrated in this selection, the development of social psychology involves human changes as well as advances in research knowledge.

Ellen Berscheid earned her Ph.D. in social psychology from the University of Minnesota in 1965, where she is currently a regents professor of psychology. Berscheid has had a long and distinguished career researching and reporting on interpersonal attraction. She is coauthor, with Elaine Hatfield, of *Interpersonal Attraction* (Addison-Wesley, 1978) and *Close Relationships* (W. H. Freeman, 1983).

This selection has been excerpted from "A Glance Back at a Quarter Century of Social Psychology," which was published in the *Journal of Personality and Social Psychology* in 1992 as part of the American Psychological Association's centennial. In it, Berscheid reviews the previous 25 years of progress in social psychology from both a personal and a professional perspective. Note that the increase of women in social psychology mirrors changes in psychology as a whole. Berscheid also points out that some of the early theories in social psychology have shaped the direction in which the discipline has been moving. As you read the other selections in this book, notice the time periods in which they were written.

Key Concept: history of social psychology

APA Citation: Berscheid, E. (1992). A glance back at a quarter century of social psychology. *Journal of Personality and Social Psychology, 63,* 525–533.

*T*he remarkable evolution social psychology has undergone over the past quarter century encompasses so many changes in the field's form and content, in the number and nature of its contributors, as well as in the context in which it is embedded, both in psychology and in society, that which of these changes can be singled out for notice in a brief, informal retrospective is necessarily a very personal and impressionistic matter. The comments that follow, which highlight only three of the many changes the field has undergone in the past few decades, meet none of the historian's claims. I hope only to give the flavor of social psychology's evolution over the past 25 years, a period which is clearly demarcated for me, for it was in 1965 that I received my doctorate in social psychology from the University of Minnesota, where I have remained ever since. . . .

Ellen Berscheid

WOMEN IN SOCIAL PSYCHOLOGY

In my personal view, then, one of the biggest changes that has taken place in the past 25 years has been the increase in the number of women social psychologists and the dramatic improvement in our working conditions (improvement but not yet equality, according to Brush, 1991). In fact, my guess is that the proportional increase of women into research positions in social psychology was greater than in any other subarea of psychology. (Unfortunately, the APA [American Psychological Association] does not have the appropriate statistics, identifying researchers and nonresearchers, that would allow documentation of this point.)

There are several possible reasons for the influx of women into social psychology, but one that should be noted on an anniversary occasion is that the men who were influential in social psychology in 1965—and they were all men, as the identities of the founding fathers of SESP [Society of Experimental Social Psychology] reflects—were far more egalitarian in outlook and values than those in any other area of psychology. The overlap in membership between Divisions 8 (the Society of Personality and Social Psychology) and 9 (the Society for the Psychological Study of Social Issues) of the APA, as well as the pervasive influence of Kurt Lewin, his students, and such other important early social psychologists as Gordon Allport would suggest that women and minorities could expect a warmer reception in social psychology than in other domains of psychology. And, for the most part, we did. Many of these men are still alive and active today, and their extracurricular contribution to social psychology through training their own female students and through the other professional roles they played at the time should be acknowledged. In addition to those who trained us and gave us jobs, one also immediately thinks of such people as Bill McGuire, then editor of *JPSP*, and Bob Krauss, then editor of the *Journal of Experimental Social Psychology*, who made special efforts to include women in the research review and editorial enterprise, as well as the rapidity (1967) with which SESP put women on its program. It is important to note that these efforts to encourage women to join the mainstream of social psychology were made long before such actions were regarded as socially chic, politically correct, or legally mandated. In short, the "culture" of social psychology in 1965 was well ahead of its time.

It can be argued that the relatively rapid entry of women into social psychology had a number of salutary consequences for the development of the field. Perhaps the most important of these was to keep the caliber of talent high while social psychology was undergoing enormous growth. By allowing the other half of the human race to participate in the enterprise—a half equal to the other in what we graduate students used to call "raw *g*"—the intellectual talent devoted to social psychological problems was not diluted in quality as it expanded in quantity, as appears to have been the case in certain other subareas of psychology that shall remain nameless here but whose graduate student applicants' Graduate Record Examination scores and GPA records at Minnesota over the years tell the tale.

Second, the influx of women into social psychology influenced the approach taken to many traditional research questions in the field. In this regard, it should be noted that because women were admitted into the mainstream and thus worked on research questions central to the discipline, there has been less "ghettoization" of women in social psychology than there has been in many other disciplines. Rather than an alternative and "feminist" view of social psychology, one that offers an opposing view of the discipline's dominant knowledge domain, there has evolved, by and large, a single social psychology that has integrated, and has been enriched by, the different experiences and views that female social psychologists have brought to their work. Because examples of such enrichment abound, they perhaps are unnecessary, but one spontaneously remembers the sighs of recognition that greeted the Deaux and Emswiller (1974) article, whose subtitle, "What is Skill for the Male is Luck for the Female," said it all for many of us. The work of Alice Eagly and her colleagues also quickly comes to mind, for when I began teaching in 1965, it was a "fact," duly reported in the social psychology texts of the day, that women were more influenceable (read "gullible," "childlike," and "uninformed") than men, a finding that seemed to fit nicely into a constellation of data said to document the submissive and dependent nature of women. Those of us using those texts could only caution our students that not all women were easily influenceable (namely, their very own instructor) and once again drag out our all-purpose and over-used example of Golda Meir—the then Prime Minister of Israel and first female political leader of a major country in modern times, whom the daily news was revealing to be no docile "Mrs. Nice Guy"—as an illustration of the hazards of generalizing to the individual case. Sistrunk and McDavid (1971), of course, dealt the first empirical blow to the idea of woman's innate influenceability, but it was Eagly's (e.g., Eagly, 1978) work that buried it.

That work, in fact, turned up a subsidiary finding with important implications for the development of the social and behavioral sciences, both then and now. Pursuing the question of women's special influenceability with the then-new technique of meta-analysis, Eagly and Carli (1981) found an association between the sex of the researcher and the outcome of the experiment, such that both male and female researchers were more likely to find results favorable to their own sex. A tendency to produce findings favorable to groups intimately associated with the researcher's own identity, through unintentional and as yet unidentified mechanisms, argues that diversification of the researcher population—apart from moral, legal, and human resource utilization considerations—

serves an important scientific goal: Diversification protects against unintended and unidentified bias in any knowledge domain that purports to be applicable to all humans....

Ellen Berscheid

INCREASE IN THE STATUS AND CENTRALITY OF SOCIAL PSYCHOLOGY WITHIN PSYCHOLOGY

Rivaling in importance the increase in the number of women within social psychology over the past quarter century has been the increase in the status and centrality of social psychology within psychology. As Zimbardo (1992) recently observed, social psychology was "long relegated to a subordinate position within psychology's status hierarchy" (p. xiv), a delicate way of saying that back in 1965, and for many years after, social psychologists were the lowest of the low. When I went off to the business school, social psychologists were having a tough time in departments of psychology. The reigning prima dons were the "experimentalists" in learning psychology, easily recognized as they flapped through the halls in their white lab coats stained with rat urine and pigeon droppings. Searching for universal laws of behavior that would span millions of years of evolutionary time, from earthworms to Homo sapiens, and often using precise mathematical models to represent their hypotheses and findings (many of which later turned out to be much ado about not very much of enduring interest), the experimental psychologists, one must admit, were doing a fine job of imitating their acknowledged betters in the "hard" sciences, especially their much admired colleagues in classical physics (most of whom, ironically, were already dead in 1965 or in a deep funk and paralyzed into inactivity by the epistemological conundrums posed by the new physics; see, for example, Capra, 1982)....

Despite our efforts to ape our betters in the world of psychology, and no doubt sometimes because of them, social psychologists were frequently the objects of laughter and derision; we were regarded as soft headed and sloppy, an embarrassment, in fact, to "serious" psychologists. No one was immune. For example, even though the Laboratory for Research in Social Relations at Minnesota was among the first and most prestigious training grounds for social psychologists, with the likes of Leon Festinger, Stanley Schachter, Hal Kelley, and Elliot Aronson as psychology faculty in residence in its early years, when we left the lab to attend our psychology classes, we frequently heard social psychology ridiculed from the lectern. As an assistant professor, in fact, the first question the then-president of the local American Association of University Professors (AAUP) asked when we were introduced was "Why do you social psychologists take the abuse?" Embarrassed that word of our pariah status had seeped out of Elliott Hall into the wider world, I retorted, "Because tomorrow belongs to us!" The bravado of that reply owed as much to the fact that I had seen the movie *Cabaret* as it did to my faith in the future, for at that time we social psychologists were haunted by dark nights of the soul and afflicted with wrenching "crises of confidence" (e.g., McGuire, 1973). Now, from the distance of 25 years and a cool look back at the hostile context in which social psychology was developing, it seems no wonder that we were frequently driven to contemplate our collective navel and to question whether we had a place in the scientific universe. . . .

In 1965 social psychology was already theory rich, but it remained to be seen whether these theories would provide the muscle and sinew the field needed to develop. Festinger (1954, 1957) had offered his theory of social comparison processes a decade earlier (in 1954), and his theory of cognitive dissonance (in 1957) was already turning the field's attention away from "groupy" phenomena (see Steiner, 1974) to matters that today would fall under the general rubric of "social cognition." Heider (1958) had already published *The Psychology of Interpersonal Relations*, which elaborated his balance theory (sketched over a decade earlier in his hard-to-read 1946 article "Attitudes and Cognitive Organization" that had purportedly influenced Festinger's concept of cognitive dissonance, although Asch, 1946, also had started people thinking about consistency as a principle of cognitive organization). In this seminal work, Heider also discussed his observation that people often try to attribute causes to events, and E. E. Jones and Davis (1965) had already begun to flesh out attribution theory. Thibaut and Kelley (1959) already had published the first version of their theory of interdependence; Homans (1961) had presented his idea of "distributive justice" in social relationships, which shortly was to be elaborated in the equity theories; Newcomb (1956) already had drawn attention to problems in the prediction of interpersonal attraction in his APA presidential address and had recently published his study of *The Acquaintance Process* (Newcomb, 1961); and Schachter (1959) had presented both *The Psychology of Affiliation* and his article "The Interaction of Cognitive and Physiological Determinants of Emotional State" (Schachter, 1964). Moreover, Asch's (1946) empirical studies of conformity phenomena and of social perception were well-known, and the "Yale school's" work on attitude change (e.g., Hovland, Janis, & Kelley, 1953) had been around for a decade, with its "incentive motivation" view currently dueling with dissonance theory on the pages of the journals. There was much more, of course, but suffice it to say that, today, the names and the content of these theories will not strike even an undergraduate in social psychology as unfamiliar. Although some of these theories and the findings they produced may have been baffling from time to time, they were never boring, and they were never wholly abandoned. All were to prove to be vital building blocks for later theorists and investigators. And all have remained alive in the sense that they have been revised frequently in response to new findings—or they have been incorporated into other theories—or the findings they spawned have remained important in themselves or have played important roles in further theory development.

Perhaps the most impressive example of the cumulative nature of social psychology lies in the attribution area. From the theoretical outlines originally sketched by Heider (1958) to E. E. Jones and Davis's (1965) formulation to Kelley's (1967) rendering of "Attribution Theory in Social Psychology" two years later, the attributionists have patiently and systematically pursued their phenomena along a very long and winding road. A powerful chronicle of attribution theory and research over the past 25 years is presented in E. E. Jones's (1990) book, *Person Perception*. If social psychology is ever again required to defend itself against the charge of noncumulativeness, submission into evidence of this book alone would get the prosecution laughed out of court. And the attributionists aren't done yet; in fact, the best may be just around the bend, for two new and highly integrative theories of person perception recently have been offered, one by Susan Fiske and her colleagues (e.g., Fiske & Neuberg, 1990) and the other by Marilynn Brewer (1988).

Not only have social psychologists not been faddish about their theories, they haven't been flighty in their selection of the social behaviors they've sought to understand. In addition to the previously mentioned work on stereotypes and prejudice, begun in social psychology's infancy with the work of Gordon Allport and Kurt Lewin, and which now constitutes a theoretically impressive and practically useful body of knowledge (e.g., see Hamilton, 1981) that continues to be the subject of much current research (e.g., Swim, Borgida, Maruyama, & Myers, 1989), social comparison is still an active research area (e.g., Wheeler & Miyake, 1992), with its fruits extended over the years to illuminate other social phenomena of interest (e.g., Tesser, Millar, & Moore, 1988). Interpersonal attraction, that rockpile of theory and research on which some of us labored as graduate students, now helps form the core of the burgeoning interpersonal relationships wing of social psychology, where the cumulative and interdisciplinary nature of the work performed in this area over the past 3 decades was traced recently by George Levinger (1990) in his address to the International Society for the Study of Personal Relationships at Oxford University. Progress in this area can be illustrated by the fact that at the University of Minnesota we have graduated from Dr. Gregor Zilstein's (a.k.a. Stanley Schachter) frightening coeds with the prospect of electric shock, from Elaine Hatfield's designing computer dances for the Student Activities Bureau's freshman orientation week, and from Elliot Aronson engineering pratfalls for otherwise competent people, to the construction of a free-standing doctoral minor in Interpersonal Relationships Research. This new program will join the forces of scholars in psychology, the Institute of Child Development, family social science, sociology, that old business school (now spiffily named the Carlson School of Management), several colleges and departments in the health sciences, and more to train graduate students and facilitate research on interpersonal relationships. As this illustrates, social psychologists not only have burrowed ever more deeply into the social phenomena that were of interest 25 years ago, but another quality of our discipline has been revealed as it's matured: its boundary-spanning nature.

Social psychologists have expanded their knowledge domain in virtually every direction. Surveying the thousands of books submitted to *Contemporary Psychology* for review consideration these past several years, for example, we were continually surprised by the number of areas in which social psychologists are currently contributing theory and research. Reflecting this state of affairs, social psychology now often finds itself hyphenated to reflect its alliances with other subareas of psychology: social-development, social-clinical, social-personality, social psychology and law, social-health, social-organizational, social-educational, social-environmental, and social-community, for examples. Few subareas of psychology interface with and inform so many other scholarly endeavors within psychology as well as in those disciplines located on psychology's perimeter.

It has become apparent, in fact, that social psychology has emerged as a central pivot for much of contemporary psychology. In this regard, it is interesting to note that even those prognosticators of the future of psychology who see it vanishing as a discipline, with many of its current internal domains being absorbed by other disciplines, do not forsee such a fate for social psychology. Scott (1991), for example, who subscribes to the notion that psychology as we know it will disintegrate, predicted that

> Social psychology will continue to expand its strong experimental base, and will increasingly fulfill its promise to address society's most vexing problems. The solutions that emerge from social psychology laboratories will inform gender and racial issues and permeate the workplace, the inner city, and the home. Social psychology will become more practice oriented, affiliating with or creating its own professional schools ... (p. 976)

If Scott is correct, it may fall to social psychologists to carry psychology's banner into the 21st century.

In sum, contemporary social psychology, with its dynamic, ever-changing and -expanding, character, is an exemplar of all the social and behavioral sciences as they have been characterized by the National Research Council:

> Taking into consideration the dynamics of specialization, the development of data, theoretical shifts, and interdisciplinary activity—and the interactions of all of these with one another—the behavioral and social sciences resemble not so much a map as a kaleidoscope, with continuous growth, shifting boundaries, and new emphases and highlights (Adams, Smelser, & Treiman, 1982, p. 26).

Dynamic. And cumulative. Could anyone have asked more of social psychology 25 years ago?

REFERENCES

Adams, R. Mc., Smelser, D. J., & Treiman, D. J. (1982). *Behavioral and social science research: A national resource (Part I)*. Washington, DC: National Academy Press.

Asch, S. E. (1946). Forming impressions of personality. *Journal of Abnormal and Social Psychology, 41*, 258–290.

Brewer, M. (1988). A dual process model of impression formation. In T. K. Srull & R. S. Wyer (Eds.), *Advances in social cognition* (Vol. 1, pp. 1–36). Hillsdale, NJ: Erlbaum.

Brush, S. G. (1991, September-October). Women in science and engineering. *American Scientist, 79*, 404–419.

Capra, F. (1982). *The turning point: Science, society and the rising culture*. New York: Simon & Schuster.

Deaux, K., & Emswiller, T. (1974). Explanation of successful performance on sex-linked tasks: What is skill for the male is luck for the female. *Journal of Personality and Social Psychology, 29*, 80–85.

Eagly, A. H. (1978). Sex differences in influenceability. *Psychological Bulletin, 85,* 86–116.

Eagly, A. H., & Carli, L. L.(1981). Sex of researchers and sex-typed communications as determinants of sex differences in influenceability: A meta-analysis of social influence studies. *Psychological Bulletin, 90,* 1–20.

Festinger, L. (1954). A theory of social comparison processes. *Human Relations, 7,* 117–140.

Festinger, L. (1957). *A theory of cognitive dissonance.* Evanston, IL: Row, Peterson.

Fiske, S. T., & Neuberg, S. L. (1990). A continuum of impression formation, from category-based to individuating processes: Influences of information and motivation on attention and interpretation. In M. P. Zanna (Ed.), *Advances in experimental social psychology* (Vol. 23, pp. 1–74). San Diego, CA: Academic Press.

Hamilton, D. L. (Ed.). (1981). *Cognitive processes in stereotyping and intergroup behavior.* Hillsdale, NJ: Erlbaum.

Heider, F. (1958). *The psychology of interpersonal relations.* New York: Wiley.

Homans, G. C. (1961). *Social behavior: Its elementary forms.* New York: Harcourt, Brace & World.

Hovland, C. I., Janis, I. L., & Kelley, H. H. (1953). *Communication and persuasion.* New Haven, CT: Yale University Press.

Jones, E. E. (1990). *Person perception.* Hillsdale, NJ: Erlbaum.

Jones, E. E., & Davis, K. E. (1965). From acts to dispositions: The attribution process in person perception. In L. Berkowitz (Ed.), *Advances in experimental social psychology, Vol. II* (pp. 219–266). San Diego, CA: Academic Press.

Kelley, H. H. (1967). Attribution theory in social psychology. In D. Levine (Ed.), *Nebraska Symposium on Motivation* (Vol. 13, pp. 192–214), Lincoln, NE: University of Nebraska Press.

Levinger, G. (1990, July). *Figure versus ground: Micro and macro perspectives on personal relationships.* Invited address to the International Society for the Study of Interpersonal Relationships, Oxford University, Oxford, England.

McGuire, W. J. (1973). The yin and yang of progress in social psychology: Seven Koan. *Journal of Personality and Social Psychology, 26,* 446–456.

Newcomb, T. M. (1956). The prediction of interpersonal attraction. *American Psychologist, 11,* 575–586.

Newcomb, T. M. (1961). *The acquaintance process.* New York: Holt, Rinehart & Winston.

Schachter, S. (1959). *The psychology of affiliation: Experimental studies of the sources of gregariousness.* Stanford, CA: Stanford University Press.

Schachter, S. (1964). The interaction of cognitive and physiological determinants of emotional state. In L. Berkowitz (Ed.), *Advances in experimental social psychology,* (Vol. 1, pp. 49–80). San Diego, CA: Academic Press.

Scott, T. R. (1991). A personal view of the future of psychology departments. *American Psychologist, 46,* 975–976.

Sistrunk, F., & McDavid, J. W. (1971). Sex variable in conformity behavior. *Journal of Personality and Social Psychology, 17,* 200–207.

Steiner, I. D. (1974). Whatever happened to the group in social psychology? *Journal of Experimental Social Psychology, 10,* 93–108.

Swim, J., Borgida, E., Maruyama, G., & Myers, D. G. (1989). Joan McKay versus John McKay: Do gender stereotypes bias evaluations? *Psychological Bulletin, 105,* 409–429.

Tesser, A., Millar, M., & Moore, J. (1988). Some affective consequences of social comparison and reflection processes: The pain and pleasure of being close. *Journal of Personality and Social Psychology, 54,* 49–61.

Thibaut, J. W., & Kelley, H. H. (1959). *The social psychology of groups.* New York: Wiley.

Wheeler, L., & Miyake, K. (1992). Social comparison in everyday life. *Journal of Personality and Social Psychology, 62,* 760–773.

Zimbardo, P. G. (1992). Foreword. In Brehm, S. S. (Ed.), *Intimate relationships* (pp. XIV–XVI). New York: McGraw-Hill.

PART TWO

Social Cognitive Processes

On the Internet . . .

Sites appropriate to Part Two

The Social Cognition Paper Archive Information Center Web site includes abstracts of papers and links to researchers of social cognition.

```
http://www.psych.purdue.edu/~esmith/
   scarch.html
```

This is the site of the International Society for Self and Identity and contains information on the self and identity in daily life, abstracts of current research, links to other resources, and information on membership.

```
http://www.soton.ac.uk/~gramzow/ISSI/
```

CHAPTER 2

Social Perception

2.1 HAROLD H. KELLEY

The Warm-Cold Variable in First Impressions of Persons

Understanding how we develop impressions of other people is important to everyday life. Often we are able to assess a person's characteristics quickly and decide whether or not we like that person. Social psychologists have been interested in person perception since the 1940s. One of the earliest studies was Harold H. Kelley's 1950 experiment on first impressions.

Kelley (b. 1921) received his Ph.D. in group psychology from the Massachusetts Institute of Technology in 1948. His thesis was on first impressions in interpersonal relationships. After holding positions at the University of Michigan, Yale University, and the University of Minnesota, Kelley accepted a position at the University of California at Los Angeles in 1961, where he remained until his retirement in 1991.

This selection is from Kelley's classic study "The Warm-Cold Variable in First Impressions of Persons," which was published in the *Journal of Personality* in 1950. In a simple and straightforward experiment, Kelley found that a single word (*warm* or *cold*) could significantly alter participants' first impression of a person and could also determine the extent to which participants interacted with that person. What are the implications of impression formation research for people's everyday interactions? Do you think people are able to control the impressions that they make on others? What variables determine person perception?

Key Concept: person perception

APA Citation: Kelley, H. H. (1950). The warm-cold variable in first impressions of persons. *Journal of Personality, 18,* 431–439.

*T*hat prior information or labels attached to a stimulus person make a difference in observers' first impressions is almost too obvious to require demonstration. The expectations resulting from such preinformation may restrict, modify, or accentuate the impressions he will have. The crucial question is: What changes in perception will accompany a given expectation? Studies of stereotyping, for example, that of Katz and Braly (2), indicate that from an ethnic label such as "German" or "Negro," a number of perceptions follow which are culturally determined. The present study finds its main significance in relation to a study by Asch (1) which demonstrates that certain crucial labels can transform the entire impression of the person, leading to attributions which are related to the label on a broad cultural basis or even, perhaps, on an autochthonous basis.

Asch read to his subjects a list of adjectives which purportedly described a particular person. He then asked them to characterize that person. He found that the inclusion in the list of what he called *central* qualities, such as "warm" as opposed to "cold," produced a widespread change in the entire impression. This effect was not adequately explained by the halo effect since it did not extend indiscriminately in a positive or negative direction to all characteristics. Rather, it differentially transformed the other qualities, for example, by changing their relative importance in the total impression. Peripheral qualities (such as "polite" versus "blunt") did not produce effects as strong as those produced by the central qualities.

The present study tested the effects of such central qualities upon the early impressions of *real* persons, the same qualities, "warm" vs "cold," being used. They were introduced as preinformation about the stimulus person before his actual appearance; so presumably they operated as expectations rather than as part of the stimulus pattern during the exposure period. In addition, information was obtained about the effects of the expectations upon the observers' behavior toward the stimulus person. An earlier study in this series has indicated that the more incompatible the observer initially perceived the stimulus person to be, the less the observer initiated interaction with him thereafter.

The second purpose of the present experiment, then, was to provide a better controlled study of this relationship....

PROCEDURE

The experiment was performed in three sections of a psychology course (Economics 70) at the Massachusetts Institute of Technology. The three sections provided 23, 16, and 16 subjects respectively. All 55 subjects were men, most of them in their third college year. In each class the stimulus person (also a male) was completely unknown to the subjects before the experimental period. One person served as stimulus person in two sections, and a second person took this role in the third section. In each case the stimulus person was introduced by the experimenter, who posed as a representative of the course instructors and who gave the following statement:

> Your regular instructor is out of town today, and since we of Economics 70 are interested in the general problem of how various classes react to different instructors, we're going to have an instructor today you've never had before, Mr. ___. Then, at the end of the period, I want you to fill out some forms about him. In order to give you some idea of what he's like, we've had a person who knows him write up a little biographical note about him. I'll pass this out to you now and you can read it before he arrives. *Please read these to yourselves and don't talk about this among yourselves until the class is over so that he won't get wind of what's going on.*

Two kinds of these notes were distributed, the two being identical except that in one the stimulus person was described among other things as being "rather cold" whereas in the other form the phrase "very warm" was substituted. The content of the "rather cold" version is as follows:

> Mr. ___ is a graduate student in the Department of Economics and Social Science here at M.I.T. He has had three semesters of teaching experience in psychology at another college. This is his first semester teaching Ec. 70. He is 26 years old, a veteran, and married. People who know him consider him to be a rather cold person, industrious, critical, practical, and determined.

The two types of preinformation were distributed randomly within each of the three classes and in such a manner that the students were not aware that two kinds of information were being given out. The stimulus person then appeared and led the class in a twenty-minute discussion. During this time the experimenter kept a record of how often each student participated in the discussion. Since the discussion was almost totally leader-centered, this participation record indicates the number of times each student initiated verbal interaction with the instructor. After the discussion period, the stimulus person left the room, and the experimenter gave the following instructions:

> Now, I'd like to get your impression of Mr. ___. This is not a test of you and can in no way affect your grade in this course. This material will not be identified as belonging to particular persons and will be kept strictly confidential. It will be of most value to us if you are completely honest in your evaluation of Mr. ___. Also, please understand that what you put down will not be used against him or cause him to lose his job or anything like that. This is not a test of him but merely a study of how different classes react to different instructors.

The subjects then wrote free descriptions of the stimulus person and finally rated him on a set of 15 rating scales.

RESULTS AND DISCUSSION

Influence of warm-cold variable on first impressions. The differences in the ratings produced by the warm-cold variable were consistent from one section to another even where different stimulus persons were used. Consequently, the data from the three sections were combined by equating means (the S.D.'s [standard deviations] were approximately equal) and the results for the total group are presented in Table 1.... From this table it is quite clear that those given the "warm" preinformation consistently rated the stimulus person more favorably than [did] those given the "cold" preinformation. Summarizing the statistically significant differences, the "warm" subjects rated the stimulus person as more considerate of others, more informal, more sociable, more popular, better natured, more humorous, and more humane....

The free report impression data were analyzed for only one of the sections. In general, there were few sizable differences between the "warm" and "cold" observers. The "warm" observers attributed more nervousness, more sincerity, and more industriousness to the stimulus person. Although the frequencies of comparable qualities are very low because of the great variety of descriptions produced by the observers, there is considerable agreement with the rating scale data.

Two important phenomena are illustrated in these free description protocols, the first of them having been noted by Asch. *Firstly*, the characteristics of the stimulus person are interpreted in terms of the precognition of warmth or coldness. For example, a "warm" observer writes about a rather shy and retiring stimulus person as follows: "He makes friends slowly but they are lasting friendships when formed." In another instance, several "cold" observers describe him as being "... intolerant: would be angry if you disagree with his views..."; while several "warm" observers put the same thing this way: "Unyielding in principle, not easily influenced or swayed from his original attitude." *Secondly*, the preinformation about the stimulus person's warmth or coldness is evaluated and interpreted in the light of the direct behavioral data about him. For example, "He has a slight inferiority complex which leads to his coldness," and "His conscientiousness and industriousness might be mistaken for coldness." Examples of these two phenomena occurred rather infrequently, and there was no way to evaluate the relative strengths of these countertendencies. Certainly some such evaluation is necessary to determine the conditions under which behavior which is contrary to a stereotyped label resists distortion and leads to rejection of the label. . . .

TABLE 1

*Comparison of "Warm" and "Cold" Observers of Average Ratings
Given Stimulus Persons*

Item	Low End of Rating Scale	High End of Rating Scale	Average Rating Warm N = 27	Cold N = 28	Level of Significance of Warm-Cold Difference
1	Knows his stuff	Doesn't know his stuff	3.5	4.6	
2	Considerate of others	Self-centered	6.3	9.6	1%
3†	Informal	Formal	6.3	9.6	1%
4†	Modest	Proud	9.4	10.6	
5	Sociable	Unsociable	5.6	10.4	1%
6	Self-assured	Uncertain of himself	8.4	9.1	
7	High intelligence	Low intelligence	4.8	5.1	
8	Popular	Unpopular	4.0	7.4	1%
9†	Good Natured	Irritable	9.4	12.0	5%
10	Generous	Ungenerous	8.2	9.6	
11	Humorous	Humorless	8.3	11.7	1%
12	Important	Insignificant	6.5	8.6	
13†	Humane	Ruthless	8.6	11.0	5%
14†	Submissive	Dominant	13.2	14.5	
15	Will go far	Will not get ahead	4.2	5.8	

†These scales were reversed when presented to the subjects.

Influence of warm-cold variable on interaction with the stimulus person. In the analysis of the frequency with which the various students took part in the discussion led by the stimulus person, a larger proportion of those given the "warm" preinformation participated than of those given the "cold" preinformation. Fifty-six per cent of the "warm" subjects entered the discussion, whereas only 32 per cent of the "cold" subjects did so. Thus the expectation of warmth not only produced more favorable early perceptions of the stimulus person but led to greater initiation of interaction with him. This relation is a low one, significant at between the 5 per cent and 10 per cent level of confidence, but it is in line with the general principle that social perception serves to guide and steer the person's behavior in his social environment.

As would be expected from the foregoing findings, there was also a relation between the favorableness of the impression and whether or not the person participated in the discussion. Although any single item yielded only a small and insignificant relation to participation, when a number are combined the trend becomes clear cut. For example, when we combine the seven items which were influenced to a statistically significant degree by the warm-cold variable, the total score bears considerable relation to participation, the relationship being significant at well beyond the 1 per cent level. A larger proportion of those having favorable total impressions participated than of those having unfavorable impressions, the biserial correlation between these variables being .34. Although this relation may be interpreted in several ways, it seems most likely that the unfavorable perception led to a curtailment of interaction....

SUMMARY

The warm-cold variable had been found by Asch to produce large differences in the impressions of personality formed from a list of adjectives. In this study the same variable was introduced in the form of expectations about a real person and was found to produce similar differences in first impressions of him in a classroom setting. In addition, the differences in first impressions produced by the different expectations were shown to influence the observers' behavior toward the stimulus person. Those observers given the favorable expectation (who, consequently, had a favorable impression of the stimulus person) tended to interact more with him than did those given the unfavorable expectation.

REFERENCES

1. Asch, S. E. Forming impressions of personality. *J. abnorm. soc. Psychol.*, 1946, **41**, 258–290.
2. Katz, D., and Braley, K. W. Verbal stereotypes and racial prejudice. In Newcomb, T. M. and Hartley, E. L. (eds.). *Readings in social psychology.* New York: Holt, 1947. Pp. 204–210.

2.2   LEON FESTINGER

A Theory of Social Comparison Processes

We are social creatures; we continually interact with others. We also use others to confirm our perceptions of reality. Through social comparison we ensure that our attitudes conform to "the norm," and we assess our abilities as they compare with those of other people. Leon Festinger's theory of social comparison has been influential in the areas of social cognition and interpersonal relationships.

Festinger (1919–1989) earned his Ph.D. in psychology from the State University of Iowa in 1942. He taught at the Massachusetts Institute of Technology, the University of Michigan, and Stanford University before going to the New School for Social Research in New York City in 1968. Festinger contributed a number of theories to social psychology, including his theory of cognitive dissonance and his theory of social comparison.

This selection is from "A Theory of Social Comparison Processes," which was published in 1954 in *Human Relations*. Festinger's theory is based on the hypothesis that people are driven to evaluate their own opinions and abilities by comparing them to those of other people. What are the conditions under which we choose to compare ourselves with others? How important is social comparison in everyday life?

Key Concept: social comparison of opinions and abilities

APA Citation: Festinger, L. (1954). A theory of social comparison processes. *Human Relations, 7,* 117–140.

*I*n this paper we shall present a further development of a previously published theory concerning opinion influence processes in social groups (1). This further development has enabled us to extend the theory to deal with other areas, in addition to opinion formation, in which social comparison is important. Specifically, we shall develop below how the theory applies to the appraisal and evaluation of abilities as well as opinions....

Hypothesis I: *There exists, in the human organism, a drive to evaluate his opinions and his abilities.*

While opinions and abilities may, at first glance, seem to be quite different things, there is a close functional tie between them. They act together in the manner in which they affect behavior. A person's cognition (his opinions and beliefs) about the situation in which he exists and his appraisals of what he is capable of doing (his evaluation of his abilities) will together have bearing on his behavior. The holding of incorrect opinions and/or inaccurate appraisals of one's abilities can be punishing or even fatal in many situations.

It is necessary, before we proceed, to clarify the distinction between opinions and evaluations since at first glance it may seem that one's evaluation of one's own ability is an opinion about it. Abilities are of course manifested only through performance which is assumed to depend upon the particular ability. The clarity of the manifestation or performance can vary from instances where there is no clear ordering criterion of the ability to instances where the performance which reflects the ability can be clearly ordered. In the former case, the evaluation of the ability does function like other opinions which are not directly testable in "objective reality." For example, a person's evaluation of his ability to write poetry will depend to a large extent on the opinions which others have of his ability to write poetry. In cases where the criterion is unambiguous and can be clearly ordered, this furnishes an objective reality for the evaluation of one's ability so that it depends less on the opinions of other persons and depends more on actual comparison of one's performance with the performance of others. Thus, if a person evaluates his running ability, he will do so by comparing his time to run some distance with the times that other persons have taken.

In the following pages, when we talk about evaluating an ability, we shall mean specifically the evaluation of that ability in situations where the performance is unambiguous and is known. Most situations in real life will, of course, present situations which are a mixture of opinion and ability evaluation.

In a previous article (1) the author posited the existence of a drive to determine whether or not one's opinions were "correct." We are here stating that this same drive also produces behavior in people oriented toward obtaining an accurate appraisal of their abilities.

The behavioral implication of the existence of such a drive is that we would expect to observe behavior on the part of persons which enables them to ascertain whether or not their opinions are correct and also behavior which enables them accurately to evaluate their abilities. It is consequently necessary to answer the question as to how persons go about evaluating their opinions and their abilities.

Hypothesis II: *To the extent that objective, non-social means are not available, people evaluate their opinions and abilities by comparison respectively with the opinions and abilities of others.*

In many instances, perhaps most, whether or not an opinion is correct cannot be immediately determined by reference to the physical world. Similarly it is frequently not possible to assess accurately one's ability by reference to the physical world. One could, of course, test the opinion that an object was fragile by hitting it with a hammer, but how is one to test the opinion that a certain political candidate is better than another, or that war is inevitable? Even when there is a possible immediate physical referent for an opinion, it is frequently not likely to be employed. The belief, for example, that tomatoes are poisonous to humans (which was widely held at one time) is unlikely to be tested. The situation is similar with respect to the evaluation of one's abilities. If the only use to which, say, jumping ability was put was to jump across a particular brook, it would be simple to obtain an accurate evaluation of one's ability in this respect. However, the unavailability of the opportunity for such clear testing and the vague and multipurpose use of various abilities generally make such a clear objective test not feasible or not useful. For example, how does one decide how intelligent one is? Also, one might find out how many seconds it takes a person to run a certain distance, but what does this mean with respect to his ability—is it adequate or not? For both opinions and abilities, to the extent that objective physical bases for evaluation are not available, subjective judgments of correct or incorrect opinion and subjectively accurate assessments of one's ability depend upon how one compares with other persons....

Hypothesis III: *The tendency to compare oneself with some other specific person decreases as the difference between his opinion or ability and one's own increases.*

A person does not tend to evaluate his opinions or his abilities by comparison with others who are too divergent from himself. If some other person's ability is too far from his own, either above or below, it is not possible to evaluate his own ability *accurately* by comparison with this other person. There is then a tendency not to make the comparison. Thus, a college student, for example, does not compare himself to inmates of an institution for the feeble minded to evaluate his own intelligence. Nor does a person who is just beginning to learn the game of chess compare himself to the recognized masters of the game....

Hypothesis IV: *There is a unidirectional drive upward in the case of abilities which is largely absent in opinions.*

With respect to abilities, different performances have intrinsically different values. In Western culture, at any rate, there is a value set on doing better and better which means that the higher the score on performance, the more desirable it is. Whether or not this is culturally determined, and hence culturally variable, is an important question but one with which we will not occupy ourselves here.

With respect to most opinions, on the other hand, in the absence of comparison there is no inherent, intrinsic basis for preferring one opinion over another. If we thought of opinions on some specific issue as ranging along a continuum, then no opinion in and of itself has any greater value than any other opinion. The value comes from the subjective feeling that the opinion is correct and valid.

Hypothesis V: *There are non-social restraints which make it difficult or even impossible to change one's ability. These non-social restraints are largely absent for opinions.*

If a person changes his mind about something, deserts one belief in favor of another, there is no further difficulty in the way of consummating the change. It is true that there are sometimes considerable difficulties in getting someone to change his mind concerning an opinion or belief. Such resistance may arise because of consistency with other opinions and beliefs, personality characteristics that make a person lean in one direction or another and the like. But the point to be stressed here is that once these resistances are overcome, there is no further restraint which would make it difficult for the change to become effective.

There are generally strong non-social restraints, however, against changing one's ability, or changing one's performance which reflects this ability. Even if a person is convinced that he should be able to run faster or should be more intelligent, and even if he is highly motivated to improve his ability in this respect, there are great difficulties in the way of consummating the change....

Hypothesis VI: *The cessation of comparison with others is accompanied by hostility or derogation to the extent that continued comparison with those persons implies unpleasant consequences.*

Thus, in the case of opinions we expect the process of making others incomparable to be associated with rejection from the group. In the case of abilities, this may or may not be the case. It would be plausible to expect that there would rarely be derogation in making those below oneself incomparable. When making those above oneself incomparable, the presence of unidirectional push upward might lead to derogation in some instances.

The asymmetry introduced in the case of abilities is another difference we may expect to find. While in the case of opinions, deviation on either side of one's own opinion would lead to the same consequences, in the case of abilities there is a difference. The process of making others incomparable results in a "status stratification" where some are clearly inferior and others are clearly superior....

Hypothesis VII: *Any factors which increase the importance of some particular group as a comparison group for some particular opinion or ability will increase the pressure toward uniformity concerning that ability or opinion within that group.*

... If an opinion or ability is of no importance to a person there will be no drive to evaluate that ability or opinion. In general, the more important the opinion or ability is to the person, the more related to behavior, social behavior in particular, and the more immediate the behavior is, the greater will be the drive for evaluation. Thus, in an election year, influence processes concerning political opinions are much more current than in other years. Likewise, a person's drive to evaluate his intellectual ability will be stronger when he must decide between going to graduate school or taking a job....

IMPLICATIONS FOR GROUP FORMATION
AND SOCIETAL STRUCTURE

The drive for self evaluation concerning one's opinions and abilities has implications not only for the behavior of persons in groups but also for the processes of formation of groups and changing membership of groups. To the extent that self evaluation can only be accomplished by means of comparison with other persons, the drive for self evaluation is a force acting on persons to belong to groups, to associate with others. And the subjective feelings of correctness in one's opinions and the subjective evaluation of adequacy of one's performance on important abilities are some of the satisfactions that persons attain in the course of these associations with other people. How strong the drives and satisfactions stemming from these sources are compared to the other needs which people satisfy in groups is impossible to say, but it seems clear that the drive for self evaluation is an important factor contributing to making the human being "gregarious".

People, then, tend to move into groups which, in their judgment, hold opinions which agree with their own and whose abilities are near their own. And they tend to move out of groups in which they are unable to satisfy their drive for self evaluation. Such movement in and out of groups is, of course, not a completely fluid affair. The attractiveness to a group may be strong enough for other reasons so that a person cannot move out of it. Or there may be restraints, for one or another reason, against leaving. In both of these circumstances, mobility from one group to another is hindered. . . .

These selective tendencies to join some and leave other associations, together with the influence process and competitive activity which arise when there is discrepancy in a group, will guarantee that we will find relative similarity in opinions and abilities among persons who associate with one another (at least on those opinions and abilities which are relevant to that association). Among different groups, we may well expect to find relative dissimilarity. It may very well be that the segmentation into groups is what allows a society to maintain a variety of opinions within it and to accommodate persons with a wide range of abilities. A society or town which was not large enough or flexible enough to permit such segmentation might not be able to accommodate the same variety. . . .

SUMMARY

If the foregoing theoretical development is correct, then social influence processes and some kinds of competitive behavior are both manifestations of the same socio-psychological process and can be viewed identically on a conceptual level. Both stem directly from the drive for self evaluation and the necessity for such evaluation being based on comparison with other persons. The differences between the processes with respect to opinions and abilities lie in the unidirectional push upward in the case of abilities, which is absent when considering opinions and in the relative ease of changing one's opinion as compared to changing one's performance.

The theory is tentatively supported by a variety of data and is readily amenable to further empirical testing. One great advantage, assuming the correctness of the theory, is that one can work back and forth between opinions and ability evaluations. Some aspects of the theory may be more easily tested in one context, some in the other. Discoveries in the context of opinions should also hold true, when appropriately operationally defined, in the context of ability evaluation.

REFERENCES

1. Festinger, L., "Informal Social Communication," *Psychological Review,* 1950, 57, 271–282.

2.3 ABRAHAM TESSER

Toward a Self-Evaluation Maintenance Model of Social Behavior

Social psychologists have been trying to explain the role of cognition in social interactions. They note, for example, that people try to behave in ways that enhance their self-image. This process affects people's attitudes and performance when interacting with others. Abraham Tesser's self-evaluation maintenance (SEM) model of social behavior has been highly influential in this area of social psychological research.

Tesser (b. 1941) earned his Ph.D. in social psychology from Purdue University in 1967. He then went to the University of Georgia, where he currently is a research professor emeritus of social psychology. Tesser has written numerous research articles in the field of interpersonal communication and attitudes, and he is the author of the textbook *Advanced Social Psychology* (McGraw-Hill, 1995). He is a former editor of the *Journal of Personality and Social Psychology: Attitudes and Social Cognition,* and he served as president of the Society for Personality and Social Psychology in 2000.

This selection is from "Toward a Self-Evaluation Maintenance Model of Social Behavior," which was published in 1988 in Leonard Berkowitz, ed., *Advances in Experimental Social Psychology, vol. 21.* In it, Tesser describes his SEM model and provides evidence of its usefulness in predicting social behavior. He demonstrates how relevance and closeness of others affects the performance of the individual as well as that of the others. Note how the processes of reflection and comparison interact in various situations. This selection provides a look at how theories in social psychology guide research studies.

Key Concept: self-evaluation maintenance model

APA Citation: Tesser, A. (1988). Toward a self-evaluation maintenance model of social behavior. In L. Berkowitz (Ed.) *Advances in experimental social psychology* (Vol. 21, pp. 181–227). New York: Academic Press.

THE SELF-EVALUATION MAINTENANCE MODEL

The SEM model assumes that (1) persons behave in a manner that will maintain or increase self-evaluation and (2) one's relationships with others have a substantial impact on self-evaluation. The SEM model is composed of two dynamic processes. Both the *reflection process* and the *comparison process* have as component variables the closeness of another and the quality of that other's performance. These two variables interact in affecting self-evaluation but do so in quite opposite ways in each of the processes.

One's self-evaluation may be raised to the extent that a close other performs very well on some activity, that is, one can bask in the reflected glory of the close other's good performance. For example, one can point out her close relationship with her friend "the concert pianist" and thereby increase her own self-evaluation. The better the other's performance and the closer the psychological relationship, the more one can gain in self-evaluation through the reflection process. The intellectual parent of the reflection process is Cialdini's work on BIRGing (Cialdini, Borden, Thorne, Walker, Freeman, & Sloan, 1976; Cialdini & Richardson, 1980).

The outstanding performance of a close other can, however, cause one's own performance to pale by comparison and decrease self-evaluation. Being close to a high-performing other invites comparison and results in one's own performance looking bad, thereby adversely affecting self-evaluation. And, again, the better the other's performance and the closer the psychological relationship, the greater the loss in self-evaluation through the comparison process. The intellectual parent of the comparison process comes from social comparison theory (e.g., Festinger, 1954; Goethals, 1984; Suls & Miller, 1977) and is most closely compatible with Wills' (1981) idea of downward comparison.

In both the reflection process and the comparison process, if closeness or the level of the other's performance decreases, the effects of the reflection and comparison processes are attenuated or perhaps even reversed. For example, if the other person has little to do with oneself (i.e., is psychologically distant), one cannot bask in the reflected glory of his/her accomplishments nor is one as likely to engage in comparison processes. Psychological closeness is like unit relatedness (Heider, 1958): friends are closer than strangers, persons with more characteristics in common are closer than persons with fewer characteristics in common, and so on. (See Campbell & Tesser, 1985, for a more complete discussion of the closeness variable.) Similarly, if the performance of the other is mediocre, one cannot increase self-evaluation by reflection nor is one as likely to suffer decreases in self-evaluation by comparison.

It should be apparent from the description that both the reflection and comparison processes depend on the same two variables but have opposite effects on self-evaluation: when closeness and performance are high there is a potential gain in self-evaluation through the reflection process but there is a potential loss through the comparison process. That being the case, the question arises: when will a close other's outstanding performance raise self-evaluation (via reflection) or lower self-evaluation (via comparison)? To answer this question, the *relevance* variable is introduced.

Individuals can recognize, value, and attend to the performance of others on a large variety of dimensions. However, any individual has a personal stake in doing well on only a small subset of performance dimensions. For example, being a good football player may be important to an individual's self-definition, but being a good speller may be inconsequential. A dimension is important to an individual's self-definition to the extent that he strives for competence on the dimension, describes himself in terms of the dimension, or freely chooses to engage in tasks that are related to the dimension. Another's performance is *relevant* to an individual's self-definition to the extent that the performance is on a dimension that is important to the individual's self-definition and to the extent that the other's performance is not so much better or worse than the individual's own performance that comparisons are rendered difficult.

According to the SEM model the relevance of another's performance to one's self-definition determines the relative importance of the reflection and comparison process. If the other's performance is highly relevant, then the comparison process will be relatively important and one will suffer by comparison to the close other's better performance. If the other's performance is minimally relevant the reflection process will be relatively important and one can enhance self-evaluation by basking in the reflected glory of a close other's better performance.

Perhaps the best way to illustrate the operation of the model is through an example. Suppose Alice and her good friend Barbara try out for the high school symphonic band and only Barbara is selected. Suppose further that doing well in music is an important part of Alice's self-definition. Relevance is high, so the comparison process should be more important than the reflection process: since Barbara is close and performs better than Alice, there is a potential loss in self-evaluation for Alice. To prevent this loss, Alice can do a variety of things: she can alter the closeness of her relationship with Barbara. She can spend less time around her or focus on ways in which the two of them are different, etc. By reducing the closeness, the impact of Barbara's better performance is reduced. Alice can also change her self-definition. She can spend less time studying music or decide that butterfly collecting is much more interesting, etc. By reducing the importance of music to her self-definition, the relevance of Barbara's performance is reduced. The reflection process becomes relatively more important with the consequence that Alice may actually gain in self-evaluation through her close friend Barbara's good performance. Finally, Alice can attempt to affect Barbara's performance. By reducing Barbara's performance she also reduces the threat of comparison. She can break Barbara's reed or hide her music for the next tryout or she can come to believe that Barbara's good performance was based on luck, etc. Or, she can attempt to alter her own performance by practicing more.

SOME RESEARCH EXAMPLES

We have completed a number of studies now that tend to corroborate each of these strategies. Below I will review several of these studies to give you a feel for the kind of research that has been done. The studies look at changes in relative performance as a function of the relevance and closeness of the other person, changes in closeness as a function of the relevance and performance of the other, and changes in relevance or self-definition as a function of the other's closeness and performance.

The Effects of Closeness and Relevance on Performance

Affecting Another's Performance.   Suppose an individual is able to facilitate or hinder another's performance. Under what conditions will she facilitate the other's performance? Under what conditions will she hinder the other's performance? The SEM model suggests that the answer to these questions is conditional. That is, helping or hurting another depends on an interactive combination of the relevance of the performance dimension and the closeness of the other. When relevance is high the comparison process is more important than the reflection process. Thus, one will suffer by the other's good performance particularly if the other is close. Therefore, in order to avoid this threat to self-evaluation, when relevance is high the closer the other the less help one would expect the other to be given. On the other hand, when relevance is low, the reflection process is more important than the comparison process. One may bask in the reflection of the other's good performance, particularly if the other is close. In order to enjoy that reflection, then, when relevance is low the closer the other the more help should be given to the other.

To test this set of hypotheses, Jon Smith and I (Tesser & Smith, 1980) designed a laboratory experiment. Male subjects were recruited and asked to bring a friend to the lab with them. Each session was composed of two pairs of friends. The four subjects were individually seated in booths around the experimenter. They were told that they would participate in a verbal task. For half the subjects, the task was described as measuring important verbal skills, leadership, et cetera (high relevance). The remaining subjects were told that the task was not related to verbal intelligence or leadership or anything of importance that we could determine (low relevance). The task was actually based on the game *Password.* Each of these subjects, in turn, was given an opportunity to guess a target word from a set of clues. The clues ostensibly came from the other three participants who chose them from a list. Since the clues were graded in difficulty, the other participant could give clues that would make it easier or more difficult to guess the target word. The first two persons to guess the target word came from each of the two friendship pairs. By experimental arrangement, these two persons were made to perform poorly. It is the subsequent behavior of these two that we keep track of. If they want to help the other perform well (i.e., better than themselves), they could give clues that are easy; if they want to "hurt" the other (i.e., make him perform less well), they could give him difficult clues. The next two persons to perform were both friend and stranger to the former participants.

Common sense suggests (as well as a number of psychological theories) that one should help one's friend. However, the SEM model prediction is not that simple. When relevance is low and one can bask in the reflected glory of another's good performance, then, certainly one should help one's friend more than a stranger. However, this relationship should be attenuated and perhaps even reversed when relevance is high.

We looked at the number of experimental sessions in which the friend was helped more than the stranger and the number of sessions in which the stranger was helped more than the friend. The prediction from the SEM model was strongly upheld. When relevance was low the friend was helped more than the stranger in 10 of the 13 sessions. When relevance was high, the stranger was helped more than the friend in 10 of the 13 sessions. . . .

Affecting Own Performance.   If one conceptualizes performance in relative terms, then comparison and reflection processes can be affected not only by changing another's performance but by changing one's own performance as well. Let us focus first on relevant performance. When a close other's performance is relevant to one's self-definition there is the potential for one to suffer lowered self-evaluation via the comparison process. One way to reduce this potential is to increase one's own efforts (behavioral) or facilitatively distort the perception of one's own performance (cognitive).

There is some preliminary evidence consistent with both of these resolutions. Tesser, Campbell, and Campbell (reported in Tesser & Campbell, 1986) looked at own actual performance among high school students. Relevance of school was defined in terms of interest in having additional education. It follows from the model that given high relevance of school, (1) the better another's performance, the more one will try and, hence, the better one's own performance; and (2) this will be particularly true if the other is close (i.e., a friend). On the other hand, given low relevance, (3) the overall impact of others' performance on one's own should be attenuated, and (4) the difference between friends and nonfriends should also be attenuated.

The effects of socioeconomic status, sex, and race were statistically removed from each respondent's own grade point average (GPA). Respondents were divided in terms of high or low interest in school. Within these groups, respondents' own "residualized" GPA was correlated with the GPA of a classmate that the respondent nominated as a friend and a classmate that the respondent did not nominate as a friend. The pattern of correlations conformed to theoretical expectations. The only correlation which was significantly more positive than zero is that among high-relevance respondents and their friends. When school is relevant, i.e., respondents want more education, the difference between the correlations for friends and nonfriends is significant. When school is not relevant, the corresponding difference in correlations is not significant. None of the other differences in correlation are significant.

There is also evidence for the distortion of one's own performance. Tesser, Campbell, and Smith (1984) compared performance ratings that fifth and sixth graders made of their own performance on a relevant activity and on an irrelevant activity with the ratings made by their teacher. If the teachers' ratings are interpreted as an "objective" benchmark then the students distorted their performance upward on the relevant activity and downward on the irrelevant activity.

Although these studies are consistent with the present viewpoint, they are correlational and there are a number of plausible alternative explanations of the results. What is needed is a more detailed theoretical analysis and more focused research. Generally, I would expect that performance which is important to one's self-definition is well practiced and actually difficult to improve. So it becomes important to specify the conditions under which threat from the comparison process will affect increased efforts to improve own performance. Since it is difficult to improve performance, attempts at actual improvement should be more likely when another's performance is unambiguously better than one's own performance (and difficult to distort) and it is difficult or costly to reduce the level of that close other's performance. Further, if one believes that effort will result in better performance, then increased task effort might be more likely as a result of the threat of comparison.

The good performance of a close other could result in increased own effort because the other's performance is "inspirational." That is, the good performance of a close other may redefine the possibilities for the self: "If he/she can do it so can I." My guess is that the inspirational effect is most likely when (1) the close other has not outperformed the self in the past and/or (2) the other's better performance relies on a new (to the self) instrumentality. Both conditions define a *possibility* for self-improvement: in the first instance, when someone who has not been better than the actor becomes better than the actor it may suggest that the actor can also improve. The introduction of a new instrumentality, the second condition, also suggests that the actor can improve himself, this time by doing things differently.

To this point we have focused on the conditions under which persons may attempt to increase their own efforts to make their performance better. The SEM model suggests that there are also circumstances under which one may actually perform at a less-than-optimal level. In dealing with the maximization of own performance we focused on the comparison process of the SEM model. People can maintain a positive self-evaluation by the reflection process as well. One can bask in the reflected glory of a close other's outstanding performance if that performance has little relevance to one's self-definition. One way of making another's performance look good is to make one's own (relative) performance look bad. This leads to the prediction that when the performance of another is low in relevance to the self the closer the other the greater the possibility that one will actually perform poorer than he/she would when that other's performance is self-relevant.

Since there is a general tendency for people to want to do well, the prediction of self-handicapping may not seem plausible. Therefore, qualifications of this prediction may be in order. For example, from an intuitive perspective the relevance of the activity to the other person should play a role. If the performance is highly relevant to the other (but low in relevance to the self), there is an added inducement to handicap one's own performance. Under high relevance to the other, one's own poorer performances provide something for the other. That is, while the self is basking in the other's (relative) accomplishment, the other is not threatened by comparison. The closer the other the more important the other's potential feelings. Therefore, the closer the other person the greater the impact of relevance-to-other on self's own performance.

Clearly, this line of thinking is speculative. A better understanding of the determinant of own effort on own self-handicapping is important from both a practical and a theoretical perspective. It would seem then that this would be a productive line of research to pursue.

The Effects of Relevance and Performance on Closeness

Now we focus on some research dealing with the effects of relevance and performance on closeness. How should relevance, or self-definition, interact with another's performance to affect closeness? Let's go back to the basic dynamics of the SEM model to make a prediction. When relevance is high the comparison process is more important than the reflection process and one will suffer by the other's good performance, particularly if the other is close. In order to avoid this potential threat to self-evaluation we would expect that when relevance is high the better the other's performance the less close or the more distance one will put between one's self and the other. On the other hand, when relevance is low and the reflection process is important there is the possibility of basking in the reflected glory of another's good performance, particularly if that other is close. Therefore, in order to experience that potential gain, when relevance is low, the better the other's performance the closer one should put oneself to another.

To test this hypothesis, we (Pleban & Tesser, 1981) returned to the laboratory. When our male subjects showed up they found one other subject already there. Both participants filled out a questionnaire which asked them to indicate how important various areas were to their self-definition. The areas consisted of things like rock music, current events, hunting and fishing, and so on. After finishing the questionnaire, the two subjects competed in a kind of college bowl competition. The experimenter, on a random basis, selected a topic that was either high or low in relevance to the subject's self-definition. The other subject, actually a confederate, had previously memorized the answers to all the questions. When the questioning began, the confederate varied his performance so that he either clearly outperformed the real subject, performed about the same, or was outperformed by the real subject. Following the question-and-answer period the subjects were given feedback about how they did. The subject learned that he had performed about average, near the 50th percentile. The subject also learned that the confederate was clearly better (performing at the 80th percentile), slightly better (performing at the 60th percentile), slightly worse (performing at the 40th percentile), or much worse (performing at the 20th percentile). Thus, we had manipulated relevance to the subjects' self-definition and the relative performance of the other.

In order to measure closeness, we asked the subjects to go into an adjoining room. The confederate sat down first and we simply measured how close or far the subject sat from the confederate. After they were seated, a questionnaire

FIGURE 1

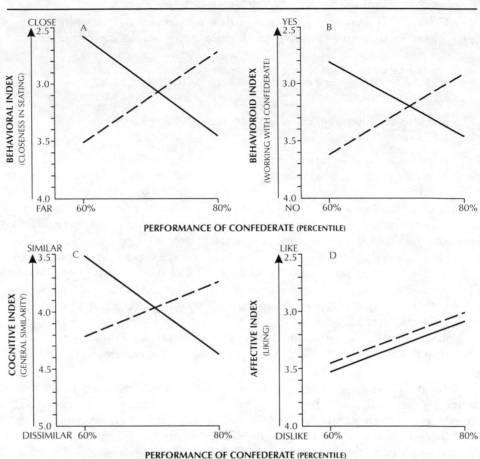

The effects of relative performance and relevance on closeness to other as indexed by behavioral, behavioroid, cognitive, and affective indices. Solid lines indicate high relevance; broken lines indicate low relevance. From Pleban and Tesser (1981).

containing alternative, paper and pencil, measures of closeness was administered. Recall our expectations: when relevance is high, the better the other's performance the less close the subject should put himself to the other. When relevance is low, the better the other's performance the closer the subject should put himself to the other.

It should be noted at the outset that level of performance made no difference when the subject outperformed the confederate. However, when the confederate outperformed the subject, each of the expectations from the SEM model was sustained. Let us look first at the behavioral index (see Fig. 1), the distance the individual sat from the confederate. As can be seen, as the confederate's performance improved from the 60th percentile to the 80th percentile the subject's distance increased when the topic was one of high relevance; the subject's distance decreased or closeness increased when the topic was of low relevance. Similar effects were obtained with the behavioroid index (Aronson & Carlsmith, 1968). "Would you want to work with this (confederate) again?" and with the cognitive index, "How much are you and this confederate alike?" There were no reliable effects on the affect index, "How attracted are you to this confederate?" Taken together these results offer some nice support for the hypotheses and also suggest that the closeness variable be defined in unit-formation terms rather than affect terms. Both the behavioral and the cognitive indices of closeness showed the predicted effect, while the affective index did not....

The Effects of Performance and Closeness on Relevance

Now let us turn to some examples of research on the determinants of self-definition or the relevance parameter. Again, the model makes some very specific predictions. Recall that the relevance parameter directly weights the comparison process and inversely weights the reflection process. When another's performance is better than one's own, one should reduce the relevance of that performance dimension. This would permit one to bask in reflected glory rather than suffer by comparison. Further, one's tendency to reduce relevance should be greater the closer the other person. In short, the better another's performance in an activity the less relevant should that activity be to one's self-definition, particularly if the other person is close.

The study to be described here has both behavioral and cognitive measures of relevance of self-definition. The laboratory study was completed in collaboration with Del Paulhus (Tesser & Paulhus, 1983). Pairs of male subjects were told that the experiment concerned the validation of a personality inventory. Half the subjects were led to believe that the two of them were scheduled at the same time because they were very much alike in a number of different ways (the close condition). The remaining subjects were led to believe that they were scheduled at the same time because they were very different from one another (the distant condition). The subjects were then seated before a microcomputer and worked on a task which they were told measured cognitive–perceptual integration. After working on the task for some time, they were given feedback. Subjects learned that they had outperformed the other subject or that the other subject had outperformed them at cognitive–perceptual integration. Thus, we had manipulated closeness and performance. (The study was actually more involved than this and dealt with the issue of public versus private self-evaluation maintenance. This issue, however, is beyond the scope of this article. See Tesser & Barbee, 1985; Tesser & Moore, 1987; and Tesser & Paulhus, 1983, for discussion.) There were three measures of relevance: an interview measure in which the subjects were asked how important cognitive–perceptual integration was to them; a questionnaire measure, again asking how important cognitive–perceptual integration was; and a behavioral measure. The behavioral measure involved surreptitiously observing the amount of time the subjects spent reading biographies of persons they believed were high in cognitive–perceptual integration versus low in cognitive–perceptual integration.

Each of the measures produced the same pattern of results. They were therefore combined and are displayed in Fig. 2. Recall our prediction: the better

FIGURE 2

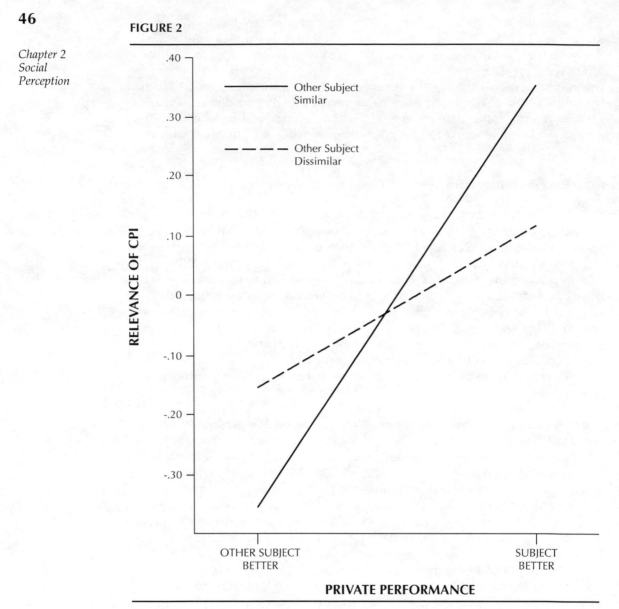

The effects of relative performance on cognitive–perceptual integration (CPI) and similarity (i.e., closeness) of other on the relevance of CPI to one's self-definition. Relevance is averaged over behavioral, interview, and questionnaire measures. From "The definition of self: Private and public self-evaluation management strategies" by A. Tesser and D. Paulhus, 1983, *Journal of Personality and Social Psychology, 44,* 672–682. Copyright 1983 by the American Psychological Association. Adapted by permission.

another does relative to the self, the less relevant should be the performance dimension, particularly when that other is close. This is precisely the pattern that was found and the interaction is significant.

REFERENCES

Aronson, E., & J. M. Carlsmith. (1968). Experimentation in social psychology. In G. Lindzey & E. Aronson (Eds.), *Handbook of social psychology, social edition* (Vol. 2). Reading, MA: Addison-Wesley.

Campbell, J. D., & Tesser, A. (1985). Self evaluation maintenance processes in relationships. In S. Duck & D. Perlman (Eds.), *Personal relationships* (Vol. 1). London: Sage.

Cialdini, R. B., Borden, R. J., Thorne, A., Walker, M. R., Freeman, S., & Sloan, L. R. (1976). Basking in reflected glory: Three (football) field studies. *Journal of Personality and Social Psychology,* **34,** 366–375.

Cialdini, R. B., & Richardson, K. D. (1980). Two indirect tactics of image management: Basking and blasting. *Journal of Personality and Social Psychology,* **39,** 406–415.

Festinger, L. (1954). A theory of social comparison processes. *Human Relations,* **7,** 117–140.

Goethals, G. B. (1984). *Social comparison theory: Psychology from the lost and found.* Paper presented at the American Psychological Association, Toronto.

Heider, F. (1958). *The psychology of interpersonal relations.* New York: Wiley.

Pleban, R., & Tesser, A. (1981). The effects of relevance and quality of another's performance on interpersonal closeness. *Social Psychology Quarterly,* **44,** 278–285.

Suls, J. M., & Miller, R. L. (Eds.). (1977). *Social comparison processes: Theoretical and empirical perspectives.* Washington, DC: Hemisphere.

Tesser, A., & Barbee, A. (1985). *Appearing competent: Self-evaluation maintenance processes.* Unpublished manuscript, University of Georgia.

Tesser, A., & Campbell, J. (1986). A self-evaluation maintenance model of student motivation. In C. Ames & R. Ames (Eds.), *Research on motivation in education: The classroom milieu.* Orlando, FL: Academic Press.

Tesser, A., Campbell, J., & Smith, M. (1984). Friendship choice and performance: Self evaluation maintenance in children. *Journal of Personality and Social Psychology,* **46,** 561–574.

Tesser, A., & Moore, J. (1987). On the convergence of public and private aspect of self. In R. Baumeister (Ed.), *Public self and private self.* Berlin: Springer-Verlag.

Tesser, A., & Paulhus, D. (1983). The definition of self: Private and public self-evaluation management strategies. *Journal of Personality and Social Psychology,* **44,** 672–682.

Tesser, A., & Smith, J. (1980). Some effects of friendship and task relevance on helping: You don't always help the one you like. *Journal of Experimental Social Psychology,* **16,** 582–590.

Wills, T. A. (1981). Downward comparison principles in social psychology. *Psychological Bulletin,* **90,** 245–271.

CHAPTER 3 The Self

3.1 ALBERT BANDURA

Self-Efficacy: Toward a Unifying Theory of Behavioral Change

It is important to have a good understanding of ourselves, including our attitudes and abilities. Albert Bandura's concept of self-efficacy focuses on our belief that we can behave in a manner that produces successful outcomes. Having the expectation that we can master a task has important implications for our self-concept and our ability to adjust to various situations.

Bandura (b. 1925) was born in Alberta, Canada, in 1925. He earned his Ph.D. in clinical psychology from the University of Iowa in 1952. He then accepted a position at Stanford University, where he is currently a professor of psychology. His research interests have focused on social cognitive theory, which assigns an important role to cognitive, vicarious, self-regulating, and self-reflective processes in human functioning. He has written numerous influential books, including *Social Foundations of Thought and Action: A Social Cognitive Theory* (Prentice Hall, 1986).

Bandura's theory of self-efficacy is described in this selection from "Self-Efficacy: Toward a Unifying Theory of Behavioral Change," which was published in *Psychological Review* in 1977. In this classic paper, he describes the factors that influence self-efficacy, including performance accomplishments, vicarious experience, verbal persuasion, and physiological arousal. In one part of the original article not included in this selection, Bandura reports that self-efficacy is important for successful behavioral change in therapy. As you read this selection, think about the variables that promote self-efficacy and how you could develop a program to help others improve their coping through enhanced self-understanding.

Key Concept: self-efficacy

APA Citation: Bandura, A. (1977). Self-efficacy: Toward a unifying theory of behavior change. *Psychological Review, 84,* 191–215.

EFFICACY EXPECTATIONS AS A MECHANISM OF OPERATION

The present theory is based on the principal assumption that psychological procedures, whatever their form, serve as means of creating and strengthening expectations of personal efficacy. Within this analysis, efficacy expectations are distinguished from response–outcome expectancies. The difference is presented schematically in Figure 1.

An outcome expectancy is defined as a person's estimate that a given behavior will lead to certain outcomes. An efficacy expectation is the conviction that one can successfully execute the behavior required to produce the outcomes. Outcome and efficacy expectations are differentiated, because individuals can believe that a particular course of action will produce certain outcomes, but if they entertain serious doubts about whether they can perform the necessary activities such information does not influence their behavior.

In this conceptual system, expectations of personal mastery affect both initiation and persistence of coping behavior. The strength of people's convictions in their own effectiveness is likely to affect whether they will even try to cope with given situations. At this initial level, perceived self-efficacy influences choice of behavioral settings. People fear and tend to avoid threatening situations they believe exceed their coping skills, whereas they get involved in activities and behave assuredly when they judge themselves capable of handling situations that would otherwise be intimidating.

Not only can perceived self-efficacy have directive influence on choice of activities and settings, but, through expectations of eventual success, it can affect coping efforts once they are initiated. Efficacy expectations determine how much effort people will expend and how long they will persist in the face of obstacles and aversive experiences. The stronger the perceived self-efficacy, the more active the efforts. Those who persist in subjectively threatening activities that are in fact relatively safe will gain corrective experiences that reinforce their sense of efficacy, thereby eventually eliminating their defensive behavior. Those who cease their coping efforts prematurely will retain their self-debilitating expectations and fears for a long time.

The preceding analysis of how perceived self-efficacy influences performance is not meant to imply that expectation is the sole determinant of behavior. Expectations alone will not produce desired performance if the component capabilities are lacking. Moreover, there are many things that people can do with certainty of success that they do not perform because they have no incentives to do so. Given appropriate skills and adequate incentives, however,

FIGURE 1

Diagrammatic Representation of the Difference Between Efficacy Expectations and Outcome Expectations

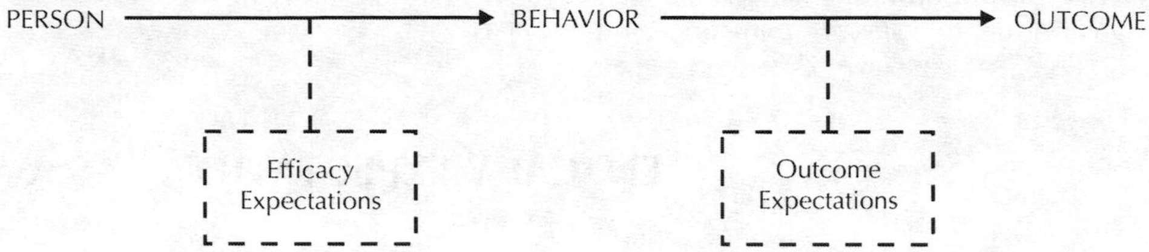

PERSON ⟶ BEHAVIOR ⟶ OUTCOME

Efficacy Expectations

Outcome Expectations

efficacy expectations are a major determinant of people's choice of activities, how much effort they will expend, and of how long they will sustain effort in dealing with stressful situations.

DIMENSIONS OF EFFICACY EXPECTATIONS

Empirical tests of the relationship between expectancy and performance of threatening activities have been hampered by inadequacy of the expectancy analysis. In most studies the measures of expectations are mainly concerned with people's hopes for favorable outcomes rather than with their sense of personal mastery. Moreover, expectations are usually assessed globally only at a single point in a change process as though they represent a static, unidimensional factor. Participants in experiments of this type are simply asked to judge how much they expect to benefit from a given procedure. When asked to make such estimates, participants assume, more often than not, that the benefits will be produced by the external ministrations rather than gained through the development of self-efficacy. Such global measures reflect a mixture of, among other things, hope, wishful thinking, belief in the potency of the procedures, and faith in the therapist. It therefore comes as no surprise that outcome expectations of this type have little relation to magnitude of behavioral change (Davison & Wilson, 1973; Lick & Bootzin, 1975).

Efficacy expectations vary on several dimensions that have important performance implications. They differ in *magnitude*. Thus when tasks are ordered in level of difficulty, the efficacy expectations of different individuals may be limited to the simpler tasks, extend to moderately difficult ones, or include even the most taxing performances. Efficacy expectations also differ in *generality*. Some experiences create circumscribed mastery expectations. Others instill a more generalized sense of efficacy that extends well beyond the specific treatment situation. In addition, expectancies vary in *strength*. Weak expectations are easily extinguishable by disconfirming experiences, whereas individuals who possess strong expectations of mastery will persevere in their coping efforts despite disconfirming experiences.

FIGURE 2

Major Sources of Efficacy Information and the Principal Sources
Through Which Different Modes of Treatment Operate

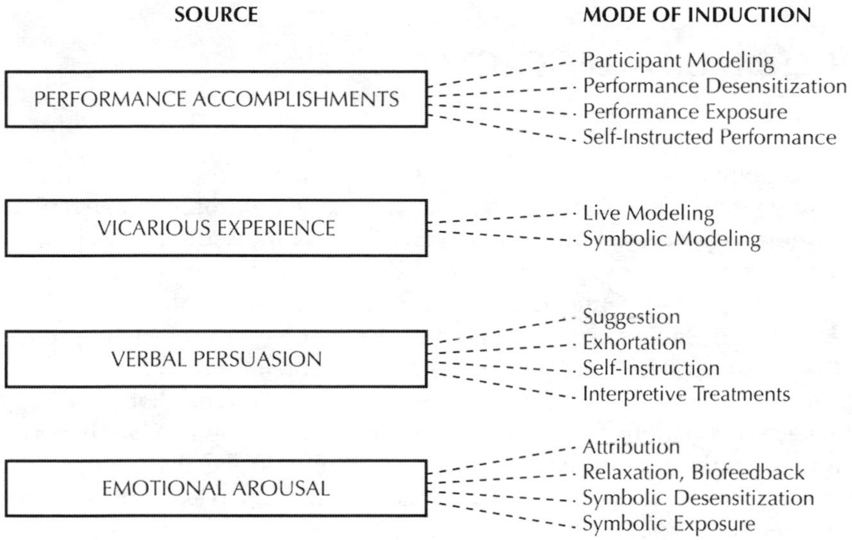

SOURCE	MODE OF INDUCTION
PERFORMANCE ACCOMPLISHMENTS	Participant Modeling Performance Desensitization Performance Exposure Self-Instructed Performance
VICARIOUS EXPERIENCE	Live Modeling Symbolic Modeling
VERBAL PERSUASION	Suggestion Exhortation Self-Instruction Interpretive Treatments
EMOTIONAL AROUSAL	Attribution Relaxation, Biofeedback Symbolic Desensitization Symbolic Exposure

An adequate expectancy analysis, therefore, requires detailed assessment of the magnitude, generality, and strength of efficacy expectations commensurate with the precision with which behavioral processes are measured. Both efficacy expectations and performance should be assessed at significant junctures in the change process to clarify their reciprocal effects on each other. Mastery expectations influence performance and are, in turn, altered by the cumulative effects of one's efforts.

SOURCES OF EFFICACY EXPECTATIONS

In this social learning analysis, expectations of personal efficacy are based on four major sources of information: performance accomplishments, vicarious experience, verbal persuasion, and physiological states. Figure 2 presents the diverse influence procedures commonly used to reduce defensive behavior and presents the principal source through which each treatment operates to create expectations of mastery. Any given method, depending on how it is applied, may of course draw to a lesser extent on one or more other sources of efficacy information. For example,... performance-based treatments not only promote behavioral accomplishments but also extinguish fear arousal, thus authenticating self-efficacy through enactive and arousal sources of information. Other methods, however, provide fewer ways of acquiring information about one's capability for coping with threatening situations. By postulating a common mechanism of operation, this analysis provides a conceptual framework within which to study behavioral changes achieved by different modes of treatment....

COGNITIVE PROCESSING OF EFFICACY INFORMATION

... At this point a distinction must be drawn between information [that people use to judge their level of self-efficacy] contained in environmental events and information as processed and transformed by the individual. The impact of information on efficacy expectations will depend on how it is cognitively appraised. A number of contextual factors, including the social, situational, and temporal circumstances under which events occur, enter into such appraisals. For this reason, even success experiences do not necessarily create strong generalized expectations of personal efficacy. Expectations that have served self-protective functions for years are not quickly discarded. When experience contradicts firmly established expectations of self-efficacy, they may undergo little change if the conditions of performance are such as to lead one to discount the import of the experience....

Results of recent studies support the thesis that generalized, lasting changes in self-efficacy and behavior can best be achieved by participant methods using powerful induction procedures initially to develop capabilities, then removing external aids to verify personal efficacy, then finally using self-directed mastery to strengthen and generalize expectations of personal efficacy (Bandura et al., 1975). Independent performance can enhance efficacy expectations in several ways: (a) It creates additional exposure to former threats, which provides participants with further evidence that they are no longer aversively aroused by what they previously feared. Reduced emotional arousal confirms increased coping capabilities. (b) Self-directed mastery provides opportunities to perfect coping skills, which lessen personal vulnerability to stress. (c) Independent performance, if well executed, produces success experiences, which further reinforce expectations of self-competency.

Extensive self-directed performance of formerly threatening activities under progressively challenging conditions at a time when treatments are usually terminated could also serve to reduce susceptibility to relearning of defensive patterns of behavior. A few negative encounters among many successful experiences that have instilled a strong sense of self-efficacy will, at most, establish discriminative avoidance of realistic threats, an effect that has adaptive value. In contrast, if people have limited contact with previously feared objects after treatment, whatever expectations of self-efficacy were instated would be weaker and more vulnerable to change. Consequently, a few unfavorable experiences are likely to reestablish defensive behavior that generalizes inappropriately....

Just as the value of efficacy information generated enactively and vicariously depends on cognitive appraisal, so does the information arising from exhortative and emotive sources. The impact of verbal persuasion on self-efficacy may vary substantially depending on the perceived credibility of the persuaders, their prestige, trustworthiness, expertise, and assuredness. The more believable the source of the information, the more likely are efficacy expectations to change. The influence of credibility on attitudinal change has, of course, received intensive study. But its effects on perceived self-efficacy remain to be investigated.

REFERENCES

Bandura, A., Jeffery, R. W., & Gajdos, E. Generalizing change through participant modeling with self-directed mastery. *Behaviour Research and Therapy*, 1975, *13*, 141–152.

Davison, G. C., & Wilson, G. T. Processes of fear-reduction in systematic desensitization: Cognitive and social reinforcement factors in humans. *Behavior Therapy*, 1973, *4*, 1–21.

Lick, J., & Bootzin, R. Expectancy factors in the treatment of fear: Methodological and theoretical issues. *Psychological Bulletin*, 1975, *82*, 917–931.

The Social Self: On Being the Same and Different at the Same Time

Our social identity helps to define who we are and how we relate to others. It includes our self-concept as well as the various groups of people with whom we identify. Much historical research in social psychology focused on the self, with less emphasis on the social aspects of identity. Recent studies, including that of Marilynn B. Brewer, have balanced personal and social factors.

Brewer (b. 1942) earned her Ph.D. in social psychology from Northwestern University in 1968. After teaching at the University of California at Los Angeles, she began her current position at Ohio State University. Brewer served as president of the Society for Personality and Social Psychology in 1990 and as president of the American Psychological Society in 1994.

This selection is from "The Social Self: On Being the Same and Different at the Same Time," which was published in *Personality and Social Psychology Bulletin* in 1991. In it, Brewer describes her model of optimal distinctiveness, in which social identity is seen as a balance between the need for similarity to others and a need for uniqueness and individuation. This approach reflects the current view in social psychology that social identity is a multidimensional concept including both self-concept and group membership. As you read this selection, think about the groups you identify with and how they help to form your own self-concept. How important is group identity versus individual uniqueness in developing a social identity?

Key Concept: optimal distinctiveness model of social identity

APA Citation: Brewer, M. B. (1991). The social self: On being the same and different at the same time. *Personality and Social Psychology Bulletin, 17,* 475–482.

Most of social psychology's theories of the self fail to take into account the significance of social identification in the definition of self. Social identities are self-definitions that are more inclusive than the individuated self-concept of most American *psychology. A model of* optimal distinctiveness *is proposed in which social identity is viewed as a reconciliation of opposing needs for assimilation and differentiation from others. According to this model, individuals avoid self-construals that are either too personalized or too inclusive and instead define themselves in terms of distinctive category memberships. Social identity and group loyalty are hypothesized to be strongest for those self-categorizations that simultaneously provide for a sense of belonging and a sense of distinctiveness. . . .*

Marilynn B. Brewer

In recent years, social psychologists have become increasingly "self"-centered. The subject index of a typical introductory social psychology text contains a lengthy list of terms such as *self-schema, self-complexity, self-verification, self-focusing, self-referencing, self-monitoring,* and *self-affirmation,* all suggesting something of a preoccupation with theories of the structure and function of self. The concept of self provides an important point of contact between theories of personality and theories of social behavior. Yet there is something peculiarly unsocial about the construal of self in American social psychology.

The *self-* terms listed above are representative of a highly *individuated* conceptualization of the self. For the most part, our theories focus on internal structure and differentiation of the self-concept rather than connections to the external world. Particularly lacking is attention to the critical importance of group membership to individual functioning, both cognitive and emotional. The human species is highly adapted to group living and not well equipped to survive outside a group context. Yet our theories of self show little regard for this aspect of our evolutionary history. As a consequence, most of our theories are inadequate to account for much human action in the form of collective behavior. The self-interested, egocentric view of human nature does not explain why individuals risk or sacrifice personal comfort, safety, or social position to promote group benefit (Caporael, Dawes, Orbell, & van de Kragt, 1989).

Even a casual awareness of world events reveals the power of group identity in human behavior. Names such as *Azerbaijan, Serbia, Lithuania, Latvia, Estonia, Tamil, Eritrea, Basques, Kurds, Welsh,* and *Quebec* are currently familiar because they represent ethnic and national identities capable of arousing intense emotional commitment and self-sacrifice on the part of individuals. Furthermore, they all involve some form of separatist action—attempts to establish or preserve distinctive group identities against unwanted political or cultural merger within a larger collective entity. People die for the sake of group distinctions, and social psychologists have little to say by way of explanation for such "irrationality" at the individual level.

SOCIAL IDENTITY AND PERSONAL IDENTITY

It is in this context that I have been interested in the concept of social identity as developed by European social psychologists, particularly Henri Tajfel and John Turner and their colleagues from the University of Bristol (e.g., Tajfel & Turner, 1986; Turner, Hogg, Oakes, Reicher, & Wetherell, 1987). Although social

FIGURE 1

Personal and Social Identities

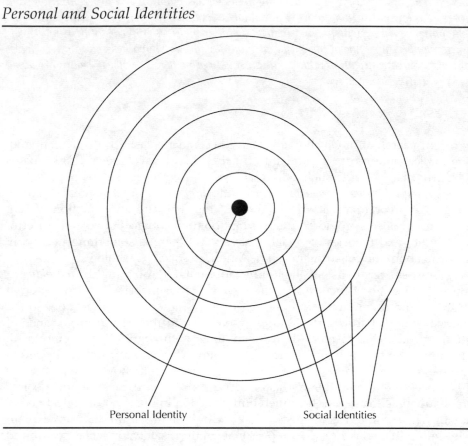

Personal Identity   Social Identities

identity theory has been introduced to U.S. social psychology, as a theory of self it is often misinterpreted. Americans tend to think of social identities as *aspects* of individual self-concept—part of internal differentiation. But the European conceptualization is one involving *extension* of the self beyond the level of the individual.

A schematic representation of social identity theory is presented in Figure 1. The concentric circles represent definitions of the self at different levels of inclusiveness within some particular domain. *Personal identity* is the individuated self—those characteristics that differentiate one individual from others within a given social context. *Social identities* are categorizations of the self into more inclusive social units that *depersonalize* the self-concept, where *I* becomes *we*. Social identity entails "a shift towards the perception of self as an interchangeable exemplar of some social category and away from the perception of self as a unique person" (Turner et al., 1987, p. 50).

The concentric circles in Figure 1 also illustrate the contextual nature of social identity. At each point in the figure, the next circle outward provides the frame of reference for differentiation and social comparison. To take a concrete example, consider my own identity within the occupation domain. At the level of personal identity is me as an individual researcher and teacher of social psychology. For this conceptualization of myself, the most immediate frame of reference for social comparison is my social psychology colleagues at UCLA. The most salient features of my self-concept in this context are those research interests, ideas, and accomplishments that distinguish me from the other social psychologists on my faculty.

My social identities, by contrast, *include* the interests and accomplishments of my colleagues. The first level of social identity is me as member of the social area within the department of psychology at UCLA. Here, the department provides the relevant frame of reference, and social comparison is with other areas of psychology. At this level the most salient features of my self-concept are those which I have in common with other members of the social area and which distinguish *us* from cognitive, clinical, and developmental psychology. At this level of self-definition my social colleague and I are interchangeable parts of a common group identity—my self-worth is tied to the reputation and outcomes of the group as a whole.

A yet higher level of social identity is the Department of Psychology within UCLA. At this level, the campus becomes the frame of reference and other departments the basis of comparison. The next level of identification is represented by UCLA as institution, with other universities providing the relevant comparison points. And, finally, there is my identification with academia as a whole, as compared with nonacademic institutions in the United States or the world.

The point to be made with this illustration is that the self-concept is *expandable and contractable* across different levels of social identity with associated *transformations* in the definition of self and the basis for self-valuation. When the definition of self changes, the meaning of self-interest and self-serving motivation also changes accordingly. . . .

OPTIMAL DISTINCTIVENESS THEORY

My position is that social identity derives from a fundamental tension between human needs for validation and similarity to others (on the one hand) and a countervailing need for uniqueness and individuation (on the other). The idea that individuals need a certain level of both similarity to and differentiation from others is not novel. It is the basis of uniqueness theory, proposed by Snyder and Fromkin (1980), as well as a number of other models of individuation (e.g., Codol, 1984; Lemaine, 1974; Maslach, 1974; Ziller, 1964). In general, these models assume that individuals meet these needs by maintaining some intermediate degree of similarity between the self and relevant others.

The theory of social identity provides another perspective on how these conflicting drives are reconciled. Social identity can be viewed as a compromise between assimilation and differentiation from others, where the need for deindividuation is satisfied within in-groups, while the need for distinctiveness is

FIGURE 2

The Optimal Distinctiveness Model

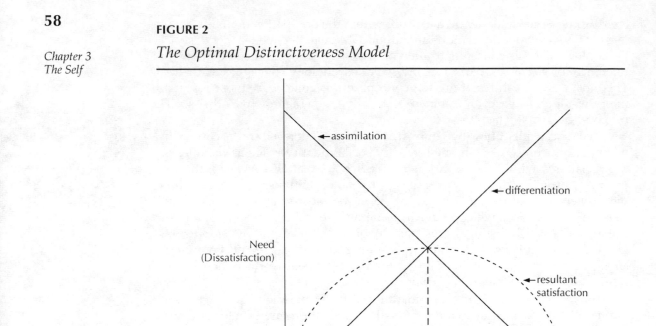

met through *inter*-group comparisons. Adolescent peer groups provide a proto-typical case. Each cohort develops styles of appearance and behavior that allow individual teenagers to blend in with their age mates while "sticking out like a sore thumb" to their parents. Group identities allow us to be the same and different at the same time.

The model underlying this view of the function of social identity is a variant of *opposing process* models, which have proved useful in theories of emotion and acquired motivation (Solomon, 1980). Instead of a bipolar con-tinuum of similarity-dissimilarity, needs for assimilation and differentiation are represented as opposing forces, as depicted in Figure 2.

As represented along the abscissa of the figure, it is assumed that within a given social context, or frame of reference, an individual can be categorized (by self or others) along a dimension of social distinctiveness-inclusiveness that ranges from uniqueness at one extreme (i.e., features that distinguish the in-dividual from any other persons in the social context) to total submersion in the social context (deindividuation) at the other. The higher the level of in-clusiveness at which self-categorization is made, the more depersonalized the self-concept becomes.

*Marilynn B.
Brewer*

Each point along the inclusiveness dimension is associated with a particular level of activation of the competing needs for assimilation and individuation. Arousal of the drive toward social assimilation is inversely related to level of inclusiveness. As self-categorization becomes more individuated or personalized, the need for collective identity becomes more intense. By contrast, arousal of self-differentiation needs is directly related to level of inclusiveness. As self-categorization becomes more depersonalized, the need for individual identity is intensified.

At either extreme along the inclusiveness dimension, the person's sense of security and self-worth is threatened. Being highly individuated leaves one vulnerable to isolation and stigmatization (even excelling on positively valued dimensions creates social distance and potential rejection). However, total de-individuation provides no basis for comparative appraisal or self-definition. As a consequence, we are uncomfortable in social contexts in which we are either too distinctive (Frable, Blackstone, & Scherbaum, 1990; Lord & Saenz, 1985) or too undistinctive (Fromkin, 1970, 1972).

In this model, equilibrium, or *optimal distinctiveness,* is achieved through identification with categories at that level of inclusiveness where the degrees of activation of the need for differentiation and of the need for assimilation are exactly equal. Association with groups that are too large or inclusive should leave residual motivation for greater differentiation of the self from that group identity, whereas too much personal distinctiveness should leave the individual seeking inclusion in a larger collective. Deviations from optimal distinctiveness in either direction—too much or too little personalization—should drive the individual to the same equilibrium, at which social identification is strongest and group loyalties most intense....

Distinctiveness and Level of Identification

The primary implication of this model of social identity is that distinctiveness per se is an extremely important characteristic of groups, independent of the status or evaluation attached to group memberships. To secure loyalty, groups must not only satisfy members' needs for affiliation and belonging *within* the group, they must also maintain clear boundaries that differentiate them from other groups. In other words, groups must maintain distinctiveness in order to survive—effective groups cannot be too large or too heterogeneous. Groups that become overly inclusive or ill-defined lose the loyalty of their membership or break up into factions or splinter groups.

To return to the concentric circle schematic of Figure 1, the optimal distinctiveness model implies that there is one level of social identity that is dominant, as the primary self-concept within a domain. In contrast to theories that emphasize the prepotency of the individuated self, this model holds that in most circumstances personal identity will *not* provide the optimal level of self-definition. Instead, the prepotent self will be a collective identity at some intermediate level of inclusiveness, one that provides both shared identity with an in-group and differentiation from distinct out-groups.

REFERENCES

Caporael, L., Dawes, R., Orbell, J., & van de Kragt, A. (1989). Selfishness examined: Cooperation in the absence of egoistic incentives. *Behavioral and Brain Sciences, 12,* 683–699.

Codol, J-P. (1984). Social differentiation and nondifferentiation. In H. Tajfel (Ed.), *The social dimension.* Cambridge: Cambridge University Press.

Frable, D., Blackstone, T., & Scherbaum, C. (1990). Marginal and mindful: Deviants in social interaction. *Journal of Personality and Social Psychology, 59,* 140–149.

Fromkin, H. L. (1970). Effects of experimentally aroused feelings of undistinctiveness upon valuation of scarce and novel experiences. *Journal of Personality and Social Psychology, 16,* 521–529.

Fromkin, H. L., (1972). Feelings of interpersonal undistinctiveness: An unpleasant affective state. *Journal of Experimental Research in Personality, 6,* 178–182.

Lemaine, G. (1974). Social differentiation and social originality. *European Journal of Social Psychology, 4,* 17–52.

Lord, C., & Saenz, D. (1985). Memory deficits and memory surfeits: Differential cognitive consequences of tokenism for tokens and observers. *Journal of Personality and Social Psychology, 49,* 918–926.

Maslach, C. (1974). Social and personal bases of individuation. *Journal of Personality and Social Psychology, 29,* 411–425.

Snyder, C. R., & Fromkin, H. L. (1980). *Uniqueness: The human pursuit of difference.* New York: Plenum.

Solomon, R. (1980). The opponent process theory of acquired motivation. *American Psychologist, 35,* 691–712.

Tajfel, H., & Turner, J. C. (1986). The social identity theory of intergroup behavior. In S. Worchel & W. Austin (Eds.), *Psychology of intergroup relations.* Chicago: Nelson-Hall.

Turner, J. C., Hogg, M., Oakes, P. Reicher, S., & Wetherell, M. (1987). *Rediscovering the social group: A self-categorization theory.* Oxford: Basil Blackwell.

Ziller, R. C. (1964). Individuation and socialization. *Human Relations, 17,* 341–360.

The Self and Social Behavior in Differing Cultural Contexts

Until the last couple of decades, much of social psychology was based on the Western cultural model, often with the assumption that all results of research based in Western culture would automatically generalize to people in any other culture. Thanks to the efforts of researchers such as Harry C. Triandis, it is now known that individuals in different cultures perceive themselves differently and have different motivations and social interactions.

Triandis (b. 1926) earned his Ph.D. in social psychology from Cornell University in 1958. He then went to the University of Illinois, where he is currently a professor emeritus of psychology. He has written extensively on cross-cultural psychology, including his book *Culture and Social Behavior* (McGraw-Hill, 1994).

This selection is from "The Self and Social Behavior in Differing Cultural Contexts," which was published in 1989 in *Psychological Review*. In it, Triandis contrasts individualism and collectivism. He finds that in individualist cultures, such as the United States, people tend to give a higher priority to personal goals. However, in collectivist cultures, such as China, people are more likely to give the highest priority to activities that help family and society. As you read this selection, consider other differences between diverse societies.

Key Concept: individualism and collectivism

APA Citation: Triandis, H. C. (1989). The self and social behavior in differing cultural contexts. *Psychological Review, 96,* 506–520.

Cultural Patterns

There is evidence of different selves across cultures (Marsella et al., 1985). However, the evidence has not been linked systematically to particular dimensions of cultural variation. This section will define three of these dimensions.

Cultural complexity.   A major difference across cultures is in cultural complexity. Consider the contrast between the human bands that existed on earth up to about 15,000 years ago and the life of a major metropolitan city today. According to archaeological evidence, the bands rarely included more than 30 individuals. The number of relationships among 30 individuals is relatively small; the number of relationships in a major metropolitan area is potentially almost infinite. The number of potential relationships is one measure of cultural complexity. Students of this construct have used many others. One can get reliable rank orders by using information about whether cultures have writing and records, fixity of residence, agriculture, urban settlements, technical specialization, land transport other than walking, money, high population densities, many levels of political integration, and many levels of social stratification. Cultures that have all of these attributes (e.g., the Romans, the Chinese of the 5th century B.C., modern industrial cultures) are quite complex. As one or more of the aforementioned attributes are missing, the cultures are more simple, the simplest including the contemporary food gathering cultures (e.g., the nomads of the Kalahari desert).

Additional measures of complexity can be obtained by examining various domains of culture. Culture includes language, technology, economic, political, and educational systems, religious and aesthetic patterns, social structures, and so on. One can analyze each of these domains by considering the number of distinct elements that can be identified in it. For example, (a) language can be examined by noting the number of terms that are available (e.g., 600 camel-related terms in Arabic; many terms about automobiles in English), (b) economics by noting the number of occupations (the U.S. Employment and Training Administration's *Dictionary of Occupational Titles* contains more than 250,000), and (c) religion by noting the number of different functions (e.g., 6,000 priests in one temple in Orissa, India, each having a different function). The subject is left to the specialists such as Carneiro (1970), Lomax and Berkowitz (1972), and Murdock and Provost (1973), who do have reliable ways of measuring the construct.

One of the consequences of increased complexity is that individuals have more and more potential ingroups toward whom they may or may not be loyal. As the number of potential ingroups increases, the loyalty of individuals to any one ingroup decreases. Individuals have the option of giving priority to their personal goals rather than to the goals of an ingroup. Also, the greater the affluence of a society, the more financial independence can be turned into social and emotional independence, with the individual giving priority to personal rather than ingroup goals. Thus, as societies become more complex and affluent, they also can become more individualistic. However, there are some moderator variables that modify this simple picture, that will be discussed later, after I examine more closely the dimension of individualism–collectivism.

Individualism–collectivism.   Individualists give priority to personal goals over the goals of collectives; collectivists either make no distinctions between personal and collective goals, or if they do make such distinctions, they subordinate their personal goals to the collective goals (Triandis, Bontempo, Villareal, Asai, & Lucca, 1988). Closely related to this dimension, in the work of Hofstede

(1980), is *power distance* (the tendency to see a large difference between those with power and those without power). Collectivists tend to be high in power distance.

Although the terms *individualism* and *collectivism* should be used to characterize cultures and societies, the terms *idiocentric* and *allocentric* should be used to characterize individuals. Triandis, Leung, Villareal, and Clack (1985) have shown that within culture (Illinois) there are individuals who differ on this dimension, and the idiocentrics report that they are concerned with achievement, but are lonely, whereas the allocentrics report low alienation and receiving much social support. These findings were replicated in Puerto Rico (Triandis et al., 1988). The distinction of terms at the cultural and individual levels of analysis is useful because it is convenient when discussing the behavior of allocentrics in individualist cultures and idiocentrics in collectivist cultures (e.g., Bontempo, Lobel, & Triandis, 1989).

In addition to subordinating personal to collective goals, collectivists tend to be concerned about the results of their actions on members of their ingroups, tend to share resources with ingroup members, feel interdependent with ingroup members, and feel involved in the lives of ingroup members (Hui & Triandis, 1986). They emphasize the integrity of ingroups over time and deemphasize their independence from ingroups (Triandis et al., 1986).

Shweder's data (see Shweder & LeVine, 1984) suggest that collectivists perceive ingroup norms are universally valid (a form of ethnocentrism). A considerable literature suggests that collectivists automatically obey ingroup authorities and are willing to fight and die to maintain the integrity of the ingroup, whereas they distrust and are unwilling to cooperate with members of outgroups (Triandis, 1972). However, the definition of the ingroup keeps shifting with the situation. Common fate, common outside threat, and proximity (which is often linked to common fate) appear to be important determinants of the ingroup/outgroup boundary. Although the family is usually the most important ingroup, tribe, coworkers, co-religionists, and members of the same political or social collective or the same aesthetic or scientific persuasion can also function as important ingroups. When the state is under threat, it becomes the ingroup.

Ingroups can also be defined on the basis of similarity (in demographic attributes, activities, preferences, or institutions) and do influence social behavior to a greater extent when they are stable and impermeable (difficult to gain membership or difficult to leave). Social behavior is a function of ingroup norms to a greater extent in collectivist than individualist cultures. (Davidson, Jaccard, Triandis, Morales, and Diaz-Guerrero, 1976).

In collectivist cultures, ingroups influence a wide range of social situations (e.g., during the cultural revolution in China, the state had what was perceived as "legitimate influence" on every collective). In some cases, the influence is extreme (e.g., the Rev. Jones's People's Temple influenced 911 members of that collective to commit suicide in 1978).

In collectivist cultures, role relationships that include ingroup members are perceived as more nurturant, respectful, and intimate than they are in individualistic cultures; those that include outgroup members are perceived to be more manipulative and exploitative in collectivist than in individualist cultures

(Sinha, 1982; Triandis, Vassiliou, & Nassiakou, 1968). In other words, more in-group social relationships are communal in the collectivist and more exchange relationships can be found in the individualist cultures. Outgroup relationships follow exchange patterns everywhere.

The distinction between communal and exchange relations (Mills & Clark, 1982) is useful. The attributes of communal and exchange relationships involve a number of contrasts, such as (a) lack of clarity versus clarity about what is to be exchanged, and when and where, (b) concern for the other person's needs versus concern for equity, (c) importance of maintaining equality of affect (if one is sad, the other is sad) as opposed to emotional detachment, (d) inequality of the benefits exchanged, and (e) benefits are not comparable versus benefits are comparable. Mills and Clark (1982) gave many examples in which exchange theory (e.g., Thibaut & Kelley, 1959) does not seem to provide adequate accounts of social behavior, makes predictions about the conditions under which exchange theory will be adequate, and tests experimentally some of these predictions. We expect that in collectivistic cultures the applicability of exchange theories will be more limited than in individualistic cultures.

As discussed earlier, over the course of cultural evolution there has been a shift toward individualism (i.e., exchange relationships). Content analyses of social behaviors recorded in written texts (Adamopoulos & Bontempo, 1986) across historical periods show a shift from communal to exchange relationships. Behaviors related to trading are characteristic of individualistic cultures, and contracts emancipated individuals from the bonds of tribalism (Pearson, 1977).

The distribution of collectivism–individualism, according to Hofstede's (1980) data, contrasts most of the Latin American, Asian, and African cultures with most of the North American and Northern and Western European cultures. However, many cultures are close to the middle of the dimension, and other variables are also relevant. Urban samples tend to be individualistic, and traditional-rural samples tend toward collectivism within the same culture (e.g., Greece in the work of Doumanis, 1983; Georgas, 1989; and Katakis, 1984). Within the United States one can find a good deal of range on this variable, with Hispanic samples much more collectivist than samples of Northern and Western European backgrounds (G. Marin & Triandis, 1985).

The major antecedents of individualism appear to be cultural complexity and affluence. The more complex the culture, the greater the number of ingroups that one may have, so that a person has the option of joining ingroups or even forming new ingroups. Affluence means that the individual can be independent of ingroups. If the ingroup makes excessive demands, the individual can leave it. Mobility is also important. As individuals move (migration, changes in social class) they join new ingroups, and they have the opportunity to join ingroups whose goals they find compatible with their own. Furthermore, the more costly it is in a particular ecology for an ingroup to reject ingroup members who behave according to their own goals rather than according to ingroup goals, the more likely are people to act in accordance with their personal goals, and thus the more individualistic is the culture. Such costs are high when the ecology is thinly populated. One can scarcely afford to reject a neighbor if one has only one neighbor. Conversely, densely populated ecologies are characterized by collectivism, not only because those who behave inappropriately can be excluded, but also because it is necessary to regulate behavior more strictly to overcome problems of crowding.

As rewards from ingroup membership increase, the more likely it is that a person will use ingroup goals as guides for behavior. Thus, when ingroups provide many rewards (e.g., emotional security, status, income, information, services, willingness to spend time with the person) they tend to increase the person's commitment to the ingroup and to the culture's collectivism.

The size of ingroups tends to be different in the two kinds of cultures. In collectivist cultures, ingroups tend to be small (e.g., family), whereas in individualist cultures they can be large (e.g., people who agree with me on important attitudes).

Child-rearing patterns are different in collectivist and individualist cultures. The primary concern of parents in collectivist cultures is obedience, reliability, and proper behavior. The primary concern of parents in individualistic cultures is self-reliance, independence, and creativity. Thus, we find that in simple, agricultural societies, socialization is severe and conformity is demanded and obtained (Berry, 1967, 1979). Similarly, in working-class families in industrial societies, the socialization pattern leads to conformity (Kohn, 1969, 1987). In more individualist cultures such as food gatherers (Berry, 1979) and very individualistic cultures such as the United States, the child-rearing pattern emphasizes self-reliance and independence; children are allowed a good deal of autonomy and are encouraged to explore their environment. Similarly, creativity and self-actualization are more important traits and are emphasized in child-rearing in the professional social classes (Kohn, 1987).

It is clear that conformity is functional in simple, agricultural cultures (if one is to make an irrigation system, each person should do part of the job in a well-coordinated plan) and in working-class jobs (the boss does not want subordinates who do their own thing). Conversely, it is disfunctional in hunting cultures, in which one must be ingenious, and in professional jobs, in which one must be creative. The greater the cultural complexity, the more is conformity to one ingroup disfunctional, inasmuch as one cannot take advantage of new opportunities available in other parts of the society.

The smaller the family size, the more the child is allowed to do his or her own thing. In large families, rules must be imposed, otherwise chaos will occur. As societies become more affluent (individualistic), they also reduce the size of the family, which increases the opportunity to raise children to be individualists. Autonomy in child-rearing also leads to individualism. Exposure to other cultures (e.g., through travel or because of societal heterogeneity) also increases individualism, inasmuch as the child becomes aware of different norms and has to choose his or her own standards of behavior....

Tight versus loose cultures. In collectivist cultures, ingroups demand that individuals conform to ingroup norms, role definitions, and values. When a society is relatively homogeneous, the norms and values of ingroups are similar. But heterogeneous societies have groups with dissimilar norms. If an ingroup member deviates from ingroup norms, ingroup members may have to make the painful decision of excluding that individual from the ingroup. Because rejection of ingroup members is emotionally draining, cultures develop tolerance for deviation from group norms. As a result, homogeneous cultures are often rigid in requiring that ingroup members behave accordingly to the ingroup norms. Such cultures are *tight*. Heterogeneous cultures and cultures in marginal positions between two major cultural patterns are flexible in dealing with ingroup members who deviate from ingroup norms. For example, Japan is considered tight, and it is relatively homogeneous. Thailand is considered loose, and it is in a marginal position between the major cultures of India and China; people are pulled in different directions by sometimes contrasting norms, and hence they must be more flexible in imposing their norms. In short, tight cultures (Pelto, 1968) have clear norms that are reliably imposed. Little deviation from normative behavior is tolerated, and severe sanctions are administered to those who deviate. *Loose* cultures either have unclear norms about most social situations or tolerate deviance from the norms. For example, it is widely reported in the press that Japanese children who return to Japan after a period of residence in the West, are criticized most severely by teachers because their behavior is not "proper." Japan is a tight culture in which deviations that would be considered trivial in the West (such as bringing Western food rather than Japanese food for lunch) are noted and criticized. In loose cultures, deviations from "proper" behavior are tolerated, and in many cases there are no standards of "proper" behavior. Theocracies are prototypical of tight cultures, but some contemporary relatively homogeneous cultures (e.g., the Greeks, the Japanese) are also relatively tight. In a heterogeneous culture, such as the United States, it is more difficult for people to agree on specific norms, and even more difficult to impose severe sanctions. Geographic mobility allows people to leave the offended communities in ways that are not available in more stable cultures. Urban environments are more loose than rural environments, in which norms are clearer and sanctions can be imposed more easily. Prototypical of loose cultures are the Lapps and the Thais. In very tight cultures, according to Pelto, one finds corporate control of property, corporate ownership of stored food and production power, religious figures as leaders, hereditary recruitment into priesthood, and high levels of taxation.

The latter list of attributes suggests that collectivism and tightness are related, but the two cultural patterns can be kept distinct for analytical purposes. It is theoretically possible for a group to be collectivist (give priority to ingroup goals) yet allow considerable deviation from group norms before imposing sanctions. For example, a group may have the norm that group goals should be given priority over personal goals, but may do nothing when individuals deviate substantially from that norm. A case reported in the Chinese press (*Peking Daily*, May 1987) is interesting: A student, whose behavior was bizarre, was assumed to be an "individualist" and was not diagnosed as mentally ill until he killed a fellow student, at which point the authorities took action. China is a collectivist, but "relatively" loose culture.

The intolerance of inappropriate behavior characteristic of tight cultures does not extend to all situations. In fact, tight cultures are quite tolerant of foreigners (they do not know better), and of drunk, and mentally ill persons. They may even have rituals in which inappropriate behavior is expected. For example, in a tight culture such as Japan one finds the office beer party as a ritual institution, where one is expected to get drunk and to tell the boss what one "really" thinks of him (it is rarely her). Similarly, in loose cultures, there are specific situations in which deviance is not tolerated. For example, in Orissa (India), a son who cuts his hair the day after his father dies is bound to be severely criticized, although the culture is generally loose.

Relationships among dimensions of cultural variation. Individualism is related to complexity according to a curvilinear function, because protoindividualism is found in nomadic groups of food gatherers. Such groups, although characterized by intensive involvement with a family or band, allow individuals to have considerable freedom of action outside the collective because it is more effective to gather food in a dispersed rather than in a collective manner. In agricultural societies one finds high levels of collectivism, and most theocracies have an agricultural basis. In modern industrial settings one finds neoindividualism, in which, again, a small group, the family or the work group, plays an important role in determining behavior, but the individual has considerable freedom of action outside the group. Because complexity increases from food gathering, to agricultural, to industrial societies, the relationship of individualism and complexity is curvilinear.

Child-rearing patterns also follow a curvilinear pattern with complexity. Simple food gathering and hunting cultures tend to socialize their children with emphasis on independence and self-reliance; agricultural, more complex cultures, tend to emphasize obedience; very complex industrial cultures, particularly among cognitive complex (professionals, upper class) subsamples, emphasize, again, independence and self reliance (Berry, 1967, 1979; Kohn, 1969, 1987).

Cultural complexity and tightness are not related; it is possible to identify types of cultures in the four quadrants defined by these two variables: Boldt (1978) has described the loose/complex quadrant as characteristic of the industrial democracies, the tight/complex quadrant as characteristic of the totalitarian industrial states, the loose/simple quadrant as characteristic of hunters and gatherers, and the tight/simple quadrant as characteristic of the agricultural simple cultures.

Finally, the relationship between collectivism and tightness is likely to be linear, but probably not very strong. Because the two constructs have different antecedents (collectivism = common fate, limited resources that must be divided in order to survive; tightness = cultural homogeneity, isolation from external cultural influences), we can expect many exceptions from the pattern of tightness and collectivism versus looseness and individualism.

REFERENCES

Adamopoulos, J., & Bontempo, R. N. (1986). Diachronic universals in interpersonal structures. *Journal of Cross-Cultural Psychology, 17,* 169–189.

Berry J. W. (1967). Independence and conformity in subsistence level societies. *Journal of Personality and Social Psychology, 7,* 415–418.

Berry, J. W. (1979). A cultural ecology of social behavior. In L. Berkowitz (Ed.), *Advances in experimental social psychology* (Vol. 12, pp. 177–207). New York: Academic Press.

Boldt, E. D. (1978). Structural tightness and cross-cultural research. *Journal of Cross-Cultural Psychology, 9,* 151–165.

Bontempo, R., Lobel, S. A., & Triandis, H. C. (1989). *Compliance and value internalization among Brazilian and U.S. students.* Manuscript submitted for publication.

Carneiro, R. L. (1970). Scale analysis, evolutionary sequences, and the ratings of cultures. In R. Naroll & R. Cohen (Eds.), *A handbook of method in cultural anthropology* (pp. 834–871). New York: Columbia University Press.

Davidson, A. R., Jaccard, J. J., Triandis, H. C., Morales, M. L., & Diaz-Guerrero, R. (1976). Cross-cultural model testing: Toward a solution of the etic-emic dilemma. *International Journal of Psychology, 11,* 1–13.

Doumanis, M. (1983). *Mothering in Greece: From collectivism to individualism.* New York: Academic Press.

Georgas, J. (1989). Changing family values in Greece: From collectivist to individualist. *Journal of Cross-Cultural Psychology, 20,* 80–91.

Hofstede, G. (1980). *Culture's consequences.* Beverly Hills, CA: Sage.

Hui, C. H., & Triandis, H. C. (1986). Individualism–collectivism: A study of cross-cultural researchers. *Journal of Cross Cultural Psychology, 17,* 225–248.

Katakis, C. D. (1984). Oi tris tautotites tis Ellinikis oikogenoias [The three identities of the Greek family]. Athens, Greece: Kedros.

Kohn, M. L. (1969). *Class and conformity.* Homewood, IL: Dorsey.

Kohn, M. L. (1987). Cross-national research as an analytic strategy. *American Sociological Review, 52,* 713–731.

Lomax, A., & Berkowitz, N. (1972). The evolutionary taxonomy of cultures. *Science, 177,* 228–239.

Marin, G., & Triandis, H. C. (1985). Allocentrism as an important characteristic of the behavior of Latin Americans and Hispanics. In R. Diaz-Guerrero (Ed.), *Cross-cultural and national studies in social psychology* (69–80). Amsterdam, The Netherlands: North Holland.

Marsella, A. J., DeVos, G., & Hsu, F. L. K. (1985). *Culture and self.* New York: Tavistock.

Mills, J., & Clark, E. S. (1982). Exchange and communal relationships. In L. Wheeler (Ed.), *Review of personality and social psychology* (Vol. 3, pp. 121–144). Beverly Hills, CA: Sage.

Murdock, G. P., & Provost, C. (1973). Measurement of cultural complexity. *Ethnology, 12,* 379–392.

Pearson, H. W. (Ed.). (1977). *The livelihood of man: Karl Polanyi.* New York: Academic Press.

Pelto, P. J. (1968, April). The difference between "tight" and "loose" societies. *Transaction,* 37–40.

Shweder, R. A., & LeVine, R. A. (1984). *Cultural theory: Essays on mind, self and emotion.* New York: Cambridge University Press.

Sinha, J. B. P. (1982). The Hindu (Indian) identity. *Dynamische Psychiatrie, 15,* 148–160.

Thibaut, J., & Kelley, H. (1959). *The social psychology of groups.* New York: Wiley.

Triandis, H. C. (1972). *The analysis of subjective culture.* New York: Wiley.

Triandis, H. C., Bontempo, R., Betancourt, H., Bond, M., Leung, K., Brenes, A., Georgas, J., Hui, C. H., Marin, G., Setiadi, B., Sinha, J. B. P., Verma, J., Spangenberg, J.,

Touzard, H., & de Montomollin, G. (1986). The measurement of etic aspects of individualism and collectivism across cultures. *Australian Journal of Psychology* (special issue on cross-cultural psychology), *38,* 257–267.

Triandis, H. C., Bontempo, R., Villareal, M. J., Asai, M., & Lucca, N. (1988). Individualism and collectivism: Cross-cultural perspectives on self-ingroup relationships. *Journal of Personality and Social Psychology, 54,* 323–338.

Triandis, H. C., Leung, K., Villareal, M. J., & Clack, F. L. (1985). Allocentric versus idiocentric tendencies: Convergent and discriminant validation. *Journal of Research in Personality, 19,* 395–415.

Triandis, H. C., Vassiliou, V., & Nassiakou, M. (1968). Three cross-cultural studies of subjective culture. *Journal of Personality and Social Psychology* [Monograph suppl.], *8*(4, pp. 1–42).

CHAPTER 4 Gender

4.1 SANDRA L. BEM

The Measurement of Psychological Androgyny

The past two decades have seen a significant increase in the efforts of psychologists to understand gender differences. An early milestone in this effort was Sandra L. Bem's development of the Bem Sex-Role Inventory (BSRI). The BSRI conceptualized two separate dimensions to determine the extent to which a person is masculine, feminine, or androgynous (having both masculine and feminine characteristics).

Bem (b. 1944) earned her Ph.D. in developmental psychology from the University of Michigan in 1968. She taught at Carnegie Mellon University and Stanford University before she went to Cornell University in 1978, where she is a professor of psychology. Her current research is presented in her book *The Lenses of Gender: Transforming the Debate on Sexual Inequality* (Yale University Press, 1993).

This selection is from "The Measurement of Psychological Androgyny," which was published in the *Journal of Consulting and Clinical Psychology* in 1974. In it, Bem describes the rationale for androgyny and the selection procedure for the items in the BSRI. Remember that $p < .05$ means that the difference is significant, or large enough to accept as real.

Later research has found that the androgynous person tends to be the most psychologically healthy. Also, psychologists have recently begun to use the terms *instrumental* and *expressive* when referring to masculinity and femininity, respectively.

Key Concept: androgyny

APA Citation: Bem, S. L. (1974). The measurement of psychological androgyny. *Journal of Consulting and Clinical Psychology, 42,* 155–162.

*B*oth in psychology and in society at large, masculinity and femininity have long been conceptualized as bipolar ends of a single continuum; accordingly, a person has had to be either masculine or feminine, but not both. This sex-role dichotomy has served to obscure two very plausible hypotheses: first, that many individuals might be "androgynous"; that is, they might be *both* masculine and feminine, *both* assertive and yielding, *both* instrumental and expressive—depending on the situational appropriateness of these various behaviors; and conversely, that strongly sex-typed individuals might be seriously limited in the range of behaviors available to them as they move from situation to situation. According to both Kagan (1964) and Kohlberg (1966), the highly sex-typed individual is motivated to keep his behavior consistent with an internalized sex-role standard, a goal that he presumably accomplishes by suppressing any behavior that might be considered undesirable or inappropriate for his sex. Thus, whereas a narrowly masculine self-concept might inhibit behaviors that are stereotyped as feminine, and a narrowly feminine self-concept might inhibit behaviors that are stereotyped as masculine, a mixed, or androgynous, self-concept might allow an individual to freely engage in both "masculine" and "feminine" behaviors.

The current research program is seeking to explore these various hypotheses, as well as to provide construct validation for the concept of androgyny (Bem, 1974). Before the research could be initiated, however, it was first necessary to develop a new type of sex-role inventory, one that would not automatically build in an inverse relationship between masculinity and femininity. This article describes that inventory.

The Bem Sex-Role Inventory (BSRI) contains a number of features that distinguish it from other, commonly used, masculinity–femininity scales, for example, the Masculinity–Femininity scale of the California Psychological Inventory (Gough, 1957). First, it includes both a Masculinity scale and a Femininity scale, each of which contains 20 personality characteristics. . . . Second, because the BSRI was founded on a conception of the sex-typed person as someone who has internalized society's sex-typed standards of desirable behavior for men and women, these personality characteristics were selected as masculine or feminine on the basis of sex-typed social desirability and not on the basis of differential endorsement by males and females as most other inventories have done. That is, a characteristic qualified as masculine if it was judged to be more desirable in American society for a man than for a woman, and it qualified as feminine if it was judged to be more desirable for a woman than for a man. Third, the BSRI characterizes a person as masculine, feminine, or androgynous as a function of the difference between his or her endorsement of masculine and feminine personality characteristics. A person is thus sex typed, whether masculine or feminine, to the extent that this difference score is high, and androgynous, to the extent that this difference score is low. Finally, the BSRI also includes a Social Desirability scale that is completely neutral with respect to sex. This scale now serves primarily to provide a neutral context for the Masculinity and Femininity scales, but it was utilized during the development of the BSRI to insure that the inventory would not simply be tapping a general tendency to endorse socially desirable traits. . . .

ITEM SELECTION

Both historically and cross-culturally, masculinity and femininity seem to have represented two complementary domains of *positive* traits and behaviors (Barry, Bacon, & Child, 1957; Erikson, 1964; Parsons & Bales, 1955). In general, masculinity has been associated with an instrumental orientation, a cognitive focus on "getting the job done"; and femininity has been associated with an expressive orientation, an affective concern for the welfare of others.

Accordingly, as a preliminary to item selection for the Masculinity and Femininity scales, a list was compiled of approximately 200 personality characteristics that seemed to the author and several students to be both positive in value and either masculine or feminine in tone. This list served as the pool from which the masculine and feminine characteristics were ultimately chosen. As a preliminary to item selection for the Social Desirability scale, an additional list was compiled of 200 characteristics that seemed to be neither masculine nor feminine in tone. Of these "neutral" characteristics, half were positive in value and half were negative.

Because the BSRI was designed to measure the extent to which a person divorces himself from those characteristics that might be considered more "appropriate" for the opposite sex, the final items were selected for the Masculinity and Femininity scales if they were judged to be more desirable in American society for one sex than for the other. Specifically, judges were asked to utilize a 7-point scale, ranging from 1 ("Not at all desirable") to 7 ("Extremely desirable"), in order to rate the desirability in American society of each of the approximately 400 personality characteristics mentioned above. (E.g., "In American society, how desirable is it for a man to be truthful?" "In American society, how desirable is it for a woman to be sincere?") Each individual judge was asked to rate the desirability of all 400 personality characteristics either "for a man" or "for a woman." No judge was asked to rate both. The judges consisted of 40 Stanford undergraduates who filled out the questionnaire during the winter of 1972 and an additional 60 who did so the following summer. In both samples, half of the judges were male and half were female.

A personality characteristic qualified as masculine if it was independently judged by both males and females in both samples to be significantly more desirable for a man than a woman ($p < .05$).[1] Similarly, a personality characteristic qualified as feminine if it was independently judged by both males and females in both samples to be significantly more desirable for a woman than for a man ($p < .05$). Of those characteristics that satisfied these criteria, 20 were selected for the Masculinity scale and 20 were selected for the Femininity scale....

A personality characteristic qualified as neutral with respect to sex and hence eligible for the Social Desirability scale (*a*) if is was independently judged by both males and females to be no more desirable for one sex than for the other ($t < 1.2$, $p > .2$) and (*b*) if male and female judges did not differ significantly in their overall desirability judgments of that trait ($t < 1.2$, $p > .2$). Of these items that satisfied these several criteria, 10 positive and 10 negative personality characteristics were selected for the BSRI Social Desirability scale in accordance with Edwards' (1964) finding that an item must be quite positive or quite negative in tone if it is to evoke a social desirability response set....

TABLE 1

Mean Social Desirability Ratings of the Masculine and Feminine Items for One's Own Sex

Sandra L. Bem

Item	Male Judges for a Man	Female Judges for a Woman
Masculine	5.59	3.46
Feminine	3.63	5.55
Difference	1.96	2.09
t	11.94*	8.88*

*$p < .001$.

After all of the individual items had been selected, mean desirability scores were computed for the masculine, feminine, and neutral items for each of the 100 judges.... [F]or both males and females, the mean desirability of the masculine and feminine items was significantly higher for the "appropriate" sex than for the "inappropriate" sex, whereas the mean desirability of the neutral items were no higher for one sex than for the other. These results are, of course, a direct consequence of the criteria used for item selection.

Table 1 separates out the desirability ratings of the masculine and feminine items for male and female judges rating their *own* sex. These own-sex ratings seem to best represent the desirability of these various items as perceived by men and women when they are asked to describe *themselves* on the inventory. That is, the left-hand column of Table 1 represents the phenomenology of male subjects taking the test and the right-hand column represents the phenomenology of female subjects taking the test. As can be seen in Table 1, not only are "sex-appropriate" characteristics more desirable for both males and females than "sex-inappropriate" characteristics, but the phenomenologies of male and female subjects are almost perfectly symmetric: that is, men and women are nearly equal in their perceptions of the desirability of sex-appropriate characteristics, sex-inappropriate characteristics, and the difference between them (t < 1 in all three comparisons).

SCORING

The BSRI asks a person to indicate on a 7-point scale how well each of the 60 masculine, feminine, and neutral personality characteristics describes himself. The scale ranges from 1 ("Never or almost never true") to 7 ("Always or almost always true") and is labeled at each point. On the basis of his responses, each person receives three major scores: a Masculinity score, a Femininity score and, most important, an Androgyny score. In addition, a Social Desirability score can also be computed.

The Masculinity and Femininity scores indicate the extent to which a person endorses masculine and feminine personality characteristics as self-descriptive. Masculinity equals the mean self-rating for all endorsed masculine items, and Femininity equals the mean self-rating for all endorsed feminine items. Both can range from 1 to 7. It will be recalled that these two scores are logically independent. That is, the structure of the test does not constrain them in any way, and they are free to vary independently.

The Androgyny score reflects the relative amounts of masculinity and femininity that the person includes in his or her self-description, and, as such, it best characterizes the nature of the person's total sex role. Specifically, the Androgyny score is defined as Student's t ratio for the difference between a person's masculine and feminine self-endorsement; that is, the Androgyny score is the difference between an individual's masculinity and femininity normalized with respect to the standard deviations of his or her masculinity and femininity scores. The use of a t ratio as the index of androgyny—rather than a simple difference score—has two conceptual advantages: first, it allows us to ask whether a person's endorsement of masculine attributes differs significantly from his or her endorsement of feminine attributes and, if it does ($|t| \geq 2.025$, $df = 38$, $p < .05$), to classify that person as significantly sex typed; and second, it allows us to compare different populations in terms of the percentage of significantly sex-typed individuals present within each.[2]

It should be noted that the greater the absolute value of the Androgyny score, the more the person is sex typed or sex reversed, with high positive scores indicating femininity and high negative scores indicating masculinity. A "masculine" sex role thus represents not only the endorsement of masculine attributes but the simultaneous rejection of feminine attributes. Similarly, a "feminine" sex role represents not only the endorsement of feminine attributes but the simultaneous rejection of masculine attributes. In contrast, the closer the Androgyny score is to zero, the more the person is androgynous. An "androgynous" sex role thus represents the equal endorsement of both masculine and feminine attributes.

The Social Desirability score indicates the extent to which a person describes himself in a socially desirable direction on items that are neutral with respect to sex. It is scored by reversing the self-endorsement ratings for the 10 undesirable items and then calculating the subject's mean endorsement score across all 20 neutral personality characteristics. The Social Desirability score can thus range from 1 to 7, with 1 indicating a strong tendency to describe oneself in a socially undesirable direction and 7 indicating a strong tendency to describe oneself in a socially desirable direction. . . .

CONCLUDING COMMENT

It is hoped that the development of the BSRI will encourage investigators in the areas of sex differences and sex roles to question the traditional assumption that it is the sex-typed individual who typifies mental health and to begin focusing on the behavioral and societal consequences of more flexible sex-role self-concepts. In a society where rigid sex-role differentiation has already out-lived its utility, perhaps the androgynous person will come to define a more human standard of psychological health.

Sandra L. Bem

NOTES

1. All significance levels in this article are based on two-tailed *t* tests.
2. A Statistical Package for the Social Sciences (SPSS) computer program for calculating individual *t* ratios is available on request from the author. In the absence of computer facilities, one can utilize the simple Androgyny difference score, Femininity–Masculinity, as the index of androgyny. Empirically, the two indices are virtually identical ($r = .98$), and one can approximate the *t*-ratio value by multiplying the Androgyny difference score by 2.322. This conversion factor was derived empirically from our combined normative sample of 917 students at two different colleges.

REFERENCES

BARRY, H., BACON, M. K., & CHILD, I. L. A cross-cultural survey of some sex differences in socialization. *Journal of Abnormal and Social Psychology,* 1957, **55**, 327–332.

BEM, S. L. Sex-role adaptability: One consequence of psychological androgyny *Journal of Personality and Social Psychology,* 1974, in press.

EDWARDS, A. L. The measurement of human motives by means of personality scales. In D. Levine (Ed.), *Nebraska symposium on motivation: 1964.* Lincoln: University of Nebraska Press, 1964.

ERIKSON, E. H. Inner and outer space: Reflections on womanhood. In R. J. Lifton (Ed.), *The woman in America.* Boston: Houghton Mifflin, 1964.

GOUGH, H. G. *Manual for the California Psychological Inventory.* Palo Alto, Calif.: Consulting Psychologists Press, 1957.

KAGAN, J. Acquisition and significance of sex-typing and sex-role identity. In M. L. Hoffman & L. W. Hoffman (Eds.), *Review of child development research.* Vol. 1. New York: Russell Sage Foundation, 1964.

KOHLBERG, L. A cognitive-developmental analysis of children's sex-role concepts and attitudes. In E. E. Maccoby (Ed.), *The development of sex differences.* Stanford, Calif.: Stanford University Press, 1966.

PARSONS, T., & BALES, R. F. *Family, socialization, and interaction process.* New York: Free Press of Glencoe, 1955.

4.2   ALICE H. EAGLY AND CAROLE CHRVALA

Sex Differences in Conformity: Status and Gender Role Interpretations

Psychologists have been interested in differences between men and women for many years. Massive research studies have been conducted on gender differences in areas such as aggression, helping, communication, and conformity. The results have sometimes been contradictory, and differences have often been subtle and difficult to observe. Alice H. Eagly has been a pioneer in the study of gender differences.

Eagly (b. 1938) earned her Ph.D. in social psychology from the University of Michigan in 1965. She taught at the University of Illinois, the University of Massachusetts–Amherst, and Purdue University before accepting her current position as a professor of psychology at Northwestern University in 1995. Carole Chrvala earned her Ph.D. from the University of Colorado in 1986. She is currently with the National Academy of Sciences at the Institute of Medicine.

This selection is from "Sex Differences in Conformity: Status and Gender Role Interpretations," which was published in *Psychology of Women Quarterly* in 1986. In it, Eagly and Chrvala present a research study on status and gender role explanations of conformity of women in group pressure situations. They found that older women conformed more than older men, but no differences were found between younger men and women. These results demonstrate how difficult it is to generalize research results.

Key Concept: sex differences in conformity

APA Citation: Eagly, A. H., & Chrvala, C. (1986). Sex differences in conformity: Status and gender role interpretations. *Psychology of Women Quarterly, 10,* 203–220.

*T*he experiment examines status and gender role explanations of the tendency for women to conform more than men in group pressure settings. Subjects believed they

*Alice H. Eagly
and Carole
Chrvala*

*were assigned to groups containing two males and two females in addition to them-
selves and received these other group members' opinions, which were represented as
deviating from the opinions that subjects had given earlier. Subjects then gave their
opinions with the other group members either having or not having surveillance over
these opinions. In addition, subjects were required to form impressions of each other's
likability or expertise. The findings indicate that subjects' sex and age affected the extent
of their conformity. Among older (19 years and older) subjects, females conformed more
with surveillance than without it, whereas surveillance did not affect males' conformity. Among younger (under 19 years) subjects, surveillance had no effects. Analysis
of sex differences revealed that older females were significantly more conforming than
older males when under surveillance as well as when subjects formed impressions of one
another's likability. Among younger subjects, there were no sex differences. These findings are discussed in terms of the theories that (a) both sex and age function as status
characteristics and (b) gender roles determine conformity.*

In group pressure conformity experiments, women tend to conform more than
men (Cooper, 1979; Eagly, 1978; Eagly & Carli, 1981; Maccoby & Jacklin, 1974).
In such settings, typified by the Sherif (1935, 1936), Asch (1956), and Crutchfield (1955) studies, subjects receive opinions from other group members and
are influenced to the extent that they change their opinions to match those of
the other members. As a recent meta-analysis of sex differences in influenceability demonstrates (Eagly & Carli, 1981), the sex difference in such group
pressure conformity experiments is significantly larger than in persuasion experiments and slightly larger than in conformity experiments not involving
group pressure.

One factor responsible for the sex difference in group pressure experiments is the surveillance that group members have over each other's opinions.
In a conformity experiment by Eagly, Wood, and Fishbaugh (1981), women
were more conforming than men only when the other group members apparently had surveillance over subjects' opinions. With surveillance, men
conformed less than women, and men's conformity with surveillance was
also significantly less than either sex's conformity without surveillance.

As Eagly et al. (1981) suggested, a promising interpretation of this sex
difference, and especially of the effect of surveillance on the sex difference, is
that sex functions as a status cue in newly formed groups (Berger, Fisek, Norman, & Zelditch, 1977; Berger, Rosenholtz, & Zelditch, 1980; Lockheed & Hall,
1976; Meeker & Weitzel-O'Neill, 1977; Ridgeway, 1978). According to this interpretation, people typically enter groups identified to each other in terms of
visible attributes that convey information about status, because the attributes
are correlated with status in natural settings. Sex is a status cue because men
generally have higher status than women in organizational hierarchies as well
as in families. Age, race, and physical attractiveness are other examples of such
status cues. Joseph Berger and his associates (e.g., Berger et al., 1980) have
called such attributes *diffuse status characteristics* because they provide a basis
for conclusions about one's competence and value across a fairly wide range of
situations. . . .

To understand further the possible contribution of status differences and gender roles to sex differences in conformity, we designed an experiment that included (a) a classification of subjects by age as well as by sex; (b) a manipulation of surveillance over subjects' opinions; and (c) a manipulation of the content (likability vs. expertise) of the impressions subjects were asked to form of other group members. Inclusion of the impression formation task not only made it possible to address an important theoretical issue by manipulating the content of these impressions, but it also greatly reduced subjects' awareness that their conformity was being assessed. This reduced awareness is a considerable advantage since subjects in classic conformity experiments were often suspicious about deception and persuasive intent (Glinski, Glinski, & Slatin, 1970; Stang, 1976; Stricker, Messick, & Jackson, 1967)....

METHOD

Subjects

A total of 91 male and 96 female Purdue University introductory psychology students served as subjects in order to fulfill a course requirement. An additional 6 males and 5 females were omitted from the analysis because they failed to attend the second session of the experiment.

Procedure

Subjects signed up for a two-session experiment on opinions about campus issues. At both sessions, subjects met in groups of 25. At the first session, a female experimenter administered two questionnaires. The first questionnaire contained 20 opinion items pertaining to campus issues. The experimenter administered each item by reading the opinion statement given at the top of each page and instructing subjects to give their opinions on a 15-point scale that ranged from *strongly agree* to *strongly disagree* and to write a "principal reason" for holding this opinion. The second questionnaire was the Personal Attributes Questionnaire (Spence & Helmreich, 1978).

At the second session (approximately three weeks later), the same experimenter explained that the study examined the way people form impressions of another person based on knowing that person's opinions. She noted that each subject had been assigned to a five-person group and would receive a Xerox copy of the eight opinions that each of the other group members had given in the first session. After reading each group member's opinion on an issue, subjects gave their impression of this member based on that opinion. The experimenter further explained that, after completing additional questionnaire measures, subjects would meet (in adjacent rooms) in their groups to discuss one of the issues. (This meeting did not actually occur.) Subjects were also instructed to prepare for the discussion by filling out a "summary sheet" for each issue on which they would summarize their own current opinion.

*Alice H. Eagly
and Carole
Chrvala*

Each subject then opened a folder that had been labeled with his or her name and responded to the written materials it contained, as paced by the experimenter. The manipulations were contained in these materials.

For each of the eight issues, the folder contained the opinions ostensibly given at the first session by the four other members of each subject's group. In fact, these opinions had been previously constructed for the experiment, and each subject received exactly the same set of opinions. Each opinion consisted of a check-mark on the 15-point rating scale and a hand-written statement giving a "principal reason" for holding the opinion. Each such opinion, given on a Xeroxed page, had been labeled with the first name (Mark, Ellen, Jim, or Beth) of one of the other group members.

Impression content.   After reading the opinions of the other group members on the first issue, subjects turned to a sheet on which they rated these group members. Subjects rated each group member either on how likeable and easy to get along with he or she was (*likability condition*) or on how well-informed and expert he or she was (*expertise condition*).

Surveillance.   Subjects then turned to a sheet on which they gave their opinion on the first issue "as a preparation for the group discussion." Lines were provided for subjects to write a summary of their views on the issue. At the bottom of the page was the same 15-point rating scale on which subjects had given their opinions at the first session. In the surveillance condition, the instructions on this page indicated that, when subjects met with their groups, they would read out loud their opinions on each issue (summary and the number checked on the rating scale) before having the discussion on one of the issues. In the no-surveillance condition, these instructions differed by (a) noting that subjects would leave these opinion sheets with the experimenter and not have them available during the discussion and (b) omitting any mention of giving opinions on each issue before beginning this discussion. In both conditions, the instructions noted that the subjects would give their final impressions of the other group members (likability or expertise, depending on condition) after the discussion. . . .

RESULTS

Opinion Conformity

The hypotheses were explored by a Sex of Subject (male versus female) × Age of Subject (older versus younger) × Surveillance of Opinions Given During Exchange (surveillance vs. no surveillance) × Impression Content (likability vs. expertise) × Time of Opinion Assessment (during exchange vs. after exchange) analysis of covariance with repeated measures on the time of assessment factor and preopinions as the covariate. The distribution of subjects' ages was dichotomized in order to include age within this design: The 87 subjects who were 18 or younger were considered younger ($M = 17.97$), and the 102 subjects who were 19 or older were considered older ($M = 19.86$). Analysis of variance indicated that subjects' preopinions did not vary across conditions and that preopinions ($M = 5.17$) differed significantly from the mean of subjects' responses on the two postopinion measures administered during the second session ($M = 7.22$), $F(1,346) = 296.99, p < .001$....

The analysis of covariance yielded a main effect for age, $F(1, 172) = 5.46$, $p < 0.25$, indicating that younger subjects conformed more ($M = 7.48$) than older subjects ($M = 7.02$). The main effect of surveillance was also significant, $F(1, 172) = 4.24, p < .05$, indicating that subjects conformed more with surveillance ($M = 7.36$) than without it ($M = 7.09$). These main effects, however, should be viewed in the context of several interactions.

The Sex × Age × Surveillance interaction proved significant, $F(1, 172) = 7.87, p < .01$. Consistent with the means shown in Table 1, the Sex × Surveillance interaction was significant among older subjects, $F(1, 172) = 4.69, p < .05$, and not among younger subjects. Examining these interactions in terms of the simple effects of sex showed that among older subjects who responded under surveillance, women conformed more than men, $F(1, 172) = 5.37, p < .025$, but there were no significant sex differences among younger subjects under surveillance or among younger or older subjects not under surveillance. Analysis of the simple effects of surveillance revealed greater conformity within (vs. without) surveillance for older female subjects, $F(1, 72) = 4.73, p < .05$, whereas surveillance had no effect on younger females or on older or younger males.

TABLE 1

The Effect of Surveillance on the Mean Opinion Conformity of Older and Younger Males and Females

	Surveillance of opinions	
Age and Sex	Surveillance	No surveillance
Older subjects		
Male subjects	6.71	7.03
Female subjects	7.86	6.68
Younger subjects		
Male subjects	7.81	7.15
Female subjects	7.50	7.42

Note: Cell *ns* = 13–30. Means are adjusted postopinion scores on a 15-point scale on which higher numbers indicate greater agreement with the other group members on the six issues. MS = 2.91

Also of interest is a marginally significant Sex × Impression Content interaction, $F(1, 172) = 2.87, p = .09$, which was qualified somewhat by a slightly weaker Sex × Age × Impression Content interaction, $F(1, 172) = 2.33, p = .13$.... [T]he Sex × Impression Content interaction was marginally significant among older subjects, $F(1, 172) = 3.24, p = .07$ but nonsignificant among younger subjects. Examining these interactions in terms of the simple effects of sex revealed that among older subjects who performed likability ratings, females conformed more than males, $F(1, 172) = 4.00$, $p < .05$, but there were no significant sex differences among younger subjects who performed likability ratings or among older or younger subjects who performed expertise ratings. Analysis of the simple effects of impression content revealed no significant effects, although older females conformed somewhat more when performing likability ratings than when performing expertise ratings, $F(1, 172) = 2.32$, $p = .13$. . . .

Alice H. Eagly and Carole Chrvala

Other Measures

As assessed by the summated measure of subjects' impressions of each of the other group members' likability or expertise, impressions were more favorable in the likability than the expertise condition ($p < .005$). Also, younger subjects formed more favorable impressions than older subjects ($p < .05$). In addition, the Sex × Age × Surveillance interaction proved significant ($p < .025$) and was accounted for primarily by the especially negative impressions formed by the older male subjects who were under surveillance.

Analysis of the ratings of other group members that subjects performed after the exchange of opinions showed that the members were rated as more competent by subjects who anticipated surveillance of their opinions than by subjects who did not anticipate surveillance ($p < .05$). No effects were obtained on perceived friendliness. In addition, subjects in the surveillance condition rated the other group members as more unbiased ($p < .01$) and as marginally more sincere ($p = .08$) than did subjects in the no-surveillance condition. Furthermore, older subjects rated the other members as more attractive than did younger subjects ($p < .01$).

The manipulation of impression content affected the perceived importance of some aspects of the interaction: Subjects who formed impression of the expertise of group members (compared with those who formed impressions of likability) judged that it was more important to be well-informed and to be expert on the issues on which they gave their opinions ($ps = .05$ or smaller). Impression content did not affect the importance of being liked by other group members or of getting along well with them.

DISCUSSION

Our experiment was designed to examine conformity sex differences in a situation of group pressure. The power of our simulated groups to exert pressure on subjects to modify their opinions was demonstrated, first of all, by the very substantial overall change in subjects' opinions toward the views advocated by the other group members. Another indication of group pressure is that subjects who believed that their opinions were under the surveillance of the other group members during the exchange of opinions conformed more than subjects who believed their opinions were not under surveillance (Deutsch & Gerard, 1955). Furthermore, those subjects who were under surveillance during the exchange conformed more at this point than they did after the exchange.

Examining the effects of sex on conformity together with the effects of age proved very informative. It was only among older subjects that we obtained the expected tendency for men to conform less than women when subjects believed that their opinions were under the surveillance of the other group members. The conformity of the younger males and females did not differ either with or without surveillance.

These findings should be considered from the perspective that age and sex affect conformity because they convey information about status. It should first be noted that the evidence that age functioned as a status characteristic is stronger than the evidence that sex functioned as a status characteristic. Overall, younger subjects tended to conform more than older subjects, whereas there was no overall tendency for females to be more conforming than males. In addition, on the ratings of the group members that subjects performed during the exchange of opinions, younger subjects acknowledged the other members' superiority by rating them more favorably than older subjects did, whereas female and male subjects did not differ on these ratings. Finally, younger subjects (but not older subjects) conformed significantly more to other group members in the opinions they gave during the exchange of opinions than in the opinions they gave (privately) after the exchange, whereas female and male subjects were not affected differently by the timing of the opinion assessment.

Evidence that sex functioned as a status characteristic was found only among the older subjects. In terms of conformity under surveillance, which is the type of conformity generally examined in the group-pressure literature, older males were less conforming than older females, whereas the younger males and females behaved similarly. The effects of surveillance on conformity suggest that these differences between older males and females should be attributed primarily to the older females' behavior: Surveillance significantly increased the conformity of the older females, but had little effect on the older males or on the younger males or females.

The findings of Eagly et al. (1981) of greater conformity among women than men only with surveillance resembles the finding obtained among the older subjects in the present experiment. The additional role of age in the present findings can be reconciled with the earlier results in terms of differing subject selection. The earlier study utilized few subjects as young as the subjects the present study classified as younger (18 years or younger), because subjects were recruited primarily from upper-level psychology courses. In the present experiment, subjects came exclusively from a fall-semester introductory psychology course.

From a status perspective, it is important to note the lack of parallelism between the effects of age and of sex. Subjects did not combine the age and sex cues in such a way that their effects aggregated, although such aggregative effects have been found with several combinations of status cues in the sociological literature on status generalization (e.g., Webster & Driskell, 1978). Had the status-lowering effects of younger age and female sex cumulated, younger females in our experiment would have behaved as if they had the lowest status. Instead, it was the older females who behaved as if they had the lowest status, if conforming more with surveillance than without it is regarded as a low-status behavior. If we focus only on conformity under surveillance, the older and younger females and the younger males behaved similarly—as if they had roughly equivalent status, lower than that of the older males.

*Alice H. Eagly
and Carole
Chrvala*

A status interpretation of these findings must include the assumption that the status-lowering effects of younger age took precedence over the status-lowering effects of female sex. As shown by the significant overall tendency for younger subjects to be more conforming than older subjects and to rate other group members more favorably, younger subjects performed as relatively low-status persons. Given the possibility of having higher status by virtue of being older, subjects then allowed sex to function as a status cue: Only the male subjects then performed as high-status persons, and females displayed their most distinctive low-status behavior by conforming significantly more when they believed themselves under surveillance.

REFERENCES

Asch, S. E. (1956). Studies of independence and conformity: I. A minority of one against a unanimous majority. *Psychological Monographs, 70,* (9, Whole No. 416).

Berger, J., Fisek, M. H., Norman, R. Z., & Zelditch, M., Jr. (1977). *Status characteristics and social interaction: An expectation states approach.* New York: American Elsevier.

Berger, J., Rosenholtz, S. J., & Zelditch, M., Jr. (1980). Status organizing processes. *Annual Review of Sociology. 6,* 479–508.

Cooper, H. M. (1979). Statistically combining independent studies: A meta-analysis of sex differences in conformity research. *Journal of Personality and Social Psychology, 37,* 131–146.

Crutchfield, R. S. (1955). Conformity and character. *American Psychologist, 10,* 191–198.

Deutsch, M., & Gerard, H. B. (1955). A study of normative and informational social influences upon individual judgment. *Journal of Abnormal and Social Psychology, 51,* 629–636.

Eagly, A. H. (1978). Sex differences in influenceability. *Psychological Bulletin, 85,* 86–116.

Eagly, A. H., & Carli, L. L. (1981). Sex of researchers and sex-typed communications as determinants of sex differences in influenceability: A meta-analysis of social influence studies. *Psychological Bulletin, 90,* 1–20.

Eagly, A. H., Wood, W., & Fishbaugh, L. (1981). Sex differences in conformity: Surveillance by the group as a determinant of male nonconformity. *Journal of Personality and Social Psychology, 40,* 384–394.

Glinski, R. J., Glinski, B. C., & Slatin, G. T. (1970). Nonnaivety contamination in conformity experiments: Sources, effects, and implications for control. *Journal of Personality and Social Psychology, 16,* 478–485.

Lockheed, M. E., & Hall, K. P. (1976). Conceptualizing sex as a status characteristic: Applications to leadership training strategies. *Journal of Social Issues, 32* (3), 111–124.

Maccoby, E. E., & Jacklin, C. N. (1974). *The psychology of sex differences.* Stanford, CA: Stanford University Press.

Meeker, B. F., & Weitzel-O'Neill, P. A. (1977). Sex roles and interpersonal behavior in task-oriented groups. *American Sociological Review, 42*, 92–105.

Ridgeway, C. L. (1978). Conformity, group-oriented motivation, and status attainment in small groups. *Social Psychology, 41*, 175–188.

Sherif, M. (1935). A study of some social factors in perception. *Archives of Psychology, 27* (187), 1–60.

Sherif, M. (1936). *The psychology of social norms.* New York: Harper.

Spence, J. T., & Helmreich, R. L. (1978). *Masculinity & femininity: Their psychological dimensions, correlates & antecedents.* Austin: University of Texas Press.

Stang, D. J. (1976). Ineffective deception in conformity research: Some causes and consequences. *European Journal of Social Psychology, 6*, 353–367.

Stricker, L. J., Messick, S., & Jackson, D. N. (1967). Suspicion of deception: Implications for conformity research. *Journal of Personality and Social Psychology, 5*, 379–389.

Webster, M., & Driskell, J. E. (1978). Status generalization: A review and some new data. *American Sociological Review, 43*, 220–236.

Individualistic and Collectivistic Perspectives on Gender and the Cultural Context of Love and Intimacy

Although Americans sometimes view their conceptualization of romantic love as universal, social psychologists have found wide differences in love beliefs among different cultures. Likewise, some research has revealed different conceptualizations of love between men and women. One cultural distinction studied by Karen K. Dion and her husband, Kenneth L. Dion, is the individualistic perspective versus the collectivistic perspective.

Karen Dion (b. 1945) and Kenneth Dion (b. 1944) earned their Ph.D.'s in psychology from the University of Minnesota in 1970. They are professors of psychology at the University of Toronto in Canada, where they have been since 1970. Although they each study other areas in social psychology, they share an interest in understanding gender and cultural influences on love.

This selection is from "Individualistic and Collectivistic Perspectives on Gender and the Cultural Context of Love and Intimacy," which was published in the *Journal of Social Issues* in 1993. In it, Dion and Dion conclude that a cultural perspective helps us to better understand gender and close relationships. Note that the authors suggest that some women in individualistic cultures have characteristics similar to those of individuals in collectivistic societies. How might this gender difference affect interactions in a close relationship such as romantic love? What are the advantages and disadvantages of individualistic and collectivistic approaches to love? In a section of the original article not included here, the authors discuss psychological intimacy and cultural influences of intimacy problems.

Key Concept: gender, culture, and love

APA Citation: Dion, K. K., & Dion, K. L. (1993). Individualistic and collectivistic perspectives on gender and the cultural context of love and intimacy. *Journal of Social Issues, 49,* 53–69.

*T*hey met, fell in love, decided to marry (or cohabit), and hoped to live happily ever after. To many North Americans, this depiction of the development of an intimate relationship between a woman and a man has been an enduring prototype, and its features seem very familiar and self-evident. This depiction, however, reflects several assumptions about the nature of intimate, opposite-sex relationships that are culturally based. These assumptions are by no means universally shared, particularly in non-Western societies; even in Western societies, this view of love, intimacy, and marriage has not always prevailed.

We have contended that a cultural perspective is needed to understand the factors contributing to the development of close relationships (Dion & Dion, 1979, 1988). The first step in theory building in this area is to identify conceptual dimensions that have the potential to provide an integrative framework. We believe that the dimensions of individualism and collectivism are key constructs with this potential for the topic of close relationships. These dimensions have been acknowledged by scholars from diverse cultural backgrounds to be of conceptual relevance for understanding the social structuring of relationships. We have previously suggested that there are cultural differences in views of self and that these differences in self-construal have implications for understanding the experience of romantic love and intimacy in heterosexual relationships (Dion & Dion, 1988).

In the present article, we present a more fully elaborated conceptual framework linking individualism and collectivism to culture-related and gender-related differences in close relationships and consider the evidence relevant to three conceptual propositions [only one of which is reprinted here]. We discuss the contrasts in the social construction of love and intimacy in two societies where individualism has been a dominant value orientation (the United States and Canada) and three Asian societies in which a collectivistic orientation has prevailed (China, India, and Japan). Our analysis is therefore most directly applicable to the manifestations of individualism and collectivism in these societies. Moreover, although we focus on the contrasts between individualism and collectivism in this article, as work in this area develops, additional conceptual and empirical analysis of culture and close relationships will be needed to compare different individualistic societies and different collectivistic societies, respectively.

INDIVIDUALISM AND COLLECTIVISM: CULTURAL PERSPECTIVES

The constructs of individualism and collectivism concern the relation between the individual and the group as reflected across many domains of social functioning (Hofstede, 1984). Individualism has been defined as "the subordination of the goals of the collectivities to individual goals" while collectivism involves the opposite, namely, "the subordination of individual goals to the goals of a collective" (Hui & Triandis, 1986, pp. 244–245). These constructs have been conceptualized at the cultural level and at the personal level, and it is important to distinguish these two levels (Kim, 1993). Societies are labeled as "individualistic" or "collectivistic" when these value orientations characterize the majority of individual members (Hui & Triandis, 1986). Within a given society, however, individual differences exist in adherence to the prevailing orientation. We have proposed using the terms *societal individualism* and *societal collectivism* to refer to these constructs at the cultural level and *psychological individualism* and *psychological collectivism* to designate these constructs at the individual level (Dion & Dion, 1991).

In his seminal work in this area, Hofstede (1984) proposed that the following features distinguished individualistic as compared to collectivistic societies. In societies characterized by individualism, the emphasis is on promoting one's self-interest and that of one's immediate family. The individual's rights rather than duties are stressed, as are personal autonomy, self-realization, individual initiative, and decision making. Personal identity is defined by the individual's attributes. Prototypic examples of individualistic societies in Hofstede's study were the United States, Australia, Great Britain, and Canada. At the personal level, individualism is characterized by valuing one's independence and showing less concern for other persons' needs and interests (Hui & Triandis, 1986).

In contrast, collectivistic societies, according to Hofstede, are characterized as stressing the importance of the individual's loyalty to the group, which in turn safeguards the interests and well-being of the individual. Other features include reduced personal privacy, a sense of personal identity based on one's place in one's group, a belief in the superiority of group compared to individual decisions, and emotional dependency on groups and organizations. Among the Asian countries and city states in Hofstede's sample characterized by the above features were Taiwan, Singapore, Hong Kong, and Pakistan. At the personal level, collectivism is manifested by concern about interpersonal bonds, greater awareness of and responsiveness to the needs of others reflecting a sense of interconnectedness, and interdependence (Hui & Triandis, 1986).

These contrasts between individualism and collectivism are reflected in the psychological concepts underlying North American compared to Asian analyses of personal and interpersonal functioning. For example, concepts that have been salient in North American personality and social psychology, such as locus of control, self-actualization, and self-esteem, can be regarded as different manifestations of individualism (Waterman, 1984). As a result of her or his personal choices across the diverse areas of life, the individual can "realize a variety of inherent potentialities and capabilities" and organize personal identity based on these choices (Roland, 1988, p. 330). In this context, a sense of self as independent is likely, characterized by features such as valuing personal uniqueness, self-expression, and the realization of personal goals (Markus & Kitayama, 1991).

Asian scholars have contended that psychological concepts emerging from an individualistic orientation constrain a full understanding of human functioning. (Western scholars, too, have been critical of the pervasive impact of individualism as shown by Bellah et al., 1985; Hogan, 1975; Sampson, 1977,

1985). Asian and some Western behavioral scientists have identified psychological constructs pertaining to interpersonal functioning that are derived from a collectivistic social structure. Based on these analyses, there is evidence that the social construction of self and other differs greatly in individualistic as contrasted with collectivistic societies. Specifically, many important concepts in Asian societies, such as *amae,* are inherently relational (Ho, 1982). They reflect a sense of self as interdependent, rather than independent (Hsu, 1971; Markus & Kitayama, 1991).

To illustrate the emphasis on interdependence that characterizes many constructs from Asian psychology, the Japanese construct of *amae,* which has been discussed extensively by Doi (1962, 1963, 1977, 1988) provides a good example. The verb form of this noun is *amaeru,* which is defined as "to depend and presume upon another's benevolence" (Doi, 1962). A Japanese person who wishes to amaeru seeks to be a passive love object and to be indulged by another. The psychological prototype of *amae* is the mother–infant relationship (Doi, 1988). According to Doi (1988) and other scholars (Morsbach & Tyler, 1986), the expression of *amae* is aimed at psychologically denying the fact of one's separation from the mother.

Doi (1988) has used the *amae* concept as a single, sovereign principle for understanding Japanese personality as well as Japanese society. The people one can *amaeru* with impunity define insiders and include one's parents, relatives, close friends, and others with whom one stands in an hierarchical relationship. According to Doi, among outsiders, one must exhibit restraint or *enryo* and suppress the expression of any dependency needs, which Japanese find unpleasant.

A second example of cultural contrasts can be found in Roland's (1988) discussion of the *familial self* in India, which he compared with the North American *individualized self.* In his analysis, the Indian conception of self is basically relational rather than autonomous. Roland suggested that the familial self developed in hierarchical relationships within the extended family in which the following qualities were present: strong emotional interdependence, reciprocal demands for intimacy and support, mutual caring, and a high degree of empathy and sensitivity to another's needs and desires within the family structure.

INDIVIDUALISM AND COLLECTIVISM: GENDER PERSPECTIVES

There are some conceptual parallels between the above discussion of cultural differences in the social construction of self–other relationships and analyses of gender differences in self–other construal within North American society. The characteristics of the relational self hypothesized to be prevalent in various Asian societies are similar to some aspects of self-construal suggested as characterizing many North American women. Various scholars have proposed that the social construction of self for many North American women is relational, while for many men, it is autonomous. Before discussing this hypothesized contrast, it should be acknowledged that individual differences in self-construal *within* gender also seem likely. Nonetheless, hypothesized gender differences in self-construal provide a provocative analytical framework. The following two examples illustrate this viewpoint. (See also Lykes, 1985, and Markus & Kitayama, 1991, for an additional example and discussion of this issue.)

Karen K. Dion and Kenneth L. Dion

Chodorow (1978) analyzed the relation between the role of women as primary care givers in the family and the development of a sense of personal identity in their daughters and sons. She argued that primary parenting by women fostered the emergence of a "sense of self... continuous with others" for girls, while boys were encouraged to develop a more autonomous and distinct sense of self (Chodorow, 1978, p. 207). She suggested that this autonomous orientation ultimately made satisfying the emotional needs of others more problematic for men than for women.

Bardwick (1980) suggested that the predominant mode of self-construal for women has been either a dependent or an interdependent mode, both of which involve the self defined in the context of relationships. The former involves a sense of dependency, both psychologically and economically, as would be the case in a traditional marriage. The latter type involves both a "sense of self" but at the same time an awareness of the reciprocal aspects of an intimate relationship. With reference to Levinson's (1978) theory of adult development in which individuation is a key developmental task, Bardwick commented that this particular view of development was "very American and very male" and contrasted markedly with a view of adulthood as a time for "meeting responsibilities within relationships" (p. 40). She suggested that an individualistic, egocentric view of self characterized only a small minority of women.

Considered together, the above conceptual analyses suggest that in some individualistic societies there are gender differences in self-construal that in turn may be related to the experience of romantic love and the capacity for intimacy in close relationships. Although the focus here is on gender differences, there are other important individual difference dimensions that also are related to the experience of love and intimacy for both women and men (see Dion & Dion, 1985; Worell, 1988).

Finally, this perspective raises some intriguing questions about the relation between gender and the experience of love and intimacy in collectivistic societies. Specifically, if the mode of self-construal is interdependent for women and for men, this social construction of self should facilitate the capacity for intimacy for both sexes. As will be evident however, in collectivistic societies both gender and cultural factors are related to the expression of intimacy in particular close relationships, such as marriage.

...[W]e propose that individualistic societies (the United States and Canada) differ from collectivistic ones (China, India, and Japan) in the social construction of love and intimacy. Moreover, we suggest that gender and cultural differences in the reported experience of love and intimacy in heterosexual relationships are related in part to differences in self-construal.

LOVE AND INTIMACY

Proposition 1: Romantic love is more likely to be considered an important basis for marriage in societies where individualism as contrasted with collectivism is a dominant cultural value.

As noted at the start of this article, marriage based on romantic love may seem like a description of the natural progression of intimacy to many North Americans. It has been suggested, however, that romantic love is most likely to emerge in particular societal contexts. For example, Averill (1985) suggested a relation between aspects of romantic love such as idealization of the lover for his or her unique qualities and "individuation of the self" (Averill, 1985, p. 101). Both during earlier periods of Western history and in some Asian societies, Averill argued that since personal identity was not highly differentiated from the group, the social context did not provide the conditions in which romantic idealization could develop.

The conceptual link between the presence of romantic love and societal individualism has been commented on by other scholars. Bellah and his colleagues discussed the pervasive impact of individualism in both the public and the private domain of American life (Bellah et al., 1985). They used the term "expressive individualism," referring to the need for self-expression and self-realization, to describe the role of individualism in the private domain of life, including intimate relationships. In this context, romantic love provided the chance for exploring and revealing dimensions of oneself, with each member of the couple seeking to share their "real selves" with one another (Bellah et al., 1985).

Interestingly, although undertaken from a very different theoretical perspective on love, similar themes emerged in Sternberg and Grajek's (1984) research on the core components of love, based on adults' completion of several psychometric measures of love across different types of relationships. Among the features of love identified as central by Sternberg and Grajek were several which pertain to intimate self-expression and personal fulfillment such as "sharing of deeply personal ideas and feelings" and "personal growth through the relationship."

In more collectivistic societies, such as China, traditionally, love and intimacy between a woman and a man were less important than other factors as a basis for marriage. Hsu (1981) suggested that the concept of romantic love did not fit particularly well with traditional Chinese society since the individual was expected to take into account the wishes of others, especially one's parents and other family members, when choosing a spouse. The Western ideal of romantic love characterized by intense feelings, disregard of others' views of one's lover, and complete mutual absorption would be regarded as disruptive. Indeed it can be argued that in many collectivistic societies, romantic love as a basis for marriage would be dysfunctional.

Consistent with this line of reasoning, family structure has been found to be related to the occurrence of romantic love as a basis for marriage and autonomous selection of one's marital partner (Lee & Stone, 1980). Analyzing cross-cultural data from 117 nonindustrial societies, Lee and Stone found that marriage based on love and choice of one's own spouse was *less* likely to occur in societies characterized by extended family systems compared to those with nuclear family structures. An extended family system can be viewed as one manifestation of greater societal collectivism.

Among recent cohorts of young adults in some Asian societies, there are signs of change toward greater valuing of love as a basis for marriage. For example in Japan, the number of "love marriages" has increased over the past four decades. However, traditional values in the parents' generation have persisted (Fukada, 1991). As of the early 1980s, Buruma (1984, p. 40) reported that up to 50% of all marriages in Japan were still arranged ones. Survey data for the latter part of the 1980s presented by De Mente (1989), however, seem to indicate stronger pressure for "love" or "love-based" marriages among young Japanese women today. Specifically, 70% of unmarried women in Japan were said to prefer to find their own husband, and an "overwhelming majority" (the exact percentage was not stated) of young Japanese women were described as preferring a love-based marriage. Similarly, in the 1980s (prior to 1989), there were signs of individualistic trends pertaining to choice of spouse in the People's Republic of China (Honig & Hershatter, 1988; Xiaohe & White, 1990).

It is intriguing to speculate about the factors that may contribute to the importance assigned romantic love as a basis for marriage in the People's Republic of China in the future. As a function of the "one child per family" policy, there are now large numbers of families in which there is only one child, and this child occupies a special and favored place in a household where traditionally the needs of the family unit were dominant. It would seem that a sense of personal uniqueness, a desire for personal gratification and fulfillment—in essence a highly individualized sense of self—are likely to develop in many of these children. Paradoxically, in a society where a relational sense of self traditionally has been the cultural norm, the family structure resulting from the "one-child" policy may ultimately foster a generation of individualists who may attach greater importance than earlier cohorts to self-discovery and personal fulfillment in their relationships with opposite-sex peers.

REFERENCES

Averill, J. R. (1985). The social construction of emotion: With special reference to love. In K. J. Gergen & K. E. Davis (Eds.), *The social construction of the person* (pp. 89–109). New York: Springer-Verlag.

Bardwick, J. (1980). The seasons of a woman's life. In D. McGuigan (Ed.), *Women's lives: New theory, research and policy* (pp. 35–55). Ann Arbor: University of Michigan Press.

Bellah, R. N., Madsen, R., Sullivan, W. M., Swidler, A., & Tipton, S. M. (1985). *Habits of the heart: Individualism and commitment in American life.* Berkeley: University of California Press.

Buruma, I. (1984). *A Japanese mirror: Heroes and villains of Japanese culture.* New York: Viking Penguin.

Chodorow, N. (1978). *The reproduction of mothering: Psychoanalysis and the sociology of gender.* Berkeley: University of California Press.

De Mente, B. (1989). *Everything Japanese.* Lincolnwood, IL: Passport Books.

Dion, K. K., & Dion, K. L. (1985). Personality, gender, and the phenomenology of romantic love. In P. R. Shaver (Ed.), *Self, situations and behavior: Review of Personality and Social Psychology* (Vol. 6, pp. 209–239). Newbury Park, CA: Sage.

Dion, K. K., & Dion, K. L. (1991). Psychological individualism and romantic love. *Journal of Social Behavior and Personality, 6,* 17–33.

Dion, K. L., & Dion, K. K. (1979). Personality and behavioural correlates of romantic love. In M. Cook & G. Wilson (Eds.), *Love and attraction* (pp. 213–220). Oxford, England and New York: Pergamon.

Dion, K. L., & Dion, K. K. (1988). Romantic love: Individual and cultural perspectives. In R. J. Sternberg & M. L. Barnes (Eds.), *The psychology of love* (pp. 264–289). New Haven, CT: Yale University Press.

Doi, T. (1962). AMAE: A key concept for understanding Japanese personality structure. In R. J. Smith & R. K. Beardsley (Eds.), *Japanese culture: Its development and characteristics* (pp. 132–139). Chicago, IL: Aldine.

Doi, T. (1963). Some thoughts on helplessness and the desire to be loved. *Psychiatry, 26,* 266–272.

Doi, T. (1977). The structure of amae. In M. Hyoe & E. G. Seidensticker (Eds.), *Guides to Japanese culture* (pp. 84–88). Tokyo: Japan Cultural Institute.

Doi, T. (1988). *The anatomy of dependence.* Tokyo and New York: Kodansha International.

Fukada, N. (1991). Women in Japan. In L. L. Adler (Ed.), *Women in cross-cultural perspective* (pp. 205–219). Westport, CT: Praeger.

Ho, D. Y. F. (1982). Asian concepts in behavioral science. *Psychologia, 25,* 228–235.

Hofstede, G. (1984). *Culture's consequences: International differences in work-related values.* Newbury Park, CA: Sage.

Hogan, R. (1975). Theoretical egocentrism and the problem of compliance. *American Psychologist, 30,* 533–540.

Honig, E., & Hershatter, G. (1988). *Personal voices: Chinese women in the 1980's.* Stanford, CA: Stanford University Press.

Hsu, F. L. K. (1971). Psychosocial homeostatis and Jen: Conceptual tools for advancing psychological anthropology. *American Anthropologist, 73,* 23–44.

Hsu, F. L. K. (1981). *Americans and Chinese: Passage to differences* (3rd ed.). Honolulu, HW: The University Press of Hawaii.

Hui, C. H., & Triandis, H. C. (1986). Individualism-collectivism: A study of cross-cultural researchers. *Journal of Cross-Cultural Psychology, 17,* 225–248.

Kim, U. (1993). *Introduction to individualism and collectivism: Conceptual clarification and elaboration.* Unpublished manuscript.

Lee, G. R., & Stone, L. H. (1980). Mate-selection systems and criteria: Variation according to family structure. *Journal of Marriage and the Family, 42,* 319–326.

Levinson, D. (1978). *The seasons of a man's life.* New York: Knopf.

Lykes, M. B. (1985). Gender and individualistic vs. collectivist bases for notions about the self. *Journal of Personality, 53,* 356–383.

Markus, H. R., & Kitayama, S. (1991). Culture and the self: Implications for cognition, emotion, and motivation. *Psychological Review, 98,* 224–253.

Morsbach, H., & Tyler, W. J. (1986). A Japanese emotion. In R. Harré (Eds.), *The social construction of emotions* (pp. 289–307). New York: Blackwell.

Roland, A. (1988). *In search of self in India and Japan.* Princeton, NJ: Princeton University Press.

Sampson, E. E. (1977). Psychology and the American ideal. *Journal of Personality and Social Psychology, 35,* 767–782.

Sampson, E. E. (1985). The decentralization of identity: Toward a revised concept of personal and social order. *American Psychologist, 40,* 1203–1211.

Sternberg, R. J., & Grajek, S. (1984). The nature of love. *Journal of Personality and Social Psychology, 47,* 312–329.

Waterman, A. S. (1984). *The psychology of individualism.* New York: Praeger.

Worell, J. (1988). Women's satisfaction in close relationships. *Clinical Psychology Review, 8,* 477–498.

Xiaohe, X., & Whyte, M. K. (1990). Love matches and arranged marriages: A Chinese replication. *Journal of Marriage and the Family, 52,* 709–722.

Karen K. Dion and Kenneth L. Dion

PART THREE

Attitudes

On the Internet . . .

Sites appropriate to Part Three

This site from the National Institute of Mental Health (NIMH) reviews information on social influence, social cognition, stereotyping and prejudice, and social and personal identity.

```
http://www.nimh.nih.gov/publicat/
    baschap5.cfm
```

The Resources for Diversity Web site contains many links to sites on multicultural issues, ethnicity and culture, disability, gender, sexuality, religion, and other diversity issues.

```
http://alabanza.com/kabacoff/Inter-Links/
    diversity.html
```

The Implicit Association Tests site was created by the University of Washington and Yale University. This site contains a series of tests that are designed to help students understand their own potential biases. Test topics include age, race, gender science, and presidential candidate choices.

```
http://www.yale.edu/implicit/index.html
```

CHAPTER 5 Attitudes and Behavior

5.1 ICEK AJZEN AND MARTIN FISHBEIN

Attitude–Behavior Relations

Attitudes are usually defined as having cognitive, emotional, and behavioral components. We usually think that our attitudes and behaviors agree with one another, but we are also aware that sometimes they do not agree. Icek Ajzen and Martin Fishbein's theory of reasoned action is designed to identify the factors that determine the degree to which attitudes and behaviors are consistent.

Ajzen earned his Ph.D. from the University of Illinois in 1969. He is currently a professor of psychology at the University of Massachusetts. Fishbein (b. 1936) received his Ph.D. in social psychology from the University of California at Los Angeles in 1961. He then accepted a position at the University of Illinois, where he is currently a professor of psychology. Ajzen and Fishbein have coauthored a number of articles on their theory of reasoned action.

This selection is from "Attitude–Behavior Relations: A Theoretical Analysis and Review of Empirical Research," which was published in *Psychological Bulletin* in 1977. In it, the authors discuss the conditions under which there is high correspondence between attitudes and behaviors. Ajzen and Fishbein define four elements that make up attitudinal and behavioral entities and then explain how they can be used to predict behavior. How can correspondence between attitudes and behaviors be increased in social psychology research? What aspects of attitude should we look at when we are making behavioral predictions?

Key Concept: correspondence of attitude and behavior

APA Citation: Ajzen, I., & Fishbein, M. (1977). Attitude–behavior relations: A theoretical analysis and review of empirical research. *Psychological Bulletin, 84*, 888–918.

ATTITUDE–BEHAVIOR CORRESPONDENCE

Attitudes are held with respect to some aspect of the individual's world, such as another person, a physical object, a behavior, or a policy. Although many definitions of attitude have been proposed, most investigators would agree that a person's attitude represents his evaluation of the entity in question. For purposes of the present review, only measures that place the individual on a bipolar evaluative or affective dimension are considered to be measures of attitude.

Behavioral criteria consist of one or more observable actions performed by the individual and recorded in some way by the investigator. Behavioral acts include attending a meeting, using birth control pills, buying a product, donating blood, and so forth. Sometimes investigators have relied on "behavioroid" measures (Aronson & Carlsmith, 1968), that is, on the individual's commitment to perform the behavior under consideration or on self-reports of behavior. Such measures are treated below as acceptable behavioral criteria only when it would have been difficult or impossible to obtain a direct measure of the behavior in question.

Attempts to predict behavior from attitudes are largely based on a general notion of consistency. It is usually considered to be logical or consistent for a person who holds a favorable attitude toward some object to perform favorable behaviors, and not to perform unfavorable behaviors, with respect to the object. Similarly, a person with an unfavorable attitude is expected to perform unfavorable behaviors, but not to perform favorable behaviors. The apparent simplicity of this notion is deceptive, since there is usually no theoretical basis for the assumption that a behavior has favorable or unfavorable implications for the object under consideration. Obviously, many behaviors have no evaluative implications for a given object. Eating hamburgers, for example, implies neither a favorable nor an unfavorable evaluation of Russia. However, an investigator might assume that an unfavorable evaluation of Russia is implied by the act of volunteering for military service and might therefore predict a relationship between attitude toward Russia and a measure of this behavior.

It can be seen that a given behavior is assumed to be consistent or inconsistent with a person's attitude on the basis of largely intuitive considerations. In the absence of an explicit and unambiguous definition of attitude–behavior consistency, therefore, many tests of the attitude–behavior relation reduce to little more than tests of the investigator's intuition. From a theoretical point of view, such tests of the relation between arbitrarily selected measures of attitude or behavior are of rather limited value.

The following analysis attempts to specify the conditions under which attitudes can or cannot be expected to predict overt behavior. Our point of departure is the notion that attitudes are held and behaviors are performed with respect to certain entities. Two important questions in research on the attitude–behavior relation can then be identified: (a) What are the entities of the attitudinal predictors and of the behavioral criteria? (b) What is the degree of correspondence between the attitudinal and the behavioral entities?

Attitudinal and Behavioral Entities

Attitudinal and behavioral entities may be viewed as consisting of four different elements: the *action*, the *target* at which the action is directed, the *context* in which the action is performed, and the *time* at which it is performed. The generality or specificity of each element depends on the measurement procedure employed.

Behavioral criteria based on single observations always involve four specific elements. That is, a given action is always performed with respect to a given target, in a given context, and at a given point in time. Criteria based on multiple observations of behavior generalize across one or more of the four elements. For example, when the behavioral observations constituting the criterion measure involve a very heterogeneous sample of targets, the target element is essentially left unspecified. However, when the different targets constitute a more homogeneous set, their common attributes determine the target element. When all targets are other human beings, for example, the target element is people in general; when the individuals serving as targets are of the same sex, religion, or race, then males, Jews, or Orientals might constitute the target element.

Similar considerations apply to the definition of the action, context, and time elements. To illustrate, when a very heterogeneous sample of behaviors is observed, the action element is left unspecified. Sometimes, however, the specific acts may represent a more general class of behaviors, such as cooperation, aggression, or altruism. Here, the action element is defined by the class of behaviors.

In conclusion, the measurement procedure determines the behavioral entity. When the same action is observed with respect to heterogeneous targets, in different contexts, and at different points in time, we obtain a behavioral index whose entity is defined only by the action element. The target serves as the entity when heterogeneous behaviors toward the same target are observed in different situations and at different points in time. In a similar manner, indices can be obtained such that the contextual element, the time element, or any combination of elements defines the entity for the behavioral criterion.

As in the case of behavioral criteria, attitudes are also directed at entities that may be defined by a single element or by combinations of two or more elements. Attitudinal predictors frequently specify only the target. Attitudes have been measured toward the church, various ethnic groups, specific persons, and so on without reference to any particular action, context, or time. However, an investigator can specify an entity in terms of any combination of elements and can obtain a measure of attitude toward that entity. For example, an evaluative semantic differential could be used to measure attitudes toward targets (Martin Luther King, Jews) toward actions (cooking dinner, cooperating), toward contexts (in St. Mary's Cathedral, at home), toward times (3:00 p.m. tomorrow, August), or toward any combination of elements (cooperating with Jews, cooking dinner at home at 3:00 p.m. tomorrow).

Correspondence Between Attitudinal and Behavioral Entities

After defining entities in terms of their elements, we can approach the question of attitude–behavior correspondence. An attitudinal predictor is said to correspond to the behavioral criterion to the extent that the attitudinal entity is identical in all four elements with the behavioral entity. For example, a measure of attitude toward a target such as "my church" (without specification of action, context, or time) corresponds directly only to a behavioral criterion based on the observation of different behaviors with respect to the person's church (e.g., donating money, attending Sunday worship services, participating in church-sponsored activities, etc.), in different contexts, and at different points in time. Similarly, when the attitude measure is an evaluation of a specific action toward a given target, such as the attitude toward "donating money to my church," the corresponding behavioral criterion is an index of monetary donations to the person's church based on multiple behavioral observations in different contexts (e.g., at home, in the church, etc.) and on different occasions. Alternatively, when the behavioral criterion is a single act, such as the person's attendance or nonattendance of next Sunday's worship service in his church at 10:00 a.m., the corresponding attitudinal predictor would be a measure of the person's evaluation of "attending my church's worship service next Sunday at 10:00 a.m."

Correspondence and the Attitude–Behavior Relation. The central thesis of this article is that the strength of an attitude–behavior relationship depends in large part on the degree of correspondence between attitudinal and behavioral entities. Although, in theory, correspondence is defined in terms of all four elements of the entities involved, for purposes of the present article, examination of the target and action elements is sufficient.

Considering target and action elements alone, two attitudinal predictors can be identified that deserve special attention. The most common measure specifies a given target (be it an object, a person, or an institution) without reference to a particular action. This predictor may be termed *attitude toward a target*. Of less frequent use is *attitude toward an action*, a predictor that specifies both action and target elements (e.g., attitude toward smoking marijuana).

A similar distinction can be made with reference to behavioral criteria. When the criterion is an index based on observations of heterogeneous behaviors with respect to a given target, only the target element is specified and the resulting measure may be called a *multiple-act criterion*. When only one behavior toward a given target is observed, both target and action elements are specified and we obtain a *single-act criterion*.

The above discussion suggests that attitudes toward targets will predict multiple-act criteria, provided that the attitudinal and behavioral entities involve the same target elements. Similarly, attitudes toward actions are expected to predict single-act criteria if the target and action elements of the attitudinal entity are identical with those of the behavioral entity (cf. Fishbein & Ajzen, 1974, 1975). . . .

Although this discussion may appear to imply that attitude measures have to be specific with respect to target, action, and context, we have argued that the problem is one of correspondence between predictor and criterion, not a problem of specificity. Of course, if the investigator chooses to observe a single action with respect to a given target in a given context in order to obtain correspondence, the attitude also has to be very specific. On the other hand, if she is really interested in a general behavioral pattern, such as discrimination toward blacks, the behavioral criterion should involve observation of different discriminatory behaviors toward various black individuals in a variety of contexts. A general measure of attitude toward blacks will correspond to such a criterion.

In conclusion, our review and theoretical analysis suggest that low and inconsistent attitude–behavior relations are attributable to low or partial correspondence between attitudinal and behavioral entities. To predict behavior from attitude, the investigator has to ensure high correspondence between at least the target and action elements of the measures he employs.

Lest attitude researchers conclude that all is well and resume their complacency, we hasten to add a few words of caution. First, attitude measurement, even by means of sophisticated instruments, may add little to our understanding of social phenomena. An investigator attempting to explain a certain phenomenon in terms of an attitudinal analysis must first define the behaviors of interest, the targets at which they are directed, and the context and time of their occurrence. Measures of attitude will serve to explain the behaviors to the extent that they involve identical target, action, context, and time elements.

Second, attempts to influence behavior by means of attitude change must also consider the degree of correspondence between the behavior that is to be changed and the attitude at which the influence attempt is directed. Demonstration of attitude change is insufficient evidence for one's ability to change behavior; only behaviors that correspond to the attitude are likely to change as a result of revisions in attitude.

Finally, high correspondence between predictors and criteria will ensure strong attitude–behavior relations only to the extent that appropriate measurement procedures are employed. For too long it has been at the investigator's discretion to select any measures deemed useful and to assign the labels *attitude* and *behavior* to them. Attitudinal and behavioral measures are often selected in an arbitrary manner, leading to apparently inconsistent research findings.

In sum, only when standard procedures are employed to scale attitudes and to select behaviors and only when attention is paid to the correspondence between attitudinal and behavioral entities will the concept of attitude be able to resume the place it was accorded by Allport (1954) as the cornerstone in the edifice of social psychology.

REFERENCES

Allport, G. W. *The nature of prejudice.* Reading, Mass.: Addison-Wesley, 1954.

Aronson, E., & Carlsmith, J. M. Experimentation in social psychology. In G. Lindzey & E. Aronson (Eds.), *Handbook of social psychology* (Vol. 2). Reading, Mass.: Addison-Wesley, 1968.

Fishbein, M., & Ajzen, I. Attitudes toward objects as predictors of single and multiple behavioral criteria. *Psychological Review,* 1974, *81,* 59–74.

Fishbein, M., & Ajzen, I. *Belief, attitude, intention, and behavior: An introduction to theory and research.* Reading, Mass.: Addison-Wesley, 1975.

5.2 RICHARD T. LaPIERE

Attitudes vs. Actions

Most people assume that their attitudes and prejudices match their actions. Likewise, many people assume that measurement of social attitudes can allow one to predict what people will do in the future. However, sometimes our private behaviors differ from our public statements. Richard T. LaPiere tested this notion by comparing the results of a survey with the actual behavior of the same population.

LaPiere (1899–1986) earned his Ph.D. from Stanford University in 1930 and spent his academic career at the University of Michigan and Stanford University. He is the author of *The Freudian Ethic* (Duell, Sloan, & Pearce, 1959).

This selection is from "Attitudes vs. Actions," which was published in *Social Forces* in 1934. In it, LaPiere presents his findings on the relationship between attitudes and behavior. Although criticized for methodological flaws and overgeneralized conclusions, LaPiere's classic study represents an early approach to research on discrimination. LaPiere's research consisted of asking people about their attitudes toward Chinese people in general and then observing people's reactions toward a specific traveling Chinese couple. LaPiere interpreted the results as evidence of a major inconsistency between attitudes and behavior. However, more recent research has indicated that there is a significantly closer relationship between attitudes and behavior. What factors might influence consistency between attitudes and behavior? As you read this selection, consider how consistent your attitudes and behaviors are in everyday situations.

Key Concept: attitudes and behavior

APA Citation: LaPiere, R. T. (1934). Attitudes vs. actions. *Social Forces, 13,* 230–237.

*B*y definition, a social attitude is a behaviour pattern, anticipatory set or tendency, predisposition to specific adjustment to designated social situations, or, more simply, a conditioned response to social stimuli. Terminological usage differs, but students who have concerned themselves with attitudes apparently agree that they are acquired out of social experience and provide the individual organism with some degree of preparation to adjust, in a well-defined way, to certain types of social situations if and when these situations arise. It would seem, therefore, that the totality of the social attitudes of a single individual would include all his socially acquired personality which is involved in the making of adjustments to other human beings.

But by derivation social attitudes are seldom more than a verbal response to a symbolic situation. For the conventional method of measuring social attitudes is to ask questions (usually in writing) which demand a verbal adjustment to an entirely symbolic situation. Because it is easy, cheap, and mechanical, the attitudinal questionnaire is rapidly becoming a major method of sociological and socio-psychological investigation. The technique is simple. Thus from a hundred or a thousand responses to the question "Would you get up to give an Armenian woman your seat in a street car?" the investigator derives the "attitude" of non-Armenian males towards Armenian females. Now the question may be constructed with elaborate skill and hidden with consummate cunning in a maze of supplementary or even irrelevant questions yet all that has been obtained is a symbolic response to a symbolic situation. The words "Armenian woman" do not constitute an Armenian woman of flesh and blood, who might be tall or squat, fat or thin, old or young, well or poorly dressed—who might, in fact, be a goddess or just another old and dirty hag. And the questionnaire response, whether it be "yes" or "no," is but a verbal reaction and this does not involve rising from the seat or stolidly avoiding the hurt eyes of the hypothetical woman and the derogatory stares of other street-car occupants. . . .

All measurement of attitudes by the questionnaire technique proceeds on the assumption that there is a mechanical relationship between symbolic and non-symbolic behavior. It is simple enough to prove that there is no *necessary* correlation between speech and action, between response to words and to the realities they symbolize. A parrot can be taught to swear, a child to sing "Frankie and Johnny" in the Mae West manner. The words will have no meaning to either child or parrot. But to prove that there is no *necessary* relationship does not prove that such a relationship may not exist. There need be no relationship between what the hotel proprietor says he will do and what he actually does when confronted with a colored patron. Yet there may be. Certainly we are justified in assuming that the verbal response of the hotel proprietor would be more likely to indicate what he would actually do than would the verbal response of people whose personal feelings are less subordinated to economic expediency. However, the following study indicates that the reliability of even such responses is very small indeed.

Beginning in 1930 and continuing for two years thereafter, I had the good fortune to travel rather extensively with a young Chinese student and his wife. Both were personable, charming, and quick to win the admiration and respect of those they had the opportunity to become intimate with. But they were foreign-born Chinese, a fact that could not be disguised. Knowing the general "attitude" of Americans towards the Chinese as indicated by the "social distance" studies which have been made, it was with considerable trepidation that I first approached a hotel clerk in their company. Perhaps the clerk's eyebrows lifted slightly, but he accommodated us without a show of hesitation. And this in the "best" hotel in a small town noted for its narrow and bigoted "attitude" towards Orientals. Two months later I passed that way again, phoned the hotel and asked if they would accommodate "an important Chinese gentleman."

Richard T.
LaPiere

The reply was an unequivocal "No." That aroused my curiosity and led to this study.

In something like ten thousand miles of motor travel, twice across the United States, up and down the Pacific Coast, we met definite rejection from those asked to serve us just once. We were received at 66 hotels, auto camps, and "Tourist Homes," refused at one. We were served in 184 restaurants and cafes scattered throughout the country and treated with what I judged to be more than ordinary consideration in 72 of them. Accurate and detailed records were kept of all these instances. An effort, necessarily subjective, was made to evaluate the overt response of hotel clerks, bell boys, elevator operators, and waitresses to the presence of my Chinese friends. The factors entering into the situations were varied as far and as often as possible. Control was not, of course, as exacting as that required by laboratory experimentation. But it was as rigid as is humanly possible in human situations. For example, I did not take the "test" subjects into my confidence fearing that their behavior might become self-conscious and thus abnormally affect the response of others towards them. Whenever possible I let my Chinese friend negotiate for accommodations (while I concerned myself with the car or luggage) or sent them into a restaurant ahead of me. In this way, I attempted to "factor" myself out. We sometimes patronized high-class establishments after a hard and dusty day on the road and stopped at inferior auto camps when in our most presentable condition.

In the end I was forced to conclude that those factors which most influenced the behavior of others towards the Chinese had nothing at all to do with race. Quality and condition of clothing, appearance of baggage (by which, it seems, hotel clerks are prone to base their quick evaluations), cleanliness and neatness were far more significant for person to person reaction in the situations I was studying than skin pigmentation, straight black hair, slanting eyes, and flat noses. And yet an air of self-confidence might entirely offset the "unfavorable" impression made by dusty clothes and the usual disorder to appearance consequent upon some hundred miles of motor travel. A supercilious desk clerk in a hotel of noble aspirations could not refuse his master's hospitality to people who appeared to take their request as a perfectly normal and conventional thing, though they might look like tin-can tourists and two of them belong to the racial category "Oriental." On the other hand, I became rather adept at approaching hotel clerks with that peculiar curb-wise manner which is so effective in provoking a somewhat scornful disregard. And then a bland smile would serve to reverse the entire situation. Indeed, it appeared that a genial smile was the most effective password to acceptance. My Chinese friends were skillful smilers, which may account, in part, for the fact that we received but one rebuff in all our experience. Finally, I was impressed with the fact that even where some tension developed due to the strangeness of the Chinese it would evaporate immediately when they spoke in unaccented English.

The one instance in which we were refused accommodations is worth recording here. The place was a small California town, a rather inferior auto-camp into which we drove in a very dilapidated car piled with camp equipment. It was early evening, the light so dim that the proprietor found it somewhat difficult to decide the genus *voyageur* to which we belonged. I left the car and spoke to him. He hesitated, wavered, said he was not sure that he had two cabins, meanwhile edging towards our car. The realization that the two occupants were Orientals turned the balance or, more likely, gave him the excuse he was looking for. "No," he said, "I don't take Japs!" In a more pretentious establishment we secured accommodations, and with an extra flourish of hospitality.

To offset this one flat refusal were the many instances in which the physical peculiarities of the Chinese served to heighten curiosity. With few exceptions this curiosity was considerately hidden behind an exceptional interest in serving us. Of course, outside of the Pacific Coast region, New York, and Chicago, the Chinese physiognomy attracts attention. It is different, hence noticeable. But the principal effect this curiosity has upon the behavior of those who cater to the traveler's needs is to make them more attentive, more responsive, more reliable. A Chinese companion is to be recommended to the white traveling in his native land. Strange features when combined with "human" speech and action seems, at times, to heighten sympathetic response, perhaps on the same principle that makes us uncommonly sympathetic towards the dog that has a "human" expression in his face.

What I am trying to say is that in only one out of 251 instances in which we purchased goods or services necessitating intimate human relationships did the fact that my companions were Chinese adversely affect us. Factors entirely unassociated with race were, in the main, the determinant of significant variations in our reception. It would appear reasonable to conclude that the "attitude" of the American people, as reflected in the behavior of those who are for pecuniary reasons presumably most sensitive to the antipathies of their white clientele, is anything but negative towards the Chinese. In terms of "social distance" we might conclude that native Caucasians are not averse to residing in the same hotels, auto-camps, and "Tourist Homes" as Chinese and will with complacency accept the presence of Chinese at an adjoining table in restaurant or cafe. It does not follow that there is revealed a distinctly "positive" attitude towards the Chinese, that whites prefer the Chinese to other whites. But the facts as gathered certainly preclude the conclusion that there is an intense prejudice towards the Chinese.

Yet the existence of this prejudice, very intense, is proven by a conventional "attitude" study. To provide a comparison of symbolic reaction to symbolic social situations with actual reaction to real social situations, I "questionnaired" the establishments which we patronized during the two year period. Six months were permitted to lapse between the time I obtained the overt reaction and the symbolic. It was hoped that the effects of the actual experience with Chinese guests, adverse or otherwise, would have faded during the intervening time. To the hotel or restaurant a questionnaire was mailed with an accompanying letter purporting to be a special and personal plea for response. The questionnaires all asked the same question, "Will you accept members of the Chinese race as guests in your establishment?" Two types of questionnaire were used. In one this question was inserted among similar queries concerning Germans, French, Japanese, Russians, Armenians, Jews, Negroes, Italians, and Indians. In the other the pertinent question was unencumbered. With persistence, completed replies were obtained from 128 of the establishments we had visited; 81 restaurants and cafes and 47 hotels, auto-camps, and "Tourist

Homes." In response to the relevant question 92 per cent of the former and 91 per cent of the latter replied "No." The remainder replied "Uncertain; depend upon circumstances." From the woman proprietor of a small auto-camp I received the only "Yes," accompanied by a chatty letter describing the nice visit she had had with a Chinese gentleman and his sweet wife during the previous summer.

A rather unflattering interpretation might be put upon the fact that those establishments who had provided for our needs so graciously were, some months later, verbally antagonistic towards hypothetical Chinese. To factor this experience out responses were secured from 32 hotels and 96 restaurants located in approximately the same regions, but uninfluenced by this particular experience with Oriental clients. In this, as in the former case, both types of questionnaires were used. The results indicate that neither the type of questionnaire nor the fact of previous experience had important bearing upon the symbolic response to symbolic social situations.

It is impossible to make direct comparison between the reactions secured through questionnaires and from actual experience. On the basis of the above data it would appear foolhardy for a Chinese to attempt to travel in the United States. And yet, as I have shown, actual experience indicates that the American people, as represented by the personnel of hotels, restaurants, etc., are not at all averse to fraternizing with Chinese within the limitations which apply to social relationships between Americans themselves....

The questionnaire is cheap, easy, and mechanical. The study of human behavior is time consuming, intellectually fatiguing, and depends for its success upon the ability of the investigator. The former method gives quantitative results, the latter mainly qualitative. Quantitative measurements are quantitatively accurate; qualitative evaluations are always subject to the errors of human judgment. Yet it would seem far more worth while to make a shrewd guess regarding that which is essential than to accurately measure that which is likely to prove quite irrelevant.

CHAPTER 6 Attitude Change

6.1 LEON FESTINGER AND JAMES M. CARLSMITH

Cognitive Consequences of Forced Compliance

One of the most important theories in social psychology is Leon Festinger's 1957 theory of cognitive dissonance. Over the past three decades numerous experiments have applied the principles of dissonance to a variety of situations. A classic experiment performed by Festinger and James M. Carlsmith in 1959 illustrates the theory. Cognitive dissonance is one of the most influential theories of attitude change.

Festinger (1919–1989) earned his Ph.D. in psychology from the State University of Iowa in 1942. He taught at the Massachusetts Institute of Technology, the University of Michigan, and Stanford University before going to the New School for Social Research in New York City in 1968. Carlsmith was also a professor of psychology at Stanford University.

This selection is from "Cognitive Consequences of Forced Compliance," which was published in 1959 in *Journal of Abnormal and Social Psychology*. In Festinger and Carlsmith's classic experiment, 71 male students performed a boring task and were then asked to tell another student that it was very interesting. The experimenters found that when a reward was offered, the students tended to believe that the boring tasks were, in fact, interesting. However, they also found that the greater the reward offered, the less this effect was produced. As you read this selection, note the elaborate care that was taken in designing this study. Also note how deception was used and how the outcome depended upon the design of the experiment. Do you think you would enjoy a job more if you were paid less? Can you think of other applications of cognitive dissonance theory?

*Leon Festinger
and James M.
Carlsmith*

Key Concept: cognitive dissonance

APA Citation: Festinger, L., and Carlsmith, J. M. (1959). Cognitive consequences of forced compliance. *Journal of Abnormal and Social Psychology, 58,* 203–210.

Recently, Festinger (1957) proposed a theory concerning cognitive dissonance from which come a number of derivations about opinion change following forced compliance. Since these derivations are stated in detail by Festinger (1957, Ch. 4), we will here give only a brief outline of the reasoning.

Let us consider a person who privately holds opinion "X" but has, as a result of pressure brought to bear on him, publicly stated that he believes "not X."

1. This person has two cognitions which, psychologically, do not fit together: one of these is the knowledge that he believes "X," the other the knowledge that he has publicly stated that he believes "not X." If no factors other than his private opinion are considered, it would follow, at least in our culture, that if he believes "X" he would publicly state "X." Hence, his cognition of his private belief is dissonant with his cognition concerning his actual public statement.

2. Similarly, the knowledge that he has said "not X" is consonant with (does fit together with) those cognitive elements corresponding to the reasons, pressures, promises of rewards and/or threats of punishment which induced him to say "not X."

3. In evaluating the total magnitude of dissonance, one must take account of both dissonances and consonances. Let us think of the sum of all the dissonances involving some particular cognition as "D" and the sum of all the consonances as "C." Then we might think of the total magnitude of dissonance as being a function of "D" divided by "D" plus "C."

Let us then see what can be said about the total magnitude of dissonance in a person created by the knowledge that he said "not X" and really believes "X." With everything else held constant, this total magnitude of dissonance would decrease as the number and importance of the pressures which induced him to say "not X" increased.

Thus, if the overt behavior was brought about by, say, offers of reward or threats of punishment, the magnitude of dissonance is maximal if these promised rewards or threatened punishments were just barely sufficient to induce the person to say "not X." From this point on, as the promised rewards or threatened punishment become larger, the magnitude of dissonance becomes smaller.

4. One way in which the dissonance can be reduced is for the person to change his private opinion so as to bring it into correspondence with what he has said. One would consequently expect to observe such opinion change after a person has been forced or induced to say something contrary to his private

opinion. Furthermore, since the pressure to reduce dissonance will be a function of the magnitude of the dissonance, the observed opinion change should be greatest when the pressure used to elicit the overt behavior is just sufficient to do it.

The present experiment was designed to test this derivation under controlled, laboratory conditions. In the experiment we varied the amount of reward used to force persons to make a statement contrary to their private views. The prediction [from 3 and 4 above] is that the larger the reward given to the subject, the smaller will be the subsequent opinion change.

PROCEDURE

Seventy-one male students in the introductory psychology course at Stanford University were used in the experiment. In this course, students are required to spend a certain number of hours as subjects (*S*s) in experiments. They choose among the available experiments by signing their names on a sheet posted on the bulletin board which states the nature of the experiment. The present experiment was listed as a two-hour experiment dealing with "Measures of Performance."

During the first week of the course, when the requirement of serving in experiments was announced and explained to the students, the instructor also told them about a study that the psychology department was conducting. He explained that, since they were required to serve in experiments, the department was conducting a study to evaluate these experiments in order to be able to improve them in the future. They were told that a sample of students would be interviewed after having served as *S*s. They were urged to cooperate in these interviews by being completely frank and honest. The importance of this announcement will become clear shortly. It enabled us to measure the opinions of our *S*s in a context not directly connected with our experiment and in which we could reasonably expect frank and honest expressions of opinion.

When the *S* arrived for the experiment on "Measures of Performance" he had to wait for a few minutes in the secretary's office. The experimenter (*E*) then came in, introduced himself to the *S* and, together, they walked into the laboratory room where the *E* said:

> This experiment usually takes a little over an hour but, of course, we had to schedule it for two hours. Since we have that extra time, the introductory psychology people asked if they could interview some of our subjects. [Offhand and conversationally.] Did they announce that in class? I gather that they're interviewing some people who have been in experiments. I don't know much about it. Anyhow, they may want to interview you when you're through here.

With no further introduction or explanation the *S* was shown the first task, which involved putting 12 spools onto a tray, emptying the tray, refilling it with spools, and so on. He was told to use one hand and to work at his own speed. He did this for one-half hour. The *E* then removed the tray and spools and placed in front of the *S* a board containing 48 square pegs. His task was to turn each peg a quarter turn clockwise, then another quarter turn, and so on. He was told again to use one hand and to work at his own speed. The *S* worked at this task for another half hour.

While the *S* was working on these tasks, the *E* sat, with a stop watch in his hand, busily making notations on a sheet of paper. He did so in order to make it convincing that this was what the *E* was interested in and that these tasks, and how the *S* worked on them, was the total experiment. From our point of view the experiment had hardly started. The hour which the *S* spent working on the repetitive, monotonous tasks was intended to provide, for each *S* uniformly, an experience about which he would have a somewhat negative opinion.

After the half hour on the second task was over, the *E* conspicuously set the stop watch back to zero, put it away, pushed his chair back, lit a cigarette, and said:

> O.K. Well, that's all we have in the experiment itself. I'd like to explain what this has been all about so you'll have some idea of why you were doing this. [*E* pauses.] Well, the way the experiment is set up is this. There are actually two groups in the experiment. In one, the group you were in, we bring the subject in and give him essentially no introduction to the experiment. That is, all we tell him is what he needs to know in order to do the tasks, and he has no idea of what the experiment is all about, or what it's going to be like, or anything like that. But in the other group, we have a student that we've hired that works for us regularly, and what I do is take him into the next room where the subject is waiting—the same room you were waiting in before—and I introduce him as if he had just finished being a subject in the experiment. That is, I say: "This is so-and-so, who's just finished the experiment, and I've asked him to tell you a little of what it's about before you start." The fellow who works for us then, in conversation with the next subject, makes these points: [The *E* then produced a sheet headed "For Group B" which had written on it: It was very enjoyable, I had a lot of fun, I enjoyed myself, it was very interesting, it was intriguing, it was exciting. The *E* showed this to the *S* and then proceeded with his false explanation of the purpose of the experiment.] Now, of course, we have this student do this, because if the experimenter does it, it doesn't look realistic, and what we're interested in doing is comparing how these two groups do on the experiment—the one with this previous expectation about the experiment, and the other, like yourself, with essentially none.

Up to this point the procedure was identical for *S*s in all conditions. From this point on they diverged somewhat. Three conditions were run, Control, One Dollar, and Twenty Dollars, as follows:

Control Condition

The *E* continued:

> Is that fairly clear? [Pause.] Look, that fellow [looks at watch] I was telling you about from the introductory psychology class said he would get here a couple of minutes from now. Would you mind waiting to see if he wants to talk to you? Fine. Why don't we go into the other room to wait? [The *E* left the *S* in the secretary's office for four minutes. He then returned and said:] O.K. Let's check and see if he does want to talk to you.

The *E* continued:

Is that fairly clear how it is set up and what we're trying to do? [Pause.] Now, I also have a sort of strange thing to ask you. The thing is this. [Long pause, some confusion and uncertainty in the following, with a degree of embarrassment on the part of the *E*. The manner of the *E* contrasted strongly with the preceding unhesitant and assured false explanation of the experiment. The point was to make it seem to the *S* that this was the first time the *E* had done this and that he felt unsure of himself.] The fellow who normally does this for us couldn't do it today —he just phoned in, and something or other came up for him—so we've been looking around for someone that we could hire to do it for us. You see, we've got another subject waiting [looks at watch] who is supposed to be in that other condition. Now Professor————, who is in charge of this experiment, suggested that perhaps we could take a chance on your doing it for us. I'll tell you what we had in mind: the thing is, if you could do it for us now, then of course you would know how to do it, and if something like this should ever come up again, that is, the regular fellow couldn't make it, and we had a subject scheduled, it would be very reassuring to us to know that we had somebody else we could call on who knew how to do it. So, if you would be willing to do this for us, we'd like to hire you to do it now and then be on call in the future, if something like this should ever happen again. We can pay you a dollar (twenty dollars) for doing this for us, that is, for doing it now and then being on call. Do you think you could do that for us?

If the *S* hesitated, the *E* said things like, "It will only take a few minutes," "The regular person is pretty reliable; this is the first time he has missed," or "If we needed you we could phone you a day or two in advance; if you couldn't make it, of course, we wouldn't expect you to come." After the *S* agreed to do it, the *E* gave him the previously mentioned sheet of paper headed "For Group B" and asked him to read it through again. The *E* then paid the *S* one dollar (twenty dollars), made out a hand-written receipt form, and asked the *S* to sign it. He then said:

O.K., the way we'll do it is this. As I said, the next subject should be here by now. I think the next one is a girl. I'll take you into the next room and introduce you to her, saying that you've just finished the experiment and that we've asked you to tell her a little about it. And what we want you to do is just sit down and get into a conversation with her and try to get across the points on that sheet of paper. I'll leave you alone and come back after a couple of minutes. O.K.?

The *E* then took the *S* into the secretary's office where he had previously waited and where the next *S* was waiting. (The secretary had left the office.) He introduced the girl and the *S* to one another saying that the *S* had just finished the experiment and would tell her something about it. He then left saying he would return in a couple of minutes. The girl, an undergraduate hired for this role, said little until the *S* made some positive remarks about the experiment and then said that she was surprised because a friend of hers had taken the experiment the week before and had told her that it was boring and that she ought to try to get out of it. Most Ss responded by saying something like "Oh, no, it's really very interesting. I'm sure you'll enjoy it." The girl, after this listened quietly, accepting and agreeing to everything the S told her. The discussion between the S and the girl was recorded on a hidden tape recorder.

After two minutes the E returned, asked the girl to go into the experimental room, thanked the S for talking to the girl, wrote down his phone number to continue the fiction that we might call on him again in the future and then said: "Look, could we check and see if that fellow from introductory psychology wants to talk to you?"

From this point on, the procedure for all three conditions was once more identical. As the E and the S started to walk to the office where the interviewer was, the E said: "Thanks very much for working on those tasks for us. I hope you did enjoy it. Most of our subjects tell us afterward that they found it quite interesting. You get a chance to see how you react to the tasks and so forth." This short persuasive communication was made in all conditions in exactly the same way. The reason for doing it, theoretically, was to make it easier for anyone who wanted to persuade himself that the tasks had been, indeed, enjoyable.

When they arrived at the interviewer's office, the E asked the interviewer whether or not he wanted to talk to the S. The interviewer said yes, the E shook hands with the S, said good-bye, and left. The interviewer, of course, was always kept in complete ignorance of which condition the S was in. The interview consisted of four questions, on each of which the S was first encouraged to talk about the matter and was then asked to rate his opinion or reaction on an 11-point scale. The questions are as follows:

1. Were the tasks interesting and enjoyable? In what way? In what way were they not? Would you rate how you feel about them on a scale from −5 to + 5 where −5 means they were extremely dull and boring, + 5 means they were extremely interesting and enjoyable, and zero means they were neutral, neither interesting nor uninteresting.

2. Did the experiment give you an opportunity to learn about your own ability to perform these tasks? In what way? In what way not? Would you rate how you feel about this on a scale from 0 to 10 where 0 means you learned nothing and 10 means you learned a great deal.

3. From what you know about the experiment and the tasks involved in it, would you say the experiment was measuring anything important? That is, do you think the results may have scientific value? In what way? In what way not? Would you rate your opinion on this matter on a scale from 0 to 10 where 0 means the results have no scientific value or importance and 10 means they have a great deal of value and importance.

4. Would you have any desire to participate in another similar experiment? Why? Why not? Would you rate your desire to participate in a similar experiment again on a scale from −5 to + 5, where −5 means you would definitely dislike to participate, + 5 means you would definitely like to participate, and 0 means you have no particular feeling about it one way or the other.

As may be seen, the questions varied in how directly relevant they were to what the S had told the girl. This point will be discussed further in connection with the results.

At the close of the interview the *S* was asked what he thought the experiment was about and, following this, was asked directly whether or not he was suspicious of anything and, if so, what he was suspicious of. When the interview was over, the interviewer brought the *S* back to the experimental room where the *E* was waiting together with the girl who had posed as the waiting *S*. (In the control condition, of course, the girl was not there.) The true purpose of the experiment was then explained to the *S* in detail, and the reasons for each of the various steps in the experiment were explained carefully in relation to the true purpose. All experimental *S*s in both One Dollar and Twenty Dollar conditions were asked, after this explanation, to return the money they had been given. All *S*s, without exception, were quite willing to return the money.

The data from 11 of the 71 *S*s in the experiment had to be discarded....

RESULTS

The major results of the experiment are summarized in Table 1 which lists, separately for each of the three experimental conditions, the average rating which the *S*s gave at the end of each question on the interview. We will discuss each of the questions on the interview separately, because they were intended to measure different things. One other point before we proceed to examine the data. In all the comparisons, the Control condition should be regarded as a baseline from which to evaluate the results in the other two conditions. The Control condition gives us, essentially, the reactions of *S*s to the tasks and their opinions about the experiment as falsely explained to them, without the experimental introduction of dissonance. The data from the other conditions may be viewed, in a sense, as changes from this baseline.

How Enjoyable the Tasks Were

The average ratings on this question, presented in the first row of figures in Table 1, are the results most important to the experiment. These results are the ones most directly relevant to the specific dissonance which was experimentally created. It will be recalled that the tasks were purposely arranged to be rather boring and monotonous. And, indeed, in the Control condition the average rating was −.45, somewhat on the negative side of the neutral point.

In the other two conditions, however, the *S*s told someone that these tasks were interesting and enjoyable. The resulting dissonance could, of course, most directly be reduced by persuading themselves that the tasks were, indeed, interesting and enjoyable. In the One Dollar condition, since the magnitude of dissonance was high, the pressure to reduce this dissonance would also be high. In this condition, the average rating was + 1.35, considerably on the positive side and significantly different from the Control condition at the .02 level[1] ($t = 2.48$).

In the Twenty Dollar condition, where less dissonance was created experimentally because of the greater importance of the consonant relations, there

TABLE 1

Average Ratings on Interview Questions for Each Condition

Leon Festinger and James M. Carlsmith

Question on Interview	Experimental Condition		
	Control (N = 20)	One Dollar (N = 20)	Twenty Dollars (N = 20)
How enjoyable tasks were (rated from -5 to +5)	-.45	+1.35	-.05
How much they learned (rated from 0 to 10)	3.08	2.80	3.15
Scientific importance (rated from 0 to 10)	5.60	6.45	5.18
Participate in similar exp. (rated from -5 to +5)	-.62	+1.20	-.25

is correspondingly less evidence of dissonance reduction. The average rating in this condition is only $-.05$, slightly and not significantly higher than the Control condition. The difference between the One Dollar and Twenty Dollar conditions is significant at the .03 level ($t = 2.22$). In short, when an S was induced, by offer of reward, to say something contrary to his private opinion, this private opinion tended to change so as to correspond more closely with what he had said. The greater the reward offered (beyond what was necessary to elicit the behavior) the smaller was the effect.

Desire to Participate in a Similar Experiment

The results from this question are shown in the last row of Table 1. This question is less directly related to the dissonance that was experimentally created for the Ss. Certainly, the more interesting and enjoyable they felt the tasks were, the greater would be their desire to participate in a similar experiment. But other factors would enter also. Hence, one would expect the results on this question to be very similar to the results on "how enjoyable the tasks were" but weaker. Actually, the result, as may be seen in the table, are in exactly the same direction, and the magnitude of the mean differences is fully as large as on the first question. The variability is greater, however, and the differences do not yield high levels of statistical significance. The difference between the One Dollar condition ($+ 1.20$) and the Control condition ($-.62$) is significant at the .08 level ($t = 1.78$). The difference between the One Dollar condition and the Twenty Dollar condition ($-.25$) reaches only the .15 level of significance ($t = 1.46$).

The Scientific Importance of the Experiment

This question was included because there was a chance that differences might emerge. There are, after all, other ways in which the experimentally created dissonance could be reduced. For example, one way would be for the S to magnify for himself the value of the reward he obtained. This, however, was unlikely in this experiment because money was used for the reward and it is undoubtedly difficult to convince oneself that one dollar is more than it really is. There is another possible way, however. The Ss were given a very good reason, in addition to being paid, for saying what they did to the waiting girl. The Ss were told it was necessary for the experiment. The dissonance could, consequently, be reduced by magnifying the importance of this cognition. The more scientifically important they considered the experiment to be, the less was the total magnitude of dissonance. It is possible, then, that the results on this question, shown in the third row of figures in Table 1, might reflect dissonance reduction.

The results are weakly in line with what one would expect if the dissonance were somewhat reduced in this manner. The One Dollar condition is higher than the other two. The difference between the One and Twenty Dollar conditions reaches the .08 level of significance on a two-tailed test ($t = 1.79$). The difference between the One Dollar and Control conditions is not impressive at all ($t = 1.21$). The result that the Twenty Dollar condition is actually lower than the Control condition is undoubtedly a matter of chance ($t = 0.58$).

How Much They Learned from the Experiment

The results on this question are shown in the second row of figures in Table 1. The question was included because, as far as we could see, it had nothing to do with the dissonance that was experimentally created and could not be used for dissonance reduction. One would then expect no differences at all among the three conditions. We felt it was important to show that the effect was not a completely general one but was specific to the content of the dissonance which was created. As can be readily seen in Table 1, there are only negligible differences among conditions. The highest t value for any of these differences is only 0.48.

REFERENCES

Festinger, L. *A theory of cognitive dissonance.* Evanston, Ill: Row Peterson, 1957.

6.2 RICHARD E. PETTY AND JOHN T. CACIOPPO

The Effects of Involvement on Responses to Argument Quantity and Quality

The cognitive approach to attitude change focuses on the thoughts people produce when they are presented with a persuasive argument. The motivation to analyze an argument carefully varies from one situation to another. Richard E. Petty and John T. Cacioppo's elaboration likelihood model of persuasion was designed to explain this variability in response to persuasive communication.

Petty (b. 1951) earned his Ph.D. in social psychology from Ohio State University in 1977. He taught at the University of Missouri until 1987, when he returned to Ohio State University as a professor and as director of the social psychology doctoral program. Petty currently serves as chair of the psychology department at Ohio State University. Cacioppo (b. 1951) also earned his Ph.D. in social psychology in 1977 from Ohio State University. He taught at the University of Notre Dame, the University of Iowa, and Ohio State University before accepting his current position at the University of Chicago in 1999.

This selection is from "The Effects of Involvement on Responses to Argument Quantity and Quality: Central and Peripheral Routes to Persuasion," which was published in 1984 in *Journal of Personality and Social Psychology*. It outlines Petty and Cacioppo's elaboration likelihood model, differentiating between the central (careful consideration) and peripheral (quick decision) routes of persuasion. The selection includes a brief experiment that applies this approach to the degree of involvement in a situation. In a longer experiment from the article that is not included in this selection, Petty and Cacioppo show that the number of arguments made has a larger impact under low involvement but that argument quality is more important under high involvement. As you read this selection, consider how argument quantity and quality affect whether you use the central or peripheral route in changing your attitude about something. How do advertisers use this information to persuade customers?

Key Concept: elaboration likelihood model of persuasion

APA Citation: Petty, R. E., & Cacioppo, J. T. (1984). The effects of involvement on responses to argument quantity and quality: Central and peripheral routes to persuasion. *Journal of Personality and Social Psychology, 46,* 69–81.

Persuasion is defined by the presentation of persuasive arguments, and the accumulated research in social psychology has generally supported the view that increasing the number of arguments in a message enhances its persuasive impact (e.g., Eagly & Warren, 1976; Maddux & Rogers, 1980; Norman, 1976). Previous analyses of this effect have suggested that increasing the number of arguments in a message enhances persuasion by giving people more information to think about. More specifically, people are postulated to generate favorable issue-relevant thoughts in response to cogent issue-relevant arguments, and the more issue-relevant arguments presented (at least up to some reasonable limit; see Calder, 1978), the more favorable thoughts that should result and the more persuasion that should occur. For example, Calder, Insko, & Yandell (1974; Experiment 2) varied the number of prosecution and defense arguments in the case materials for a hypothetical trial and found that persuasion generally followed the preponderance of arguments. In addition to attitude measures, these authors included a measure of subjects' idiosyncratic thoughts about the trial (see Brock, 1967) and concluded that "beliefs are derived from thoughts about the communication; and these thoughts themselves are partially a function of the amount of objective information on either side of the case" (Calder et al., 1974, p. 86; see also Chaiken, 1980, and Insko, Lind, & LaTour, 1976, for additional evidence consistent with this view).

Although increasing the number of arguments may enhance persuasion by increasing favorable issue-relevant thoughts in some instances, we have suggested that increasing the number of arguments in a message can induce attitude change even if people are *not* thinking about the arguments at all (Petty, Cacioppo, & Goldman, 1981). If people are unmotivated or are unable to think about the message, and no other salient cues are available, they might invoke the simple but reasonable decision rule, "the more arguments the better," and their attitudes might change in the absence of thinking about or scrutinizing the arguments. Accordingly, persuasion may require only that people realize that the message contains either relatively few or relatively many arguments. A major goal of this article is to provide empirical evidence for the view that the number of arguments in a message can affect persuasion either by affecting issue-relevant thinking or by serving as a simple acceptance cue.

CENTRAL AND PERIPHERAL ROUTES TO PERSUASION

In a recent review of the attitude-change literature (Petty & Cacioppo, 1981), we proposed that, even though the many different theories of persuasion have different terminologies, postulates, underlying motives, and particular effects

Richard E. Petty and John T. Cacioppo

that they specialize in explaining, most approaches to persuasion emphasize one of two distinct routes to attitude change. One, called the *central route*, says that attitude change results from a person's careful consideration of information that reflects what that person feels are the true merits of a particular attitudinal position. According to this view, if under scrutiny the message arguments are found to be cogent and compelling, favorable thoughts will be elicited that will result in attitude change in the direction of the advocacy. If the arguments are found to be weak and specious, they will be counterargued and the message will be resisted—or boomerang (change opposite to that intended) may even occur. To the extent that increasing the number of arguments in a message affects persuasion by enhancing issue-relevant cognitive activity, the central route to persuasion has been followed.

However, people are not always motivated to think about the information to which they are exposed, nor do they always have the ability to do so, yet attitudes may change nonetheless. Attitude changes that occur via the second or *peripheral route* do not occur because the person has diligently considered the pros and cons of the issue; they occur because the person associates the attitude issue or object with positive or negative cues or makes a simple inference about the merits of the advocated position based on various simple cues in the persuasion context. For example, rather than carefully evaluating the issue-relevant arguments, a person may accept an advocacy simply because it is presented during a pleasant lunch or because the message source is an expert. Similarly, a person may reject an advocacy simply because the position presented appears to be too extreme or because the source is unattractive. These cues (e.g., good food, expert and attractive sources, extreme positions) may shape attitudes or allow a person to decide what attitudinal position to adopt without the need for engaging in any extensive thought about the arguments presented. To the extent that a person agrees with a recommendation because of the simple perception that there are a lot of arguments to support it, the peripheral route to persuasion has been followed.

As we noted earlier, previous researchers have made the reasonable suggestion that the number of arguments in a message affects agreement by giving recipients more to think about (central route; see Calder et al., 1974; Chaiken, 1980; Insko et al., 1976) but have not tested the possibility that the number of arguments in a message might serve as a peripheral cue to the validity of the advocacy. Social psychological studies of leadership have strongly supported the view that attitudes and beliefs may be affected by the mere number of things that a person says (e.g., Bavelas, Hastorf, Gross, & Kite, 1965; Stang, 1973)....

Similar effects have been observed in the persuasion literature. For example, in two experiments Cook (1969) varied the number of arguments in a message (1 vs. 8 in Experiment 1; 2 vs. 10 in Experiment 2) and the expertise of the message source. Although both experiments used similar topics (cultural truisms), in the first experiment subjects' attitudes were affected more by the expertise than by the number of arguments manipulation, and in the second study the opposite occurred. One possible explanation for this result is that in Experiment 1 the expertise manipulation was more salient than the number-of-arguments manipulation, but in Experiment 2 the reverse was true. In fact, the descriptions of the high- and low-expert sources averaged 87 words in the first study and only 7 words in the second experiment. These results suggest quite reasonably that when two peripheral cues compete, the more salient cue has more impact.

According to the central/peripheral analysis of attitude change, people should follow the central route to persuasion when their motivation and ability to think about the issue-relevant arguments presented are relatively high, but the peripheral route should be followed when either motivation or ability to scrutinize the message arguments is relatively low. Many variables have been shown to affect persuasion by enhancing or reducing the motivation and/or the ability to think about issue-relevant arguments (see Petty & Cacioppo, 1981, 1983, for reviews). Recent research suggests that if people have the ability to think about a message (i.e., the message is not too complex, few distractions are present, etc.), one important motivational moderator of the route to persuasion is the personal relevance of the advocacy. As an issue increases in personal relevance or consequences, it becomes more important and adaptive to form a reasoned and veridical opinion, and people become more motivated to devote the cognitive effort required to evaluate the issue-relevant arguments that are presented. Thus, when a message is high in personal relevance, the quality of the issue-relevant arguments in the message is an important determinant of persuasion (Petty & Cacioppo, 1979b). When personal relevance is low, however, people are less motivated to engage in the considerable cognitive work necessary to evaluate the issue-relevant arguments and they rely more on peripheral cues to evaluate the advocacy. Thus, when a message is low in relevance, variables such as the expertise or the likableness of the message source have a greater impact on attitude change than the nature of the arguments provided (Chaiken, 1980; Petty et al., 1981; Petty, Cacioppo, & Schumann, 1983).

The central/peripheral analysis suggests that manipulating the number of arguments in a message can induce persuasion via either the central or the peripheral route. Specifically, increasing the number of arguments in a message might enhance persuasion by invoking a simple decision rule, "the more the better," when the personal relevance of a message is low, because people are unmotivated to exert the cognitive effort necessary to evaluate the merits of the arguments (peripheral route). However, increasing the number of arguments in a message might enhance persuasion by affecting issue-relevant thinking when the personal relevance of a message is high, because when the advocacy has personal consequences, it is adaptive to exert the effort necessary to evaluate the true merits of the proposal (central route).

PILOT STUDY

To provide an exploratory test of the idea that the number of arguments in a message could affect persuasion by either the central or the peripheral route, 46 undergraduates were asked to read one of three messages that they were led to believe had either high or low personal relevance. All of the messages concerned a faculty proposal to increase student tuition. In the high-involvement conditions, the message advocated that the tuition be increased at the students'

*Richard E.
Petty and John
T. Cacioppo*

own university, whereas in the low-involvement conditions, the message advocated that the tuition be increased at a distant, but comparable, university. The message that subjects read contained either three cogent arguments (e.g., part of the increased revenue could be used to decrease class size at the university, which would facilitate teacher/student interaction), three specious arguments (e.g., part of the increased revenue could be used to improve the blackboards at the university, which would impress campus visitors), or three cogent and three specious arguments (with the cogent arguments presented first). After reading the message, subjects made a slash on a 64-mm line to indicate the extent to which they agreed with the idea of raising tuition.

If the number of arguments in a message served as a peripheral cue to the validity of the message under low involvement, then subjects exposed to the six-argument message should express more agreement with the tuition increase than subjects exposed to either of the messages with three arguments. On the other hand, if subjects evaluated the nature of the arguments under high involvement, then the six-argument message should produce a level of agreement intermediate to the messages containing three strong and three weak arguments. A 2 × 3 (Involvement × Message) analysis of variance (ANOVA) on the attitude measure produced a main effect for message type, $F(2, 40) = 11.27$, $p < .001$, and an Involvement × Message interaction, $F(2, 40) = 2.72$, $p < .07$, that was consistent with our hypothesis. A Neuman-Keuls analysis of this interaction revealed that under low involvement, three strong arguments did not elicit significantly more agreement than three weak arguments, but six arguments (3 strong plus 3 weak) elicited significantly more agreement than either of the three argument conditions ($ps < .05$). Under high involvement, however, three strong arguments elicited significantly more agreement than three weak arguments ($p < .05$), but the six-argument message did not produce significantly more agreement than did the three strong arguments (although it did produce more agreement than the 3 weak arguments). These results are consistent with the view that under low involvement, people do not evaluate the message arguments, but the number of arguments in a message serves as a peripheral cue as to the worth of the advocacy. Thus, under low involvement, attitudes were affected by the mere number of arguments presented, and quality was unimportant (peripheral route). Under high involvement, however, people were motivated to think about the issue-relevant information presented and thus argument quality was more important than number (central route)....

DISCUSSION

The present research provided initial evidence for the view that increasing the number of arguments in a message can affect attitude change either by enhancing issue-relevant thinking or by serving as a relatively simple acceptance cue. Thus, in the present studies it was observed that if college students were evaluating a relatively low-involvement proposal to raise tuition at a distant university ... the students found the proposal to be more acceptable the more arguments that were presented in support of it. The quality of the arguments didn't have much impact. On the other hand, when the proposal concerned a relatively immediate increase in tuition... at their own university, acceptance of the proposal depended more on the quality than on the number of issue-relevant arguments provided.

Previous persuasion studies exploring the effects of increasing the number of arguments have not manipulated quality of arguments, and thus it was not possible to tell if the greater agreement engendered by increasing the number of arguments resulted from increased thinking about the arguments or if the greater agreement resulted from the operation of a simple acceptance cue. The present data suggest that a manipulation of number of arguments can affect attitudes with or without issue-relevant thinking. If the arguments presented are thought about and are strong, then it is likely that the more arguments presented up to some limit (see Calder, 1978), the more favorable cognitions and the more agreement that will result. On the other hand, even if the arguments are not thought about, increasing the number of arguments can still increase agreement because people may employ the simple inference, the more the better, or make the assumption that the more arguments, the more carefully researched the proposal must be....

The accumulated research on persuasion clearly indicates that neither the central nor the peripheral approaches can account for the diversity of attitude-change results observed (cf., Cialdini, Petty, & Cacioppo, 1981; Eagly & Himmelfarb, 1978). A general framework for understanding attitude change must consider that in some situations people are avid seekers and manipulators of information, whereas at other times people are best described as "cognitive misers" who eschew any difficult information-processing activity (McGuire, 1969). Given that there are two relatively distinct routes to persuasion, an important question for future research concerns the differential consequences, if any, of the attitude changes induced under each route. We have suggested that there may be two very important consequences of the route to persuasion (Petty & Cacioppo, 1980; 1983).

First, attitude changes induced via the central route may persist longer than changes induced via the peripheral route (Chaiken, 1980; Cialdini, Levy, Herman, Kozlowski, & Petty, 1976). When an attitude change is based on an extensive foundation of issue-relevant beliefs, and these beliefs are rehearsed, the attitude change is likely to persist because the issue-relevant beliefs are likely to remain salient (especially if they are self-generated; see Greenwald, 1968; Slamecka & Graf, 1978). Furthermore, even if a few of the favorable conditions elicited at the time of message exposure are forgotten, others are likely to remain. On the other hand, attitude changes that result from one prominent cue (e.g., an attractive source) or one simple inference (e.g., if there are so many arguments, it must be good), would appear to be more vulnerable to forgetting. These changes are likely to endure only if the person has been exposed to the persuasive message many times, rendering the cue or inference relatively permanent. Even then, however, such attitude changes would appear to be highly susceptible to counterpropaganda, because the person has so little on which to base a positive or a negative opinion. Thus, the new attitude would be difficult to defend if challenged severely.

A second consequence of the two routes to persuasion is that attitudes formed or changed via the central route may be more predictive of behavior than attitudes formed or changed via the peripheral route (Pallak et al., 1983; Petty et al., 1983). People may have more confidence in attitudes that are based on issue-relevant thinking rather than on peripheral cues, and thus they may be more willing to act on these attitudes. In addition, attitudes based on issue-relevant thinking may be more salient in memory than attitudes based on peripheral cues, and thus people may be more able to act on them (see Fazio & Zanna, 1981).

Richard E. Petty and John T. Cacioppo

REFERENCES

Bavelas, A., Hastorf, A. H., Gross, A. E., & Kite, W. R. (1965). Experiments on the alteration of group structure. *Journal of Experimental Social Psychology, 1,* 55–70.

Brock, T. C. (1967). Communication discrepancy and intent to persuade as determinants of counterargument production. *Journal of Experimental Social Psychology; 3,* 269–309.

Calder, B. J. (1978). Cognitive response, imagery, and scripts: What is the cognitive basis of attitude? *Advances in Consumer Research, 5,* 630–634.

Calder, B. J., Insko, C. A., & Yandell, B. (1974). The relation of cognitive and memorial processes to persuasion in a simulated jury trial. *Journal of Applied Social Psychology, 4,* 62–93.

Chaiken, S. (1980). Heuristic versus systematic information processing and the use of source versus message cues in persuasion. *Journal of Personality and Social Psychology, 39,* 752–766.

Cialdini, R. B., Levy, A., Herman, P., Kozlowski, L., & Petty, R. (1976). Elastic shifts of opinion: Determinants of direction and durability. *Journal of Personality and Social Psychology, 34,* 663–672.

Cialdini, R. B., Petty, R. E., & Cacioppo, J. T. (1981). Attitude and attitude change. *Annual Review of Psychology, 32,* 357–404.

Cook, T. D. (1969). Competence, counterarguing, and attitude change. *Journal of Personality, 37,* 342–358.

Eagly, A. H., & Himmelfarb, S. (1978). Attitudes and opinions. *Annual Review of Psychology, 29,* 517–554.

Eagly, A. H., & Warren, R. (1976). Intelligence, comprehension, and opinion change. *Journal of Personality, 44,* 226–242.

Fazio, R. H., & Zanna, M. P. (1981). Direct experience and attitude behavior consistency. In L. Berkowitz (Ed.), *Advances in experimental social psychology* (Vol. 14, pp. 161–202). New York: Academic.

Greenwald, A. G. (1968). Cognitive learning, cognitive response to persuasion, and attitude change. In A. Greenwald, T. Brock, & T. Ostrom (Eds.), *Psychological foundations of attitudes* (pp. 148–170). New York: Academic.

Insko, C. A., Lind, E. A., & LaTour, S. (1976). Persuasion, recall, and thoughts. *Representative Research in Social Psychology, 7,* 66–78.

Maddux, J. E., & Rogers, R. W. (1980). Effects of source expertness, physical attractiveness, and supporting arguments on persuasion. A case of brains over beauty. *Journal of Personality and Social Psychology, 38,* 235–244.

McGuire, W. J. (1969). The nature of attitudes and attitude change. In G. Lindzey & E. Aronson (Eds.), *The handbook of social psychology* (2nd ed., Vol. 3, pp. 136–314). Reading, MA: Addison-Wesley.

Norman, R. (1976). When what is said is important: A comparison of expert and attractive sources. *Journal of Experimental Social Psychology, 12,* 294–300.

Pallak, S. R., Murroni, E., & Koch, J. (1983). Communicator attractiveness and expertise, emotional versus rational appeals, and persuasion. *Social Condition, 2,* 122–141.

Petty, R. E., & Cacioppo, J. T. (1979b). Issue-involvement can increase or decrease persuasion by enhancing message-relevant cognitive responses. *Journal of Personality and Social Psychology, 37,* 1915–1926.

Petty, R. E., & Cacioppo, J. T. (1980). Effects of issue involvement on attitudes in an advertising context. In G. Gorn & M. Goldberg (Eds.), *Proceedings of the Division 23 Program* (pp. 75–79). Montreal, Canada: American Psychological Association.

Petty, R. E., & Cacioppo, J. T. (1981). *Attitudes and persuasion: Classic and contemporary approaches.* Dubuque, IA: Wm. C. Brown.

Petty, R. E., & Cacioppo, J. T. (1983). Central and peripheral routes to persuasion: Application to advertising. In L. Percy & A. Woodside (Eds.), *Advertising and consumer psychology* (pp. 3–23). Lexington, MA: D.C. Heath.

Petty, R. E., Cacioppo, J. T., & Goldman, R. (1981). Personal involvement as a determinant of argument-based persuasion. *Journal of Personality and Social Psychology, 41,* 847–855.

Petty, R. E., Cacioppo, J. T., & Schumann, D. (1983). Central and peripheral routes to advertising effectiveness: The moderating role of involvement. *Journal of Consumer Research, 10,* 134–148.

Slamecka, N. J., & Graf, P. (1978). The generation effect: Delineation of a phenomenon. *Journal of Experimental Psychology: Human Learning and Memory, 4,* 592–604.

Stang, D. J. (1973). Effect of interaction rate on ratings of leadership and liking. *Journal of Personality and Social Psychology, 27,* 405–408.

6.3 SANG-PIL HAN AND SHARON SHAVITT

Persuasion and Culture: Advertising Appeals in Individualistic and Collectivistic Societies

Social psychologists have recently become interested in the effects of culture on persuasion. In this selection, Sang-pil Han and Sharon Shavitt investigate the differences of persuasive advertising in individualistic and collectivistic cultures.

Han earned a Ph.D. in social psychology from the University of Illinois and currently holds a position at Han Yang University in Korea. Shavitt (b. 1959) earned her Ph.D. in social psychology in 1985 from Ohio State University. In 1987, after a postdoctoral fellowship at Indiana University, she went to the University of Illinois, where she is currently a professor of psychology.

This selection is from "Persuasion and Culture: Advertising Appeals in Individualistic and Collectivistic Societies," which was published in the *Journal of Experimental Social Psychology* in 1994. In it, Han and Shavitt explore differences between advertising in the United States (an individualistic culture) and advertising in Korea (a collectivistic culture) by comparing product advertisements from magazines. Do you think comparing other forms of advertising (television, for example) would reveal similar differences? In a second study not included here, Han and Shavitt found that advertisements that emphasized individualistic benefits were more effective in the United States, while those that emphasized group benefits were more successful in Korea. Why might the results of this research be of interest to an international company?

Key Concept: persuasion and culture

APA Citation: Han, S., & Shavitt, S. (1994). Persuasion and culture: Advertising appeals in individualistic and collectivistic societies. *Journal of Experimental Social Psychology, 30*, 326–350.

T wo studies examined the extent to which a core dimension of cultural variability, individualism–collectivism (Hofstede, 1980, 1983; Triandis, 1990), is reflected in the types of persuasive appeals that tend to be used and that tend to be effective in different countries. Study 1 demonstrated that magazine advertisements in the United States, an individualistic culture, employed appeals to individual benefits and preferences, personal success, and independence to a greater extent than did advertisements in Korea, a collectivistic culture. Korean advertisements employed appeals emphasizing ingroup benefits, harmony, and family integrity to a greater extent than did U.S. ads. Study 2 [not reprinted here], a controlled experiment conducted in the two countries, demonstrated that in the U.S. advertisements emphasizing individualistic benefits were more persuasive, and ads emphasizing family or ingroup benefits were less persuasive than they were in Korea. In both studies, however, product characteristics played a role in moderating these overall differences: Cultural differences emerged strongly in Studies 1 and 2 for advertised products that tend to be purchased and used with others, but were much less evident for products that are typically purchased and used individually.

Individualism–collectivism is perhaps the most basic dimension of cultural variability identified in cross-cultural research. Concepts related to this dimension have been employed in several social science domains (cf. Triandis, McCusker, & Hui, 1990), and the individualism–collectivism dimension has come to be regarded as "central to an understanding of cultural values, of work values, of social systems, as well as in the studies of morality, the structure of constitutions, and cultural patterns" (Triandis, Brislin, & Hui, 1988). Several recent studies have suggested that individualism and collectivism are contrasting cultural syndromes that are associated with a broad pattern of differences in individuals' social perceptions and social behavior, including differences in the definition of self and its perceived relation to ingroups and outgroups (Markus & Kitayama, 1991), in the endorsement of values relevant to individual vs group goals (Triandis et al., 1990), and in the pattern and style of social interactions (cf. Triandis, 1990).

However, little is known about the implications of these cultural differences for another social process that is fundamental to every culture: persuasion. Persuasive communications transmit and reflect the values of a culture. Persuasive messages are used to obtain the compliance that achieves the personal, political, and economic ends valued in the culture. Although social influence has always been a central arena of research in social psychology, little is understood about what differences exist in the types of persuasive appeals used in different cultures (see Burgoon, Dillard, Doran, & Miller, 1982; Glenn, Witmeyer, & Stevenson, 1977). Even less is known about the effectiveness of different appeal types in different cultures.

What types of persuasive appeals are prevalent in individualistic versus collectivistic cultures? And how do members of these different cultures differ in the extent to which they are persuaded by these appeals? This paper presents an exploration of these questions.

Our studies focused on cross-cultural differences in advertising, a form of persuasive communication that is highly prevalent in many societies, both individualist and collectivist. The studies examined how this core dimension of cultural variability is reflected in the types of advertising appeals employed in two countries (the United States and Korea) that have been shown to differ greatly on the individualism-collectivism dimension (Hofstede, 1980, 1983). The research also investigated the relative *effectiveness* of individualistic and collectivistic advertising appeals in the United States and Korea. Moreover, the research looks beyond overall cultural differences in advertising content and persuasiveness to identify factors that may moderate these differences.

Individualism and Collectivism.   Individualism-collectivism is perhaps the broadest and most widely used dimension of cultural variability for cultural comparison (Gudykunst and Ting-Toomey, 1988). Hofstede (1980) described individualism–collectivism as the relationship between the individual and the collectivity that prevails in a given society. In individualist cultures, individuals tend to prefer independent relationships to others and to subordinate ingroup goals to their personal goals. In collectivistic cultures, on the other hand, individuals are more likely to have interdependent relationships to their ingroups and to subordinate their personal goals to their ingroup goals. Individualistic cultures are associated with emphases on independence, achievement, freedom, high levels of competition, and pleasure. Collectivistic cultures are associated with emphases on interdependence, harmony, family security, social hierarchies, cooperation, and low levels of competition (see Triandis, 1989, 1990; Triandis et al., 1990, for supporting evidence and discussions of the antecedents and consequences of individualism and collectivism).

Individualistic and collectivistic cultures are characterized by important differences in members' social perceptions and social behavior. Members of these cultures have very different construals of the self, of others, and of the interdependence of the two (Markus & Kitayama, 1991). The self is defined in terms of ingroup memberships (e.g., family and ethnic identity) to a greater extent in collectivistic cultures than individualistic cultures. Moreover, there is evidence suggesting that members of collectivistic cultures perceive their ingroups to be more homogeneous than their outgroups, whereas the reverse is true among persons in individualistic societies (Triandis et al., 1990). These cultural differences in the perceived relation of the self to others have been shown to have many other cognitive, emotional, and behavioral consequences (see Markus & Kitayama, 1991).

The individualistic cultural pattern is found in most northern and western regions of Europe and in North America, whereas the collectivistic cultural pattern is common in Asia, Africa, Latin America, and the Pacific (Hofstede, 1980, 1983). In the present studies, the United States and Korea were selected to represent individualistic and collectivistic cultures, respectively. These countries were selected based on Hofstede's (1980, 1983) studies of individualism–collectivism in over 50 countries, which indicated that the United States is highly individualistic with a score of 91 on a 100-point individualism scale, whereas Korea is clearly on the collectivistic side with a score of 18.

Persuasion and Culture.   We expected that advertisements in the United States and Korea would reflect their indigenous individualistic or collectivistic cultural orientation. We also expected that the persuasiveness of certain types of ad appeals would differ in these two cultures. There are several reasons to hypothesize a link between these cultural patterns and persuasion processes.

First, previous content analyses of advertising have demonstrated differences between countries in the prevalence of various types of ad content, including emotional content, informative content, comparative content, and the use of humor (e.g., Hong, Muderrisoglu, & Zinkhan, 1987; Madden, Caballero, & Matsukubo, 1986; Martenson; 1987; Miracle, 1987; Renforth & Raveed, 1983; Tansey, Hyman, & Zinkhan, 1990; Weinberger & Spotts, 1989; Zandpour, Chang, & Catalano, 1992), although ads have not always been found to reflect their indigenous cultures (e.g., Marquez, 1975; Mueller, 1987). The roles of individualism and collectivism have not been investigated in these content analyses, although the findings have suggested that cultural factors often influence the types of ads employed in different countries.

... [R]esearch has shown that perceived social norms, roles, and values are major determinants of behavioral intentions in collectivist cultures, whereas individual likes and dislikes as well as perceived costs and benefits are weighted more heavily by individualists (Davidson, Jaccard, Triandis, Morales, & Diaz-Guerrero, 1976). This suggests that persuasive appeals that emphasize social norms and roles versus individual preferences and benefits may be more effective in changing behavioral intentions in collectivistic versus individualistic cultures.

Based on these findings, we expected that different types of advertising appeals would tend to be employed and to be effective in the U.S. and Korea. Specifically, appeals emphasizing family expectations, relations with ingroups, and group benefits—i.e., collectivistic appeals—would be more prevalent in Korean advertising, whereas messages emphasizing a concern with individual benefits, personal success, and independence—i.e., individualistic appeals—would be more prevalent in American advertising. We also expected that ads emphasizing these culturally relevant values would be more persuasive than ads emphasizing other values.

Moderating Factors.   Although cultural orientation may be reflected in the prevalence and effectiveness of different types of appeals overall, these cultural differences may be moderated by other factors.

Product characteristics.   Products differ in the goals that are associated with them and, therefore, in the types of benefits that are sought from them. As a result, appeals addressing different types of benefits are effective for different types of products (Shavitt, 1990).

Shared versus personal product categories appeared to be potentially important in moderating differences between individualistic and collectivistic cultures. *Shared products* were defined as ones for which the decision making process involved in purchase and the pattern of product usage are likely to include family members or friends (e.g., home appliances, groceries, and furniture). *Personal products,* conversely, were defined as ones for which the purchase decision and product usage are usually done by an individual (e.g., fashion apparel, cosmetics, personal care products).

How would these product characteristics moderate cultural differences in the content and persuasiveness of appeals? Shared products, which offer benefits both for the individual and for the group, could plausibly be advertised both in terms of individualistic and collectivistic appeals. For such products, cultural differences in the value placed on individual versus collective benefits could be manifested in the types of appeals that are typically employed and that are persuasive. In contrast, personal products which offer primarily personal benefits and are typically used individually, are not likely to be convincingly promoted in terms of group-oriented or collectivistic appeals. Instead, they are likely to be promoted in terms of individual benefits, even in cultures where group benefits are highly valued. Thus, the nature of the product may constrain the degree to which cultural differences in individualism–collectivism are likely to be manifested in advertising (see Shavitt, Lowrey, & Han, 1992, for a similar point about how products constrain individual differences in advertising effectiveness).

Involvement. The concept of involvement has played a central role in theory and research on advertising and persuasion. Involvement has been defined and operationalized in a variety of ways (see Greenwald & Leavitt, 1984; Johnson & Eagly, 1989). The present research focused on involvement as the extent to which the information in a message is potentially important or personally relevant to outcomes desired by the message recipient (e.g., Petty & Cacioppo, 1986). Persuasion processes under conditions of high involvement differ from those under low involvement. Many studies have shown that involvement can moderate the effects of other message factors, including message content, on attitude change (e.g., Kahle & Homer, 1985; Petty & Cacioppo, 1979; Petty, Cacioppo, & Schumann, 1983)....

STUDY 1

The first study assessed the extent to which advertising content in the U.S. and Korea reflects its indigenous individualistic or collectivistic cultural pattern. By examining the role of product characteristics, the study also attempted to identify conditions under which these cultural differences are most likely to emerge.

Method

Sample of Advertisements. One popular news magazine and one women's magazine in each country were chosen for the study. The periodicals selected as being representative of American news and women's magazines were *Newsweek* and *Redbook,* respectively. The comparable magazines for Korea were *Wolgan Chosun* and *Yosong Donga.* In order to achieve sample comparability, the two magazines were selected from each country based on their similarity in format and target audience (Mueller, 1987). The time span studied was January 1987 through December 1988. Every third month's issue was included in the sample. Two hundred product ads from each country were randomly selected from the sample.

Coding of Advertisements.   A manual for coding the ads was developed from theory-based factors identified by previous research on individualism-collectivism (Hofstede, 1980; Hui, 1984; Triandis et al., 1986, 1988). The individualistic classification included, (1) appeals about individuality or independence, (2) reflections of self-reliance with hedonism or competition, (3) emphasis on self-improvement or self-realization, and (4) emphasis on the benefits of the product to the consumer (you). The collectivistic classification included, (1) appeals about family integrity, (2) focus on group integrity or group well-being, (3) concerns about others or support of society, (4) focus on interdependent relationships with others, and (5) focus on group goals. A fuller description of the coding scheme is presented in Appendix A.

The advertisements of each country were evaluated by four judges. For each country's ads, coding was performed by two native speakers from that country (Americans for U.S. ads and Koreans for Korean ads). In addition, two bilingual coders coded both the U.S. and Korean ads. These bilingual coders were native Koreans, who lived in the United States for several years and were fluent in English. Coders were ignorant of the purposes of the study, and independently rated the degree of individualistic or collectivistic content for each of the ads on two 3-point scales [1 = not at all individualistic (collectivistic), 2 = somewhat, 3 = very]. Discrepancies in coding were settled by a fifth judge for the U.S. data, and by discussion among coders for the Korean data. The average correlation between the Korean coders' ratings was $r = .80$, and the average correlation of the American coders' ratings was $r = .84$, which are within acceptable ranges suggested by Kassarjian (1977). Moreover, the bilinguals' coding was highly correlated both with Koreans' coding of Korean ads (mean $r = .85$) and with Americans' coding of U.S. ads (mean $r = .82$), suggesting that possible cross-cultural differences in interpreting the meaning of ad content did not pose a serious threat to the reliability of the coding.

Selection of Personal vs Shared Products.   Personal vs. shared product categories were determined on the basis of a survey in which 24 American students and 24 Korean students rated 44 consumer products and services in terms of, (1) the decision making process involved in purchase (1 = never discuss with their family or friends whether to purchase, 5 = always discuss), and (2) usage pattern (1 = used mostly individually, 5 = used mostly with other members of family or friends). The correlations between the two mean scores across all products were high (American data, $r = .81$; Korean data, $r = .74$), and no differences were obtained between countries in the mean rating of the personal products or in the mean rating of the shared products. Thus, an average of the two items across all 48 respondents was used to classify products as personal or shared. Although many products could perhaps be classified as personal in some situations and shared in others, we believe that our classification adequately captured basic differences in the way the products tend to be purchased and used.

TABLE 1

Individualism and Collectivism Ratings in U.S. and Korean Advertisements

Sang-pil Han
and Sharon
Shavitt

	U.S. ads[a,b]	Korean ads[a,b]	Overall[c,d]
Individualism ratings			
Personal products	2.07	1.91	1.99
Shared products*	1.88	1.50	1.69
Overall*	1.98	1.70	
Collectivism ratings			
Personal products*	1.11	1.32	1.22
Shared products*	1.25	1.89	1.57
Overall*	1.19	1.61	

Note. Ratings were made on two 3-point scales, where 1 indicated "not at all individualistic (or collectivistic)" and 3 "very."
*Mean ratings for U.S. and Korean ads differed significantly at $p < .005$.
[a]For personal products, individualism and collectivism ratings differed significantly at $p < .005$.
[b]For shared products, individualism and collectivism ratings differed significantly at $p < .005$.
[c]Individualism ratings for personal and shared products differed significantly at $p < .005$.
[d]Collectivism ratings for personal and shared products differed significantly at $p < .005$.

Results

U.S. ads were expected to be rated as more individualistic and less collectivistic than Korean ads. However, product category was expected to moderate these effects such that the differences between countries would be greater for shared than for personal products.

Table 1 shows the mean ratings of individualism and collectivism as a function of country and product category. An analysis of variance with country (United States vs Korea) and product type (personal vs shared) as between-subjects factors and rating type (individualism vs collectivism ratings) as a within-subject factor yielded a significant main effect of rating type ($F(1, 396) = 72.21; p < .0001$) indicating that, overall, ads tended to be rated higher in individualism than in collectivism. More importantly, a significant interaction of country $\times$ rating type emerged ($F(1, 396) = 44.69; p < .001$) indicating as expected that the relative ratings of ads on individualism and collectivism differed for U.S. vs Korean ads. Simple main effects tests demonstrated that U.S. ads were rated significantly higher in individualism than Korean ads ($F(1, 398) = 14.98; p < .001$), whereas Korean ads were rated significantly higher in collectivism than U.S. ads ($F(1, 398) = 42.86; p < .001$).

The interaction of product category $\times$ rating type was also significant ($F(1, 396) = 39.10; p < .0001$), indicating that the relative ratings of ads for individualism and collectivism differed for personal vs shared products. Simple effects tests indicated that ads for personal products were rated significantly higher in individualism than ads for shared products ($F(1, 398) = 17.78; p < .0001$), whereas ads for shared products were rated significantly higher in collectivism than ads for personal products (F (1, 398) $= 27.95$; $p < .0001$).

However, as expected, the two-way interactions were qualified by a country $\times$ product category $\times$ rating type interaction ($F(1, 392) = 11.42$; $p < .001$), indicating as expected that product category moderated the differences in the ratings of Korean vs U.S. ads. That is, the differences were greater for shared than for personal products. Further analysis revealed that the interaction of country $\times$ rating type was significant within each product category, indicating that ratings of U.S. versus Korean ads differed reliably for both product types (personal products: $F(1, 194) = 7.35$; $p < .01$; shared products: $F(1, 202) = 42.76$; $p < .0001$). But within-group comparisons suggested as expected that cultural differences in advertising were much more evident for shared products than for personal products. For personal products, individualism ratings were higher than collectivism ratings for *both* U.S. and Korean ads (U.S. ads: $t(96) = 11.58$; $p < .001$; Korean ads: $t(98) = 5.36$; $p < .001$). In contrast, for shared products, individualism ratings were higher than collectivism ratings for U.S. ads ($t(102) = 7.73$; $p < .001$), whereas collectivism ratings were higher than individualism ratings for Korean ads ($t(100) = 2.93$; $p < .005$).

Discussion

The data supported the hypothesis that individualism–collectivism, a basic dimension of cultural variability, is reflected in the content of advertising in different cultures. As expected, U.S. ads were rated as more individualistic and less collectivistic than Korean ads. That is, U.S. ads were more likely than Korean ads to emphasize self-reliance, self-improvement, and personal rewards, and less likely to emphasize family well-being, ingroup goals, and interdependence.

Importantly, this overall difference was not uniform across products. Cross-cultural differences emerged for both product categories, but were greater for shared than for personal products. The ratings of U.S. and Korean ads suggested that personal products tended to be promoted more in terms of individualistic than collectivistic appeals in both countries. This was as expected, since personal products offer predominantly personal or individually experienced benefits, and thus are unlikely to be promoted with group-oriented appeals. However, shared products tended to be promoted differently in the two countries—more in terms of individualistic appeals in the United States and more in terms of collectivistic appeals in Korea. This may be because shared products, which offer both individual and collective benefits, can be convincingly promoted in terms of either type of benefit, allowing cultural differences in the value placed on these benefits to influence the types of appeals that are employed....

The present research examined how individualism–collectivism, a core dimension of cultural variability, is reflected in the advertising appeals employed in the United States and Korea, countries that have been shown to differ on this dimension (Hofstede, 1980, 1983). It also investigated the relative effectiveness of ad appeals emphasizing culturally relevant values versus appeals targeting other values. On the basis of the converging pattern of results from a content analysis and an experimental investigation conducted in two countries, it is evident that cultural differences in individualism-collectivism play an important role in persuasion processes both at the societal and the individual level, influencing the prevalence and the effectiveness of different types of advertising appeals....

Limitations in the Generalizability of the Results. Some limitations must be kept in mind in interpreting these results. First, our research involved only one country from each culture. Although the United States and Korea differ greatly in terms of individualism and collectivism, they do not necessarily represent all aspects of this dimension. Collectivism or individualism can take different forms in different countries (see Triandis et al., 1990). Thus, the present findings should be viewed as preliminary. Further research is needed including other individualistic and collectivistic countries in order to establish further the role of this dimension in persuasion processes....

APPENDIX A

Scoring Criteria for Cultural Variation

1. Criteria for Classification as Individualistic Appeals.

- Appeals about individuality or independence

    - "The art of being unique"
    - "She's got a style all her own"

- Reflections of self-reliance with hedonism or competition (mostly expressed in pictures, not in headlines)

    - "Alive with pleasure!"
    - "Self-esteem"

- Emphasis on self-improvement or self-realization

    - "My own natural color's come back. Only better, much better"
    - "You, only better"

- Emphasis on the benefits of the product to the consumer (you)

  - "How to protect the most personal part of the environment. Your skin."
  - "A quick return for your investment"

- Focus on ambition

  - "A leader among leaders"
  - "Local hero"

- Focus on personal goals

  - "With this new look I'm ready for my new role"
  - "Make your way through the crowd"

2. Criteria for Classification as Collectivistic Appeals.

- Appeals about family integrity

  - "A more exhilarating way to provide for your family"

- Focus on group integrity or group well-being

  - "We have a way of bringing people closer together"
  - "Ringing out the news of business friendships that really work"

- Concerns about others or support of society

  - "We share our love with seven wonderful children"
  - "We devote ourselves to contractors"

- Focus on interdependent relationships to others

  - "Successful partnerships"
  - "Celebrating a half-century of partnership"

- Focus on group goals

  - "The dream of prosperity for all of us"
  - "Sharing is beautiful"

- References to harmony with others

  - "Your business success: Harmonization with Sunkyong"

- Focus on others' happiness

    - "Mom's love—Baby's happiness"

- Paying attention to the views of others

    - "Our family agrees with the selection of home-furnishings"

REFERENCES

Burgoon, M., Dillard, J., Doran, N., & Miller, M. (1982). Cultural and situational influences on the process of persuasive strategy selection. *International Journal of Intercultural Relations*, **6**, 85–100.

Davidson, A. R., Jaccard, J. J., Triandis, H. C., Morales, M. L., & Diaz-Guerrero, R. (1976). Cross-cultural model testing: Toward a solution of the emic–etic dilemma. *International Journal of Psychology*, **11**, 1–13.

Glenn, E. S., Witmeyer, D., & Stevenson, K. A. (1977). Cultural styles of persuasion. *International Journal of Intercultural Relations*, **3**, 52–65.

Greenwald, A. G., & Leavitt, C. (1984). Audience involvement in advertising: Four levels. *Journal of Consumer Research*, **11**, 581–592.

Gudykunst, W. B., & Ting-Toomey, S. (1988). *Culture and interpersonal communication.* Newbury Park, CA: Sage.

Hofstede, G. (1980). *Culture's consequences: International differences in work-related values.* Beverly Hills, CA: Sage.

Hofstede, G. (1983). Dimensions of national cultures in fifty countries and three regions. In J. Deregowski et al. (Eds.) *Explications in cross-cultural psychology.* Lisse, The Netherlands: Swets and Zeitlinger.

Hong, J., Muderrisoglu, A., & Zinkhan, G. (1987). Cultural differences and advertising expression: A comparative content analysis of Japanese and U.S. magazine advertising. *Journal of Advertising*, **16**(1), 55–62.

Hui, C. H. (1984). *Individualism-collectivism: Theory, measurement and its relation to reward allocation.* Unpublished doctoral dissertation. University of Illinois at Urbana-Champaign.

Johnson, B. T., & Eagly, A. H. (1989). Effects of involvement on persuasion: A meta-analysis. *Psychological Bulletin*, **106**, 290–314.

Kahle, L. R., & Homer, P. M. (1985). Physical attractiveness of the celebrity endorser: A social adaptation perspective. *Journal of Consumer Research*, **11**, 954–961.

Kassarjian, H. H. (1977). Content analysis in consumer research. *Journal of Consumer Research*, **4**, 8–18.

Madden, C., Caballero, M., & Matsukubo, S. (1986). Analysis of information content in U.S. and Japanese magazine advertising. *Journal of Advertising*, **15**(3), 38–45.

Markus, H. R., & Kitayama, S. (1991). Culture and the self: Implications for cognition, emotion, and motivation. *Psychological Review*, **98**, 224–253.

Marquez, F. T. (1975). The relationship of advertising and culture in the Philippines. *Journalism Quarterly*, **52**(3), 436–442.

Martenson, R. (1987). Advertising strategies and information content in American and Swedish advertising. *International Journal of Advertising, 6,* 133–144.

Miracle, G. (1987). Feel-do-learn: An alternative sequence underlying Japanese response to television commercials. In F. Feasley (Ed.), *Proceedings of the 1987 conference of the American Academy of Advertising* (pp. 73–78).

Mueller, B. (1987). Reflections of culture: An analysis of Japanese and American advertising appeals. *Journal of Advertising Research, 27,* 51–59.

Petty, R. E., & Cacioppo, J. T. (1979). Issue involvement can increase or decrease persuasion by enhancing message-relevant cognitive responses. *Journal of Personality and Social Psychology, 37,* 1915–1926.

Petty, R. E., & Cacioppo, J. T. (1986). *Communication and persuasion: Central and peripheral routes to attitude change.* New York: Springer-Verlag.

Petty, R. E., Cacioppo, J. T., & Schumann, D. (1983). Central and peripheral routes to advertising effectiveness: The moderating role of involvement. *Journal of Consumer Research, 10,* 134–148.

Renforth, W., & Raveed, S. (1983). Consumer information cues in television advertising: A cross country analysis. *Journal of the Academy of Marketing Science, 11*(3), 216–225.

Shavitt, S. (1990). The role of attitude objects in attitude functions. *Journal of Experimental Social Psychology, 26,* 124–148.

Shavitt, S., Lowrey, T. M., & Han, S. (1992). Attitude functions in advertising: The interactive role of products and self-monitoring. *Journal of Consumer Psychology, 1*(4), 337–364.

Tansey, R., Hyman, M. R., & Zinkhan, G. M. (1990). Cultural themes in Brazilian and U.S. auto ads: A cross-cultural comparison. *Journal of Advertising, 19*(2), 30–39.

Triandis, H. C. (1989). The self and social behavior in differing cultural contexts. *Psychological Review, 96*(3), 506–520.

Triandis, H. C. (1990). Cross-cultural studies of individualism and collectivism. In J. Berman (Ed.), *Nebraska symposium on motivation.* Lincoln: University of Nebraska Press.

Triandis, H. C., Bontempo, R., Betancourt, H., Bond, M., Leung, K., Brenes, A., Georgas, J., Hui, C. H., Marin, G., Setiadi, B., Sinha, J. B. P., Verma, J., Spangenberg, J., Touzard, H., & de Montmollin, G. (1986). The measurement of etic aspects of individualism and collectivism across cultures. *Australian Journal of Psychology, 38*(3), 257–267.

Triandis, H. C., Bontempo, R., Villareal, M. J., Asai, M., & Lucca, N. (1988). Individualism and collectivism: Cross-cultural perspectives on self-ingroup relationships. *Journal of Personality and Social Psychology, 54,* 323–338.

Triandis, H. C., Brislin, R., & Hui, C. H. (1988). Cross-cultural training across the individualism-collectivism divide. *International Journal of Intercultural Relations, 12,* 269–289.

Triandis, H. C., McCusker, C., & Hui, C. H. (1990). Multimethod probes of individualism and collectivism. *Journal of Personality and Social Psychology, 59,* 1006–1020.

Weinberger, M. B., & Spotts, H. E. (1989). Humor in U.S. versus U.K. TV commercials: A comparison. *Journal of Advertising, 18*(2), 39–44.

Zandpour, F., Chang, C., & Catalano, J. (1992). Stories, symbols, and straight talk: A comparative analysis of French, Taiwanese, and U.S. TV Commercials. *Journal of Advertising Research, 32*(1), 25–38.

CHAPTER 7 Prejudice and Discrimination

7.1 GORDON W. ALLPORT

What Is the Problem?

Prejudice has long been a problem in society. Prejudice is an unjustified attitude that involves a fixed way of looking at a person or object. Social psychologists such as Gordon W. Allport have studied the causes of prejudice and have contributed to its reduction.

Allport (1897–1967) earned his Ph.D. from Harvard University in 1921. He spent time in Turkey, Germany, and England, and briefly taught at Dartmouth College before returning to teach at Harvard University, where he remained the rest of his life. He published many books, including *Pattern and Growth in Personality* (Addison-Wesley, 1961).

This selection is from chapter 1, "What Is the Problem?" of Allport's book *The Nature of Prejudice* (Addison-Wesley, 1954). Through vivid examples, Allport describes the difficulty of defining prejudice. He felt that it is important to understand the problem before a solution can be implemented. Allport's book continues to provide an excellent introduction to the problem of prejudice. What is a good definition of prejudice? Can it account for all the kinds of prejudice felt and shown today?

Key Concept: definition of prejudice

APA Citation: Allport, G. W. (1954). *The nature of prejudice.* Cambridge, MA: Addison-Wesley. [Chapter 1, What is the problem?]

DEFINITION

The word *prejudice*, derived from the Latin noun *praejudicium*, has, like most words, undergone a change of meaning since classical times. There are three stages in the transformation.

1. To the ancients, *praejudicium* meant a *precedent*—a judgment based on previous decisions and experiences.
2. Later, the term, in English, acquired the meaning of a judgment formed before due examination and consideration of the facts—a premature or hasty judgment.
3. Finally the term acquired also its present emotional flavor of favorableness or unfavorableness that accompanies such a prior and unsupported judgment.

Perhaps the briefest of all definitions of prejudice is: *thinking ill of others without sufficient warrant*. This crisp phrasing contains the two essential ingredients of all definitions—reference to unfounded judgment and to a feeling-tone. It is, however, too brief for complete clarity.

In the first place, it refers only to *negative* prejudice. People may be prejudiced in favor of others; they may think *well* of them without sufficient warrant. The wording offered by the New English Dictionary recognizes positive as well as negative prejudice:

> A feeling, favorable or unfavorable, toward a person or thing, prior to, or not based on, actual experience.

While it is important to bear in mind that biases may be *pro* as well as *con*, it is none the less true that *ethnic* prejudice is mostly negative. A group of students was asked to describe their attitudes toward ethnic groups. No suggestion was made that might lead them toward negative reports. Even so, they reported eight times as many antagonistic attitudes as favorable attitudes.... Accordingly, we shall be concerned chiefly with prejudice *against*, not with prejudice *in favor of*, ethnic groups.

The phrase "thinking ill of others" is obviously an elliptical expression that must be understood to include feelings of scorn or dislike, of fear and aversion, as well as various forms of antipathetic conduct: such as talking against people, discriminating against them, or attacking them with violence.

Similarly, we need to expand the phrase "without sufficient warrant." A judgment is unwarranted whenever it lacks basis in fact. A wit defined prejudice as "being down on something you're not up on."

It is not easy to say how much fact is required in order to justify a judgment. A prejudiced person will almost certainly claim that he has sufficient warrant for his views. He will tell of bitter experiences he has had with refugees, Catholics, or Orientals. But, in most cases, it is evident that his facts are scanty and strained. He resorts to a selective sorting of his own few memories, mixes them up with hearsay, and overgeneralizes. No one can possibly know *all* refugees, Catholics, or Orientals. Hence any negative judgment of these groups *as a whole* is, strictly speaking, an instance of thinking ill without sufficient warrant.

Sometimes, the ill-thinker has no first-hand experience on which to base his judgment. A few years ago most Americans thought exceedingly ill of Turks —but very few had ever seen a Turk nor did they know any person who had seen one. Their warrant lay exclusively in what they had heard of the Armenian massacres and of the legendary crusades. On such evidence they presumed to condemn all members of a nation.

Ordinarily, prejudice manifests itself in dealing with individual members of rejected groups. But in avoiding a Negro neighbor, or in answering "Mr. Greenberg's" application for a room, we frame our action to accord with our categorical generalization of the group as a whole. We pay little or no attention to individual differences, and overlook the important fact that Negro X, our neighbor, is not Negro Y whom we dislike for good and sufficient reason; that Mr. Greenberg, who may be a fine gentleman, is not Mr. Bloom, whom we have good reason to dislike.

So common is this process that we might define prejudice as:

> an avertive or hostile attitude toward a person who belongs to a group, simply because he belongs to that group, and is therefore presumed to have the objectionable qualities ascribed to the group.

This definition stresses the fact that while ethnic prejudice in daily life is ordinarily a matter of dealing with individual people it also entails an unwarranted idea concerning a group as a whole.

Returning to the question of "sufficient warrant," we must grant that few if any human judgments are based on absolute certainty. We can be reasonably, but not absolutely, sure that the sun will rise tomorrow, and that death and taxes will finally overtake us. The sufficient warrant for any judgment is always a matter of probabilities. Ordinarily our judgments of natural happenings are based on firmer and higher probabilities than our judgments of people. Only rarely do our categorical judgments of nations or ethnic groups have a foundation in high probability.

Take the hostile view of Nazi leaders held by most Americans during World War II. Was it prejudiced? The answer is No, because there was abundant available evidence regarding the evil policies and practices accepted as the official code of the party. True, there may have been good individuals in the party who at heart rejected the abominable program; but the probability was so high that the Nazi group constituted an actual menace to world peace and to humane values that a realistic and justified conflict resulted. The high probability of danger removes an antagonism from the domain of prejudice into that of realistic social conflict.

In the case of gangsters, our antagonism is not a matter of prejudice, for the evidence of their antisocial conduct is conclusive. But soon the line becomes hard to draw. How about an ex-convict? It is notoriously difficult for an ex-convict to obtain a steady job where he can be self-supporting and self-respecting. Employers naturally are suspicious if they know the man's past record. But often they are more suspicious than the facts warrant. If they looked further they might find evidence that the man who stands before them is genuinely reformed, or even that he was unjustly accused in the first place. To shut the door merely because a man has a criminal record has *some* probability in its favor, for many prisoners are never reformed; but there is also an element of unwarranted prejudgment involved. We have here a true borderline instance.

We can never hope to draw a hard and fast line between "sufficient" and "insufficient" warrant. For this reason we cannot always be sure whether we are dealing with a case of prejudice or nonprejudice. Yet no one will deny that often we form judgments on the basis of scant, even nonexistent, probabilities.

Overcategorization is perhaps the commonest trick of the human mind. Given a thimbleful of facts we rush to make generalizations as large as a tub. One young boy developed the idea that all Norwegians were giants because he was impressed by the gigantic stature of Ymir in the saga, and for years was fearful lest he meet a living Norwegian. A certain man happened to know three Englishmen personally and proceeded to declare that the whole English race had the common attributes that he observed in these three.

There is a natural basis for this tendency. Life is so short, and the demands upon us for practical adjustments so great, that we cannot let our ignorance detain us in our daily transactions. We have to decide whether objects are good or bad by classes. We cannot weigh each object in the world by itself. Rough and ready rubrics, however coarse and broad, have to suffice.

Not every overblown generalization is a prejudice. Some are simply *misconceptions,* wherein we organize wrong information. One child had the idea that all people living in Minneapolis were "monopolists." And from his father he had learned that monopolists were evil folk. When in later years he discovered the confusion, his dislike of dwellers in Minneapolis vanished.

Here we have the test to help us distinguish between ordinary errors of prejudgment and prejudice. If a person is capable of rectifying his erroneous judgments in the light of new evidence he is not prejudiced. *Prejudgments become prejudices only if they are not reversible when exposed to new knowledge.* A prejudice, unlike a simple misconception, is actively resistant to all evidence that would unseat it. We tend to grow emotional when a prejudice is threatened with contradiction. Thus the difference between ordinary prejudgments and prejudice is that one can discuss and rectify a prejudgment without emotional resistance.

Taking these various considerations into account, we may now attempt a final definition of negative ethnic prejudice.... Each phrase in the definition represents a considerable condensation of the points we have been discussing:

> Ethnic prejudice is an antipathy based upon a faulty and inflexible generalization. It may be felt or expressed. It may be directed toward a group as a whole, or toward an individual because he is a member of that group.

The net effect of prejudice, thus defined, is to place the object of prejudice at some disadvantage not merited by his own misconduct....

We have said that an adequate definition of prejudice contains two essential ingredients. There must be an *attitude* of favor or disfavor; and it must be related to an overgeneralized (and therefore erroneous) *belief*. Prejudiced statements sometimes express the attitudinal factor, sometimes the belief factor. In the following series the first item expresses attitude, the second, belief:

> I can't abide Negroes. Negroes are smelly.

> I wouldn't live in an apartment house with Jews. There are a few exceptions, but in general all Jews are pretty much alike.

> I don't want Japanese-Americans in my town. Japanese-Americans are sly and tricky.

Is it important to distinguish between the attitudinal and belief aspects of prejudice? For some purposes, no. When we find one, we usually find the other. Without some generalized beliefs concerning a group as a whole, a hostile attitude could not long be sustained. In modern researches it turns out that people who express a high degree of antagonistic attitudes on a test for prejudice, also show that they believe to a high degree that the groups they are prejudiced against have a large number of objectionable qualities.

But for some purposes it is useful to distinguish attitude from belief. For example, . . . certain programs designed to reduce prejudice succeed in altering beliefs but not in changing attitudes. Beliefs, to some extent, can be rationally attacked and altered. Usually, however, they have the slippery propensity of accommodating themselves somehow to the negative attitude which is much harder to change. The following dialogue illustrates the point:

> **Mr. X:** The trouble with the Jews is that they only take care of their own group.
> **Mr. Y:** But the record of the Community Chest campaign shows that they give more generously, in proportion to their numbers, to the general charities of the community, than do non-Jews.
> **Mr. X:** That shows they are always trying to buy favor and intrude into Christian affairs. They think of nothing but money; that is why there are so many Jewish bankers.
> **Mr. Y:** But a recent study shows that the percentage of Jews in the banking business is negligible, far smaller than the percentage of non-Jews.
> **Mr. X:** That's just it; they don't go in for respectable business; they are only in the movie business or run night clubs.

Thus the belief system has a way of slithering around to justify the more permanent attitude. The process is one of *rationalization*—of the accommodation of beliefs to attitudes.

It is well to keep these two aspects of prejudice in mind, for in our subsequent discussions we shall have occasion to make use of the distinction. But wherever the term *prejudice* is used without specifying these aspects, the reader may assume that both attitude and belief are intended.

ACTING OUT PREJUDICE

What people actually do in relation to groups they dislike is not always directly related to what they think or feel about them. Two employers, for example may dislike Jews to an equal degree. One may keep his feelings to himself and may hire Jews on the same basis as any workers—perhaps because he wants to gain goodwill for his factory or store in the Jewish community. The other may translate his dislike into his employment policy, and refuse to hire Jews. Both men are prejudiced, but only one of them practices *discrimination*. As a rule discrimination has more immediate and serious social consequences than has prejudice.

It is true that any negative attitude tends somehow, somewhere, to express itself in action. Few people keep their antipathies entirely to themselves. The more intense the attitude, the more likely it is to result in vigorously hostile action....

From the point of view of social consequences much "polite prejudice" is harmless enough—being confined to idle chatter. But unfortunately, the fateful progression is, in this century, growing in frequency. The resulting disruption in the human family is menacing. And as the peoples of the earth grow ever more interdependent, they can tolerate less well the mounting friction.

7.2 MUZAFER SHERIF

Superordinate Goals in the Reduction of Intergroup Conflict

The reduction of prejudice is an ongoing goal of many social psychologists. Muzafer Sherif, for example, has studied prejudice in conflict situations between groups of adolescents. His findings indicate not only that conflict increases hostility between groups but also that hostility is reduced when groups are forced to work together to solve a common problem. The contact theory of prejudice reduction, which is evident in Sherif's work, suggests that cooperation among opponents to reach goals is important.

Sherif (1906–1988) was born in Turkey and moved to the United States in 1929. After earning his Ph.D. from Columbia University in 1935, he became interested in attitudes and intergroup conflict. He was a professor at the University of Oklahoma when he conducted the research published in *The Robber's Cave Experiment: Intergroup Conflict and Cooperation* (University Press of New England, 1954).

This selection is from "Superordinate Goals in the Reduction of Intergroup Conflict," which was published in *The American Journal of Sociology* in 1958. In it, Sherif summarizes his study of conflict and cooperation among boys at a summer camp. This research has served as a model for studying the development and consequent reduction of prejudice in groups. As you read this selection, notice the techniques that Sherif used to promote intergroup harmony and decide if they would work in groups with which you are familiar.

Key Concept: reduction of prejudice through contact

APA Citation: Sherif, M. (1958). Superordinate goals in the reduction of intergroup conflict. *American Journal of Sociology, 63,* 349–356.

*T*his paper summarizes an experimental study on intergroup relations, with emphasis on the reduction of conflict between groups. In the first phase, two groups were *established independently by introducing specified conditions for interaction; in the second phase, the groups were brought into functional contact in conditions perceived by the members of the respective groups as competitive and frustrating. Members developed unfavorable attitudes and derogatory stereotypes of the other group; social distance developed to the point of mutual avoidance, even in pleasant activities. In the final phase of the experiment the measure that proved effective in reducing tension between groups was the introduction of goals which were compellingly shared by members of the groups and which required the collaborative efforts of all.*

In the past, measures to combat the problems of intergroup conflicts, proposed by social scientists as well as by such people as administrators, policy-makers, municipal officials, and educators, have included the following: introduction of legal sanctions; creation of opportunities for social and other contacts among members of conflicting groups; dissemination of correct information to break down false prejudices and unfavorable stereotypes; appeals to the moral ideals of fair play and brotherhood; and even the introduction of rigorous physical activity to produce catharsis by releasing pent-up frustrations and aggressive complexes in the unconscious. Other measures proposed include the encouragement of co-operative habits in one's own community, and bringing together in the cozy atmosphere of a meeting room the leaders of antagonistic groups.

Many of these measures may have some value in the reduction of intergroup conflicts, but, to date, very few generalizations have been established concerning the circumstances and kinds of intergroup conflict in which these measures are effective. Today measures are applied in a somewhat trial-and-error fashion. Finding measures that have wide validity in practice can come only through clarification of the nature of intergroup conflict and analysis of the factors conducive to harmony and conflict between groups under given conditions.

The task of defining and analyzing the nature of the problem was undertaken in a previous publication. One of our major statements was the effectiveness of superordinate goals for the reduction of intergroup conflict. "Superordinate goals" we defined as goals which are compelling and highly appealing to members of two or more groups in conflict but which cannot be attained by the resources and energies of the groups separately. In effect, they are goals attained only when groups pull together....

A RESEARCH PROGRAM

A program of research has been under way since 1948 to test experimentally some hypotheses derived from the literature of intergroup relations. The first large-scale intergroup experiment was carried out in 1949, the second in 1953, and the third in 1954. The conclusions reported here briefly are based on the 1949 and 1954 experiments and on a series of laboratory studies carried out as co-ordinate parts of the program.

The methodology, techniques, and criteria for subject selection in the experiments must be summarized here very briefly. The experiments were carried out in successive stages: (1) groups were formed experimentally; (2) tension and conflict were produced between these groups by introducing conditions conducive to competitive and reciprocally frustrating relations between them; and (3) the attempt was made toward reduction of the intergroup conflict. This stage of reducing tension through introduction of superordinate goals was attempted in the 1954 study on the basis of lessons learned in the two previous studies.

At every stage the subjects interacted in activities which appeared natural to them at a specially arranged camp site completely under our experimental control. They were not aware of the fact that their behavior was under observation. No observation or recording was made in the subjects' presence in a way likely to arouse the suspicion that they were being observed. There is empirical and experimental evidence contrary to the contention that individuals cease to be mindful when they know they are being observed and that their words are being recorded.

In order to insure validity of conclusions, results obtained through observational methods were cross-checked with results obtained through sociometric technique, stereotype ratings of in-groups and out-groups, and through data obtained by techniques adapted from the laboratory. Unfortunately, these procedures cannot be elaborated here. The conclusions summarized briefly are based on results cross-checked by two or more techniques.

The production of groups, the production of conflict between them, and the reduction of conflict in successive stages were brought about through the introduction of problem situations that were real and could not be ignored by individuals in the situation. Special "lecture methods" or "discussion methods" were not used. For example, the problem of getting a meal through their own initiative and planning was introduced when participating individuals were hungry.

Facing a problem situation which is immediate and compelling and which embodies a goal that cannot be ignored, group members *do* initiate discussion and *do* plan and carry through these plans until the objective is achieved. In this process the discussion becomes *their* discussion, the plan *their* plan, the action *their* action. In this process discussion, planning, and action have their place, and, when occasion arises, lecture or information has its place, too. The sequence of these related activities need not be the same in all cases.

The subjects were selected by rigorous criteria. They were healthy, normal boys around the age of eleven and twelve, socially well adjusted in school and neighborhood, and academically successful. They came from a homogeneous sociocultural background and from settled, well-adjusted families of middle or lower-middle class and Protestant affiliations. No subject came from a broken home. The mean I.Q. was above average. The subjects were not personally acquainted with one another prior to the experiment. Thus, explanation of results on the basis of background differences, social maladjustment, undue childhood frustrations, or previous interpersonal relations was ruled out at the beginning by the criteria for selecting subjects.

The first stage of the experiments was designed to produce groups with distinct structure (organization) and a set of norms which could be confronted with intergroup problems. The method for producing groups from unacquainted individuals with similar background was to introduce problem situations in which the attainment of the goal depended on the co-ordinated activity of all individuals. After a series of such activities, definite group structures or organizations developed.

The results warrant the following conclusions for the stage of group formation: When individuals interact in a series of situations toward goals which appeal to all and which require that they co-ordinate their activities, group structures arise having hierarchical status arrangements and a set of norms regulating behavior in matters of consequence to the activities of the group.

Once we had groups that satisfied our definition of "group," relations between groups could be studied. Specified conditions conducive to friction or conflict between groups were introduced. This negative aspect was deliberately undertaken because the major problem in intergroup relations today is the reduction of existing intergroup frictions. (Increasingly, friendly relations between groups is not nearly so great an issue.) The factors conducive to intergroup conflict give us realistic leads for reducing conflict.

A series of situations was introduced in which one group could achieve its goals only at the expense of the other group—through a tournament of competitive events with desirable prizes for the winning group. The results of the stage of intergroup conflict supported our main hypotheses. During interaction between groups in experimentally introduced activities which were competitive and mutually frustrating, members of each group developed hostile attitudes and highly unfavorable stereotypes toward the other group and its members. In fact, attitudes of social distance between the groups became so definite that they wanted to have nothing further to do with each other. This we take as a case of experimentally produced "social distance" in miniature. Conflict was manifested in derogatory name-calling and invectives, flare-ups of physical conflict, and raids on each other's cabins and territory. Over a period of time, negative stereotypes and unfavorable attitudes developed.

At the same time there was an increase in in-group solidarity and co-operativeness. This finding indicates that co-operation and democracy within groups do not necessarily lead to democracy and co-operation with out-groups, if the directions and interests of the groups are conflicting.

Increased solidarity forged in hostile encounters, in rallies from defeat, and in victories over the out-group is one instance of a more general finding: Intergroup relations, both conflicting and harmonious, *affected the nature of relations within the groups involved.* Altered relations between groups produced significant changes in the status arrangements *within* groups, in some instances resulting in shifts at the upper status levels or even a change in leadership. Always, consequential intergroup relations were reflected in new group values or norms which signified changes in practice, word, and deed within the group. Counterparts of this finding are not difficult to see in actual and consequential human relations. Probably many of our major preoccupations, anxieties, and activities in the past decade are incomprehensible without reference to the problems created by the prevailing "cold war" on an international scale. . . .

INTRODUCTION OF SUPERORDINATE GOALS

After establishing the ineffectiveness, even the harm, in intergroup contacts which did not involve superordinate goals, we introduced a series of superordinate goals. Since the characteristics of the problem situations used as superordinate goals are implicit in the two main hypotheses for this stage, we shall present these hypotheses:

1. When groups in a state of conflict are brought into contact under conditions embodying superordinate goals, which are compelling but cannot be achieved by the efforts of one group alone, they will tend to co-operate toward the common goals.
2. Co-operation between groups, necessitated by a series of situations embodying superordinate goals, will have a cumulative effect in the direction of reducing existing conflict between groups.

The problem situations were varied in nature, but all had an essential feature in common—they involved goals that could not be attained by the efforts and energies of one group alone and thus created a state of interdependence between groups: combating a water shortage that affected all and could not help being "compelling"; securing a much-desired film, which could not be obtained by either group alone but required putting their resources together; putting into working shape, when everyone was hungry and the food was some distance away, the only means of transportation available to carry food.

The introduction of a series of such superordinate goals was indeed effective in reducing intergroup conflict: (1) when the groups in a state of friction interacted in conditions involving superordinate goals, they did co-operate in activities leading toward the common goal and (2) a series of joint activities leading toward superordinate goals had the cumulative effect of reducing the prevailing friction between groups and unfavorable stereotypes toward the out-group.

These major conclusions were reached on the basis of observational data and were confirmed by sociometric choices and stereotype ratings administered first during intergroup conflict and again after the introduction of a series of superordinate goals. Comparison of the sociometric choices during intergroup conflict and following the series of superordinate goals shows clearly the changed attitudes toward members of the out-group. Friendship preferences shifted from almost exclusive preferences for in-group members toward increased inclusion of members from the "antagonists." Since the groups were still intact following co-operative efforts to gain superordinate goals, friends were found largely within one's group. However, choices of out-group members grew, in one group, from practically none during intergroup conflict to 23 per cent. Using chi square, this difference is significant ($P < .05$). In the other group, choices of the out-group increased to 36 per cent, and the difference is significant ($P < .001$). The findings confirm observations that the series of superordinate goals produced increasingly friendly associations and attitudes pertaining to out-group members.

Observations made after several superordinate goals were introduced showed a sharp decrease in the name-calling and derogation of the out-group common during intergroup friction and in the contact situations without superordinate goals. At the same time the blatant glorification and bragging about the in-group, observed during the period of conflict, diminished. These observations were confirmed by comparison of ratings of stereotypes (adjectives) the subjects had actually used in referring to their own group and the out-group during conflict with ratings made after the series of superordinate goals. Ratings of the out-group changed significantly from largely unfavorable ratings to largely favorable ratings. The proportions of the most unfavorable ratings found appropriate for the out-group that is, the categorical verdicts that "all of them are stinkers" or "... smart alecks" or "... sneaky"—fell, in one group, from 21 per cent at the end of the friction stage to 1.5 per cent after interaction oriented toward superordinate goals. The corresponding reduction in these highly unfavorable verdicts by the other group was from 36.5 to 6 per cent. The over-all differences between the frequencies of stereotype ratings made in relation to the out-group during intergroup conflict and following the series of superordinate goals are significant for both groups at the .001 level (using chi-square test).

Ratings of the in-group were not so exclusively favorable, in line with observed decreases in self-glorification. But the differences in ratings of the in-group were not statistically significant, as were the differences in ratings of the out-group.

Our findings demonstrate the effectiveness of a series of superordinate goals in the reduction of intergroup conflict, hostility, and their by-products. They also have implications for other measures proposed for reducing intergroup tensions.

It is true that lines of communication between groups must be opened before prevailing hostility can be reduced. But, if contact between hostile groups takes place without superordinate goals, the communication channels serve as media for further accusations and recriminations. When contact situations involve superordinate goals, communication is utilized in the direction of reducing conflict in order to attain the common goals.

Favorable information about a disliked out-group tends to be ignored, rejected, or reinterpreted to fit prevailing stereotypes. But, when groups are pulling together toward superordinate goals, true and even favorable information about the out-group is seen in a new light. The probability of information being effective in eliminating unfavorable stereotypes is enormously enhanced.

When groups co-operate in the attainment of superordinate goals, leaders are in a position to take bolder steps toward bringing about understanding and harmonious relations. When groups are directed toward incompatible goals, genuine moves by a leader to reduce intergroup tension may be seen by the membership as out of step and ill advised. The leader may be subjected to severe criticism and even loss of faith and status in his own group. When compelling superordinate goals are introduced, the leader can make moves to further co-operative efforts, and his decisions receive support from other group members.

In short, various measures suggested for the reduction of intergroup conflict—disseminating information, increasing social contact, conferences of leaders acquire new significance and effectiveness when they become part and parcel of interaction processes between groups oriented toward superordinate goals which have real and compelling value for all groups concerned.

Muzafer Sherif

**7.3 JOHN F. DOVIDIO AND
SAMUEL L. GAERTNER**

Affirmative Action, Unintentional Racial Biases, and Intergroup Relations

Despite the efforts of psychologists to understand and to reduce prejudice, it continues to be present in our society. However, as opposed to the traditional form of prejudice, which was direct, more recent forms of prejudice are often indirect and more subtle. John F. Dovidio and Samuel L. Gaertner have been working toward understanding modern aversive prejudice.

Dovidio (b. 1951) earned his Ph.D. in social psychology from the University of Delaware in 1977. He then accepted a position at Colgate University, where he is currently a professor of psychology. Gaertner (b. 1942) earned his Ph.D. in social psychology from the City University of New York in 1970. He then went to work at the University of Delaware, where he is presently a professor of psychology. Dovidio and Gaertner coedited the book *Prejudice, Discrimination, and Racism* (Academic Press, 1986).

This selection is from "Affirmative Action, Unintentional Racial Biases, and Intergroup Relations," which was published in *Journal of Social Issues* in 1996. In it, Dovidio and Gaertner describe modern aversive racism and review research studies that demonstrate its effects in various settings. As you read this selection, consider how a program might be developed to reduce the level of aversive prejudice. How can we become more aware of modern aversive racism in our lives?

Key Concept: prejudice

APA Citation: Dovidio, J. F., & Gaertner, S. L. (1996). Affirmative action, unintentional racial biases, and intergroup relations. *Journal of Social Issues, 52,* 51–75.

The nature of prejudice appears to have changed. Whereas traditional forms of prejudice are direct and overt, contemporary forms are indirect and subtle. Aversive racism (see Dovidio & Gaertner, 1991; Dovidio, Mann, & Gaertner, 1989; Gaertner & Dovidio, 1986; Kovel, 1970) has been identified as a modern form of prejudice that characterizes the racial attitudes of many Whites who endorse egalitarian values, who regard themselves as nonprejudiced, but who discriminate in subtle, rationalizable ways. Most of the work on aversive racism that will be discussed here involves Whites' attitudes toward Blacks. Elsewhere we have demonstrated the generalizability of these processes to attitudes toward Latinos (Dovidio, Gaertner, Anastasio, & Sanitioso, 1992) and women (Dovidio & Gaertner, 1983).

According to the aversive racism perspective, many people who consciously and sincerely support egalitarian principles and believe themselves to be nonprejudiced also unconsciously harbor negative feelings and beliefs about Blacks. These feelings and beliefs, which may be based in part on almost unavoidable cognitive (e.g., informational processing biases that result when people are categorized into ingroups and outgroups; see Hamilton & Trolier, 1986), motivational (e.g., personal or group interest), and sociocultural processes (e.g., social learning; see Gaertner & Dovidio, 1986).

The feelings of aversive racists toward Blacks are characterized by mildly negative feelings, such as fear, disgust, and uneasiness, that tend to motivate avoidance rather than intentionally destructive or hostile behavior, which is more likely to characterize the traditional, old-fashioned form of racism. Relative to the more overt, traditional racists (see Kovel, 1970), aversive racists do not represent the open flame of racial hatred nor do they usually *intend* to act out of bigoted beliefs or feelings. Instead, that bias is expressed in subtle and indirect ways that do not threaten the aversive racist's nonprejudiced self-image. When a negative response can be rationalized on the basis of some factor other than race, bias against Blacks is likely to occur; when these rationalizations are less available, bias is less likely to be manifested. In addition, whereas aversive racists may be very guarded about behaving in anti-Black ways, their biases may be more likely unintentionally manifested in pro-White behaviors (i.e., ingroup favoritism rather than outgroup derogation).

Consistent with the aversive racism perspective, other theories of contemporary racism and sexism also hypothesize that bias is currently expressed more subtly than in the past. One such approach is symbolic racism theory (Kinder & Sears, 1981; McConahay & Hough, 1976; Sears, 1988; Sears, Citrin, & van Laar, 1995; Sears, Hensler, & Speer, 1979; Sears & Allen, 1984) or modern racism (McConahay, 1986) theory. Work on symbolic (Sears, 1988) and modern (McConahay, 1986) racism evolved from the conceptual and practical problems that arose from the weak relationships between traditional self-report prejudice items and racially relevant behaviors, such as voting intentions, that were being obtained in survey data. According to symbolic racism theory, negative feelings toward Blacks that Whites acquire early in life persist into adulthood but are expressed indirectly and symbolically, in terms of opposition to busing or resistance to preferential treatment, rather than directly or overtly, as in support for segregation. The items and theory that were developed focused on "the expression in terms of abstract ideological symbols and symbolic behaviors of the feeling that blacks are violating cherished values and making illegitimate demands for changes in the *status quo*" (McConahay & Hough, 1976, p. 23). These "cherished values" were those, such as personal freedom, that were associated with a politically conservative ideology.

McConahay's (1986) theory of modern racism accepted the basic tenets of symbolic racism but amplified the definition "to add the belief that discrimination no longer exists and that the cherished values are those associated with 'equality' or 'equality of opportunity'" (pp. 95–96). McConahay (1986) further proposed that because modern racism involves the rejection of traditional racist beliefs and the displacement of anti-Black feelings onto more abstract social and political issues, modern racists, like aversive racists, are relatively unaware of their racist feelings. Swim, Aikin, Hall, and Hunter (1995) have extended these notions to contemporary prejudice toward women.

Whereas symbolic and modern racism are subtle forms of contemporary racism that seem to exist among political conservatives, aversive racism is more strongly associated with liberals. In addition, we have proposed that because of the sensitivity of aversive racists to race-related issues, it may not be possible to assess individual differences in aversive racism using self-report measures of prejudice (Gaertner & Dovidio, 1986). Kleinpenning and Hagendoorn (1993), believing otherwise however, have suggested that aversive racism can be assessed through self-reports of how pleasant or unpleasant social interactions (e.g., as classmates) or intimate relations (e.g., as marriage partners) with members of other groups would be. They conceptualize forms of racism on a continuum, beginning with aversive racism (which they regard as the mildest form), and followed by symbolic racism and then old-fashioned racism. Kleinpenning and Hagendoorn (1993) conclude that prejudice is a cumulative dimension that begins with avoidance of minorities in private contexts (aversive prejudice) and runs through beliefs that minority groups receive more social and economic benefits than they deserve (symbolic prejudice) to full-blown racist ideologies portraying minorities as being genetically inferior (old-fashioned prejudice).

EMPIRICAL EVIDENCE

Although contemporary forms of bias may be expressed subtly and often unintentionally, the effects may be profound. Across a number of paradigms, we have found consistent evidence of the impact of aversive racism in Whites' responses to Blacks (see Gaertner & Dovidio, 1986). For example, one of our early studies (Gaertner & Dovidio, 1977) demonstrated its influence in an emergency situation.

*John F. Dovidio
and Samuel L.
Gaertner*

In one early test of the aversive racism perspective, we investigated whether or not high and low prejudice-scoring White students would help Black or White victims in emergency situations depending upon the clarity of norms regarding intervention (Gaertner & Dovidio, 1977). White subjects were led to believe they were the only bystanders or were among three witnesses (all White) to an emergency involving a Black or White victim. According to Darley and Latané (1968), the normatively appropriate behavior, helping, is clearly defined when a bystander is the only witness to an emergency. In contrast, the appropriate response when other bystanders are believed to be present is less clear and obvious: The presumed presence of other bystanders allows bystanders to diffuse responsibility (Darley & Latané, 1968), to relieve feelings of obligation to help by coming to the conclusion that someone else will act.

Gaertner and Dovidio (1977) found that the White bystanders who believed they were the only witnesses to the emergency were as likely to help Black victims as White victims. When other White bystanders were present, however, Whites were more likely to diffuse responsibility and less likely to intervene to aid the Black victim than the White victim—here they helped the Black victim *half as often* as they helped the White victim. Thus, in the situation in which socially appropriate behavior was clearly defined, White subjects behaved in accordance with their generally nonprejudiced self-images and did not discriminate against the Black victim; when witnesses could rationalize nonintervention, White bystanders discriminated against Black victims. Whereas the situational context was a strong predictor of bias, traditional measures of racial attitudes were not. Neither self-report of prejudice nor authoritarianism correlated overall with responses to the Black victim when bystanders were alone or in the presence of others.

The impact of aversive racism continues to persist today. Its consequences are evident in more considered, deliberative judgments as well as in spontaneous expression of behavior.

Evaluative Judgments

The principles and processes associated with aversive racism may be manifested in situations involving personnel selection. For instance, in a recent study (Dovidio, 1995), White students were recruited ostensibly to help select resident (dormitory) advisors, highly prestigious and competitive student positions, for the coming semester. When the information provided about candidates was unambiguous (i.e., uniformly positive or uniformly negative), Black and White applicants were treated equivalently. However, when the candidate's record was more ambiguous—involving a combination of positive and negative information—White applicants were endorsed more strongly than Black applicants. As in the emergency helping study, contextual ambiguity, not self-reported racial attitudes, predicted whether or not discrimination against Blacks would occur....

WHEN IS EQUAL OPPORTUNITY UNEQUAL?

Even when equal access for employment is provided in principle, subtle, perhaps unconscious, expressions of bias related to aversive racism, like more blatant forms, may limit opportunities for Blacks and other minorities in practice. We have hypothesized that aversive racism is more intensely manifested in situations in which Whites may be directly or symbolically threatened by the advancement of Blacks to positions of status and control.

Acceptance of Competence

In one study, for instance, we investigated the relationship between status and bias in the context of a decision with implications for participants—making admissions decisions for their university (Kline & Dovidio, 1982). Applicant qualifications were systematically varied: Participants evaluated a poorly qualified applicant, a moderately qualified candidate, or a highly qualified applicant. In addition, the race of the applicant was manipulated by a photograph attached to the file. The central question concerned how this picture would affect participants' admissions decisions.

Discrimination against the Black applicant occurred, but, as expected, it did not occur equally in all conditions. Students rated the poorly qualified Black and White applicants equally low. They showed some bias when they evaluated the moderately qualified White applicant slightly higher than the comparable African-American candidate. Discrimination against the Black applicant was most apparent, however, when the applicants were *highly* qualified. This bias can also be interpreted as a pro-White manifestation of aversive racism (Gaertner et al., 1996). Although White students evaluated the highly qualified African-American applicant very positively, they judged the highly qualified White applicant—with exactly the same credentials—as even better. Thus, a situation that appears to offer equal opportunity to very well-qualified applicants still favors Whites over Blacks because of subtle and pervasive biases.

This study also included individual items that contributed to the overall evaluative score—scaled according to how directly they related to the information presented in the applicant's transcript. The less directly related the item was to the transcript information, the greater the bias ($r = .69$). These results are consistent with the finding that Whites tend to evaluate Blacks less favorably than Whites on subjective dimensions of work performance (Kraiger & Ford, 1985) and support Goddard's (1986) observation in applied settings that "vague, ill-defined, subjective criteria lend themselves to all kinds of biased judgments" (p. 34).

Maintaining the Status Quo

Whereas blatant racial and ethnic prejudices relate to support for policies that unconditionally restrict the rights and opportunities of minority groups, subtle racism is associated with support for the *status quo* or for restrictions when other justifications (e.g., lack of credentials) are available (Pettigrew & Meertens, 1995). Thus, in other research we investigated the possibility that the generally articulated issue of relative competence is a rationalization in which a nonracial factor, competence, is used by Whites to object to the advancement of Blacks in ways that increase the likelihood that Whites will be subordinated to minority groups.

This reasoning also has relevance to reactions to affirmative action. Consistent with the aversive racism framework, resistance to affirmative action is not commonly expressed directly, but rather mainly as concerns about individual freedom or about unfair distribution of rewards. Nevertheless, although common protests by Whites regarding affirmative action seem to express mainly the concern that *qualified* Whites will be disadvantaged relative to *less qualified* Blacks, it is possible that the reversal of the traditional role relationship, in which Whites occupied positions of superior status, represents the primary threat to Whites.

The results of two separate studies comparing the reactions of White male and female participants to a Black male partner (Dovidio & Gaertner, 1981) and a White female partner (Dovidio & Gaertner, 1983) relative to a White male partner produced convergent findings. Specifically, relative status, rather than relative ability, was the primary determinant of positive behaviors toward Black male and White female partners. Regardless of their competence, Black male and White female supervisors were responded to *less favorably* than were Black male or White female subordinates. In contrast, in both studies White male supervisors were responded to somewhat *more positively* than were White male subordinates.

How could participants in these experiments rationalize not responding as positively to competent Black and female supervisors? Participants' post-experimental evaluations of their partners revealed that their behaviors may have been mediated by perceptions of *relative* intelligence (competence). Although participants' ratings indicated that they accepted high-ability White male partners as being somewhat more intelligent than themselves, participants described even high-ability Black partners as significantly less intelligent than themselves and high-ability female partners as no more intelligent than themselves. To the extent that majority group members are reluctant to believe Blacks and women are higher or equal in competence compared to themselves, they are likely to perceive programs that foster the advancement of members of these groups over themselves and members of their group as unfair preferential treatment. This biased perception of relative competence also decreases the likelihood that passive equal employment opportunity programs can insure truly equitable treatment of disadvantaged groups by the majority group.

Subtle Bias and the Glass Ceiling

Aversive racism and contemporary forms of sexism are difficult to identify definitively in complex organizations because they are subtle and other explanations are usually possible. In fact, aversive racism is generally manifested *only* when other explanations that can rationalize bias are present. Thus, we cannot say that simply because disparities exist in organizations, racism is the cause. But, where racism exists, disparities will exist. These disparities generally reflect the patterns we have discovered in the laboratory. Across organizations as diverse as the armed forces, federal government, and Fortune 1000 companies, greater racial disparities occur at higher status levels. In addition, these patterns have persisted over the past decade.

Across the different branches of the military in 1988, African Americans who were identified as qualified for officer promotions succeeded at significantly lower rates than did White candidates. Consistent with our laboratory demonstrations, disparities in promotion rates tended to increase with higher ranks. Within the Navy, for example, in 1988 African Americans represented 13% of the force, but only 5% of the officers and 1.5% of the admirals. We have also examined patterns of disparities for various segments of federal employees and found similar evidence: Blacks are generally less well represented in higher grades (e.g., GS 16–18) than in lower grades. Furthermore, these disparities have remained relatively stable across time as well.

A recent Department of Labor survey of Fortune 1000 companies provides independent evidence of the "glass ceiling effect" for Blacks and other minorities in industry. Representations of minorities consistently declined with higher occupational status. A Department of Commerce survey further confirmed substantial income disparities between African-American and White men. In 1989, African-American men with a high school education earned $6230 less per year than White men with comparable education ($20,280 vs. $26,510). The gap was even larger ($9710) between college-educated African-American and White men ($31,380 vs. $41,090).

Thus, across a range of settings we see consistent patterns of disparities in occupational advancement and income. We acknowledge that the "glass ceiling effect" can occur for a wide range of reasons and that the leap from laboratory to organizations is a large one. Nevertheless, the pattern of disparities that we see in organizations conforms to our predictions.

REFERENCES

Darley, J. M., & Latané, B. (1968). Bystander intervention in emergencies: Diffusion of responsibility. *Journal of Personality and Social Psychology, 8,* 377–383.

Dovidio, J. F. (1995). *Bias in evaluative judgments and personnel selection: The role of ambiguity.* Unpublished manuscript. Department of Psychology, Colgate University, Hamilton, NY.

Dovidio, J. F., & Gaertner, S. L. (1981). The effects of race, status, and ability on helping behavior. *Social Psychology Quarterly, 44,* 192–203.

Dovidio, J. F., & Gaertner, S. L. (1983). The effects of sex, status, and ability on helping behavior. *Journal of Applied Social Psychology, 13,* 191–205.

Dovidio, J. F., & Gaertner, S. L. (1991). Changes in the nature and expression of racial prejudice. In H. Knopke, J. Norrell, & R. Rogers (Eds.), *Opening doors: An appraisal of race relations in contemporary America* (pp. 201–241). Tuscaloosa, AL: University of Alabama Press.

Dovidio, J. F., Gaertner, S. L., Anastasio, P. A., & Sanitioso, R. (1992). Cognitive and motivational bases of bias: The implications of aversive racism for attitudes toward Hispanics. In S. Knouse, P. Rosenfeld, & A. Culbertson (Eds.). *Hispanics in the workplace* (pp. 75–106). Newbury Park, CA: Sage.

Dovidio, J. F., Mann, J. A., & Gaertner, S. L. (1989). Resistance to affirmative action: The implication of aversive racism. In F. A. Blanchard & F. J. Crosby (Eds.), *Affirmative action in perspective* (pp. 83–102). New York: Springer-Verlag.

Gaertner, S. L., & Dovidio, J. F. (1977). The subtlety of White racism, arousal, and helping behavior. *Journal of Personality and Social Psychology, 35,* 691–707.

Gaertner, S. L., & Dovidio, J. F. (1986). The aversive form of racism. In J. F. Dovidio & S. L. Gaertner (Eds.), *Prejudice, discrimination, and racism* (pp. 61–89). Orlando, FL: Academic Press.

Gaertner, S. L., Dovidio, J. F., Banker, B., Rust, M., Nier, J., Mottola, G., & Ward, C. (1996). Does racism necessarily mean anti-Blackness? Aversive racism and pro-Whiteness. In M. Fine, L. Powell, L. Weis, & M. Wong (Eds.), *Off White* (pp. 167–178). London: Routledge.

Goddard, R. W. (1986, October). Post-employment: The changing current in discrimination charges. *Personnel Journal, 65,* 34–40.

Hamilton, D. L., & Trolier, T. K. (1986). Stereotypes and stereotyping: An overview of the cognitive approach. In J. F. Dovidio & S. L. Gaertner (Eds.), *Prejudice, discrimination, and racism* (pp. 127–163). Orlando, FL: Academic Press.

Kinder, D. R., & Sears, D. O. (1981). Prejudice and politics: Symbolic racism versus threats to "the good life." *Journal of Personality and Social Psychology, 40,* 414–431.

Kleinpenning, G., & Hagendoorn, L. (1993). Forms of racism and the cumulative dimension of ethnic attitudes. *Social Psychology Quarterly, 56,* 21–36.

Kline, B. B., & Dovidio, J. F. (1982, April). *Effects of race, sex, and qualifications on predictions of a college applicant's performance.* Paper presented at the annual meeting of the Eastern Psychological Association, Baltimore, MD.

Kovel, J. (1970). *White racism: A psychohistory.* New York: Pantheon.

Kraiger, K., & Ford, J. K. (1985). A meta-analysis of ratee effects in performance ratings. *Journal of Applied Psychology, 70,* 56–65.

McConahay, J. B. (1986). Modern racism, ambivalence, and the modern racism scale. In J. F. Dovidio & S. L. Gaertner (Eds.), *Prejudice, discrimination, and racism* (pp. 91–125). Orlando, FL: Academic Press.

McConahay, J. B., & Hough, J. C. (1976). Symbolic racism. *Journal of Social Issues, 32*(2), 23–45.

Pettigrew, T. F., & Meertens, R. W. (1995). Subtle and blatant prejudice in Western Europe. *European Journal of Social Psychology, 25,* 57–76.

Sears, D. O. (1988). Symbolic racism. In P. A. Katz & D. A. Taylor (Eds.), *Eliminating racism: Profiles in controversy* (pp. 53–84). New York: Plenum Press.

Sears, D. O., & Allen, H. M., Jr. (1984). The trajectory of local desegregation controversies and Whites' opposition to busing. In M. B. Brewer & N. Miller (Eds.), *Groups in contact: The psychology of desegregation* (pp. 123–151). New York: Academic Press.

Sears, D. O., Citrin, J., & van Laar, C. (1995, September). *Black exceptionalism in a multicultural society.* Paper presented at the joint meeting of the Society for Experimental Psychology and the European Association of Experimental Social Psychology, Washington, DC.

Sears, D. O., Hensler, C. P., & Speer, L. K. (1979). Whites' opposition to "busing": Self-interest or symbolic politics? *American Political Science Review, 73,* 369–384.

Swim, J. K., Aikin, K. J., Hall, W. S., & Hunter, B. A. (1995). Sexism and racism: Old-fashioned and modern prejudices. *Journal of Personality and Social Psychology, 68,* 199–214.

PART FOUR

Social Interaction and Relationships

On the Internet . . .

Sites appropriate to Part Four

The 1,001 Ways to Be Romantic Web site literally presents 1,001 ways to be romantic, from the book of the same name. Some of the suggestions are silly, while others provide practical advice on romantic love.

```
http://www.godek.com/1001.html
```

This site provides a brief history of close relationships and of social cognition. It also provides numerous references pertinent to the topic.

```
http://artsci.wustl.edu/~msahrend/
   SC2.html#agenda
```

This site from the Center for Evolutionary Psychology at the University of California, Santa Barbara, contains a paper describing evolutionary psychology. A great deal of background information is also included.

```
http://www.psych.ucsb.edu/research/cep/
```

CHAPTER 8 Interpersonal Attraction

8.1 KAREN DION, ELLEN BERSCHEID, AND ELAINE WALSTER

What Is Beautiful Is Good

Social psychologists have attempted to explain why individuals like certain other individuals. Research indicates that there are three major influences on interpersonal attractiveness: proximity, similarity, and physical attractiveness. In general, physical attractiveness has been found to be the main determinant of whom we decide to get to know better. Pioneers in this area are Karen Dion, Ellen Berscheid, and Elaine Walster (now Hatfield).

Dion (b. 1945) earned her Ph.D. in psychology from the University of Minnesota in 1970 and then moved to the University of Toronto, where she is currently a professor of psychology. Berscheid (b. 1936) earned her Ph.D. in social psychology from the University of Minnesota in 1965, where she is currently a regents professor of psychology. Walster (b. 1937) earned her Ph.D. in social psychology in 1963 from Stanford University. She taught at the University of Minnesota and the University of Wisconsin before going to the University of Hawaii in 1981.

This selection is from "What Is Beautiful Is Good," which was published in the *Journal of Personality and Social Psychology* in 1972. In it, the authors describe an experiment showing that physically attractive people are perceived as having more socially desirable traits and are expected to be more successful in life than are unattractive people. This research suggests that people stereotype physically attractive people as having the best of all worlds. Note that the *F* values in the article refer to the Analysis of Variance Statistical Test, which is designed to measure the significance of the results.

How would you explain the results of the experiment? Why would attractive individuals have more positive traits than unattractive ones?

Key Concept: physical attractiveness and interpersonal attraction

APA Citation: Dion, K., Berscheid, E., and Walster, E. (1972). What is beautiful is good. *Journal of Personality and Social Psychology, 24,* 285–290.

A person's physical appearance, along with his sexual identity, is the personal characteristic that is most obvious and accessible to others in social interaction. The present experiment was designed to determine whether physically attractive stimulus persons, both male and female are (a) assumed to possess more socially desirable personality traits than physically unattractive stimulus persons and (b) expected to lead better lives (e.g., be more competent husbands and wives, be more successful occupationally, etc.) than unattractive stimulus persons. Sex of Subject × Sex of Stimulus Person interactions along these dimensions also were investigated. The present results indicate a "what is beautiful is good" stereotype along the physical attractiveness dimension with no Sex of Judge × Sex of Stimulus interaction. The implications of such a stereotype on self-concept development and the course of social interaction are discussed.

... The present study was an attempt to determine if a physical attractiveness stereotype exists and, if so, to investigate the content of the stereotype along several dimensions. Specifically, it was designed to investigate (a) whether physically attractive stimulus persons, both male and female, are assumed to possess more *socially desirable personality traits* than unattractive persons and (b) whether they are expected to *lead better lives* than unattractive individuals. With respect to the latter, we wished to determine if physically attractive persons are generally expected to be better husbands and wives, better parents, and more successful socially and occupationally than less attractive persons.

Because it seemed possible that jealousy might attenuate these effects (if one is jealous of another, he may be reluctant to accord the other the status that he feels the other deserves), and since subjects might be expected to be more jealous of attractive stimulus persons of the same sex than of the opposite sex, we examined the Sex of Subject × Sex of Stimulus person interactions along the dimensions described above.

METHOD

Subjects

Sixty students, 30 males and 30 females, who were enrolled in an introductory course in psychology at the University of Minnesota participated in this experiment. Each had agreed to participate in return for experimental points to be added to their final exam grade.

Procedure

... The subjects were told that standard sets of photographs would be used as the basis for personality inferences. The individuals depicted in the photographs were said to be part of a group of college students currently enrolled at other universities who were participating in a longitudinal study of personality development scheduled to continue into adulthood. It would be possible, therefore, to assess the accuracy of each subject's judgments against information currently available on the stimulus persons and also against forthcoming information.

Stimulus Materials. Following the introduction, each subject was given three envelopes. Each envelope contained one photo of a stimulus person of approximately the subject's own age. One of the three envelopes that the subject received contained a photograph of a physically attractive stimulus person; another contained a photograph of a person of average attractiveness; and the final envelope contained a photograph of a relatively unattractive stimulus person. Half of our subjects received three pictures of girls; the remainder received pictures of boys.

To increase the generalizability of our findings and to insure that the general dimension of attractiveness was the characteristic responded to (rather than unique characteristics such as hair color, etc.), 12 different sets of three pictures each were prepared. Each subject received and rated only 1 set. Which 1 of the 12 sets of pictures the subject received, the order in which each of the three envelopes in the set were presented, and the ratings made of the person depicted, were all randomly determined.

Dependent Variables. The subjects were requested to record their judgments of the three stimulus persons in several booklets. The first page of each booklet cautioned the subjects that this study was an investigation of accuracy of person perception and that we were not interested in the subjects' tact, politeness, or other factors usually important in social situations. It was stressed that it was important for the subject to rate the stimulus persons frankly.

The booklets tapped impressions of the stimulus person along several dimensions. First, the subjects were asked to open the first envelope and then to rate the person depicted on 27 different *personality traits* (which were arranged in random order).[1] The subjects' ratings were made on 6-point scales, the ends of which were labeled by polar opposites (i.e., exciting–dull). When these ratings had been computed, the subject was asked to open the second envelope, make ratings, and then open the third envelope.

In a subsequent booklet, the subjects were asked to assess the stimulus persons on five additional personality traits.[2] These ratings were made on a slightly different scale. The subjects were asked to indicate which stimulus person possessed the "most" and "least" of a given trait. The stimulus person thought to best represent a positive trait was assigned a score of 3; the stimulus person thought to possess an intermediate amount of the trait was assigned a score of 2; and the stimulus person thought to least represent the trait was assigned a score of 1.

In a previous experiment... , a subset of items was selected to comprise an index of the *social desirability* of the personality traits assigned to the stimulus person. The subjects' ratings of each stimulus person on the appropriate items were simply summed to determine the extent to which the subject perceived each stimulus person as socially desirable.

In order to assess whether or not attractive persons are expected to lead happier and more successful lives than unattractive persons, the subjects were asked to estimate which of the stimulus persons would be most likely, and which least likely, to have a number of different life experiences. The subjects were reminded again that their estimates would eventually be checked for accuracy as the lives of the various stimulus persons evolved. The subjects' estimates of the stimulus person's probable life experiences formed indexes of the stimulus person's future happiness in four areas: (*a*) marital happiness (Which stimulus persons is most likely to ever be divorced?); (*b*) parental happiness (Which stimulus person is most likely to be a good parent?); (*c*) social and professional happiness (Which stimulus person is most likely to experience deep personal fulfillment?); and (*d*) total happiness (sum of Indexes *a, b*, and *c*).

A fifth index, an occupational success index, was also obtained for each stimulus person. The subjects were asked to indicate which of the three stimulus persons would be most likely to engage in 30 different occupations. (The order in which the occupations were presented and the estimates made was randomized.) The 30 occupations had been chosen such that three status levels of 10 different general occupations were represented, three examples of which follow: Army sergeant (low status); Army captain (average status); Army colonel (high status). Each time a high-status occupation was foreseen for a stimulus person, the stimulus person was assigned a score of 3; when a moderate status occupation was foreseen, the stimulus person was assigned a score of 2; when a low-status occupation was foreseen, a score of 1 was assigned. The average status of occupations that a subject ascribed to a stimulus person constituted the score for that stimulus person in the occupational status index.

RESULTS AND DISCUSSION

Manipulation Check

It is clear that our manipulation of the relative attractiveness of the stimulus persons depicted was effective. The six unattractive stimulus persons were seen as less attractive than the average stimulus persons, who, in turn, were seen as less attractive than the six attractive stimulus persons. The stimulus persons' mean rankings on the attractiveness dimension were 1.22, 2.02, and 2.87, respectively. These differences were statistically significant ($F = 939.32$).[3]

*Karen Dion
et al.*

It will be recalled that it was predicted that the subjects would attribute more socially desirable personality traits to attractive individuals than to average or unattractive individuals. It also was anticipated that jealousy might attenuate these effects. Since the subjects might be expected to be more jealous of stimulus persons of the same sex than of the opposite sex, we blocked both on sex of subject and sex of stimulus person. If jealousy attenuated the predicted main effect, a significant Sex of Subject × Sex of Stimulus Person interaction should be secured in addition to the main effect.

All tests for detection of linear trend and interaction were conducted via a multivariate analysis of variance. (This procedure is outlined in Hays, 1963.)

The means relevant to the hypothesis that attractive individuals will be perceived to possess more socially desirable personalities than others are reported in Table 1. Analyses reveal that attractive individuals were indeed judged to be more socially desirable than are unattractive ($F = 29.61$) persons. The Sex of Subject × Sex of Stimulus Person interaction was insignificant (interaction $F = .00$). Whether the rater was of the same or the opposite sex as the stimulus person, attractive stimulus persons were judged as more socially desirable.

Furthermore, it was also hypothesized that the subjects would assume that attractive stimulus persons are likely to secure more prestigious jobs than those of lesser attractiveness, as well as experiencing happier marriages, being better parents, and enjoying more fulfilling social and occupational lives.

The means relevant to these predictions concerning the estimated future life experiences of individuals of varying degrees of physical attractiveness are also depicted in Table 1. As shown in the table, there was strong support for all of the preceding hypotheses save one. Attractive men and women were expected to attain more prestigious occupations than were those of lesser attractiveness ($F = 42.30$), and this expectation was expressed equally by raters of the same or the opposite sex as the stimulus person (interaction $F = .25$).

The subjects also assumed that attractive individuals would be more competent spouses and have happier marriages than those of lesser attractiveness ($F = 62.54$). (It might be noted that there is some evidence that this may be a correct perception. Kirkpatrick and Cotton (1951), reported that "well-adjusted" wives were more physically attractive than "badly adjusted" wives. "Adjustment," however, was assessed by friends' perceptions, which may have been affected by the stereotype evident here.)

According to the means reported in Table 1, it is clear that attractive individuals were not expected to be better parents ($F = 1.47$). In fact, attractive persons were rated somewhat lower than any other group of stimulus persons as potential parents, although no statistically significant differences were apparent.

TABLE 1

Traits Attributed to Various Stimulus Others

Trait ascription	Unattractive stimulus person	Average stimulus person	Attractive stimulus person
Social desirability of the stimulus person's personality	56.31	62.42	65.39
Occupational status of the stimulus person	1.70	2.02	2.25
Marital competence of the stimulus person	.37	.71	1.70
Parental competence of the stimulus person	3.91	4.55	3.54
Social and professional happiness of the stimulus person	5.28	6.34	6.37
Total happiness of the stimulus person	8.83	11.60	11.60
Likelihood of marriage	1.52	1.82	2.17

The higher the number, the more socially desirable, the more prestigious an occupation, etc., the stimulus person is expected to possess.

As predicted, attractive stimulus persons were assumed to have better prospects for happy social and professional lives ($F = 21.97$). All in all, the attractive stimulus persons were expected to have more total happiness in their lives than those of lesser attractiveness ($F = 24.20$).

The preceding results did not appear to be attenuated by a jealousy effect (Sex of Subject $\times$ Stimulus Person interaction $Fs = .01, .07, .21,$ and $.05,$ respectively).

The subjects were also asked to estimate the likelihood that the various stimulus persons would marry early or marry at all. Responses were combined into a single index. It is evident that the subjects assumed that the attractive stimulus persons were more likely to find an acceptable partner than those of lesser attractiveness ($F = 35.84$). Attractive individuals were expected to marry earlier and to be less likely to remain single. Once again, these conclusions were reached by all subjects, regardless of whether they were of the same or opposite sex of the stimulus person (interaction $F = .01$).

The results suggest that a physical attractiveness stereotype exists and that its content is perfectly compatible with the "What is beautiful is good" thesis. Not only are physically attractive persons assumed to possess more socially desirable personalities than those of lesser attractiveness, but it is presumed that their lives will be happier and more successful.

NOTES

1. The subjects were asked how altruistic, conventional, self-assertive, exciting, stable, emotional, dependent, safe, interesting, genuine, sensitive, outgoing, sexually permissive, sincere, warm, sociable, competitive, obvious, kind, modest, strong, serious, sexually warm, simple, poised, bold, and sophisticated each stimulus person was.
2. The subjects rated stimulus persons on the following traits: friendliness, enthusiasm, physical attractiveness, social poise, and trustworthiness.
3. Throughout this report, $df = 1/55$.

REFERENCES

Hays, W. L. *Statistics for psychologists.* New York: Holt, Rinehart & Winston, 1963.

Kirkpatrick, C., & Cotton, J. Physical attractiveness, age, and marital adjustment. *American Sociological Review,* 1951, **16,** 81–86.

The Strategies of Human Mating

The focus of social psychology has become increasingly multicultural in recent years as researchers look for universal laws of human behavior. The evolutionary approach to courtship and mate selection argues that men and women throughout the world have different reproductive strategies. David M. Buss of the University of Michigan, in collaboration with 50 other researchers around the world, surveyed over 10,000 men and women in 37 countries on their mating preferences. Buss has used the survey results to develop a theory of mate selection.

Buss received his Ph.D. in psychology from the University of California at Berkeley in 1981. He taught at Harvard University and the University of Michigan prior to accepting his current position at the University of Texas in 1996. His evolutionary theory of human mate selection is detailed in his book *The Evolution of Desire: Strategies of Human Mating* (Basic Books, 1994).

This selection is from "The Strategies of Human Mating," which was published in *American Scientist* in 1994. In it, Buss outlines his theory and provides research results—obtained predominantly through surveys—that support the conclusion that, universally, men and women desire certain characteristics in a mate that are unique to each sex. How might an understanding of differences in sexual preference help men and women in their interpersonal relationships?

Key Concept: cross-cultural theory of mate selection

APA Citation: Buss, D. M. (1994). The strategies of human mating. *American Scientist, 82,* 238–249.

What do men and women want in a mate? Is there anything consistent about human behavior when it comes to the search for a mate? Would a Gujarati of India be attracted to the same traits in a mate as a Zulu of South Africa or a college student in the midwestern United States?

As a psychologist working in the field of human personality and mating preferences, I have come across many attempts to answer such questions and provide a coherent explanation of human mating patterns. Some theories have suggested that people search for mates who resemble archetypical images of the opposite-sex parent (à la Freud and Jung), or mates with characteristics that are either complementary or similar to one's own qualities, or mates with whom to make an equitable exchange of valuable resources.

These theories have played important roles in our understanding of human mating patterns, but few of them have provided specific predictions that can be tested. Fewer still consider the origins and functions of an individual's mating preferences. What possible function is there to mating with an individual who is an archetypical image of one's opposite-sex parent? Most theories also tend to assume that the processes that guide the mating preferences of men and women are identical, and no sex-differentiated predictions can be derived. The context of the mating behavior is also frequently ignored; the same mating tendencies are posited regardless of circumstances.

Despite the complexity of human mating behavior, it is possible to address these issues in a single, coherent theory. David Schmitt of the University of Michigan and I have recently proposed a framework for understanding the logic of human mating patterns from the standpoint of evolutionary theory. Our theory makes several predictions about the behavior of men and women in the context of their respective sexual strategies. In particular, we discuss the changes that occur when men and women shift their goals from short-term mating (casual sex) to long-term mating (a committed relationship).

Some of the studies we discuss are based on surveys of male and female college students in the United States. In these instances, the sexual attitudes of the sample population may not be reflective of the behavior of people in other cultures. In other instances, however, the results represent a much broader spectrum of the human population. In collaboration with 50 other scientists, we surveyed the mating preferences of more than 10,000 men and women in 37 countries over a six-year period spanning 1984 through 1989. Although no survey, short of canvassing the entire human population, can be considered exhaustive, our study crosses a tremendous diversity of geographic, cultural, political, ethnic, religious, racial and economic groups. It is the largest survey ever on mate preferences.

What we found is contrary to much current thinking among social scientists, which holds that the process of choosing a mate is highly culture-bound. Instead, our results are consistent with the notion that human beings, like other animals, exhibit species-typical desires when it comes to the selection of a mate. These patterns can be accounted for by our theory of human sexual strategies.

COMPETITION AND CHOICE

Sexual-strategies theory holds that patterns in mating behavior exist because they are evolutionarily advantageous. We are obviously the descendants of people who were able to mate successfully. Our theory assumes that the sexual strategies of our ancestors evolved because they permitted them to survive and produce offspring. Those people who failed to mate successfully because they did not express these strategies are not our ancestors. One simple example is the urge to mate, which is a universal desire among people in all cultures and which is undeniably evolutionary in origin.

Although the types of behavior we consider are more complicated than simply the urge to mate, a brief overview of the relevant background should be adequate to understand the evolutionary logic of human mating strategies.

As with many issues in evolutionary biology, this background begins with the work of Charles Darwin.

Darwin was the first to show that mate preferences could affect human evolution. In his seminal 1871 treatise, *The Descent of Man and Selection in Relation to Sex*, Darwin puzzled over characteristics that seemed to be perplexing when judged merely on the basis of their relative advantage for the animal's survival. How could the brilliant plumage of a male peacock evolve when it obviously increases the bird's risk of predation? Darwin's answer was sexual selection, the evolution of characteristics that confer a reproductive advantage to an organism (rather than a survival advantage). Darwin further divided sexual selection into two processes: intrasexual competition and preferential mate choice.

Intrasexual competition is the less controversial of the two processes. It involves competition between members of the same sex to gain preferential access to mating partners. Characteristics that lead to success in these same-sex competitions—such as greater strength, size, agility, confidence or cunning—can evolve simply because of the reproductive advantage gained by the victors. Darwin assumed that this is primarily a competitive interaction between males, but recent studies suggest that human females are also very competitive for access to mates.

Preferential mate choice, on the other hand, involves the desire for mating with partners that possess certain characteristics. A consensual desire affects the evolution of characteristics because it gives those possessing the desired characteristics an advantage in obtaining mates over those who do not possess the desired characteristics. Darwin assumed that preferential mate choice operates primarily through females who prefer particular males. (Indeed, he even called this component of sexual selection *female choice*.)

Darwin's theory of mate-choice selection was controversial in part because Darwin simply assumed that females desire males with certain characteristics. Darwin failed to document how such desires might have arisen and how they might be maintained in a population.

The solution to the problem was not forthcoming until 1972, when Robert Trivers, then at Harvard University, proposed that the relative parental investment of the sexes influences the two processes of sexual selection. Specifically, the sex that invests more in offspring is selected to be more discriminating in choosing a mate, whereas the sex that invests less in offspring is more competitive with members of the same sex for sexual access to the high-investing sex. Parental-investment theory accounts, in part, for both the origin and the evolutionary retention of different sexual strategies in males and females.

Consider the necessary *minimum* parental investment by a woman. After internal fertilization, the gestation period lasts about nine months and is usually followed by lactation, which in tribal societies typically can last several years. In contrast, a man's minimum parental investment can be reduced to the contribution of sperm, an effort requiring as little time as a few minutes. This disparity in parental investment means that the replacement of a child who dies (or is deserted) typically costs more (in time and energy) for women than men. Parental-investment theory predicts that women will be more choosy and selective about their mating partners. Where men can provide resources, women should desire those who are able and willing to commit those resources to her and her children.

SEXUAL STRATEGIES

Our evolutionary framework is based on three key ingredients. First, human mating is inherently strategic. These strategies exist because they solved specific problems in human evolutionary history. It is important to recognize that the manifestation of these strategies need not be through conscious psychological mechanisms. Indeed, for the most part we are completely unaware of *why* we find certain qualities attractive in a mate. A second component of our theory is that mating strategies are context-dependent. People behave differently depending on whether the situation presents itself as a short-term or long-term mating prospect. Third, men and women have faced different mating problems over the course of human evolution and, as a consequence, have evolved different strategies.

... [S]exual strategies theory consists of nine hypotheses. We can test these hypotheses by making several predictions about the behavior of men and women faced with a particular mating situation. Even though we make only a few predictions for each hypothesis, it should be clear that many more predictions can be derived to test each hypothesis. We invite the reader to devise his or her own tests of these hypotheses.

Hypothesis 1: Short-Term Mating Is More Important for Men Than Women. This hypothesis follows from the fact that men can reduce their parental investment to the absolute minimum and still produce offspring. Consequently, short-term mating should be a key component of the sexual strategies of men, and much less so for women. We tested three predictions based on this hypothesis in a sample of 148 college students (75 men and 73 women) in the midwestern United States.

First, we predict that men will express a greater interest in seeking a short-term mate than will women. We asked the students to rate the degree to which they were currently seeking a short-term mate (defined as a one-night stand or a brief affair) and the degree to which they were currently seeking a long-term mate (defined as a marriage partner). They rated their interests on a 7-point scale, where a rating of 1 corresponds to a complete lack of interest and a 7 corresponds to a high level of interest.

We found that although the sexes do not differ in their stated proclivities for seeking a long-term mate (an average rating of about 3.4 for both sexes), men reported a significantly greater interest (an average rating of about 5) in seeking a short-term sexual partner than did women (about 3). The results also showed that at any given time men are more interested in seeking a short-term mate rather than a long-term mate, whereas women are more interested in seeking a long-term mate than a short-term mate.

Second we predict that men will desire a greater number of mates than is desired by women. We asked the same group of college students how many sexual partners they would ideally like to have during a given time interval and during their lifetimes. In this instance men consistently reported that they desired a greater number of sex partners than reported by the women for every interval of time. For example, the average man desired about eight sex partners during the next two years, whereas the average woman desired to have one sex partner. In the course of a lifetime, the average man reported the desire to have about 18 sex partners, whereas the average woman desired no more that 4 or 5 sex partners.

A third prediction that follows from this hypothesis is that men will be more willing to engage in sexual intercourse a shorter period of time after first meeting a potential sex partner. We asked the sample of 148 college students the following question: "If the conditions were right, would you consider having sexual intercourse with someone you viewed as desirable if you had known that person for *(a time period ranging from one hour to five years)*?" For each of 10 time intervals the students were asked to provide a response ranging from -3 (definitely not) to 3 (definitely yes).

After a period of 5 years, the men and women were equally likely to consent to sexual relations, each giving a score of about 2 (probably yes). For all shorter time intervals, men were consistently more likely to consider sexual intercourse. For example, after knowing a potential sex partner for only one week, the average man was still positive about the possibility of having sex, whereas women said that they were highly unlikely to have sex with someone after knowing him for only one week.

The issue was addressed in a novel way by Russell Clark and Elaine Hatfield of the University of Hawaii. They designed a study in which college students were approached by an attractive member of the opposite sex who posed one of three questions after a brief introduction: "Would you go out on a date with me tonight?" "Would you go back to my apartment with me tonight?" or "Would you have sex with me tonight?"

Of the women who were approached, 50 percent agreed to the date, 6 percent agreed to go to the apartment and none agreed to have sex. Many women found the sexual request from a virtual stranger to be odd or insulting. Of the men approached, 50 percent agreed to the date, 69 percent agreed to go back to the woman's apartment and 75 percent agreed to have sex. In contrast to women, many men found the sexual request flattering. Those few men who declined were apologetic about it, citing a fiancee or an unavoidable obligation that particular evening. Apparently, men are willing to solve the problem of partner number by agreeing to have sex with virtual strangers.

[Hypotheses 2 through 9, the discussions of which are not reprinted here, are as follows:

David M. Buss

Hypothesis 2: Men seeking a short-term mate will solve the problem of identifying women who are sexually accessible.

Hypothesis 3: Men seeking a short-term mate will minimize commitment and investment.

Hypothesis 4: Men seeking a short-term mate will solve the problem of identifying fertile women.

Hypothesis 5: Men seeking a long-term mate will solve the problem of identifying reproductively valuable women.

Hypothesis 6: Men seeking a long-term mate will solve the problem of paternity confidence.

Hypothesis 7: Women seeking a short-term mate will prefer men willing to impart immediate resources.

Hypothesis 8: Women will be more selective than men in choosing a short-term mate.

Hypothesis 9: Women seeking a long-term mate will prefer men who can provide resources for her offspring.

As with Hypothesis 1, Buss makes and tests several predictions based on these hypotheses.—Ed.]

CONCLUSION

The results of our work and that of others provide strong evidence that the traditional assumptions about mate preferences—that they are arbitrary and culture-bound—are simply wrong. Darwin's initial insights into sexual selection have turned out to be scientifically profound for people, even though he understood neither their functional-adaptive nature nor the importance of relative parental investment for driving the two components of sexual selection.

Men and women have evolved powerful desires for particular characteristics in a mate. These desires are not arbitrary, but are highly patterned and universal. The patterns correspond closely to the specific adaptive problems that men and women have faced during the course of human evolutionary history. These are the problems of paternity certainty, partner number and reproductive capacity for men, and the problems of willingness and ability to invest resources for women.

It turns out that a woman's physical appearance is the most powerful predictor of the occupational status of the man she marries. A woman's appearance is more significant than her intelligence, her level of education or even her original socioeconomic status in determining the mate she will marry. Women who possess the qualities men prefer are most able to translate their preferences into actual mating decisions. Similarly, men possessing what women want—the ability to provide resources—are best able to mate according to their preferences.

Some adaptive problems are faced by men and women equally: identifying mates who show a proclivity to cooperate and mates who show evidence of having good parenting skills. Men do not look at women simply as sex objects, nor do women look at men simply as success objects. One of our most robust observations was that both sexes place tremendous importance on mutual love and kindness when seeking a long-term mate.

The similarities among cultures and between sexes implies a degree of psychological unity or species typicality that transcends geographical, racial, political, ethnic and sexual diversity. Future research could fruitfully examine the ecological and historical sources of diversity, while searching for the adaptive functions of the sexual desires that are shared by all members of our species.

8.3 MICHAEL R. CUNNINGHAM

Measuring the Physical in Physical Attractiveness

Social psychologists have found that physical attractiveness is important in a variety of social situations. It appears likely that facial features have a major impact on attractiveness ratings. Over the past couple of decades, Michael R. Cunningham has refined the measurement of human facial features in an attempt to better understand interpersonal attraction. In recent years, Cunningham and his colleagues have sought cross-cultural support for this hypothesis.

Cunningham (b. 1950) earned his Ph.D. in social psychology from the University of Minnesota in 1977. He taught at the University of Georgia and Elmhurst College before accepting his current position at the University of Louisville in 1986.

This study is from "Measuring the Physical in Physical Attractiveness: Quasi-Experiments on the Sociobiology of Female Facial Beauty," which was published in the *Journal of Personality and Social Psychology* in 1986. In this experiment, Cunningham investigated the female facial features (neonate, mature, and expressive) that males consider attractive. To what degree are attractiveness preferences innate? Do you think that these preferences are different in other cultures? In a second study not included here, Cunningham found that subjects rated attractive females higher than less attractive females in perceived character traits such as brightness, sociability, and assertiveness.

Key Concept: physical attraction

APA Citation: Cunningham, M. R. (1986). Measuring the physical in physical attractiveness: Quasi-experiments on the sociobiology of female facial beauty. *Journal of Personality and Social Psychology, 50,* 925–935.

*T*wo quasi-experiments investigated the relation between specific adult female facial features and the attraction, attribution, and altruistic responses of adult males. Precise measurements were obtained of the relative size of 24 facial features in an international sample of photographs of 50 females. Male subjects provided ratings of the attractiveness of each of the females. Positively correlated with attractiveness ratings

*were the neonate features of large eyes, small nose, and small chin; the maturity fea-
tures of prominent cheekbones and narrow cheeks; and the expressive features of high
eyebrows, large pupils, and large smile. A second study asked males to rate the personal
characteristics of 16 previously measured females. The males were also asked to indicate the females for whom they would be most inclined to perform altruistic behaviors,
and select for dating, sexual behavior, and childrearing. The second study replicated the
correlations of feature measurements with attractiveness. Facial features also predicted
personality attributions, altruistic inclinations, and reproductive interest. Sociobiolog-
ical interpretations are discussed.*

Charles Darwin (1871) noted that "In civilized life, man is largely, but
by no means exclusively, influenced in the choice of his wife by external appearance." Social psychologists have confirmed Darwin's (1871) observations
on the importance of physical attractiveness in social behavior. Physical attractiveness has been found to influence heterosexual dating, peer acceptance,
teacher behavior, altruism, attitude change, employment interviews, jury decisions, marriage happiness, and income (Berscheid & Walster, 1974; Cash, 1981;
Hatfield & Sprecher, 1986). Although female facial attractiveness appears to be
relatively stable both during childhood (Sussman, Mueser, Grau, & Yarnold,
1983) and adulthood (Livson, 1979), the social significance of the features of the
face have not been examined in extensive detail (Liggett, 1974).

There may be several causes for the sporadic research attention directed
towards the human face as a stimulus. The pseudosciences of phrenology and
physiognomy may have made measuring the face seem disreputable to some
scientists. Those who did work on the topic quickly became aware of the complexity of the face as a stimulus (Goldstein, 1983). Some research on the perception of personality from faces produced data on dozens of physiognomic and
evaluative dimensions but lacked a guiding theory to render them fully coherent, whereas other research tended to use only a limited number of globally
defined variables (Hirschberg, Jones, & Haggerty, 1978; Iliffe, 1960; Lucker &
Graber, 1980; Milord, 1978; Secord, 1958; Taylor & Thompson, 1955; Terry, 1977).
Perhaps the major deterrent to the systematic investigation of facial physical
attractiveness was the belief that beauty was in the eyes of the beholder, and
that there were no cross-culturally universal standards for what constituted
an attractive female face. Darwin (1871) was struck by cultural differences in
preference for different skin colors and amounts of body hair, as well as such
practices as teeth filing and lip ornamentation. Ford and Beach (1951) documented the cross-cultural variability in admired body weight, breast size, and
other aspects of the female physique, suggesting little consensus in aesthetic
preferences. Berscheid and Walster (1974) quoted Darwin's statement that "It is
certainly not true that there is in the mind of man any universal standards of
beauty with respect to the human body." Even within the West, there seemed
to be substantial individual personality differences in preferences for various
human body forms or physiques (Beck, Ward-Hull, & McLear, 1976; Lavrakas,
1975; Scodel, 1957; Wiggins, Wiggins, & Conger, 1968). Yet variability in some
aspects of preferred physique or ornamentation does not preclude the possibility of other universally alluring characteristics (Horvath, 1981; Lott, 1979),

so that certain facial configurations could be intrinsically attractive. Darwin (1871) adopted a more agnostic position on the issue of universal standards of facial beauty than he did with respect to the body, noting that "Mr. Winwood Reade... who has had ample opportunities for observation, not only with the Negroes of the west coast of Africa, but those of the interior who have never associated with Europeans is convinced that their ideas of beauty are, *on the whole,* the same as ours." Research with Western subjects disclosed significant consistency in evaluating attractiveness (Hatfield & Sprecher 1986; Iliffe, 1960). The females judged to be most attractive may have such similar facial features that they were hard to distinguish one from another (Light, Hollander, & Kayra-Stuart, 1981). Cross-cultural investigations on the judgment of facial attractiveness tended to highlight societal differences, but rough agreements in facial aesthetic preferences were shown by Asian-American and Caucasian females (Wagatsuma & Kieinke, 1979), Chinese, Indian, and English females judging Greek males (Thakerar & Iwawaki, 1979), South African and American males and females (Morse, Gruzen & Reis, 1976), and blacks and whites judging males and females from both races (Cross & Cross, 1971).

There is evidence for cross-species standards of facial attractiveness. Ethologists such as Lorenz (1943) and Eibl-Eibesfeldt (1970) noted that neonates in a wide range of species share such features as large eyes and forehead, smaller, rounded nose and chin, softer skin and a coloration which differed from that of more mature members of their species. These neonate features seemed to elicit instinctive protective and caretaking responses from adults. Humans also manifested more positive responses to stereotypic and even supernormal infants than to the features of older individuals (Alley, 1983; Sternglanz, Gray, & Murakami, 1977). Further, the closer that a human infant approximated the facial configuration of the ideal infant, the more positive were adult evaluations. Hildebrandt and Fitzgerald (1978) measured the size of various facial features of infants, and found that larger eye height and width, larger forehead height, and larger cheeks were positively correlated with cuteness ratings, whereas larger nose width, ear height, and mouth height were negatively associated with perceived cuteness.

The fact that the same facial features which were associated with infantile features in other species were correlated with perceived cuteness in human babies did not prove that an instinct caused the human response to infant features. If human adults have a preference for neonate features in the young for whatever reason the same preference may be evident in judgments of adults. In fact, Korthase and Trenholme (1982) demonstrated that younger appearing adults were seen as more attractive than older, more mature appearing adults. Younger individuals may have been preferred because neonate features elicited positive caretaking responses. Alternatively, neonate features may have conveyed the appearance of youth, health, and an extended period of fertility (Symons, 1979).

The Korthase and Trenholme (1982) results dovetailed with the investigations of child attractiveness; younger features were more attractive than older ones. Yet there is reason to believe that some mature features may be related to perceived attractiveness. In comparison with an infant, an adult's face has a relatively small forehead and eyes, and a large nose, cheekbones, jaw, and chin (Enlow; 1982). Guthrie (1976) and Keating, Mazur; and Segall, 1981) suggested that maturity features may convey an image of status, power, and dominance. Responsivity to a few mature features such as high cheekbones or cheeks which have lost some of their baby fat may have evolved to discourage pedophilia and insure that advances were made only to postpubescent females.

The architecture of the face which is involved in the expression of positive emotion may also contribute to attractiveness ratings. A smile indicates joy, friendliness (Kraut & Johnston, 1979), and sometimes submissive appeasement. Because individuals who were smiling received more positive attractiveness ratings than nonsmiling targets (Mueser, Grau, Sussman, & Rosen, 1984), individuals who have particularly large smiles may receive even higher attractiveness ratings. Because raised eyebrows often signal interest, greeting, and submission (Eibl-Eibesfeidt, 1970; Nakdimen, 1984), individuals whose eyebrows are set high on their foreheads may convey the image of a positive attitude and receive more positive ratings than their low-browed peers. Finally, dilated pupils have been found to elicit increased attractiveness ratings (Hess, 1965).

The present quasi-experiments were designed to investigate the specific features in adult human female faces which stimulate positive attractiveness ratings by adult males. Three categories of variables were used:

1. Neonate features: Congruent with the research on child cuteness, it was predicted that more attractive women would have larger foreheads, larger eyes, wider set eyes, smaller nose, smaller chin, and larger lips. Eye size was expected to be particularly powerful because it has been found to influence recognition memory for faces (McKelvie, 1976).

2. Mature features: The use of a separate category of mature features may seem arbitrary, because the maturity of a feature may be inversely rated to its apparent neoteny. Yet because mature features may serve a distinct functional role in the perception of attractiveness, a separate category was used. Based on ethological observations (Guthrie, 1976; Keating, Mazur, & Segall, 1981), it was expected that higher, wider cheekbones, and narrower cheeks would be related to greater perceived attractiveness.

3. Expressive features: It was predicted that individuals whose features were particularly effective at signaling positive emotions, with larger smiles, higher eyebrows, and larger pupils, would be seen as more attractive.

To provide wide variation in facial feature configurations, and to provide possible insights into cross-cultural standards of attractiveness, the pool of stimuli included faces from 28 countries. Because age has an effect on attractiveness judgments, the target stimuli were restricted to college age females.

Method

Subjects. Seventy-five undergraduate males, who happened to be Caucasian, volunteered to participate in this study as part of a requirement of an introductory psychology course at a small Midwestern college.

Stimulus materials. Fifty black and white photographs were used as Stimuli. Photographs were presented in a standard 4×5 cm size mounted on 8×12 cm cards. Twenty-three of the pictures portrayed graduating Caucasian seniors from a yearbook of a women's college. These photos were randomly selected except for the stipulations that the women be smiling and not wearing glasses. All faces appeared to be free of facial hair, disfigurement, or asymmetry. Twenty-seven photographs were taken from the yearbook section of a Miss Universe international beauty pageant program. The photographs portrayed individuals in normal clothing and makeup, so that they did not look like beauty pageant contestants. The photographs of the contestants matched those of the college seniors in lighting, pose, clothing, and image size. Because the contestants had been selected for their beauty and talent in their country of origin, their features might provide a clue to cross-cultural standards of attractiveness. The international contestants were randomly selected except for the criterion that the women be smiling and no contest regalia be visible. In this group of portraits, 14 were Caucasian, 7 were Negro, and 6 were Oriental. During debriefing it was determined that none of the subjects suspected that some of the photographs portrayed beauty contestants.

Procedure. Individual subjects were asked by a female experimenter to judge the photographs based on their estimates of the physical attractiveness of each female. Six numbered boxes were used for categories ranging from *extremely attractive* to *extremely unattractive.* No limit was placed on the number of photographs which could be placed in each box. So that the evaluation be based on objective aspects of attractiveness, participants were asked to try not to be influenced by racial or ethnic factors, or whether they would like to go out with the woman.

Concurrent with the collection of attractiveness ratings, precise measurements of the size of various facial features were made using a micrometer accurate to .05 mm. Because hundreds of measurements could be made on the complex topography of the face, measurement choices were based on the theoretical hypotheses noted earlier. The female experimenter, who was blind to the hypotheses, and the author made independent sets of physiognomic measurements, which correlated .863. Differences greater than 1.00 mm were resolved by a second measurement by the author, otherwise the female experimenter's measurements were used.

To control for minor variations in facial image size, the predictor measurements were standardized as ratios to the indicated horizontal or vertical axis. Thus, what is later referred to as height of eyes, for example, represents the ratio of the eye height to the overall length of the face.

Results

The mean physical attractiveness rating for each target female was calculated by averaging across the evaluations provided by the male subjects. Correlations between the size of the various facial features and the physical attractiveness ratings are presented in Table 1.

A number of neonate feature measurements were associated with attractiveness ratings. Higher and wider eyes, greater distance between eyes, a smaller chin, and a smaller overall nose size were correlated with more positive ratings. The width of the nose at tip and the length of the nose were unrelated to attractiveness. Forehead height was also unrelated to attractiveness. The width of the nose at the nostrils was positively associated with attractiveness ratings. This was attributable to the correlation of nose width with smile width ($r[48] = .46, p < .01$). The muscles that stretched the mouth into a broad smile apparently also expanded the width of the nostrils. When the effect of smile width was partialed out, the association between width of nose at nostrils and attractiveness diminished to insignificance ($\beta = .11, t = .77, ns$).

The maturity features of prominent cheekbones and narrower cheeks were positively linked to attractiveness, whereas midface length was unrelated to attractiveness. The expressive features of higher eyebrows, larger smile, and dilated pupils were also positively linked to attractiveness ratings. Dilated pupils were correlated with attractiveness even when the effects of iris size were controlled.

To exclude the possibility that the observed feature-attractiveness relations were due to some unique factors associated with the beauty contestants, the correlations between facial measurements and attractiveness were calculated separately for the college senior photographs. Because of the reduced range and diminished statistical power, fewer correlations were significant, but eye height, eye width, distance between the eyes, cheekbone width, cheek width, and eyebrow height were significantly associated with male attractiveness judgments. The few differences, such as with lower lip thickness and pupil width may be attributed to sample fluctuation.

Several additional analyses were conducted to further examine the relation between feature size and beauty. Correlations of the direct measurements of feature size, uncorrected by the size of the head, were found to bear roughly the same relation to attraction as the corrected measurements. Lip size was found to be uncorrelated with attractiveness when only Caucasian target females were analyzed (upper lip, $r[35] = -.16, ns$: lower lip, $r[35] = .08, ns$). Darkness of hair color ($r = .18, ns$) and darkness of skin color ($r = .005, ns$), were unrelated to attractiveness. Tests for curvilinear relations between feature measurements and attractiveness ratings were considered. Although it was likely that exophthalmic eyes or a minuscule chin would have been unattractive, such extreme features were absent in the collection of target photos.

A multiple regression analysis was conducted using the significant facial feature measurements, except for the redundant standardized pupil width, to predict attractiveness ratings for all targets. The resulting prediction equation was highly significant ($R = .77, F [12, 37] = 4.37, p < .0001$). Separate regressions equation using only the group of neonate ($R = .63$), only mature ($R = .61$),

TABLE 1

*Correlations of Feature Measurement Ratios With Mean
Attractiveness Ratings*

*Michael R.
Cunningham*

Feature	Complete sample (n = 50)	College senic (n = 23)
Neonate features		
Forehead height, eyebrow to hairline	−.09	.08
Upperhead height, pupil to top of head	.16	.01
Eye height	.50*	.42*
Eye width	.41*	.48*
Iris width	.17	.02
Separation of eyes	.29*	.47*
Nose tip width	−.05	−.23
Nostril width	.33*	.32
Nose length	−.02	−.28
Nose area	−.34*	−.31
Upper lip thickness	−.06	−.14
Lower lip thickness	.11	−.19
Chin length	−.38*	−.24
Mature features		
Cheekbone width	.58*	.50*
Cheek width	−.47*	−.55*
Mid-face length	.06	.11
Expressive features		
Eyebrow height	.46*	.37*
Pupil width	.42*	−.24
Standardized pupil width	.30*	.24
Smile height	.23	.14
Smile width	.53*	.19

* $p < .05$.

and only expressive features ($R = .63$) were also highly significant. Because the predictors were not independent, partial correlations were conducted. It was determined that the groups of neonate ($R = .34$), mature ($R = .25$), and expressive ($R = .23$) features each were significantly associated with attractiveness independently of the effects of the other two groups of predictors. The optimal multiple regression analysis used the neonate features of eye height ($\beta = .24$, $t = 2.03$, $p < .05$), and nose area ($\beta = .28$, $t = 2.48$, $p < .02$), the mature feature of narrow cheek width ($\beta = .35$, $t = 2.96$, $p < .005$), and the expressive feature of smile width ($\beta = .28$, $t = 2.44$, $p < .02$); it was found to be as effective ($R =$

.73, $F[4, 45] = 12.46$, $p < .0001$) as the full set and accounted for 52.5% of the variance in mean attractiveness ratings.

The nonwhite beauty pageant contestants received further attention to determine the attractiveness standards used in other cultures to govern representatives to international beauty competition. In comparison with the American college seniors, the Black and Oriental beauty contestants had significantly greater eye height ($F[1, 34] = 18.43$, $p < .0001$), eye width ($F[1, 34] = 18.76$, $p < .0001$) and distances between their eyes ($F[1, 34] = 15.40$, $p < .0001$), wider nostrils ($F[1, 34] = 21.91$, $p < .0001$), marginally longer noses ($F[1, 34] = 2.96$, $p = .09$), larger upper lips ($F[1, 34] = 13.40$, $p < .0001$), larger lower lips ($F[1, 34] = 9.25$, $p < .005$), smaller chins ($F[1, 34] = 10.13$, $p < .003$), somewhat wider cheekbones ($F[1, 34] = 3.76$, $p = .06$), somewhat narrower cheeks ($F[1, 34] = 3.78$, $p = .06$), higher eyebrows ($F[1, 34] = 28.94$, $p < .0001$), and wider smile ($F[1, 34] = 6.67$, $p < .01$). There were no differences between the Black and Oriental pageant contestants, compared with the American college seniors in nose tip width ($F[1, 34] = .69$, *ns*), nose area ($F[1, 34] = .11$, *ns*), height of smile ($F[1, 34] = 1.64$, *ns*), and pupil width ($F[1, 34] = 2.00$, *ns*). Thus, the Black and Oriental beauty contestants possessed ethnically distinct features, but also displayed most of the facial features associated with attractiveness in Caucasians.

Discussion

Quasi-Experiment 1 demonstrated that males were attracted to females possessing the neonate features of large eyes, small nose area, small chin, and widely spaced eyes. The males were also attracted to females with the mature features of wide cheekbones and narrow cheeks, and the expressive features of highly set eyebrows, wide pupils, and a large smile. Beautiful features seemed to be those which deviate in specific ways from what is typical in the population (cf. Galton, 1907; Light et al., 1981). Such features are the focus of cosmetic, orthodontic (Korabik, 1981), and rhinoplastic alteration (Cash & Horton, 1983), further attesting to their importance.

Forehead size was uncorrelated with attractiveness ratings. This may have been due to measurement error caused by hairstyle covering the forehead. Both forehead and nose shape may prove more influential with profile portraits. Lip size was also unrelated to attractiveness, perhaps because lip size differences were minimized by the smiling pose. Nostril width was positively associated with attractiveness, but this was found to be attributable to the effect of smiling. Hair and skin color were unrelated to attractiveness ratings, but the use of black and white photographs may have minimized differences due to pigmentation.

Black and Oriental beauty pageant contestants were found to possess most of the patterns of neonate, mature, and expressive features associated with attractiveness in Caucasians. Although contestants were chosen by their native countries, the Miss Universe contest panel of judges were multinational, and the pageant was held in Japan, perhaps those facial features found to be attractive in this investigation were universally attractive. Alternatively, because the Miss Universe pageant derived substantial revenues from sales of television time, chiefly in Western nations, it was possible that the Black and Oriental contestants were chosen as their nation's representatives only because they approximated Western standards of beauty rather than those of their native lands.

The present data cannot exclude the possibility that the use of Western standards governed the choice of beauty pageant contestants in non-Western nations. Perhaps there is a culture in which small eyes, a large nose, narrow cheekbones, wide cheeks, a long chin, low eyebrows, and a small smile represents the epitome of beauty. Ultimately, the issue of cross-cultural universality can be settled only by obtaining the attractiveness ratings of non-Western individuals judging photographs which vary along the dimensions discussed here. Studies using very young subjects may also provide insight into noncultural factors in attractiveness judgments (Brooks & Lewis, 1976).

REFERENCES

Alley, T. R. (1983). Infantile head shape as an elicitor of adult protection. *Merrill-Palmer Quarterly, 29*, 411–427.

Beck, S. P., Ward-Hull, C. I., & McLear, P. M. (1976). Variables related to women's somatic preferences of the male and female body. *Journal of Personality and Social Psychology, 34*, 1200–1210.

Berschied, E., & Walster, E. (1974). Physical attractiveness. In L. Berkowitz (Ed.), *Advances in experimental social psychology*. New York: Academic Press.

Brooks, J., & Lewis, M. (1976). Infants' response to strangers: Midget, adult, and child. *Child Development, 47*, 323–332.

Cash, T. F. (1981). Physical attractiveness: An annotated bibliography of theory and research in the behavioral sciences. *JSAS Catalog of Selected Documents in Psychology, 11*, 1–284. (Ms. No. 2370)

Cash, T. F., & Horton, C. E. (1983). Aesthetic surgery: Effects of rhinoplasty on the social perception of patients by others. *Plastic and Reconstructive Surgery, 72*, 543–548.

Cross, J. F., & Cross, J. (1971). Age, sex, race, and the perception of facial beauty. *Developmental Psychology, 5*, 433–439.

Darwin, C. (1871). *The descent of man, and selection in relation to sex.* London: John Murray.

Eibl-Eibesfeldt, I. (1970). *Ethology, the biology of behavior.* New York: Holt, Rinehart, & Winston.

Enlow, D. M. (1982). *Handbook of facial growth* (2nd ed.). Philadelphia: Saunders.

Ford, C. S., & Beach, F. A. (1951). *Patterns of Sexual Behavior.* New York: Harper & Row.

Galton, F. (1907). *Inquiries into human faculties and its development* (2nd ed.). New York: Elsevier North Holland.

Goldstein, A. G. (1983). Behavioral scientists' fascination with faces. *Journal of Nonverbal Behavior, 7*, 223–254.

Guthrie, R. D. (1976). *Body hotspots.* New York: Van Nostrand Reinhold.

Hatfield, E., & Sprecher, S. (1986). *Mirror, mirror . . . The importance of looks in everyday life.* New York: SUNY Press.

Hess, L. H. (1965). Attitude and pupil size. *Scientific American, 212*, 46–54.

Hildebrandt, K. A., & Fitzgerald, H. E. (1978). Adults' responses to infants varying in perceived cuteness. *Behavioral Processes, 3*, 159–172.

Hirschberg, N., Jones, L. E., & Haggerty, M. (1978). What's in a face: Individual differences in face perception. *Journal of Research in Personality, 12,* 488–499.

Horvath, T. (1981). Physical attractiveness: The influence of selected torso parameters. *Archives of Sexual Behavior, 10,* 21–24.

Iliffe, A. H. (1960). A study of preferences in feminine beauty. *British Journal of Psychology, 51,* 267–273.

Keating, C. F., Mazur, A., & Segall, M. H. (1981). A cross-cultural exploration of physiognomic traits of dominance and happiness. *Ethology and Sociobiology, 2,* 41–48.

Korabik, K. (1981). Changes in physical attractiveness and interpersonal attraction. *Basic and Applied Social Psychology, 2,* 59–65.

Korthase, K. M., & Trenholme, I. (1982). Perceived age and perceived physical attractiveness. *Perceptual & Motor Skills, 54,* 1251–1258.

Kraut, R. E., & Johnston, R. E. (1979). Social and emotional messages of smiling: An ethological approach. *Journal of Personality and Social Psychology, 37,* 1539–1553.

Lavrakas, P. J. (1975). Female preferences for male physiques. *Journal of Research on Personality, 9,* 324–334.

Liggett, J. (1974). *The human face.* New York: Stein & Day.

Light, L. L., Hollander, S., & Kayra-Stuart, F. (1981). Why attractive people are harder to remember. *Personality and Social Psychology Bulletin, 7,* 269–276.

Livson, N. (1979). The physically attractive woman at age 40: Precursors in adolescent personality and adult correlates from a longitudinal study. In M. Cook & G. Wilson (Eds.), *Love and attraction.* New York: Pergamon Press.

Lorenz, K. (1943). Die angeborenen formen moglicher arfahrung. *Zietschrift Für Tierpsychologie, 5,* 233–409.

Lott, D. F. (1979). A possible role for generally adaptive features in mate selection and sexual stimulation. *Psychological Reports, 45,* 539–546.

Lucker, G. W., & Graber, L. W. (1980). Physiognomic features and facial appearance judgments in children. *Journal of Psychology, 104,* 261–168.

McKelvie, S. J. (1976). The role of the eyes and mouth in the memory of a face. *American Journal of Psychology, 2,* 311–323.

Milford, J. T. (1978). Aesthetic aspects of faces: A (somewhat) phenomenological analysis using multidimensional scaling methods. *Journal of Personality and Social Psychology, 36,* 205–216.

Morse, S. T., Gruzen, J., & Reis, H. (1976). The "eye of the beholder": A neglected variable in the study of physical attractiveness. *Journal of Personality, 44,* 209–225.

Mueser, K. T., Grau, B. W., Sussman, M. S., & Rosen, A. J. (1984). You are only as pretty as you feel: Facial expression as a determinant of physical attractiveness. *Journal of Personality and Social Psychology, 46,* 469–478.

Nakdimen, K. A. (1984). The physiognomic basis of sexual stereotyping. *American Journal of Psychiatry, 14,* 499–503.

Scodel, A. (1957). Heterosexual somatic preference and fantasy dependency. *Journal of Consulting Psychology, 21,* 371–374.

Secord, P. F. (1958). Facial features and inference processes in interpersonal perception. In R. Tagiuri & L. Petrullo (Eds), *Person perception and interpersonal behavior.* Stanford, CA: Stanford University Press.

Sternglanz, S. H., Gray, J. L., & Murakami, M. (1977). Adult preferences for infantile facial features: An ethological approach. *Animal Behavior, 25,* 108–115.

Sussman, S., Mueser, K. T., Grau, B. W., & Yarnold, P. R. (1983). Stability of females' facial attractiveness during childhood. *Journal of Personality and Social Psychology, 44,* 1231–1233.

Symons, D. (1979). *The evolution of human sexuality.* New York: Oxford Univ. Press.

Taylor, C., & Thompson, G. G. (1955). Age trends in preferences for certain facial proportions. *Child Development, 26,* 97–102.

Terry, R. (1977). Further evidence on components of facial attractiveness. *Perceptual & Motor Skills, 45,* 130.

Thakerar, J. M., & Iwawaki, S. (1979). Cross-cultural comparisons in interpersonal attraction of females toward males. *Journal of Social Psychology, 108,* 121–122.

Wagatsuma, E., & Kleinke, C. L. (1979). Ratings of facial beauty by Asian-American and Caucasian females. *Journal of Social Psychology, 109,* 299–300.

Wiggins, J. S., Wiggins, N., & Conger, J. C. (1968). Correlates of heterosexual somatic preference. *Journal of Personality and Social Psychology, 10,* 82–90.

Some Evidence for Heightened Sexual Attraction Under Conditions of High Anxiety

How do we fall in love? Researchers have suggested that people need to learn the cultural definition of love, choose an appropriate person, and experience physiological arousal. Others have suggested that people label their arousal according to their environment. In a classic experiment, Donald G. Dutton and Arthur P. Aron tested the notion that arousal might be interpreted as sexual attraction.

Dutton (b. 1943) received his Ph.D. in social psychology from the University of Toronto in 1970 and then accepted a position at the University of British Columbia in Vancouver, where he is currently a professor of psychology. Aron (b. 1945) earned his Ph.D. in social psychology from the University of Toronto in 1970. He taught at the University of British Columbia, Maharishi University, and the University of California at Santa Cruz before accepting his current position at the State University of New York at Stony Brook.

This selection is from "Some Evidence for Heightened Sexual Attraction Under Conditions of High Anxiety," which was published in *Journal of Personality and Social Psychology* in 1974. In it, Dutton and Aron report on research in which they found that after male residents of Vancouver were interviewed by an attractive young woman on a precariously swaying suspension bridge, the men showed more sexual imagery in stories they subsequently wrote and were more interested in calling the woman on the phone than were men who were interviewed on a solid bridge. In additional research not included here, Dutton and Aron found that male college students who were anticipating being shocked in an experiment showed increased sexual imagery scores compared to those who were anticipating someone else being shocked. As you read this selection, think about the influence of anxiety on sexual attractiveness in everyday situations. How else might anxiety be interpreted in these situations?

*Donald G.
Dutton and
Arthur P. Aron*

Key Concept: anxiety and sexual attraction

APA Citation: Dutton, D. G., & Aron, A. P. (1974). Some evidence for heightened sexual attraction under conditions of high anxiety. *Journal of Personality and Social Psychology, 30,* 510–517.

M*ale passersby were contacted either on a fear-arousing suspension bridge or a non-fear-arousing bridge by an attractive female interviewer who asked them to fill out questionnaires containing Thematic Apperception Test [TAT] pictures. Sexual content of stories written by subjects on the fear-arousing bridge and tendency of these subjects to attempt postexperimental contact with the interviewer were both significantly greater. No significant differences between bridges were obtained on either measure for subjects contacted by a male interviewer....*

There is a substantial body of indirect evidence suggesting that sexual attractions occur with increased frequency during states of strong emotion. For example, heterosexual love has been observed to be associated both with hate (James, 1910; Suttie, 1935) and with pain (Ellis, 1936). A connection between "aggression" and sexual attraction is supported by Tinbergen's (1954) observations of intermixed courting and aggression behaviors in various animal species....

Aron (1970)... argued that an aggression–sexuality link exists, but it is only a special case of a more general relationship between emotional arousal of all kinds and sexual attraction. To demonstrate this point, he designed a study in which instead of anger, residual emotion from intense role playing was the independent variable. In this experiment, each of 40 male subjects role played with the same attractive female confederate in either a highly emotional or a minimally emotional situation. Subjects enacting highly emotional roles included significantly more sexual imagery in stories written in response to TAT-like stimuli ($p < .01$) and indicated significantly more desire to kiss the confederate ($p < .05$) than did subjects in the control condition. One possible explanation is suggested by Schachter's theory of emotion (Schachter, 1964; Schachter & Singer, 1962). He argued that environmental cues are used, in certain circumstances, to provide emotional labels for unexplained or ambiguous states of arousal. However, it is notable that much of the above-cited research indicates that a sexual attraction–strong emotion link may occur even when the emotions are unambiguous. Accordingly, taking into account both the Schachter position and findings from sexual attraction research in general, Aron (1970) hypothesized that strong emotions are relabeled as sexual attraction whenever an acceptable object is present, and emotion-producing circumstances do not require the full attention of the individual.

The present series of experiments is designed to test the notion that an attractive female is seen as more attractive by males who encounter her while they experience a strong emotion (fear) than by males not experiencing a strong emotion. Experiment 1 is an attempt to verify this proposed emotion–sexual attraction link in a natural setting....

EXPERIMENT 1

Method

Subjects. Subjects were males visiting either of two bridge sites who fit the following criteria: (*a*) between 18 and 35 years old and (*b*) unaccompanied by a female companion. Only one member of any group of potential subjects was contacted. A total of 85 subjects were contacted by either a male or a female interviewer.

Site. The experiment was conducted on two bridges over the Capilano River in North Vancouver, British Columbia, Canada. The "experimental" bridge was the Capilano Canyon Suspension Bridge, a five-foot-wide, 450-foot-long, bridge constructed of wooden boards attached to wire cables that ran from one side to the other of the Capilano Canyon. The bridge has many arousal-inducing features such as (*a*) a tendency to tilt, sway, and wobble, creating the impression that one is about to fall over the side; (*b*) very low handrails of wire cable which contribute to this impression; and (*c*) a 230-foot drop to rocks and shallow rapids below the bridge. The "control" bridge was a solid wood bridge further upriver. Constructed of heavy cedar, this bridge was wider and firmer than the experimental bridge, was only 10 feet above a small, shallow rivulet which ran into the main river, had high handrails, and did not tilt or sway.

Procedure. As subjects crossed either the control or experimental bridge, they were approached by the interviewer.

FEMALE INTERVIEWER   The interviewer explained that she was doing a project for her psychology class on the effects of exposure to scenic attractions on creative expression. She then asked potential subjects if they would fill out a short questionnaire. The questionnaire contained six filler items such as age, education, prior visits to bridge, etc., on the first page. On the second page, subjects were instructed to write a brief, dramatic story based upon a picture of a young woman covering her face with one hand and reaching with the other. The instructions and the picture... employed were adapted from Murray's (1943) *Thematic Apperception Test Manual....* If the subject agreed, the questionnaire was filled out on the bridge.

Stories were later scored for manifest sexual content according to a slightly modified version of the procedure employed by Barclay and Haber (1965). Scores ranged from 1 (no sexual content) to 5 (high sexual content) according to the most sexual reference in the story. Thus, for example, a story with any mention of sexual intercourse received 5 points; but if the most sexual reference was "girl friend," it received a score of 2; "kiss" counted 3; and "lover," 4.

On completion of the questionnaire, the interviewer thanked the subject and offered to explain the experiment in more detail when she had more time. At this point, the interviewer tore the corner off a sheet of paper, wrote down her name and phone number, and invited each subject to call, if he wanted to talk further. Experimental subjects were told that the interviewer's name was Gloria and control subjects, Donna, so that they could easily be classified when they called. On the assumption that curiosity about the experiment should be equal between control and experimental groups, it was felt that differential calling rates might reflect differential attraction to the interviewer.

MALE INTERVIEWER   The procedure with the male interviewer was identical to that above. Subjects were again supplied with two fictitious names so that if they phoned the interviewer, they could be classified into control or experimental groups.

Results

Check on Arousal Manipulation.   Probably the most compelling evidence for arousal on the experimental bridge is to observe people crossing the bridge. Forty percent of subjects observed crossing the bridge walked very slowly and carefully, clasping onto the handrail before taking each step. A questionnaire was administered to 30 males who fit the same criteria as the experimental subjects. Fifteen males on the experimental bridge were asked, "How fearful do you think the average person would be when he crossed this bridge?" The mean rating was 79 on a 100-point scale where 100 was equal to extremely fearful. Fifteen males on the control bridge gave a mean rating of 18 on the same scale ($t = 9.7$, $df = 28$, $p < .001$, two-tailed). In response to the question "How fearful were you while crossing the bridge?" experimental-bridge males gave a rating of 65 and control-bridge males a rating of 3 ($t = 10.6$, $p < .001$, $df = 28$, two-tailed). Hence, it can be concluded that most people are quite anxious on the experimental bridge but not on the control bridge. To prevent suspicion, no checks on the arousal of experimental subjects could be made.

Thematic Apperception Test Responses.

FEMALE INTERVIEWER   On the experimental bridge, 23 of 33 males who were approached by the female interviewer agreed to fill in the questionnaire. On the control bridge, 22 of 33 agreed. Of the 45 questionnaires completed, 7 were unusable either because they were incomplete or written in a foreign language. The remaining 38 questionnaires (20 experimental and 18 control) had their TAT stories scored for sexual imagery by two scorers who were experienced with TAT scoring. (Although both were familiar with the experimental hypothesis, questionnaires had been coded so that they were blind as to whether any given questionnaire was written by a control or experimental subject.) The interrater reliability was +.87.

Subjects in the experimental group obtained a mean sexual imagery score of 2.47 and those in the control group, a score of 1.41 ($t = 3.19$, $p < .01$; $df = 36$, two-tailed). Thus, the experimental hypothesis was verified by the imagery data.

MALE INTERVIEWER Twenty-three out of 51 subjects who were approached on the experimental bridge agreed to fill in the questionnaire. On the control bridge 22 out of 42 agreed. Five of these questionnaires were unusable, leaving 20 usable in both experimental and control groups. These were rated as above. Subjects in the experimental group obtained a mean sexual imagery score of .80 and those in the control group, .61 ($t = .36$. *ns*). Hence the pattern of result obtained by the female interviewer was not reproduced by the male interviewer.

Behavioral Data.

FEMALE INTERVIEWER In the experimental group, 18 of the 23 subjects who agreed to the interview accepted the interviewer's phone number. In the control group, 16 out of 22 accepted. A second measure of sexual attraction was the number of subjects who called the interviewer. In the experimental group 9 out of 18 called, in the control group 2 out of 16 called ($x^2 = 5.7$, $p < .02$). Taken in conjunction with the sexual imagery data, this finding suggests that subjects in the experimental group were more attracted to the interviewer.

MALE INTERVIEWER In the experimental group, 7 out of 23 accepted the interviewer's phone number. In the control group, 6 out of 22 accepted. In the experimental group, 2 subjects called; in the control group, 1 subject called. Again, the pattern of results obtained by the female interviewer was not replicated by the male.

Although the results of this experiment provide prima facie support for an emotion–sexual attraction link, the experiment suffers from interpretative problems that often plague field experiments. The main problem with the study is the possibility of different subject populations on the two bridges. First, the well-advertised suspension bridge is a tourist attraction that may have attracted more out-of-town persons than did the nearby provincial park where the control bridge was located. This difference in subject populations may have affected the results in two ways. The experimental subjects may have been less able to phone the experimenter (if they were in town on a short-term tour) and less likely to hold out the possibility of further liaison with her. If this were the case, the resulting difference due to subject differences would have operated *against* the main hypothesis. Also, this difference in subject populations could not affect the sexual imagery scores unless one assumed the experimental bridge subjects to be more sexually deprived than controls. The results using the male interviewer yielded no significant differences in sexual imagery between experimental and control subjects; however, the possibility still exists that sexual deprivation could have interacted with the presence of the attrac-

*Donald G.
Dutton and
Arthur P. Aron*

tive female experimenter to produce the sexual imagery results obtained in this experiment. . . .

The theoretical implications of these results are twofold. In the first place, they provide additional support in favor of the theoretical positions from which the original hypothesis was derived: the Schachter and Singer (1962) tradition of cognitive labeling of emotions and the Aron (1970) conceptual framework for sexual attraction processes. In the second place, these data seem to be inconsistent with (or at least unpredictable by) standard theories of interpersonal attraction. Both the reinforcement (Byrne, 1969) and the cognitive consistency (Festinger, 1957; Heider, 1958) points of view would seem to predict that a negative emotional state associated with the object would *decrease* her attractiveness; and neither theory would seem to be easily capable of explaining the arousal of a greater sexual emotion in the experimental condition of the present experiments.

REFERENCES

Aron, A. Relationship variables in human heterosexual attraction. Unpublished doctoral dissertation, University of Toronto, 1970.

Barclay, A. M., & Haber, R. N. The relation of aggressive to sexual motivation. *Journal of Personality,* 1965, **33,** 462–475.

Byrne, D. Attitudes and attraction. In L. Berkowitz (Ed.), *Advances in experimental social psychology.* Vol 4. New York: Academic Press, 1969.

Ellis, H. *Studies in the Psychology of Sex.* New York: Random House, 1936.

Festinger, L. *A theory of cognitive dissonance.* Evanston, Ill.: Row, Peterson, 1957.

Heider, F. *The psychology of interpersonal relations.* New York: Wiley, 1958.

James, W. *The principles of psychology.* Vol. 2. New York: Holt, 1910.

Murray, H. A. *Thematic Apperception Test manual.* Cambridge, Mass.: Harvard University Press, 1943.

Schachter, S. The interaction of cognitive and physiological determinants of emotional state. In L. Berkowitz (Ed.), *Advances in experimental social psychology.* Vol. 1. New York: Academic Press, 1964.

Schachter, S., & Singer, J. E. Cognitive, social and physiological components of the emotional state. *Psychological Review,* 1962, **69,** 379–399.

Suttie, I. D. *The origins of love and hate.* London: Kegan Paul, 1935.

Tinbergen, N. The origin and evolution of courtship and threat display. In J. S. Huxley, A. C. Hardy, & E. B. Ford (Eds.), *Evolution as a process.* London: Allen & Unwin, 1954.

CHAPTER 9 Love

9.1   ROBERT J. STERNBERG

The Ingredients of Love

Although love is an extremely important human emotion, only recently have social psychologists attempted to study it scientifically. Researchers recognize that there are different kinds of love, making it difficult to generalize the results of studies on the subject. In an attempt to distinguish among the various kinds of love, psychologist Robert J. Sternberg has proposed a triangular theory in which love consists of intimacy, passion, and decision/commitment.

Sternberg (b. 1949) earned his Ph.D. in experimental psychology from Stanford University in 1975 and then accepted his current position as IBM Professor of Psychology at Yale University. Although well known for his research in the emotional aspects of love, Sternberg's major area of study has been in intelligence and thinking. The American Psychological Association awarded him the Distinguished Scientific Award for Early Career Contribution to Psychology in 1981.

This selection is from chapter 2, "The Ingredients of Love," of Sternberg's book *The Triangle of Love: Intimacy, Passion, Commitment* (Basic Books, 1988). In it, Sternberg describes, in an informal, practical style, how the three ingredients of intimacy, passion, and commitment combine to form eight possible kinds of love. As you read this selection, evaluate Sternberg's theory of love. Can you identify any other ingredients that should be included in this theory?

Key Concept: triangular theory of love

APA Citation: Sternberg, R. J. (1988). *The triangle of love: Intimacy, passion, commitment.* New York: Basic Books. [Chapter 2, The ingredients of love]

Robert J.
Sternberg

A substantial body of evidence suggests that the components of intimacy, passion, and commitment play a key role in love over and above other attributes. Even before I collected the first bit of data to test my theory, I had several reasons for choosing these three components as the building blocks for it.

First, many of the other aspects of love prove, on close examination, to be either parts or manifestations of these three components. Communication, for example, is a building block of intimacy, as is caring or compassion. Were one to subdivide intimacy and passion and commitment into their own subparts, the theory would eventually contain so many elements as to become unwieldy. There is no one, solely correct fineness of division. But a division into three components works well in several ways. . . .

Second, my review of the literature on couples in the United States, as well as in other lands, suggested that, whereas some elements of love are fairly time-bound or culture-specific, the three I propose are general across time and place. The three components are not equally weighted in all cultures, but each component receives at least some weight in virtually any time or place.

Third, the three components do appear to be distinct, although, of course, they are related. You can have any one without either or both of the others. In contrast, other potential building blocks for a theory of love—for example, nurturance and caring—tend to be difficult to separate, logically as well as psychologically.

Fourth, . . . many other accounts of love seem to boil down to something similar to my own account, or a subset of it. If we take away differences in language and tone, the spirit of many other theories converges with mine.

Finally, and perhaps most important, the theory works. . . .

INTIMACY

In the context of the triangular theory, intimacy refers to those feelings in a relationship that promote closeness, bondedness, and connectedness. My research with Susan Grajek . . . indicates that intimacy includes at least ten elements:

1. *Desiring to promote the welfare of the loved one.* The lover looks out for the partner and seeks to promote his or her welfare. One may promote the other's welfare at the expense of one's own—but in the expectation that the other will reciprocate when the time comes.
2. *Experiencing happiness with the loved one.* The lover enjoys being with his or her partner. When they do things together, they have a good time and build a store of memories upon which they can draw in hard times. Furthermore, good times shared will spill over into the relationship and make it better.
3. *Holding the loved one in high regard.* The lover thinks highly of and respects his or her partner. Although the lover may recognize flaws in the partner, this recognition does not detract from the overall esteem in which the partner is held.

4. *Being able to count on the loved one in times of need.* The lover feels that the partner is there when needed. When the chips are down, the lover can call on the partner and expect that he or she will come through.

5. *Having mutual understanding with the loved one.* The lovers understand each other. They know each other's strengths and weaknesses and how to respond to each other in a way that shows genuine empathy for the loved one's emotional states. Each knows where the other is "coming from."

6. *Sharing oneself and one's possessions with the loved one.* One is willing to give of oneself and one's time, as well as one's things, to the loved one. Although all things need not be joint property, the lovers share their property as the need arises. And, most important, they share themselves.

7. *Receiving emotional support from the loved one.* The lover feels bolstered and even renewed by the loved one, especially in times of need.

8. *Giving emotional support to the loved one.* The lover supports the loved one by empathizing with, and emotionally supporting, him or her in times of need.

9. *Communicating intimately with the loved one.* The lover can communicate deeply and honestly with the loved one, sharing innermost feelings.

10. *Valuing the loved one.* The lover feels the great importance of the partner in the scheme of life.

These are only some of the possible feelings one can experience through the intimacy of love; moreover, it is not necessary to experience all of these feelings in order to experience intimacy. To the contrary, our research indicates that you experience intimacy when you sample a sufficient number of these feelings, with that number probably differing from one person and one situation to another. You do not usually experience the feelings independently, but often as one overall feeling. . . .

Intimacy probably starts in self-disclosure. To be intimate with someone, you need to break down the walls that separate one person from another. It is well known that self-disclosure begets self-disclosure: if you want to get to know what someone else is like, let him or her learn about you. But self-disclosure is often easier in same-sex friendships than in loving relationships, probably because people see themselves as having more to lose by self-disclosure in a loving relationship. And odd as it may sound, there is actually evidence that spouses may be less symmetrical in self-disclosure than are strangers, again probably because the costs of self-disclosure can be so high in love. . . .

Intimacy, then, is a foundation of love, but a foundation that develops slowly, through fits and starts, and is difficult to achieve. Moreover, once it starts to be attained, it may, paradoxically, start to go away because of the threat it poses. It poses a threat in terms not only of the dangers of self-disclosure but of the danger one starts to feel to one's existence as a separate, autonomous being. Few people want to be "consumed" by a relationship, yet many people start to feel as if they are being consumed when they get too close to another human being. The result is a balancing act between intimacy and autonomy which goes on throughout the lives of most couples, a balancing act in which a completely stable equilibrium is often never achieved. But this in itself is not necessarily bad: the swinging back and forth of the intimacy pendulum provides some of the excitement that keeps many relationships alive.

PASSION

The passion component of love includes what Elaine Hatfield and William Walster refer to as a "state of intense longing *for union* with the other." Passion is largely the expression of desires and needs—such as for self-esteem, nurturance, affiliation, dominance, submission, and sexual fulfillment. The strengths of these various needs vary across persons, situations, and kinds of loving relationship. For example, sexual fulfillment is likely to be a strong need in romantic relationships but not in filial ones. These needs manifest themselves through psychological and physiological arousal, which are often inseparable from each other.

Passion in love tends to interact strongly with intimacy, and often they fuel each other. For example, intimacy in a relationship may be largely a function of the extent to which the relationship meets a person's need for passion. Conversely, passion may be aroused by intimacy. In some close relationships with members of the opposite sex, for example, the passion component develops almost immediately; and intimacy, only after a while. Passion may have drawn the individuals into the relationship in the first place, but intimacy helps sustain the closeness in the relationship. In other close relationships, however, passion, especially as it applies to physical attraction, develops only after intimacy. Two close friends of the opposite sex may find themselves eventually developing a physical attraction for each other once they have achieved a certain emotional intimacy. . . .

Most people, when they think of passion, view it as sexual. But any form of psychophysiological arousal can generate the experience of passion. For example, an individual with a high need for affiliation may experience passion toward an individual who provides him or her with a unique opportunity to affiliate. For example, Debbie grew up in a broken home, with no extended family to speak of, and two parents who were constantly at war with each other and eventually divorced when she was an adolescent. Debbie felt as though she never had a family, and when she met Arthur, her passion was kindled. What he had to offer was not great sex but a large, warm, closely knit family that welcomed Debbie with open arms. Arthur was Debbie's ticket to the sense of belongingness she had never experienced but had always craved, and his ability to bring belongingness into her life aroused her passion for him. . . .

For other people, the need for submission can be the ticket to passion. . . . Social workers are often frustrated when, after months spent getting a battered woman to leave her husband, the woman ultimately goes back to the batterer. To some observers, her return may seem incomprehensible; to others, it may seem like a financial decision. But often it is neither. Such a woman has had the misfortune to identify abuse with being loved and, in going back to the abuse, is returning to what is, for her, love as she has learned it.

These patterns of response have been established through years of observation and sometimes first-hand experience, which cannot be easily undone by a social worker or anyone else in a few months. Probably the strangest learning mechanism for the buildup of passionate response is the mechanism of *intermittent reinforcement*, the periodic, sometimes random rewarding of a particular response to a stimulus. If you try to accomplish something, and sometimes are rewarded for your efforts and sometimes not, you are being intermittently reinforced. Oddly enough, intermittent reinforcement is even more powerful at developing or sustaining a given pattern of behavior than is continuous reinforcement. You are more likely to lose interest in or desire for something, and to become bored, if you are always rewarded when you seek it than if you are sometimes rewarded, but sometimes not. Put another way, sometimes the fun is in wanting something rather than in getting it. And if you are never rewarded for a given pattern of behavior, you are likely to give up on it ("extinguish," as learning theorists would say), if only because of the total frustration you experience when you act in that particular way.

Passion thrives on the intermittent reinforcement that is intense at least in the early stages of a relationship. When you want someone, sometimes you feel as if you are getting closer to him or her, and sometimes you feel you are not—an alternation that keeps the passion aroused....

DECISION AND COMMITMENT

The decision/commitment component of love consists of two aspects—one short-term and one long-term. The short-term aspect is the decision to love a certain other, whereas the long-term one is the commitment to maintain that love. These two aspects of the decision/commitment component of love do not necessarily occur together. The decision to love does not necessarily imply a commitment to that love. Oddly enough, the reverse is also possible, where there is a commitment to a relationship in which you did not make the decision, as in arranged marriages. Some people are committed to loving another without ever having admitted their love. Most often, however, a decision precedes the commitment both temporally and logically. Indeed, the institution of marriage represents a legalization of the commitment to a decision to love another throughout life.

While the decision/commitment component of love may lack the "heat" or "charge" of intimacy and passion, loving relationships almost inevitably have their ups and downs, and in the latter, the decision/commitment component is what keeps a relationship together. This component can be essential for getting through hard times and for returning to better ones. In ignoring it or separating it from love, you may be missing exactly that component of a loving relationship that enables you to get through the hard times as well as the easy ones. Sometimes, you may have to trust your commitment to carry you through to the better times you hope are ahead.

The decision/commitment component of love interacts with both intimacy and passion. For most people, it results from the combination of intimate involvement and passionate arousal; however, intimate involvement or passionate arousal can follow from commitment, as in certain arranged marriages or in close relationships in which you do not have a choice of partners. For example, you do not get to choose your mother, father, siblings, aunts, uncles, or cousins. In these close relationships, you may find that whatever intimacy or passion you experience results from your cognitive commitment to the relationship, rather than the other way around. Thus, love can start off as a decision.

The expert in the study of commitment is the UCLA psychologist Harold Kelley.... For Kelley, commitment is the extent to which a person is likely to stick with something or someone and see it (or him or her) through to the finish. A person who is committed to something is expected to persist until the goal underlying the commitment is achieved. A problem for contemporary relationships is that two members of a couple may have different ideas about what it means to stick with someone to the end or to the realization of a goal. These differences, moreover, may never be articulated. One person, for example, may see the "end" as that point where the relationship is no longer working, whereas the other may see the end as the ending of one of the couple's lives. In a time of changing values and notions of commitment, it is becoming increasingly common for couples to find themselves in disagreement about the exact nature and duration of their commitment to each other. When marital commitments were always and automatically assumed to be for life, divorce was clearly frowned upon. Today, divorce is clearly more acceptable than it was even fifteen years ago, in part because many people have different ideas about how durable and lasting the marital commitment need be.

Difficulties in mismatches between notions of commitment cannot always be worked out by discussing mutual definitions of it, because these may change over time and differently for the two members of a couple. Both may intend a life-long commitment at the time of marriage, for example; but one of them may have a change of mind—or heart—over time....

KINDS OF LOVING

How do people love, and what are some examples of ways in which they love? A summary of the various kinds of love captured by the triangular theory is shown in table 1.

Intimacy Alone: Liking

... Liking results when you experience only the intimacy component of love without passion or decision/commitment. The term *liking* is used here in a nontrivial sense, to describe not merely the feelings you have toward casual acquaintances and passers-by, but rather the set of feelings you experience in relationships that can truly be characterized as friendships. You feel closeness,

TABLE 1

Taxonomy of Kinds of Love

Kind of Love	Intimacy	Passion	Decision/ Commitment
Non-love	–	–	–
Liking	+	–	–
Infatuated love	–	+	–
Empty love	–	–	+
Romantic love	+	+	–
Companionate love	+	–	+
Fatuous love	–	+	+
Consummate love	+	+	+

Note: + = component present; – = component absent.

bondedness, and warmth toward the other, without feelings of intense passion or long-term commitment. Stated another way, you feel emotionally close to the friend, but the friend does not arouse your passion or make you feel that you want to spend the rest of your life with him or her.

It is possible for friendships to have elements of passionate arousal or long-term commitment, but such friendships go beyond mere liking. You can use the absence test to distinguish mere liking from love that goes beyond liking. If a typical friend whom you like goes away, even for an extended period of time, you may miss him or her but do not tend to dwell on the loss. You can pick up the friendship some years later, often in a different form, without even having thought much about the friendship during the intervening years. When a close relationship goes beyond liking, however, you actively miss the other person and tend to dwell on or be preoccupied with his or her absence. The absence has a substantial and fairly long-term effect on your life. When the absence of the other arouses strong feelings of intimacy, passion, or commitment, the relationship has gone beyond liking.

Passion Alone: Infatuated Love

Tom met Lisa at work. One look at her was enough to change his life: he fell madly in love with her. Instead of concentrating on his work, which he hated, he would think about Lisa. She was aware of this, but did not much care for Tom. When he tried to start a conversation with her, she moved on as quickly as possible....

Tom's "love at first sight" is infatuated love or, simply, infatuation. It results from the experiencing of passionate arousal without the intimacy and decision/commitment components of love. Infatuation is usually obvious, although it tends to be somewhat easier for others to spot than for the person who is experiencing it. An infatuation can arise almost instantaneously and dissipate as quickly. Infatuations generally manifest a high degree of psychophysiological arousal and bodily symptoms such as increased heartbeat or even palpitations of the heart, increased hormonal secretions, and erection of genitals....

Decision/Commitment Alone: Empty Love

John and Mary had been married for twenty years, for fifteen of which Mary had been thinking about getting a divorce, but could never get herself to go through with it....

Mary's kind of love emanates from the decision that you love another and are committed to that love even without having the intimacy or the passion associated with some loves. It is the love sometimes found in stagnant relationships that have been going on for years but that have lost both their original mutual emotional involvement and physical attraction. Unless the commitment to the love is very strong, such love can be close to none at all. Although in our society we see empty love generally as the final or near-final stage of a long-term relationship, in other societies empty love may be the first stage of a long-term relationship. As I have said, in societies where marriages are arranged, the marital partners start with the commitment to love each other, or to try to do so, and not much more. Here, *empty* denotes a relationship that may come to be filled with passion and intimacy, and thus marks a beginning rather than an end.

Intimacy + Passion: Romantic Love

Susan and Ralph met in their junior year of college. Their relationship started off as a good friendship, but rapidly turned into a deeply involved romantic love affair. They spent as much time together as possible, and enjoyed practically every minute of it. But Susan and Ralph were not ready to commit themselves permanently to the relationship: both felt they were too young to make any long-term decisions, and that until they at least knew where they would go after college, it was impossible to tell even how much they could be together....

Ralph and Susan's relationship combines the intimacy and passion components of love. In essence, it is liking with an added element: namely, the arousal brought about by physical attraction. Therefore, in this type of love, the man and woman are not only drawn physically to each other but are also bonded emotionally. This is the view of romantic love found in classic works of literature, such as *Romeo and Juliet*....

Intimacy + Commitment: Companionate Love

In their twenty years of marrige, Sam and Sara had been through some rough times. They had seen many of their friends through divorces, Sam through several jobs, and Sara through an illness that at one point had seemed as though it might be fatal. Both had friends, but there was no doubt in either of their minds that they were each other's best friend. When the going got rough, each of them knew he or she could count on the other. Neither Sam nor Sara felt any great passion in their relationship, but they had never sought out others. . . .

Sam and Sara's kind of love evolves from a combination of the intimacy and decision/commitment components of love. It is essentially a long-term, committed friendship, the kind that frequently occurs in marriages in which physical attraction (a major source of passion) has waned. . . .

Passion + Commitment: Fatuous Love

When Tim and Diana met at a resort in the Bahamas, they were each on the rebound. Tim's fiancé had abruptly broken off their engagement. . . . Diana was recently divorced, the victim of the "other woman." Each felt desperate for love, and when they met each other, they immediately saw themselves as a match made in heaven. . . . The manager of the resort, always on the lookout for vacation romances as good publicity, offered to marry them at the resort and to throw a lavish reception at no charge, other than cooperation in promotional materials. After thinking it over, Tim and Diana agreed. . . .

Fatuous love, as in the case of Tim and Diana, results from the combination of passion and decision/commitment without intimacy, which takes time to develop. It is the kind of love we sometimes associate with Hollywood, or with a whirlwind courtship, in which a couple meet one day, get engaged two weeks later, and marry the next month. This love is fatuous in the sense that the couple commit themselves to one another on the basis of passion without the stabilizing element of intimate involvement. Since passion can develop almost instantaneously, and intimacy cannot, relationships based on fatuous love are not likely to last.

Intimacy + Passion + Commitment: Consummate Love

Harry and Edith seemed to all their friends to be the perfect couple. And what made them distinctive from many such "perfect couples" is that they pretty much fulfilled the notion. They felt close to each other, they continued to have great sex after fifteen years, and they could not imagine themselves happy over the long term with anyone else. . . .

Consummate, or complete, love like Edith and Harry's results from the combination of the three components in equal measure. It is a love toward which many of us strive, especially in romantic relationships. Attaining consummate love is analogous, in at least one respect, to meeting your goal in a weight-reduction program: reaching your ideal weight is often easier than maintaining it. Attaining consummate love is no guarantee that it will last; indeed, one may become aware of the loss only after it is far gone. Consummate love, like other things of value, must be guarded carefully. . . .

Jack saw his colleague Myra at work almost every day. They interacted well in their professional relationship, but neither was particularly fond of the other. Neither felt particularly comfortable talking to the other about personal matters; and after a few tries, they decided to limit their conversations to business.

Non-love, as in the relationship of Jack and Myra, refers simply to the absence of all three components of love. Non-love characterizes many personal relationships, which are simply casual interactions that do not partake of love or even liking.

Robert J.
Sternberg

"I Love You More Today Than Yesterday"

Most people would agree that love is an important emotion in their lives. Yet until a few decades ago, psychologists did not conduct serious research into love. This lack of attention has recently been rectified by social psychologists such as Susan Sprecher, who has been studying how love develops in romantic partners.

Sprecher earned her Ph.D. in sociology from the University of Wisconsin in 1985. She then accepted a position at Illinois State University, where she is currently a professor of sociology. Her research has focused on the social psychology of interpersonal relationships, and she is coauthor, with Kathleen McKinney, of *Sexuality* (Sage, 1993).

This selection is from the research report " 'I Love You More Today Than Yesterday': Romantic Partners' Perceptions of Changes in Love and Related Affect Over Time," which was published in *Journal of Personality and Social Psychology* in 1999. In it, Sprecher describes her research on feelings of romantic love among dating couples over multiple periods of time. As you read this selection, note the difficulty of measuring actual emotion compared to the perception of emotion. Remember: any statistical test is significant if probability (*p*) is less than .05.

Key Concept: development of romantic love

APA Citation: Sprecher, S. (1999). "I love you more today than yesterday": Romantic partners' perceptions of changes in love and related affect over time. *Journal of Personality and Social Psychology, 76,* 46–53.

Partners in romantic relationships provided reports on perceived changes in their love, commitment, and satisfaction and completed contemporaneous scales on the same relationship phenomena multiple times over several years. At each wave of the longitudinal study, participants whose relationships had remained intact perceived that their love and related phenomena had increased since they had last participated in the study. However, their scores on contemporaneous scales did not generally increase over time. Analyses indicated that participants' reports of change were related to actual change in love, commitment, and satisfaction scores and with future relationship stability. Furthermore, participants who experienced a breakup during the longitudinal study reported an overall decrease in their positive affect in the months prior to the breakup.

Do intimate partners really love each other more with time, as suggested by the title of this article? Do they perceive that their love is increasing? Because close relationships are extended in length, partners' love and other feelings for each other are likely to change over time and be perceived to change. However, the temporal course of love and related relationship phenomena (e.g., satisfaction) has rarely been studied. In this investigation, a sample of romantic couples (all were dating at the beginning of the study) were surveyed five times over a 4-year period about their relationship. At each wave of the study, the participants completed contemporaneous scales of love, commitment, and satisfaction, and they also reported how the same relationship phenomena had changed since they had last participated in the study. As a result, both actual and perceived changes are examined, as well as the association between the two....

METHOD

The data came from a longitudinal study conducted at a Midwestern university with a sample of romantic heterosexual couples. The initial sample consisted of both partners of 101 dating couples who completed a self-administered questionnaire in the fall of 1988 (Time 1). Follow-ups were conducted in the spring of 1989 (Time 2) and the spring–summer of 1990, 1991, and 1992 (Times 3, 4, and 5, respectively). The sample size decreased with each wave, because when couples broke up they completed one last questionnaire (about the breakup) and then did not participate further in the study. By Time 5, 59% ($n = 60$) of the couples had ended their relationships.

Participants

Dating couples were recruited through announcements in classes, advertisements in the student newspaper, and posters placed around campus. The mean age of the participants at Time 1 was 20 years. Most participants in the sample were Caucasian (87%) and of the middle or upper-middle class (87%). The mean number of months the couples had been dating when the study began was 18.7; the range was from 1 month to 55 months. Of the 41 couples who were still together at Time 5, 29 (71%) had married.

Procedure

At Time 1, couples were scheduled to complete a self-administered questionnaire (separately) at a campus location. In the follow-ups, participants who were still attending classes at the university came to the campus to complete a questionnaire (partners from couples who broke up came at different times). Participants who had moved away were mailed the questionnaire and a stamped, self-addressed return envelope. Among the couples who remained together over the study ($n = 41$), there was very little nonresponse. Thirty-eight of the women and 36 of the men participated in all five waves of the study. A higher rate of nonresponse occurred in the final contact (the breakup questionnaire) for the subsample of couples who broke up ($n = 60$), although the response rate was still very high (86%).

Measurement

Beginning at Time 2, the questionnaire for the intact couples contained a set of questions that measured their subjective perceptions of changes in their relationships for the period of time since the last data collection (which was 6 months at Time 2 and approximately 1 year at Times 3–5). Participants were asked, "How do you think each of the following has changed—if at all—in the past year?" Couples, upon breaking up, were asked to respond for the period of time prior to the breakup. Although several relationship phenomena were listed, the focus of this study was on change in love and related affect. The particular items analyzed were listed in the following ways: "love and affection for this person," "commitment to the relationship," and "satisfaction in the relationship." Each item was followed by a 7-point response scale ranging from 1 = *decreased* to 4 = *same* (i.e., no change) to 7 = *increased*. Because the three items were highly intercorrelated (mean $r = .81$ for men and .72 for women at Time 2), an index of perceived change, represented by the mean response to the three items, was created. The higher the score on this index, the more the participant perceived his or her positive feelings to increase over time. The alpha coefficient for this index was .93 for men and .84 for women, on the basis of the intact sample at Time 2.

At each wave of the study, participants who were in intact relationships also completed a lengthy questionnaire about those relationships, which included scales that measured their current love, commitment, and satisfaction. Love was assessed by the 10-item Braiker and Kelley (1979) love scale (each item was followed by a 7-point response scale: Time 1 alpha was .85 for men and .81 for women). Commitment was measured by 4 items from the Lund (1985) commitment scale and one additional global item of commitment (each item was followed by a 7-point response scale; Time 1 alpha was .89 for men and .78 for women). Satisfaction was assessed by the 7-item Hendrick (1988) Relationship Assessment Scale (each item was followed by a 5-point response scale; Time 1 alpha was .81 for men and .75 for women). For each scale, a higher score indicated greater love, commitment, and satisfaction, respectively.

In addition, an index of contemporaneous feelings comparable to the three-item index of perceived change was created by combining, from each scale, one item that referred most directly to the specific affect. These items were "To what extent do you love _____ at this stage"; "How committed are you to your partner"; and "In general, how satisfied are you with your relationship?" The latter item, which had a 5-point response scale, was first multiplied by a factor of 1.4 to make it a 7-point response scale similar to the other two items. Time 1 alpha for this index of contemporaneous feelings was .79 for men and .77 for women.

RESULTS

Perceptions of Change in the Stable Couples

The participants in intact relationships at Time 2 ($n = 84$ couples) reported there were increases in their love and related affect for their partner since they had completed the first questionnaire (6 months earlier), in support of Hypothesis 1. The mean response to the index of perceived change was 5.22 for men and 5.62 for women. These mean scores were significantly above the midpoint, *no change*, as indicated by *t* tests for a single sample. The score for women was significantly higher than that for men, paired $t(79) = -3.05, p < .01$.

The subsamples of intact couples surveyed at Times 3, 4, and 5 also perceived increases in love and related affect (see means in Table 1). In each case, the mean score to the index of perceived change was significantly higher than the midpoint (which represented no change). Women's scores were significantly higher ($p < .05$) than men's at Times 3 and 5 (as well as at Time 1, as reported above). Partners perceived similar changes in relationship phenomena only at some of the waves. The interpartner correlation for the index of perceived change was .63 ($p < .001$) at Time 2, .36 ($p < .01$) at Time 3, .26 (*ns*) at Time 4, and .17 (*ns*) at Time 5. Table 1 also presents the mean scores for each retrospective item (i.e., love and affection, commitment, and satisfaction). At each wave, participants reported that each specific affect had increased since they had last participated in the study.

I also examined whether the reports of change varied over time for the subsample of participants who remained in their relationship throughout the entire study and who participated at every wave ($n = 35$ men and 38 women from the 41 couples). A repeated measures analysis (within a multivariate analysis of variance) indicated no significant changes over time in scores on the index of perceived change for either the men or the women. A consistent overall positive change was reported at each wave for this group of most stable couples.

Hypothesis 1 also stated that stable couples would perceive greater increases in love and related affect than would actually be found in an analysis of changes in scores on contemporaneous scales between waves of the study.... [T]he scores on the index of contemporaneous feelings did not change significantly between any adjacent waves of the study for the groups of stable couples as a whole. Furthermore, between most waves, there were no significant changes in scores on the love, commitment, and satisfaction scales. The significant changes between Times 1 and 2 were actually negative rather than positive (in love for men and satisfaction for both men and women). The only significant increases were between Times 4 and 5, and these were for commitment and satisfaction for women. These results, when considered in conjunction with the results presented above for the reports of change, provide support for the prediction in Hypothesis 1 that the amount of change reported by participants is greater than actual change (as evidenced in change in contemporaneous scores).

TABLE 1

Perception of Changes in Love, Commitment, and Satisfaction for Men and Women in Intact Couples at Four Waves of the Study and in the Breakup Sample

	Sample				
	Intact	Intact	Intact	Intact	
Measure	*Time 2*	*Time 3*	*Time 4*	*Time 5*	*Breakup*
n (couples)	84	62	48	41	58
Three-item index of perceived change					
Men	5.22	5.44	5.51	5.62	3.32
Women	5.62	5.82	5.81	6.06	3.44
Specific items					
Love and affection					
Men	5.44	5.68	5.50	5.82	3.92_a
Women	5.94	5.89	5.81	6.10	4.15_a
Commitment					
Men	5.21	5.55	5.65	5.87	3.22
Women	5.65	5.89	5.90	6.23	3.37
Satisfaction					
Men	5.04	5.08	5.39	5.18	2.76
Women	5.26	5.69	5.73	5.85	2.82

Note: The above mean responses are based on a response scale ranging from 1 (*decreased*) to 7 (*increased*), where 4 = *same* or *no change*. The exact sample size for each analysis varied as a function of the number of participants at each wave (both partners did not participate at every wave) and the amount of missing data on each variable. With the exception of the means that are marked with the subscript a (for the breakup sample), each mean was significantly different from 4, the midpoint representing the perception of no change.

I also considered the possibility that the most stable couples (those who stayed together throughout the longitudinal study) would experience increases in scores on contemporaneous scales over time. In fact, scores on the index of contemporaneous feelings did increase over time for men, linear $F(1,34) = 4.47$, $p < .05$ (means at Time 1 = 6.39, at Time 2 = 6.43, at Time 3 = 6.44, at Time 4 = 6.55, at Time 5 = 6.66), although not for women, linear $F(1,37) = 0.89$, *ns* (means at Time 1 = 6.70, at Time 2 = 6.63, at Time 3 = 6.77, at Time 4 = 6.66, at Time 5 = 6.77). However, the means were higher for women than for men in this subsample even early in the study. An analysis of the three specific scales indicated that commitment increased significantly over time for this subsample: linear $F(1,34) = 9.52$, $p < .01$, for men, and linear $F(1,37) = 6.32$, $p < .05$, for women. (For a table of these means, write to Susan Sprecher.)

Perceived Change Among the Breakup Couples

The second hypothesis stated that breakup couples will perceive that their love, commitment, and satisfaction decreased in the period prior to the breakup. Data were available after the breakup for both partners of 47 couples and one partner from 11 other couples who ended their relationships. Among this breakup sample, the mean score on the index of perceived change was 3.32 for men and 3.44 for women. These scores were significantly below the midpoint of 4 (*no change*) and in the direction of the anchor *decreased*. The difference between men and women was not significant, and there was little similarity between ex-partners in perceptions of change ($r = -.08$). The final column of Table 1 also presents the mean scores for the individual items on change (love, commitment, satisfaction) for the subsample of breakup couples. Love was reported to decrease the least; in fact, the mean for this item for both men and women was at 4, *no change*. (Follow-up analyses indicated that this mean score was the result of most participants scoring at or near the midpoint of *no change* rather than a result of a bimodal distribution on the item.)

Because participants in the breakup sample did not complete the contemporaneous scales of love, commitment, and satisfaction in their breakup questionnaire, it was not possible to determine in any straightforward way whether they over- or underestimated the change that occurred in their relationships prior to breaking up. However, it can be assumed that positive affect decreases for couples just prior to a breakup.

Associations Between Reports of Change and the Contemporaneous Measures

The final issue examined was the degree to which participants' beliefs about past changes in their love and related affect are associated with current feelings in the relationship and with future outcomes, including actual changes in feelings and the stability of the relationship. Only the analyses conducted with the three-item index of perceived change and the three-item index of contemporaneous feelings are presented. (The analyses were also conducted with the love, commitment, and satisfaction scales and the corresponding individual reports of change, but unless noted, the results were very similar.)

First, I found that those individuals who reported more positive change for the period since the last data collection also experienced more positive current feelings. At Waves 2–5, scores on the index of perceived change were significantly correlated with scores on the index of contemporaneous feelings (correlations ranged from .64 to .71 for men and from .33 to .65 for women)....

DISCUSSION

Perceived and Actual Change in Stable Couples

Hypothesis 1 predicted that the romantic partners in stable relationships perceive that their love, commitment, and satisfaction increase over time. This hypothesis was strongly supported. For the intact samples at Times 2, 3, 4, and 5, men and women perceived that their positive feelings (e.g., love) for their partner had increased since they had last participated in the study (these reports of change were not requested at Time 1). Thus, with each passing year participants believed that their love (and commitment and satisfaction) had grown. These results are consistent with other findings in the literature indicating that people perceive their relationship and partner in idealistic ways (e.g., Murray & Holmes, 1993; Murray et al., 1996; Van Lange & Rusbult, 1995). It is also possible that people's definition of love and related affect changes over time so that compared with the type of love (commitment or satisfaction) that they are currently experiencing, what they recall experiencing at an earlier time may seem to have a different and lesser quality.

Although the participants in intact relationships at each wave perceived that their love, commitment, and satisfaction were increasing over time, there was little evidence that these affects, as measured by contemporaneous measures, were actually increasing between waves of the study, also in support of Hypothesis 1. The exception was that in the most stable couples (those who stayed together throughout the study), an overall increase was found for affect, particularly commitment. The general lack of change in contemporaneous scores between waves, however, may be due to ceiling effects reached in the measures early in the study, which made it difficult for significant differences to be evidenced.

Perceived Change Among the Breakup Couples

Most of the individuals whose relationships dissolved during the longitudinal study completed one additional questionnaire after the breakup, which included items asking how their love and related phenomena had changed before the breakup. These participants reported overall decreases in their positive feelings (especially satisfaction and commitment) prior to the breakup. These results are consistent with the research indicating that decreases in commitment, satisfaction, and other positive feelings in the relationship occur before relationship breakdown (e.g., Rusbult, 1983). In addition, however, for some individuals the reported decrease in positive affect for the period prior to the breakup may reflect attempts, in postdissolution rumination, to make sense of the breakup (Duck, 1982).

Of the positive feelings, satisfaction was perceived to decrease the most, whereas love was perceived to decrease the least. These results suggest that people do not end their relationships because of the disappearance of love, but because of a dissatisfaction or unhappiness that develops, which may then cause love to stop growing. Research on emotional reactions after a breakup

(Sprecher, 1994) has also found that love does not dissipate completely in the process of relationship dissolution.

Associations Between Reports of Change and Contemporaneous Measures

Evidence was found in this study that beliefs about increases in love and related phenomena were associated with current feelings in the relationship and future positive outcomes. First, I found at each wave of the study that included collection of reports of change (Waves 2–5) that individuals in intact relationships who reported increases in their positive feelings since they had last participated in the study were also likely to experience current high levels of love, commitment, and satisfaction with their partner. However, these analyses were based on reports of perceived change and contemporaneous measures completed at the same time point, and thus the participants' current relationship states may have influenced how they recalled change. As suggested by Ross's (1989) theory of emotions, individuals who are in a current state of happiness and love are likely to report they experienced an increase in their positive feelings if they believe that such affect increases over time in dating relationships.

REFERENCES

Braiker, H. B., & Kelley, H. H. (1979). Conflict in the development of close relationships. In R. L. Burgess & T. L. Huston (Eds.), *Social exchange in developing relationships* (pp. 135–168). New York: Academic Press.

Duck, S. (1982). A topography of relationship disengagement and dissolution. In S. Duck (Ed.), *Personal relationships: Vol. 4. Dissolving personal relationships* (pp. 1–30). New York: Academic Press.

Hendrick, S. S. (1988). A generic measure of relationship satisfaction. *Journal of Marriage and the Family, 50,* 93–98.

Lund, M. (1985). The development of investment and commitment scales for predicting continuity of personal relationships. *Journal of Social and Personal Relationships, 2,* 3–23.

Murray, S. L., & Holmes, J. G. (1993). Seeing virtues in faults: Negativity and the transformation of interpersonal narratives in close relationships. *Journal of Personality and Social Psychology, 65,* 707–722.

Murray, S. L., Holmes, J. G., & Griffin, D. W. (1996). The benefits of positive illusions: Idealization and the construction of satisfaction in close relationships. *Journal of Personality and Social Psychology, 70,* 79–98.

Ross, M. A. (1989). The relation of implicit theories to the construction of personal histories. *Psychological Review, 96,* 341–357.

Rusbult, C. E. (1983). A longitudinal test of the investment model: The development (and deterioration) of satisfaction and commitment in heterosexual involvements. *Journal of Personality and Social Psychology, 45,* 101–117.

Sprecher, S. (1994). Two ideas to the breakup of dating relationships. *Personal Relationships, 1,* 199–222.

Van Lange, P. A. M., & Rusbult, C. E. (1995). My relationship is better than—and not as bad as—yours is: The perception of superiority in close relationships. *Personality and Social Psychology Bulletin, 21,* 32–44.

9.3 CINDY HAZAN AND PHILLIP SHAVER

Romantic Love Conceptualized as an Attachment Process

Although attachment and love have long been studied by psychologists as separate concepts, only recently have serious attempts been made to study love as an attachment process. There are differences in attachment style among infants, and some researchers argue that these differences could form the framework for understanding the process of romantic love. Cindy Hazan and Phillip Shaver are social psychologists who have been exploring love from the attachment perspective.

Hazan earned her Ph.D. in social psychology from the University of Denver in 1988, then accepted her current position at Cornell University. Shaver (b. 1944) earned his Ph.D. in social psychology from the University of Michigan in 1970. He taught at New York University, the State University of New York at Buffalo, and the University of Denver before accepting his current position as chair of the psychology department at the University of California at Davis.

This selection is from "Romantic Love Conceptualized as an Attachment Process," which was published in the *Journal of Personality and Social Psychology* in 1987. Through a newspaper survey, Hazan and Shaver found that the proportion of people who characterized themselves as being secure, avoidant, or anxious/ambivalent in their most important relationships was fairly similar to the proportion of infants reportedly having these attachment styles. How would you categorize your love style? As you read this selection, consider the implications for romantic love partners and how the information could promote better understanding between partners. A second study not included here, in which the subjects were college students, replicated the results of the first study.

Key Concept: attachment and romantic love

APA Citation: Hazan, C., & Shaver, P. (1987). Romantic love conceptualized as an attachment process. *Journal of Personality and Social Psychology, 52,* 511–524.

*O*ne of the landmarks of contemporary psychology is Bowlby's (1969, 1973, 1980) three-volume exploration of attachment, separation, and loss, the processes by which affectional bonds are forged and broken. Bowlby's major purpose was to describe and explain how infants become emotionally attached to their primary caregivers and emotionally distressed when separated from them, although he also contended that "attachment behavior [characterizes] human beings from the cradle to the grave" (1979, p. 129). In recent years, laboratory and naturalistic studies of infants and children (summarized by Bretherton, 1985, and Maccoby, 1980) have provided considerable support for attachment theory, which was proposed by Bowlby and elaborated by several other investigators. The purpose of this article is to explore the possibility that this theory, designed primarily with infants in mind, offers a valuable perspective on adult romantic love. We will suggest that romantic love is an attachment process (a process of becoming attached), experienced somewhat differently by different people because of variations in their attachment histories.

For our purpose, which is to create a coherent framework for understanding love, loneliness, and grief at different points in the life cycle, attachment theory has several advantages over existing approaches to love (Shaver, Hazan, & Bradshaw, in press). First, although many researchers (e.g., Rubin, 1973; Hatfield & Sprecher, 1985) have attempted to assess love with unidimensional scales, love appears to take multiple forms (e.g., Dion & Dion, 1985; Hendrick & Hendrick, 1986; Lee, 1973; Steck, Levitan, McLane, & Kelley, 1982; Sternberg, 1986; Tennov, 1979). Attachment theory explains how at least some of these forms develop and how the same underlying dynamics, common to all people, can be shaped by social experience to produce different relationship styles. Second, although various authors have portrayed certain forms of love as healthy and others as unhealthy, or at least problematic (e.g., Hindy & Schwarz, 1984; Tennov, 1979), they have not said how the healthy and unhealthy forms fit together in a single conceptual framework. Attachment theory not only provides such a framework, but it also explains how both healthy and unhealthy forms of love originate as reasonable adaptations to specific social circumstances. The portrait of love offered by attachment theory includes negative as well as positive emotions: for example, fear of intimacy (discussed by Hatfield, 1984), jealousy (e.g., Hindy & Schwarz, 1985), and emotional ups and downs (Tennov, 1979) as well as caring (Rubin, 1973), intimacy (Sternberg, 1986), and trust (Dion & Dion, 1985). Third, attachment theory deals with separation and loss and helps explain how loneliness and love are related (Shaver & Rubenstein, 1980; Parkes & Weiss, 1983; Weiss; 1973). Finally, attachment theory links adult love with socioemotional processes evident in children and nonhuman primates; it places love within an evolutionary context (Wilson, 1981). (See Sternberg & Barnes, in press, for an anthology of recent approaches to the study of adult love.)

... The formation during early childhood of a smoothly functioning (i.e., secure) attachment relationship with a primary caregiver, although the norm in our society, is by no means guaranteed. Research by Ainsworth and others suggests that a mother's sensitivity and responsiveness to her infant's signals and needs during the first year of life are important prerequisites. Mothers who are slow or inconsistent in responding to their infant's cries or who regularly intrude on or interfere with their infant's desired activities (sometimes to force affection on the infant at a particular moment) produce infants who cry more than usual, explore less than usual (even in the mother's presence), mingle attachment behaviors with overt expressions of anger, and seem generally anxious. If, instead, the mother consistently rebuffs or rejects the infant's attempts to establish physical contact, the infant may learn to avoid her. On the basis of their observations, Ainsworth, Blehar, Waters, and Wall (1978) delineated three styles or types of attachment, often called *secure, anxious/ambivalent,* and *avoidant.* Infants in the anxious/ambivalent category frequently exhibit the behaviors Bowlby called *protest,* and the avoidant infants frequently exhibit the behaviors he called *detachment.* A major goal of this article is to apply this three-category system to the study of romantic love.

In their description of the three attachment styles, Ainsworth et al. (1978) referred to infants' expectations concerning their mothers' accessibility and responsiveness. This fits with Bowlby's claim that infants and children construct inner working models of themselves and their major social-interaction partners. Because the expectations incorporated in these models are some of the most important sources of continuity between early and later feelings and behaviors, they deserve special attention. According to Bowlby, working models (which we will also call *mental models)* and the behavior patterns influenced by them are central components of personality. The claim of cross-situational and cross-age continuity is still controversial but is supported by a growing list of longitudinal studies from infancy through the early elementary school years (Dontas, Maratos, Fafoutis, & Karangelis, 1985; Erickson, Sroufe, & Egeland, 1985; Main, Kaplan, & Cassidy, 1985; Sroufe, 1983; Waters, Wippman, & Sroufe, 1979). This evidence for continuity adds plausibility to the notion that a person's adult style of romantic attachment is also affected by attachment history.

Continuity, according to Bowlby (1973), is due primarily to the persistence of interrelated mental models of self and social life in the context of a fairly stable family setting:

> Confidence that an attachment figure is, apart from being accessible, likely to be responsive can be seen to turn on at least two variables: (a) whether or not the attachment figure is judged to be the sort of person who in general responds to calls for support and protection; [and] (b) whether or not the self is judged to be the sort of person towards whom anyone, and the attachment figure in particular is likely to respond in a helpful way. Logically these variables are independent. In practice they are apt to be confounded. As a result, the model of the attachment figure and the model of the self are likely to develop so as to be complementary and mutually confirming. (Bowlby, 1973, p. 238)

LOVE AS ATTACHMENT

So far, no one has attempted to conceptualize the entire range of romantic love experiences in a way that parallels the typology developed by Ainsworth and her colleagues. Nor has anyone with an interest in romantic relationships pursued Bowlby's idea that continuity in relationship style is a matter of mental models of self and social life. Finally, no one has explored the possibility that the specific characteristics of parent-child relationships identified by Ainsworth et al. as the probable causes of differences in infant attachment styles are also among the determinants of adults' romantic attachment styles. These are the major aims of this article.

We derived the following hypotheses by applying Bowlby's and Ainsworth's ideas and findings as literally as possible to the domain of adult love.

Hypothesis 1

Given the descriptions of the secure, avoidant, and anxious/ambivalent styles, we expected roughly 60% of adults to classify themselves as secure and the remainder to split fairly evenly between the two insecure types, with perhaps a few more in the avoidant than in the anxious/ambivalent category. In a summary of American studies of the three types of infants, Campos, Barrett, Lamb, Goldsmith, and Stenberg (1983) concluded that 62% are secure, 23% are avoidant, and 15% are anxious/ambivalent. Given a diverse sample of American adults, we thought it reasonable to expect approximately the same proportions.

Hypothesis 2

Just as the feelings an infant presumably experiences in the relationship with his or her mother are thought to reflect the quality of attachment to her; we expected that different types of respondents—secure, avoidant, and anxious/ambivalent—would experience their most important love relationships differently. We predicted that the most important love experience of a secure adult would be characterized by trust, friendship, and positive emotions. For avoidant adults, love was expected to be marked by fear of closeness and lack of trust. Anxious/ambivalent adults were expected to experience love as a preoccupying, almost painfully exciting struggle to merge with another person. This last style is similar to what Hindy and Schwarz (1984) called anxious romantic attachment and Tennov (1979) called limerence.

Hypothesis 3

Respondents' working models of self and relationships were also expected to differ according to attachment style. Secure types should believe in enduring love, generally find others trustworthy, and have confidence that the self is likable. Avoidant types should be more doubtful of the existence or durability of

214

romantic love and believe that they do not need a love partner in order to be happy. Anxious/ambivalent types should fall in love frequently and easily but have difficulty finding true love. They should also have more self-doubts than the other two types because, unlike avoidant respondents, they do not repress or attempt to hide feelings of insecurity.

Hypothesis 4

Because attachment style is thought to develop in infancy and childhood, we expected respondents of the three types to report different attachment histories. According to the theory, secure respondents should remember their mothers as dependably responsive and caring; avoidant respondents should report that their mothers were generally cold and rejecting; and anxious/ambivalent respondents should remember a mixture of positive and negative experiences with their mothers. As less research has been conducted with fathers, we tentatively expected the findings related to them to be roughly similar to the findings for mothers.

Hypothesis 5

Finally, because the attachment needs of insecure respondents are unlikely to be fully met, avoidant and anxious/ambivalent respondents should be especially vulnerable to loneliness. The avoidant types, however, may defend against or attempt to hide this vulnerable feeling and so report less loneliness than anxious/ambivalent respondents do.

STUDY 1

In an initial effort to test the attachment-theory approach to romantic love, we designed a "love quiz" to be printed in a local newspaper. As explained by Shaver and Rubenstein (1983), the newspaper questionnaire method has been used in a wide variety of studies, always with results that approximate those from more expensive, more strictly representative surveys. The main difference between newspaper survey respondents and participants in representative sample surveys is that the former have slightly higher education levels. Also, depending on the topic, newspaper surveys tend to draw more female than male respondents. Neither of these biases seemed to preclude a valuable initial test of our ideas, and the gains in sample size and heterogeneity appeared to outweigh the cost of mild unrepresentativeness.

A single-item measure of the three attachment styles was designed by translating Ainsworth et al.'s (1978) descriptions of infants into terms appropriate to adult love. The love-experience questionnaire, which we will describe in detail, was based on previous adult-love measures and extrapolations from the literature on infant-caregiver attachment. The measure of working models was based on the assumption that conscious beliefs about romantic love—

concerning, for example, whether it lasts forever and whether it is easy or difficult to find—are colored by underlying, and perhaps not fully conscious, mental models. The measure of attachment history was a simple adjective checklist used to describe childhood relationships with parents and the parents' relationship with each other.

Method

Subjects.   Analyses reported here are based on the first 620 of over 1,200 replies received within a week following publication of the questionnaire. (The major findings were stable after the first few hundred, 50 additional replies were not keypunched.) Of these 620 replies, 205 were from men and 415 were from women. The subjects ranged in age from 14 to 82, with a median age of 34 and a mean of 36. Average household income was $20,000 to $30,000; average education level was "some college." Just over half (51%) were Protestant, 22% were Catholic, 3% were Jewish, 10% were atheist or agnostic, and 13% were "other." Ninety-one percent were "primarily heterosexual," 4% were "primarily homosexual," and 2% were "primarily bisexual" (3% chose not to answer). Forty-two percent were married at the time of the survey; 28% were divorced or widowed, 9% were "living with a lover" and 31% were dating. (Some checked more than one category.)

Measures and procedure.   The questionnaire appeared in the July 26, 1985, issue of the *Rocky Mountain News* on the first and second pages of the Lifestyles section. Besides being highly visible there, it was referred to in a banner headline at the top of the paper's front page: "Tell us about the love of your life; experts ask 95 questions about your most important romance." The instructions included the following sentences: "The questionnaire is designed to look at the most important love relationship you have ever had, why you got involved in it, and why it turned out the way it did . . . It may be a past or a current relationship, but choose only the most important one." Given that there was only enough room to ask about one relationship, we decided to have subjects focus on the one they considered most important.

The questionnaire was divided into three parts. The first contained 56 statements concerning the subject's most important relationship, for example, "I (considered/consider) _____ one of my best friends" and "I (loved/love) _____ so much that I often (felt/feel) jealous." (The blank referred to the most important lover's name.) Responses were recorded by circling *SD, D, A,* or *SA* to indicate points along a *strongly disagree* to *strongly agree* continuum. The 56 statements, 4 each for 14 a priori subscales, were adapted from previous love questionnaires (Dion & Dion, 1985; Hatfield & Sprecher, 1985; Hindy & Schwarz, 1984; Lasswell & Lobsenz, 1980; Rubin, 1973; Steffen, McLaney, & Hustedt, 1984) or suggested by the literature on infant-caretaker attachment (e.g, Ainsworth et al., 1978).

A principal-components analysis followed by equimax rotation was performed on the 56-item measure. Thirteen factors had eigen-values greater than 1.0, and 12 corresponded to a priori scales. Items loading above .40 on 1 of the

TABLE 1

Information on Love-Experience Scales

Cindy Hazan
and Phillip
Shaver

Scale name	Sample item	No. of items	α
Happiness	My relationship with_____(made/makes) me very happy.	4	.84
Friendship	I (considered/consider)_____ one of my best friends.	4	.78
Trust	I (felt/feel) complete trust in _____.	4	.83
Fear of closeness	I sometimes (felt/feel) that getting too close to_____ could mean trouble.	3	.64
Acceptance	I (was/am) well aware of_____'s imperfections but it (did/does) not lessen my love.	2	.67
Emotional extremes	I (felt/feel) almost as much pain as joy in my relationship with_____.	3	.81
Jealousy	I (loved/love)_____ so much that I often (felt/feel) jealous.	4	.82
Obsessive preoccupation	Sometimes my thoughs (were/are) uncontrollably on_____.	3	.70
Sexual attraction	I (was/am) very physically attracted to_____.	4	.80
Desire for union	Sometimes I (wished/wish) that_____ and I were a single unit, a "we" without clear boundaries.	3	.79
Desire for reciprocation	More than anything, I (wanted/want) _____ to return my feelings.	3	.70
Love at first sight	Once I noted_____, I was hooked.	4	.70

12 predicted factors were analyzed for reliability, and items that reduced coefficient alpha were deleted. Table 1 provides the names of the 12 scales and a sample item, the number of items retained, and coefficient alpha for each. Alpha ranged from .64 to .84 with a mean of .76, which seemed adequate for preliminary tests of the hypotheses....

Results and Discussion

Frequencies of the three attachment styles. Hypothesis 1 concerned whether newspaper readers could meaningfully classify themselves as avoidant, anxious/ambivalent, or secure in their most important romantic relationship, given fairly simple descriptions of the three attachment styles, and in particular whether the frequencies of the types would be similar to those found in studies of infants and young children. Table 2 shows how the alternatives were worded and provides the percentage of subjects endorsing each description.

TABLE 2

Adult Attachment Types and Their Frequencies (Newspaper Sample)

Question: Which of the following best describes your feelings?
Answers and percentages:
Secure (N = 319, 56%): I find it relatively easy to get close to others and am comfortable depending on them and having them depend on me. I don't often worry about being abandoned or about someone getting to close to me.

Avoidant (N = 145, 25%): I am somewhat uncomfortable being close to others; I find it difficult to trust them completely, difficult to allow myself to depend on them. I am nervous when anyone gets too close, and often, love partners want me to be more intimate that I feel comfortable being.

Anxious/Ambivalent (N = 110, 19%): I find that others are reluctant to get as close as I would like. I often worry that my partner doesn't really love me or won't want to stay with me. I want to merge completely with another person, and this desire sometimes scares people away.

Note: Twenty-one subjects failed to answer this question, and 25 checked more than one answer alternative.

Just over half (56%) classified themselves as secure, whereas the other half split fairly evenly between the avoidant and anxious/ambivalent categories (25% and 19%, respectively). These figures are similar to proportions reported in American studies of infant-mother attachment (Campos et al., 1983, summarized the proportions obtained in these studies as 62% secure, 23% avoidant, and 15% anxious/ambivalent). Our results suggest, but of course do not prove, that subjects' choices among the alternatives were nonrandom and may have been determined by some of the same kinds of forces that affect the attachment styles of infants and children. The remainder of the results argue for the validity of subjects' self-classifications.

Differences in love experiences. The second hypothesis predicted that subjects with different self-designated attachment styles would differ in the way they characterized their most important love relationship. Table 3 presents the mean subscale scores (each with a possible range of 1 to 4) for each attachment type, along with the *F* ratio from a one-way analysis of variance (ANOVA) on scores for each subscale.

In line with the hypothesis, secure lovers described their most important love experience as especially happy, friendly, and trusting. They emphasized being able to accept and support their partner despite the partner's faults.

TABLE 3

Love-Subscale Means for the Three Attachment Types (Newspaper Sample)

Cindy Hazan
and Phillip
Shaver

Scale name	Avoidant	Anxious/ ambivalent	Secure	$F(2,571)$	
Happiness	3.19$_a$	3.31$_a$	3.51$_b$	14.21	***
Friendship	3.18$_a$	3.19$_a$	3.50$_b$	22.96	***
Trust	3.11$_a$	3.13$_a$	3.43$_b$	16.21	***
Fear of closeness	2.30$_a$	2.15$_a$	1.88$_b$	22.65	***
Acceptance	2.86$_a$	3.03$_b$	3.01$_b$	4.66	**
Emotional extremes	2.75$_a$	3.05$_b$	2.36$_c$	27.54	***
Jealousy	2.57$_a$	2.88$_b$	2.17$_c$	43.91	***
Obsessive preoccupation	3.01$_a$	3.29$_b$	3.01$_a$	9.47	***
Sexual attraction	3.27$_a$	3.43$_b$	3.27$_a$	4.08	*
Desire for union	2.81$_a$	3.25$_b$	2.69$_a$	22.67	***
Desire for reciprocation	3.24$_a$	3.55$_b$	3.22$_a$	14.90	***
Love at first sight	2.91$_a$	3.17$_b$	2.97$_a$	6.00	**

Note: Within each row, means with different subscripts differ at the .05 level of significance according to a Scheffé test.
$^*p < .05.$
$^{**}p < .01.$
$^{***}p < .001.$

Moreover, their relationships tended to endure longer: 10.02 years, on the average, compared with 4.86 years for the anxious/ambivalent subjects and 5.97 years for the avoidant subjects, $F(2, 568) = 15.89$, $p < .001$. This was the case even though members of all three groups were 36 years old on the average. Only 6% of the secure group had been divorced, compared with 10% of the anxious/ambivalent group and 12% of the avoidant group, $F(2, 573) = 3.36$, $p < .05$.

The avoidant lovers were characterized by fear of intimacy, emotional highs and lows, and jealousy. They never produced the highest mean on a positive love-experience dimension. The anxious/ambivalent subjects experienced love as involving obsession, desire for reciprocation and union, emotional highs and lows, and extreme sexual attraction and jealousy. They provided a close fit to Tennov's (1979) description of limerence and Hindy and Schwarz's (1984) conception of anxious romantic attachment, suggesting that the difference between what Tennov called love and limerence is the difference between secure and anxious/ambivalent attachment.

Although the average love experiences of people in the three different attachment categories differed significantly, for most of the subscales all three types scored on the same side of the midpoint (2.50), emotional extremes and jealousy being the only exceptions. Thus, there appears to be a core experience of romantic love shared by all three types, with differences in emphasis and patterning between the types. The results also support the ideas that love is a multidimensional phenomenon and that individuals differ in more ways than the intensity of their love experiences. Especially noteworthy was the fact that the ordering of means for the different attachment styles differed for different dimensions. For the dimensions of happiness, friendship, trust, and fear of closeness, secure subjects differed significantly from avoidant and anxious/ambivalent subjects but these two insecure groups did not differ from each other. On the dimensions of obsessive preoccupation, sexual attraction, desire for union, desire for reciprocation, and love at first sight, anxious/ambivalent subjects differed significantly from avoidant and secure subjects, who did not differ from each other. On the acceptance dimension, avoidant subjects (the least accepting) differed from anxious/ambivalent and secure subjects, and on emotional extremes and jealousy, all three groups were statistically distinct. This variety of patterns supports the claim that there are three different love styles, not simply three points along a love continuum....

GENERAL DISCUSSION

Five hypotheses concerning adult love and loneliness were derived from attachment theory and research. The first was the simplest prediction we could make regarding the relative frequencies of the three attachment styles: that they would be about as common in adulthood as they are in infancy. The results supported this hypothesis. Across both studies, approximately 56% of the subjects classified themselves as secure, approximately 24% as avoidant, and approximately 20% as anxious/ambivalent. Campos et al. (1983) estimated the figures for infancy as 62% secure, 23% avoidant, and 15% anxious/ambivalent. Of course, it is unlikely that our single-item measure of attachment style measures exactly the same thing that Ainsworth et al. (1978) coded from behavioral observations of infant-mother dyads, and it would be naive to think that a style adopted in infancy remains unchanged or unelaborated all through life. Still, the search for connections between attachment in childhood and attachment in adulthood must begin somewhere, and our simple measure and straightforward hypothesis fared surprisingly well in their initial tests....

Because many social psychologists are likely to misread our approach as Freudian, it may be worthwhile to contrast Freudian conceptions of infant-adult continuity on the one hand with attachment theory's conception on the other: Unlike the Freudian conception, according to which the supposed irrationalities of adult love indicate regression to infancy or fixation at some earlier stage of psychosexual development, attachment theory includes the idea that social development involves the continual construction, revision, integration, and abstraction of mental models. This idea, which is similar to the notion of scripts and schemas in cognitive social psychology (e.g., Fiske & Taylor, 1984), is compatible with the possibility of change based on new information and experiences, although change may become more difficult with repeated, uncorrected use of habitual models or schemas.

Freud argued his case beautifully, if not persuasively, by likening the unconscious to the city of Rome, which has been ravaged, revised, and rebuilt many times over the centuries. In the case of the unconscious, according to Freud, it is as if all the previous cities still exist, in their original form and on the same site. Bowlby's conception is more in line with actual archeology. The foundations and present shapes of mental models of self and social life still bear similarities and connections to their predecessors—some of the important historical landmarks, bridges, and crooked streets are still there. But few of the ancient structures exist unaltered or in mental isolation, so simple regression and fixation are unlikely.

The attachment-theory approach to romantic love suggests that love is a biological as well as a social process, based in the nervous system and serving one or more important functions. This view runs counter to the increasingly popular idea that romantic love is a historical-cultural invention, perhaps a creation of courtly lovers in 13th-century Europe (e.g., Averill, 1985; de Rougement, 1940). This is obviously a matter for serious cross-cultural and historical research, but in the absence of strong evidence to the contrary, we hypothesize that romantic love has always and everywhere existed as a biological potential, although it has often been precluded as a basis for marriage. There are explicit records of romantic love in all of the great literate civilizations of early historic times, from Egypt and China to Greece and Rome (Mellen, 1981).

Finally, we should make clear that by calling romantic love an attachment process we do not mean to imply that the early phase of romance is equivalent to being attached. Our idea, which requires further development, is that romantic love is a biological process designed by evolution to facilitate attachment between adult sexual partners who, at the time love evolved, were likely to become parents of an infant who would need their reliable care.

The noticeable decrease in fascination and preoccupation as lovers move from the romantic (attaching) phase to what can become a decades-long period of secure attachment is evident not only in the case of romantic love but also in early childhood, when most secure children begin to take parental support for granted (barring unexpected separations). As Berscheid (1983) has shown in her analysis of the apparent unemotionality of many marriages, disruptions such as divorce and widowhood often "activate the attachment system," to use Bowlby's phrase, and reveal the strength of attachment bonds that were previously invisible. Loneliness and grieving are often signs of the depth of broken attachments.

In sum, love and loneliness are emotional processes that serve biological functions. Attachment theory portrays them in that light and urges us to go beyond simpler and less theoretically integrative models involving concepts such as attitude (e.g., Rubin, 1973) and physiological arousal (Berscheid & Walster, 1974). For that reason, the attachment approach seems worth pursuing even if future study reveals (as it almost certainly will) that adult romantic love requires additions to or alterations in attachment theory. It would not be surprising to find that adult love is more complex than infant-caretaker attachment, despite fundamental similarities.

REFERENCES

Ainsworth, M. D. S., Blehar, M. C., Waters, E., & Wall, S. (1978). *Patterns of attachment: A psychological study of the strange situation.* Hillsdale, NJ: Erlbaum.

Averill, J. R. (1985). The social construction of emotion: With special reference to love. In K. J. Gergen & K. E. Davis (Eds.), *The social construction of the person* (pp. 89–109). New York: Springer-Verlag.

Berscheid, E. (1983). Compatibility and emotion. In W. Ickes (Ed.), *Compatible and incompatible relationships* (pp. 143–161). New York: Springer-Verlag.

Berscheid, E., & Walster, E. (1974). A little bit above love. In T. L. Huston (Ed.), *Foundations of interpersonal attraction* (pp. 355–381). New York: Academic Press.

Bowlby, J. (1969). *Attachment and loss: Vol. 1. Attachment.* New York: Basic Books.

Bowlby, J. (1973). *Attachment and loss: Vol. 2. Separation: Anxiety and anger.* New York: Basic Books.

Bowlby, J. (1979). *The making and breaking of affectional bonds.* London: Tavistock.

Bowlby, J. (1980). *Attachment and loss: Vol. 3. Loss.* New York: Basic Books.

Bretherton, I. (1985). Attachment theory: Retrospect and prospect. *Monographs of the Society for Research in Child Development, 50*(1 & 2), 3–35.

Campos, J. J., Barrett, K. C., Lamb, M. E., Goldsmith, H. H., & Stenberg, C. (1983). Socioemotional development. In M. M. Haith & J. J. Campos (Eds.), *Handbook of child psychology: Vol. 2. Infancy and psychobiology* (pp. 783–915). New York: Wiley.

de Rougement, D. (1940). *Love in the Western world.* New York: Harcourt.

Dion, K. K., & Dion, K. L. (1985). Personality, gender, and the phenomenology of romantic love. In P. Shaver (Ed.), *Review of personality and social psychology* (Vol. 6, pp. 209–239). Beverly Hills, CA: Sage.

Dontas, C., Maratos, O., Fafoutis, M., & Karangelis, A. (1985). Early social development in institutionally reared Greek infants: Attachment and peer interaction. *Monographs of the Society for Research in Child Development, 50*(1 & 2), 136–146.

Erickson, M. F., Sroufe, L. A., & Egeland, B. (1985). The relationship between quality of attachment and behavior problems in preschool in a high-risk sample. *Monographs of the Society for Research in Child Development, 50*(1 & 2), 146–166.

Fiske, S. T., & Taylor, S. E. (1984). *Social cognition.* Reading, MA: Addison-Wesley.

Hatfield, E. (1984). The dangers of intimacy. In V. J. Derlega (Ed.), *Communication, intimacy, and close relationships* (pp. 207–220). New York: Academic Press.

Hatfield, E., & Sprecher, S. (1985). *Measuring passionate love in intimate relations.* Unpublished manuscript, University of Hawaii at Manoa.

Hendrick, C., & Hendrick, S. (1986). A theory and method of love. *Journal of Personality and Social Psychology, 50,* 392–402.

Hindy, C. G., & Schwarz, J. C. (1984). *Individual differences in the tendency toward anxious romantic attachments.* Paper presented at the Second International Conference on Personal Relationships, Madison, WI.

Hindy, C. G., & Schwarz, J. C. (1985). *"Lovesickness" in dating relationships: An attachment perspective.* Paper presented at the annual convention of the American Psychological Association, Los Angeles.

Lasswell, M., & Lobsenz, N. M. (1980). *Styles of loving: Why you love the way you do.* New York: Doubleday.

Lee, J. A. (1973). *The colors of love: An exploration of the ways of loving.* Don Mills, Ontario, Canada: New Press.

Maccoby, E. E. (1980). *Social development: Psychological growth and the parent-child relationship.* New York: Harcourt Brace Jovanovich.

Main, M., Kaplan, N., & Cassidy, J. (1985). Security in infancy, childhood, and adulthood: A move to the level of representation. *Monographs of the Society for Research in Child Development, 50*(1 & 2), 66–104.

Mellen, S. L. W. (1981). *The evolution of love.* San Francisco: Freeman.

Parkes, C. M., & Weiss, R. S. (1983). *Recovery from bereavement.* New York: Basic Books.

Rubin, Z. (1973). *Liking and loving: An invitation to social psychology.* New York: Holt, Rinehart & Winston.

Shaver, P., Hazan, C., & Bradshaw, D. (in press). Love as attachment: The integration of three behavioral systems. In R. Sternberg & M. Barnes (Eds.), *The anatomy of love.* New Haven, CT: Yale University Press.

Shaver, P., & Rubinstein, C. (1980). Childhood attachment experience and adult loneliness. In L. Wheeler (Ed.), *Review of personality and social psychology* (Vol. 1, pp. 42–73). Beverly Hills, CA: Sage.

Shaver, P., & Rubenstein, C. (1983). Research potential of newspaper and magazine surveys. In H. T. Reis (Ed.), *Naturalistic approaches to studying social interaction* (pp. 75–91). San Francisco: Jossey-Bass.

Sroufe, L. A. (1983). Infant-caregiver attachment and patterns of adaptation in preschool: The roots of maladaptation and competence. In M. Perlmutter (Ed.), *Minnesota Symposium on Child Psychology* (Vol. 16, pp. 41–83). Hillsdale, NJ: Erlbaum.

Steffen, J. J., McLaney, M. A., & Hustedt, T. K. (1984). *The development of a measure of limerence.* Unpublished manuscript, University of Cincinnati, Ohio.

Steck, L., Levitan, D., McLane, D., & Kelly, H. H. (1982). Care, need, and conceptions of love. *Journal of Personality and Social Psychology, 43,* 481–491.

Sternberg, R. J. (1986). A triangular theory of love. *Psychological Review, 93,* 119–135.

Sternberg, R. J., & Barnes, M. (in press). *The anatomy of love.* New Haven, CT: Yale University Press.

Tennov, D. (1979). *Love and limerence: The experience of being in love.* New York: Stein & Day.

Waters, E., Wippman, J., & Sroufe, L. A. (1979). Attachment, positive affect, and competence in the peer group: Two studies in construct validation. *Child Development, 50,* 821–829.

Weiss, R. S. (1973). *Loneliness: The experience of emotional and social isolation.* Cambridge, MA: MIT Press.

Wilson, G. (1981). *The Coolidge effect: An evolutionary account of human sexuality.* New York: Morrow.

PART FIVE

Social Influence and Group Processes

On the Internet . . .

Sites appropriate to Part Five

The Influence at Work Web site focuses on persuasion, compliance, and propaganda. This site provides introductory material as well as research material. Practical examples and applications are also included.

> http://www.influenceatwork.com/index.html

This Primer of Practical Persuasion and Influence site contains essays on a variety of topics, such as attitude-behavior consistency, routes of persuasion, attribution, and compliance.

> http://www.as.wvu.edu/~sbb/comm221/
>   primer.htm

This home page for the Society for the Psychological Study of Social Issues provides information about current research in social psychology as well as abstracts from issues of the *Journal of Social Issues.*

> http://www.spssi.org

The Stanford Prison Experiment Site describes a simulation study of the psychology of imprisonment that was conducted at Stanford University. This site includes a slide show of the actual study, discussion questions, and links related to group processes and prisons.

> http://www.prisonexp.org

CHAPTER 10 Social Influence

10.1 STANLEY MILGRAM

Behavioral Study of Obedience

Obedience is a type of social influence in which an individual exhibits the behavior required by a command from someone else. We are taught as children to obey parents and teachers, and as we grow up we learn to obey employers, law enforcement officers, and a variety of other authority figures. One of the best-known studies on obedience was performed by Stanley Milgram at Yale University.

Milgram (1933–1984) studied under social psychologist Solomon E. Asch and earned his Ph.D. from Harvard University in 1960. He taught at Yale University and Harvard University before accepting a position at the Graduate Center of the City University of New York in 1967. Milgram, a very creative social psychologist, studied social communication, prejudice, interpersonal relationships, and obedience. Milgram's research on obedience was published in his book *Obedience to Authority* (Harper & Row, 1974).

This selection is from "Behavioral Study of Obedience," which was published in the *Journal of Abnormal and Social Psychology* in 1963. It presents the results of the first in a series of Milgram's obedience experiments: a large percentage of his subjects delivered what they believed to be the maximum level of electric shocks to a "learner" (who was actually

Milgram's accomplice), despite the learner's screaming protests, because an authority figure told them to do so. This study has been a subject of controversy during the past three decades because of its ethical considerations as well as its social implications. As you read this selection, consider the extent to which you obey in today's society.

Key Concept: obedience

APA Citation: Milgram, S. (1963). Behavioral study of obedience. *Journal of Abnormal and Social Psychology, 67*, 371–378.

Obedience is as basic an element in the structure of social life as one can point to. Some system of authority is a requirement of all communal living, and it is only the man dwelling in isolation who is not forced to respond, through defiance or submission, to the commands of others. Obedience, as a determinant of behavior, is of particular relevance to our time. It has been reliably established that from 1933–45 millions of innocent persons were systematically slaughtered on command. Gas chambers were built, death camps were guarded, daily quotas of corpses were produced with the same efficiency as the manufacture of appliances. These inhumane policies may have originated in the mind of a single person, but they could only be carried out on a massive scale if a very large number of persons obeyed orders....

General Procedure

A procedure was devised which seems useful as a tool for studying obedience (Milgram, 1961). It consists of ordering a naive subject to administer electric shock to a victim. A simulated shock generator is used, with 30 clearly marked voltage levels that range from 15 to 450 volts. The instrument bears verbal designations that range from Slight Shock to Danger: Severe Shock. The responses of the victim, who is a trained confederate of the experimenter, are standardized. The orders to administer shocks are given to the naive subject in the context of a "learning experiment" ostensibly set up to study the effects of punishment on memory. As the experiment proceeds the naive subject is commanded to administer increasingly more intense shocks to the victim, even to a point of reaching the level marked Danger: Severe Shock. Internal resistances become stronger, and at a certain point the subject refuses to go on with the experiment. Behavior prior to this rupture is considered "obedience," in that the subject complies with the commands of the experimenter. The point of rupture is the act of disobedience. A quantitative value is assigned to the subject's performance based on the maximum intensity shock he is willing to administer before he refuses to participate further. Thus for any particular subject and for any particular experimental condition the degree of obedience may be specified with a numerical value. The crux of the study is to systematically vary the factors believed to alter the degree of obedience to the experimental commands....

METHOD

Subjects

The subjects were 40 males between the ages of 20 and 50, drawn from New Haven and surrounding communities. Subjects were obtained by a newspaper advertisement and direct mail solicitation. Those who responded to the appeal believed they were to participate in a study of memory and learning at Yale University. A wide range of occupations is represented in the sample. Typical subjects were postal clerks, high school teachers, salesmen, engineers, and laborers. Subjects ranged in educational level from one who had not finished elementary school, to those who had doctorate and other professional degrees. They were paid $4.50 for their participation in the experiment. However, subjects were told that payment was simply for coming to the laboratory, and that the money was theirs no matter what happened after they arrived....

Personnel and Locale

The experiment was conducted on the grounds of Yale University in the elegant interaction laboratory. (This detail is relevant to the perceived legitimacy of the experiment. In further variations, the experiment was dissociated from the university, with consequences for performance.) The role of experimenter was played by a 31-year-old high school teacher of biology. His manner was impassive, and his appearance somewhat stern throughout the experiment. He was dressed in a gray technician's coat. The victim was played by a 47-year-old accountant, trained for the role; he was of Irish-American stock, whom most observers found mild-mannered and likeable.

Procedure

One naive subject and one victim (an accomplice) performed in each experiment. A pretext had to be devised that would justify the administration of electric shock by the naive subject. This was effectively accomplished by the cover story. After a general introduction on the presumed relation between punishment and learning, subjects were told:

> But actually, we know *very little* about the effect of punishment on learning, because almost no truly scientific studies have been made of it in human beings.
>
> For instance, we don't know how *much* punishment is best for learning—and we don't know how much difference it makes as to who is giving the punishment, whether an adult learns best from a younger or an older person than himself—or many things of that sort.

So in this study we are bringing together a number of adults of different occupations and ages. And we're asking some of them to be teachers and some of them to be learners.

We want to find out just what effect different people have on each other as teachers and learners, and also what effect *punishment* will have on learning in this situation.

Therefore, I'm going to ask one of you to be the teacher here tonight and the other one to be the learner.

Does either of you have a preference?

Subjects then drew slips of paper from a hat to determine who would be the teacher and who would be the learner in the experiment. The drawing was rigged so that the naive subject was always the teacher and the accomplice always the learner. (Both slips contained the word "Teacher.") Immediately after the drawing, the teacher and learner were taken to an adjacent room and the learner was strapped into an "electric chair" apparatus.

The experimenter explained that the straps were to prevent excessive movement while the learner was being shocked. The effect was to make it impossible for him to escape from the situation. An electrode was attached to the learner's wrist, and electrode paste was applied "to avoid blisters and burns." Subjects were told that the electrode was attached to the shock generator in the adjoining room.

In order to improve credibility the experimenter declared, in response to a question by the learner: "Although the shocks can be extremely painful, they cause no permanent tissue damage."

Learning Task.   The lesson administered by the subject was a paired-associate learning task. The subject read a series of word pairs to the learner, and then read the first word of the pair along with four terms. The learner was to indicate which of the four terms had originally been paired with the first word. He communicated his answer by pressing one of four switches in front of him, which in turn lit up one of four numbered quadrants in a answer-box located atop the shock generator.

Shock Generator.   The instrument panel consists of 30 lever switches set in a horizontal line. Each switch is clearly labeled with a voltage designation that ranges from 15 to 450 volts. There is a 15-volt increment from one switch to the next going from left to right. In addition, the following verbal designations are clearly indicated for groups of four switches going from left to right: Slight Shock, Moderate Shock, Strong Shock, Intense Shock, Extremely Intense Shock, Danger: Severe Shock. (Two switches after this last designation are simply marked XXX.)

Upon depressing a switch: a pilot light corresponding to each switch is illuminated in bright red; an electric buzzing is heard; an electric blue light, labeled "voltage energizer," flashes; the dial on the voltage meter swings to the right; various relay clicks are sounded.

The upper left-hand corner of the generator is labeled Shock generator, Type ZLB, Dyson Instrument Company, Waltham, Mass. Output 15 Volts–450 Volts.

Details of the instrument were carefully handled to insure an appearance of authenticity. The panel was engraved by precision industrial engravers, and all components were of high quality. No subject in the experiment suspected that the instrument was merely a simulated shock generator.

Sample Shock. Each naive subject is given a sample shock on the shock generator, prior to beginning his run as teacher. This shock is always 45 volts, and is applied by pressing the third switch of the generator. The shock is applied to the wrist of the naive subject, and has its source in a 45-volt battery wired into the generator. This further convinces the subject of the authenticity of the generator.

Shock Instructions. The subject is told to administer a shock to the learner each time he gives a wrong response. Moreover—and this is the key command —the subject is instructed to "move one level higher on the shock generator each time the learner flashes a wrong answer." He is also instructed to announce the voltage level before administering a shock. This serves to continually remind subjects of the increasing intensity of shocks administered to the learner.

Preliminary and Regular Run. Pretests revealed that the procedure of reading words and administering shocks requires some practice before it can be handled smoothly. Therefore, immediately preceding the regular run, the teacher is given a preliminary series of 10 words to read to the learner. There are 3 neutral words in the practice series (i.e., words that the learner answers correctly), so that shocks are administered for 7 of the words, with the maximum shock of 105 volts (moderate shock). Almost all subjects master the procedure by the time the preliminary run is over.

Subjects are then presented with a second list, and are told that the procedure is the same as for the first list; the experimenter adds however:

> When you get to the bottom of the list, repeat it over again, and continue giving shocks, until the learner has learned all the pairs correctly.

The experimenter instructs the subject to,

> start from 15 volts and increase the shock level one step each time the learner gives a wrong answer.

Feedback from the Victim. In all conditions the learner gives a predetermined set of responses to the word pair test, based on a schedule of approximately three wrong answers to one correct answer. In the present experimental condition no vocal response or other sign of protest is heard from the learner until Shock Level 300 is reached. When the 300-volt shock is administered, the learner pounds on the wall of the room in which he is bound to the electric chair. The pounding can be heard by the subject. From this point on, the learner's answers no longer appear on the four-way panel.

At this juncture, subjects ordinarily turn to the experimenter for guidance. The experimenter instructs the subject to treat absence of a response as a wrong answer, and to shock the subject according to the usual schedule. He advises the subjects to allow 5–10 seconds before considering no response as a wrong answer, and to increase the shock level one step each time the learner fails to respond correctly. The learner's pounding is repeated after the 315-volt shock is administered; afterwards he is not heard from, nor do his answers reappear on the four-way signal box.

Experimenter Feedback. At various points in the experiment the subject may turn to the experimenter for advice on whether he should continue to administer shocks. Or he may indicate that he does not wish to go on. It was important to standardize the experimenter's responses to these inquiries and reactions.

If the subject indicated his unwillingness to go on, the experimenter responded with a sequence of "prods," using as many as necessary to bring the subject into line.

Prod 1: Please continue. *or* Please go on.

Prod 2: The experiment requires that you continue.

Prod 3: It is absolutely essential that you continue.

Prod 4: You have no other choice, you *must* go on.

The prods were always made in sequence: Only if Prod 1 had been unsuccessful, could Prod 2 be used. If the subject still refused to obey the experimenter after Prod 4, the experiment was terminated. The experimenter's tone of voice was at all times firm, but not impolite. The sequence was begun anew on each occasion that the subject balked or showed reluctance to follow orders.

Special prods. If the subject asked if the learner was liable to suffer permanent physical injury, the experimenter said:

Although the shocks may be painful, there is no permanent tissue damage, so please go on. [Followed by Prods 2, 3, and 4 if necessary.]

If the subject said that the learner did not want to go on, the experimenter replied:

Whether the learner likes it or not, you must go on until he has learned all the word pairs correctly. So please go on. [Followed by Prods 2, 3, and 4 if necessary]

Dependent Measures

The primary dependent measure for any subject is the maximum shock he administers before he refuses to go any further. In principle this may vary from 0 (for a subject who refuses to administer even the first shock) to 30 (for a subject who administers the highest shock on the generator). A subject who breaks off the experiment at any point prior to administering the thirtieth shock level is termed a *defiant subject*. One who complies with experimental command fully, and proceeds to administer all shock levels commanded, is termed an *obedient* subject. . . .

Interview and Dehoax. Following the experiment, subjects were interviewed; open-ended questions, projective measures, and attitude scales were employed. After the interview, procedures were undertaken to assure that the subject would leave the laboratory in a state of well being. A friendly reconciliation was arranged between the subject and the victim, and an effort was made to reduce any tensions that arose as a result of the experiment.

RESULTS

Preliminary Notions

Before giving an account of the experimental results, it is instructive to consider how persons predict others will perform when commanded to administer powerful shocks to another person. Fourteen Yale seniors, all psychology majors, were provided with a detailed description of the experimental situation. They were asked to reflect carefully on it, and to predict the behavior of 100 hypothetical subjects. More specifically, they were instructed to plot the distribution of obedience of "100 Americans of diverse occupations, and ranging in age from 20 to 50 years," who were placed in the experimental situation.

There was considerable agreement among the respondents on the expected behavior of hypothetical subjects. All respondents predicted that only an insignificant minority would go through to the end of the shock series. (The estimates ranged from 0 to 3%, i.e, the most "pessimistic" member of the class predicted that of 100 persons, 3 would continue through to the most potent shock available on the shock generator—450 volts.) The class mean was 1.2%. The question was also posed informally to colleagues of the author, and the most general feeling was that few if any subjects would go beyond the designation Very Strong Shock.

Result of Experiment I

Subjects Accept Situation. With few exceptions subjects were convinced of the reality of the experimental situation, that they were administering shocks to another person, and the most potent shocks were extremely painful. In the post-experimental interview subjects were asked: "How painful to the learner were the last few shocks that you administered to him?" Subjects were instructed to indicate their answers on a printed 14-point scale ranging from "Not at all painful" to "Extremely painful." The modal response was 14 (Extremely painful) with the mean at 13.42.

Signs of Extreme Tension. Many subjects showed signs of nervousness in the experimental situation, and especially upon administering the more powerful shocks. In a large number of cases the degree of tension reached extremes that are rarely seen in sociopsychological laboratory studies. Subjects were observed to sweat, tremble, stutter, bite their lips, groan, and dig their fingernails into their flesh. These were characteristic rather than exceptional responses to the experiment.

One sign of tension was the regular occurrence of nervous laughing fits. Fourteen of the 40 subjects showed definite signs of nervous laughter and smiling. The laughter seemed entirely out of place, even bizarre. Full-blown, uncontrollable seizures were observed for 3 subjects. On one occasion we observed a seizure so violently convulsive that it was necessary to call a halt to the experiment. The subject, a 46-year-old encyclopedia salesman, was seriously embarrassed by his untoward and uncontrollable behavior. In the post-experimental interviews subjects took such pains to point out that they were not sadistic types, and that the laughter did not mean they enjoyed shocking the victim.

Distribution of Scores. It had been conjectured that persons would not, in general, agree to administer shocks beyond the level designated Very Strong Shock. The distribution of maximum shocks for this experiment is shown in Table 1. The obtained distribution of scores deviates radically from the prediction.

Upon command of the experimenter, each of the 40 subjects went beyond the expected breakoff point. No subject stopped prior to administering Shock Level 20. (At this level—300 volts—the victim kicks on the wall and no longer provides answers to the teacher's multiple-choice questions.)

Of the 40 subjects, 5 refused to obey the experimental commands beyond the 300-volt level. Four more subjects administered one further shock, and then refused to go on. Two broke off at the 330-volt level, and 1 each at 345, 360, and 375 volts. Thus a total of 14 subjects defied the experimenter. It is instructive to reprint their remarks at the point of defiance, as transcribed from the tape recordings:

> [0124] I think he's trying to communicate, he's knocking.... Well it's not fair to shock the guy... these are terrific volts. I don't think this is very humane.... Oh, I can't go on with this; no this isn't right. It's a hell of an experiment. The guy is suffering in there. No, I don't want to go on. This is crazy. [Subject refused to administer more shocks.]

> [0123] He's banging in there. I'm gonna chicken out. I'd like to continue, but I can't do that to a man.... I'm sorry I can't do that to a man. I'll hurt his heart. You take your check.... No really, I couldn't do it.

These subjects were frequently in a highly agitated and even angered state. Sometimes, verbal protest was at a minimum, and the subject simply got up from his chair in front of the shock generator, and indicated that he wished to leave the laboratory.

Of the 40 subjects, 26 obeyed the orders of the experimenter to the end, proceeding to punish the victim until they reached the most potent shock available on the shock generator. At that point, the experimenter called a halt to the sessions. (The maximum shock is labeled 450 volts, and is two steps beyond the designation: Danger: Severe Shock.) Although obedient subjects continued to administer shocks, they often did so under extreme stress. Some expressed

TABLE 1

Distribution of Breakoff Points

Verbal designation and voltage indication	Number of subjects for whom this was maximum shock
Slight Shock	
15	0
30	0
45	0
60	0
Moderate Shock	
75	0
90	0
105	0
120	0
Strong Shock	
135	0
150	0
165	0
180	0
Very Strong Shock	
195	0
210	0
225	0
240	
Intense Shock	
255	0
270	0
285	0
300	5
Extreme Intensity Shock	
315	4
330	2
345	1
360	1
Danger: Severe Shock	
375	1
390	0
405	0
420	0
XXX	
435	0
450	26

reluctance to administer shocks beyond the 300-volt level, and displayed fears similar to those who defied the experimenter; yet they obeyed.

After the maximum shocks had been delivered, and the experimenter called a halt to the proceedings, many obedient subjects heaved sighs of relief, mopped their brows, rubbed their fingers over their eyes, or nervously fumbled cigarettes. Some shook their heads, apparently in regret. Some subjects had remained calm throughout the experiment, and displayed only minimal signs of tension from beginning to end.

DISCUSSION

The experiment yielded two findings that were surprising. The first finding concerns the sheer strength of obedient tendencies manifested in this situation. Subjects have learned from childhood that it is a fundamental breach of moral conduct to hurt another person against his will. Yet, 26 subjects abandon this tenet in following the instructions of an authority who has no special powers to enforce his commands. To disobey would bring no material loss to the subject; no punishment would ensue. It is clear from the remarks and outward behavior of many participants that in punishing the victim they are often acting against their own values. Subjects often expressed deep disapproval of shocking a man in the face of his objections, and others denounced it as stupid and senseless. Yet the majority complied with the experimental commands. This outcome was surprising from two perspectives: first, from the standpoint of predictions made in the questionnaire described earlier. (Here, however, it is possible that the remoteness of the respondents from the actual situation, and the difficulty of conveying to them the concrete details of the experiment, could account for the serious underestimation of obedience.)

But the results were also unexpected to persons who observed the experiment in progress, through one-way mirrors. Observers often uttered expressions of disbelief upon seeing a subject administer more powerful shocks to the victim. These persons had a full acquaintance with the details of the situation, and yet systematically underestimated the amount of obedience that subjects would display.

The second unanticipated effect was the extraordinary tension generated by the procedures. One might suppose that a subject would simply break off or continue as his conscience dictated. Yet, this is very far from what happened. There were striking reactions of tension and emotional strain.

REFERENCES

Milgram, S. Dynamics of obedience. Washington: National Science Foundation, 25 January 1961. (Mimeo)

Compliance Without Pressure: The Foot-in-the-Door Technique

Compliance is a type of social influence in which an individual changes his or her behavior because of a direct request from someone else. The compliance technique of first making a small request and then making a large request is called the foot-in-the-door technique. Jonathan L. Freedman and Scott C. Fraser conducted a classic study that illustrates this technique.

Freedman earned his Ph.D. in social psychology from Yale University in 1961. He taught at Stanford University and Columbia University before accepting his current position at the University of Toronto. Fraser (b. 1943) earned his Ph.D. in social psychology from New York University in 1973. He currently works at Pacific Western University and the Neuropsychological Foundation. Fraser was an undergraduate student when he worked with Freedman.

This selection is from "Compliance Without Pressure: The Foot-in-the-Door Technique," which was published in 1966 in the *Journal of Personality and Social Psychology*. In a very creative experiment, Freedman and Fraser first asked homemakers to answer a few questions about household soap products and then a couple of days later asked them if five men could come to their house to classify all their household products. Notice how carefully the procedure is described in this selection. Consider why the foot-in-the-door technique is so effective in everyday compliance situations. Have you experienced or used this technique? If so, with what results?

Key Concept: foot-in-the-door compliance technique

APA Citation: Freedman, J. L., and Fraser, S. C. (1966). Compliance without pressure: The foot-in-the-door technique. *Journal of Personality and Social Psychology, 4*, 195–202.

*H*ow can a person be induced to do something he would rather not do? This question is relevant to practically every phase of social life, from stopping at a traffic light to stopping smoking, from buying Brand X to buying savings bonds, from supporting the March of Dimes to supporting the Civil Rights Act.

One common way of attacking the problem is to exert as much pressure as possible on the reluctant individual in an effort to force him to comply. This technique has been the focus of a considerable amount of experimental research. Work on attitude change, conformity, imitation, and obedience has all tended to stress the importance of the degree of external pressure. The prestige of the communicator (Kelman & Hovland, 1953), degree of discrepancy of the communication (Hovland & Pritzker, 1957), size of the group disagreeing with the subject (Asch, 1951), perceived power of the model (Bandura, Ross, & Ross, 1963), etc., are the kinds of variables that have been studied. This impressive body of work, added to the research on rewards and punishments in learning, has produced convincing evidence that greater external pressure generally leads to greater compliance with the wishes of the experimenter. The one exception appears to be situations involving the arousal of cognitive dissonance in which, once discrepant behavior has been elicited from the subject, the greater the pressure that was used to elicit the behavior, the less subsequent change occurs (Festinger & Carlsmith, 1959). But even in this situation one critical element is the amount of external pressure exerted.

Clearly, then, under most circumstances the more pressure that can be applied, the more likely it is that the individual will comply. There are, however, many times when for ethical, moral, or practical reasons it is difficult to apply much pressure when the goal is to produce compliance with a minimum of apparent pressure, as in the forced-compliance studies involving dissonance arousal. And even when a great deal of pressure is possible, it is still important to maximize the compliance it produces. Thus, factors other than external pressure are often quite critical in determining degree of compliance. What are these factors?

Although rigorous research on the problem is rather sparse, the fields of advertising, propaganda, politics, etc., are by no means devoid of techniques designed to produce compliance in the absence of external pressure (or to maximize the effectiveness of the pressure that is used, which is really the same problem). One assumption about compliance that has often been made either explicitly or implicitly is that once a person has been induced to comply with a small request he is more likely to comply with a larger demand. This is the principle that is commonly referred to as the foot-in-the-door or gradation technique and is reflected in the saying that if you "give them an inch, they'll take a mile." It was, for example, supposed to be one of the basic techniques upon which the Korean brainwashing tactics were based (Schein, Schneier, & Barker, 1961), and, in a somewhat different sense, one basis for Nazi propaganda during 1940 (Bruner, 1941). It also appears to be implicit in many advertising campaigns which attempt to induce the consumer to do anything relating to the product involved, even sending back a card saying he does not want the product....

The basic paradigm was to ask some subjects (Performance condition) to comply first with a small request and then 3 days later with a larger, related request. Other subjects (One-Contact condition) were asked to comply only with the large request. The hypothesis was that more subjects in the Performance condition than in the One-Contact condition would comply with the larger request.

Two additional conditions were included in an attempt to specify the essential difference between these two major conditions. The Performance subjects were asked to perform a small favor, and, if they agreed, they did it. The question arises whether the act of agreeing itself is critical or whether actually carrying it out was necessary. To assess this a third group of subjects (Agree-Only) was asked the first request, but, even if they agreed, they did not carry it out. Thus, they were identical to the Performance group except that they were not given the opportunity of performing the request.

Another difference between the two main conditions was that at the time of the larger request the subjects in the Performance condition were more familiar with the experimenter than were the other subjects. The Performance subjects had been contacted twice, heard his voice more, discovered that the questions were not dangerous, and so on. It is possible that this increased familiarity would serve to decrease the fear and suspicion of a strange voice on the phone and might accordingly increase the likelihood of the subjects agreeing to the larger request. To control for this a fourth condition was run (Familiarization) which attempted to give the subjects as much familiarity with the experimenter as in the Performance and Agree-Only conditions with the only difference being that no request was made.

The major prediction was that more subjects in the Performance condition would agree to the large request than in any of the other conditions, and that the One-Contact condition would produce the least compliance. Since the importance of agreement and familiarity was essentially unknown, the expectation was that the Agree-Only and Familiarization conditions would produce intermediate amounts of compliance.

METHOD

The prediction stated above was tested in a field experiment in which housewives were asked to allow a survey team of five or six men to come into their homes for 2 hours to classify the household products they used. This large request was made under four different conditions: after an initial contact in which the subject had been asked to answer a few questions about the kinds of soaps she used, and the questions were actually asked (Performance condition); after an identical contact in which the questions were not actually asked (Agree-Only condition); after an initial contact in which no request was made (Familiarization condition); or after no initial contact (One-Contact condition). The dependent measure was simply whether or not the subject agreed to the large request.

Procedure

The subjects were 156 Palo Alto, California, housewives, 36 in each condition, who were selected at random from the telephone directory. An additional 12 subjects distributed about equally among the three two-contact conditions could not be reached for the second contact and are not included in the data analysis. Subjects were assigned randomly to the various conditions, except that the Familiarization condition was added to the design after the other three conditions had been completed. All contacts were by telephone by the same experimenter who identified himself as the same person each time. Calls were made only in the morning. For the three groups that were contacted twice, the first call was made on either Monday or Tuesday and the second always 3 days later. All large requests were made on either Thursday or Friday.

At the first contact, the experimenter introduced himself by name and said that he was from the California Consumers' Group. In the Performance condition he then proceeded:

> We are calling you this morning to ask if you would answer a number of questions about what household products you use so that we could have this information for our public service publication, "The Guide." Would you be willing to give us this information for our survey?

If the subject agreed, she was asked a series of eight innocuous questions dealing with household soaps (e.g., "What brand of soap do you use in your kitchen sink?") She was then thanked for her cooperation, and the contact terminated.

Another condition (Agree-Only) was run to assess the importance of actually carrying out the request as opposed to merely agreeing to it. The only difference between this and the Performance condition was that, if the subject agreed to answer the questions, the experimenter thanked her, but said that he was just lining up respondents for the survey and would contact her if needed.

A third condition was included to check on the importance of the subject's greater familiarity with the experimenter in the two-contact conditions. In this condition the experimenter introduced himself, described the organization he worked for and the survey it was conducting, listed the questions he was asking, and then said that he was calling merely to acquaint the subject with the existence of his organization. In other words, these subjects were contacted, spent as much time on the phone with the experimenter as the Performance subjects did, heard all the questions, but neither agreed to answer them nor answered them.

In all of these two-contact conditions some subjects did not agree to the requests or even hung up before the requests were made. Every subject who answered the phone was included in the analysis of the results and was contacted for the second request regardless of her extent of cooperativeness during the first contact. In other words, no subject who could be contacted the appropriate number of times was discarded from any of the four conditions.

The large request was essentially identical for all subjects. The experimenter called, identified himself, and said either that his group was expanding

TABLE 1

Percentage of Subjects Complying With Large Request in Experiment I

*Jonathan L.
Freedman and
Scott C. Fraser*

Condition	%
Performance	52.8
Agree-Only	33.3
Familiarization	27.8*
One-Contact	22.2**

Note: N = 36 for each group. Significance levels represent differences from the Performance condition.
* p < .07.
**p < .02.

its survey (in the case of the two-contact conditions) or that it was conducting a survey (in the One-Contact condition). In all four conditions he then continued:

> The survey will involve five or six men from our staff coming into your home some morning for about 2 hours to enumerate and classify all the household products that you have. They will have to have full freedom in your house to go through the cupboards and storage places. Then all this information will be used in the writing of the reports for our public service publication, "The Guide."

If the subject agreed to the request, she was thanked and told that at the present time the experimenter was merely collecting names of people who were willing to take part and that she would be contacted if it were decided to use her in the survey. If she did not agree, she was thanked for her time. This terminated the experiment.

RESULTS

Apparently even the small request was not considered trivial by some of the subjects. Only two thirds of the subjects in the Performance and Agree-Only conditions agreed to answer the questions about household soaps. It might be noted that none of those who refused the first request later agreed to the large request, although as stated previously all subjects who were contacted for the small request are included in the data for those groups.

Our major prediction was that subjects who had agreed to and carried out a small request (Performance condition) would subsequently be more likely to comply with a larger request than would subjects who were asked only the larger request (One-Contact condition). As may be seen in Table 1, the results support the prediction. Over 50% of the subjects in the Performance condition agreed to the larger request, while less than 25% of the One-Contact condition agreed to it. Thus it appears that obtaining compliance with a small request does tend to increase subsequent compliance. The question is what aspect of the initial contact produces this effect.

One possibility is that the effect was produced merely by increased familiarity with the experimenter. The Familiarization control was included to assess the effect on compliance of two contacts with the same person. The group had as much contact with the experimenter as the Performance group, but no request was made during the first contact. As the table indicates, the Familiarization group did not differ appreciably in amount of compliance from the One-Contact group, but was different from the Performance group ($\chi^2 = 3.70, p < .07$). Thus, although increased familiarity may well lead to increased compliance, in the present situation the differences in amount of familiarity apparently were not great enough to produce any such increase; the effect that was obtained seems not to be due to this factor.

Another possibility is that the critical factor producing increased compliance is simply agreeing to the small request (i.e., carrying it out may not be necessary). The Agree-Only condition was identical to the Performance condition except that in the former the subjects were not asked the questions. The amount of compliance in this Agree-Only condition fell between the Performance and One-Contact conditions and was not significantly different from either of them. This leaves the effect of merely agreeing somewhat ambiguous, but it suggests that the agreement alone may produce part of the effect.

REFERENCES

Asch, S. E. Effects of group pressure upon the modification and distortion of judgments. In H. Guetzkow (Ed.), *Groups, leadership and men; research in human relations.* Pittsburgh: Carnegie Press, 1951. Pp. 177–190.

Bandura, A., Ross, D., & Ross, S. A. A comparative test of the status envy, social power, and secondary reinforcement theories of identificatory learning. *Journal of Abnormal and Social Psychology,* 1963, **67,** 527–534.

Bruner, J. The dimensions of propaganda: German short-wave broadcasts to America. *Journal of Abnormal and Social Psychology,* 1941, **36,** 311–337.

Festinger, L., & Carlsmith, J. Cognitive consequences of forced compliance. *Journal of Abnormal and Social Psychology,* 1959, **58,** 203–210.

Hovland, C. I., & Pritzker, H. A. Extent of opinion change as a function of amount of change advocated. *Journal of Abnormal and Social Psychology,* 1957, **54,** 257–261.

Kelman, H. C., & Hovland, C. I. "Reinstatement" of the communicator in delayed measurement of opinion change. *Journal of Abnormal and Social Psychology,* 1953, **48,** 327–335.

Schein, E. H., Schneier, I., & Barker, C. H. *Coercive pressure.* New York: Norton, 1961.

10.3 ROBERT B. CIALDINI ET AL.

Low-Ball Procedure for Producing Compliance: Commitment Then Cost

Getting others to comply with our requests is an important part of everyday social interaction. Salespeople, in particular, have a great need to extract compliance from their customers. Social psychologists, including Robert B. Cialdini and his colleagues, have been investigating various procedures that might encourage compliance in people.

Cialdini (b. 1945) earned his Ph.D. in social psychology in 1970 from the University of North Carolina and is currently a professor of psychology at Arizona State University. He has written extensively on social influence, including *Influence: Science and Practice,* 4th ed. (Allyn & Bacon, 2001). John T. Cacioppo (b. 1951) earned his Ph.D. in social psychology from Ohio State University in 1977. He taught at the University of Notre Dame, the University of Iowa, and Ohio State University before accepting his current position at the University of Chicago in 1999. Rodney Bassett (b. 1951) received a Ph.D. from Ohio State University in 1977, then went to work at Roberts Wesleyan College, where he is currently a professor of psychology. John A. Miller was on the faculty at Ohio State University when the research described in this selection was conducted.

This selection is from the research study "Low-Ball Procedure for Producing Compliance: Commitment Then Cost," which was published in *Journal of Personality and Social Psychology* in 1978. In it, Cialdini et al. describe their experiments on the effectiveness of the low-ball technique for generating compliance. Essentially, the low-ball procedure involves inducing someone to make a decision to perform a behavior and then making the behavior more costly. How effective do you think the low-ball procedure is? Have you ever used it to obtain compliance from someone?

Key Concept: low-ball compliance procedure

APA Citation: Cialdini, R. B., Cacioppo, J. T., Bassett, R., & Miller, J. A. (1978). Low-ball procedure for producing compliance: Commitment then cost. *Journal of Personality and Social Psychology, 36,* 463–476.

*T*he low-ball technique, a tactic often used by automobile sales dealers to produce compliance from customers, was examined in a set of three experiments. In all
three studies, a requester who induced subjects to make an initial decision to perform a
target behavior and who then made performance of the behavior more costly obtained
greater final compliance than a requester who informed subjects of the full costs of the
target behavior from the outset. The low-ball phenomenon—that an active preliminary
decision to take an action tends to persevere even after the costs of performing the action
have been increased—was found to be reliable (Experiment 1) [and] different from the
foot-in-the-door effect (Experiment 2)....

The Low-Ball Technique

It is the purpose of the present article to use such an investigatory sequence in an examination of the relationship of certain social psychological
concepts to compliance behavior like that typically obtained through a contemporary sales practice. There is a tactic, reputedly widespread (Carlson, 1973;
Consumer Reports, 1974), that is used by some sales organizations to produce
compliance from their customers. The technique, called "throwing a low-ball"
or "low-balling," is especially prevalent among new-car dealers. The critical
component of the procedure is for the salesperson to induce the customer to
make an *active decision* to buy one of the dealership's cars by offering an extremely good price, perhaps as much as $300 below competitors' prices. Once
the customer has made the decision for a specific car (and has even begun completing the appropriate forms), the salesperson removes the price advantage in
one of a variety of ways. For example, the customer may be told that the originally cited price did not include an expensive option that the customer had
assumed was part of the offer. More frequently, however, the initial price offer
is rescinded when the salesperson "checks with the boss," who does not allow
the deal because "we'd be losing money." Sometimes, the original agreement
is voided by the used-car manager, who offers a trade-in price substantially
below the inflated one suggested by the salesperson in the initial negotiation.
In each instance, the result is the same: The reason that the customer made
a favorable purchase decision is removed, and the performance of the target
behavior (i.e., buying that specific automobile) is rendered more costly. The increased cost is such that the final price is equivalent to, or sometimes slightly
above, that of the dealer's competitors. Yet, car dealership lore has it that more
customers will remain with their decision to purchase the automobile, even at
the adjusted figure, than would have bought it had the full price been revealed
before a purchase decision had been obtained. The essence of the low-ball procedure, then, is for a requester to induce another to make a behavioral decision
concerning a target action. It is assumed that the decision will persist even after circumstances have changed to make performance of the target action more
costly.

The first step in an examination of the low-ball technique and its relationship to compliance involves a demonstration of the effectiveness of the

tactic. Does it really work, or have automobile dealers, in the absence of evidence from controlled procedures, deluded themselves as to the compliance-producing power of low-balling? In order to provide experimental evidence concerning the reliability of low-ball procedures in enhancing compliance, a small field study was conducted. The study implemented the low-ball strategy by obtaining a decision from subjects to execute a target behavior and then raising the cost of performing that behavior. The low-ball procedure was contrasted with a control procedure in which subjects were informed of the full cost of the target behavior before being requested to perform it.

EXPERIMENT 1

Method

Subjects and procedure.   Subjects were 63 students of both sexes enrolled in introductory psychology classes at a large state university. The subjects were randomly selected from class rolls and phoned by an experimental confederate. The confederate, who was blind to the experimental hypothesis, solicited subject participation in a psychology experiment by using either low-ball or control procedures. In both conditions, the confederate introduced herself as follows:

> My name is _____. I'm calling for the Psychology Department to schedule Psychology 100 students for an experiment on thinking processes. The experiment concerns the way people organize facts. We can give you 1 hour of credit for your participation in this experiment.

At this point, the experimental script diverged for the two conditions.

Control condition.   Before they were asked if they would be willing to participate, subjects in the control condition were informed that the experiment would take place at 7:00 a.m. Specifically, the confederate said:

> The room in which the experiment is being held is used during the day and evening by other people in the department; so we are running this experiment at 7:00 in the morning on Wednesdays and Fridays. Can I put you down for Wednesday or Friday morning at 7:00?

If a subject said "No," he or she was debriefed and thanked. If the subject said "Yes," an appointment was made and the subject's name taken.

Low-ball condition.   Subjects in this condition were asked if they wished to participate after the experimental requirements were only partially described. If a subject agreed, he or she was *then* informed of the 7:00 a.m. starting time and was again asked if he or she was willing to participate. Specifically, the confederate said, "Would you be willing to participate?" A subject who said

"No," was debriefed and thanked. If a subject inquired about a time, the confederate replied,

> Well, we have more than one time during the week, but right now I'm just interested in finding out if you wish to participate.

If the subject said "Yes," the confederate continued as follows:

> The room in which the experiment is being held is used during the day and evening by other people in the department; so we are running this experiment at 7:00 in the morning on Wednesdays and Fridays. Can I put you down for Wednesday or Friday morning at 7:00?

Unless the experimental appointment was for the following day, all subjects agreeing to participate were called again the night before the appointment to remind them of the experiment. If a subject was not home, a message was left.

Two dependent measures were taken. The first, measuring verbal compliance, was the percentage of subjects who made an appointment to participate in the study at one of the two specified times; the other, measuring behavioral compliance, was the percentage of subjects who actually appeared for their 7:00 a.m. appointments. Those subjects who appeared did indeed participate in an experiment on thinking processes at that time. At the completion of the thinking-processes experiment, subjects were fully informed of the procedures of both studies.

Results

The data on verbal compliance with the confederate's request confirm the effectiveness of the low-ball strategy, in that 56% (19/34) of the low-ball condition subjects made an appointment to participate, whereas only 31% (9/29) of the control condition subjects did so, $\chi^2(1) = 4.14$, $p < .05$. The superiority of the low-ball procedure was demonstrated to an even greater extent on the more important, practical measure of behavioral compliance, in that 53% (18/34) of the low-ball condition subjects who were called actually appeared at the appointed time as compared to only 24% (7/29) of the control condition subjects, $\chi^2(1) = 5.40$, $p < .024$. A high percentage of subjects in both conditions who complied verbally with the request complied behaviorally as well; this percentage was somewhat, but not significantly, higher in the low-ball condition, 95% (18/19) versus 79% (7/9). There were no significant differences due to sex of subject.

Discussion

The results of our analogue of the low-ball technique indicate that the sequence of obtaining an active decision from a target person to perform an action and only then providing information about the full costs of the action is an effective way to produce compliance with a request to perform the fully described action. Armed with such evidence from controlled, experimental procedures, our confidence that the low-ball strategy does really work and is not merely a sales myth can be increased. Given that increased confidence, the next step in the examination of the technique would seem to be the demonstration of its generality to a naturalistic context unlike that of Experiment 1. That is, although Experiment 1 was a field study and the experimenter was blind to the hypothesis, the study did use as subjects introductory psychology students who interacted with a requester whom they perceived as an experimenter; consequently, experimental demand influences (Orne, 1962) may conceivably have been implicated. Further, if the technique is cross-situationally robust, it should induce compliance in settings and with types of behavior quite unlike those to which it is customarily applied; for example, in contrast to the typical sales context, we should be able to establish the tactic's effectiveness in a charity context and on altruistic action. To these ends, it was decided to conduct a second study that was wholly unrelated, in the subject's mind, to psychological experimentation and that used a form of benevolence as the target behavior.

Another purpose of Experiment 2 was to provide evidence that the low-ball technique was different from an established compliance tactic that could be seen as similar, if not identical, to low-balling. That is, it might be argued that the low-ball sequence in which a requester secures an active decision to perform a target behavior and then raises the cost of performing the behavior is just a version of the foot-in-the-door procedure (Freedman & Fraser, 1966). A requester uses the foot-in-the-door technique by inducing an individual to perform an initial favor and subsequently asking that individual to comply with a larger, second request. While both techniques seek to gain performance of a costly action by first obtaining accession to an apparently less costly request, there is at least one important difference. With the low-ball tactic, the behavior requested initially (e.g., buying a certain car, participating in a certain experiment) is in fact the target behavior; only the cost of carrying out that specific behavior changes. With the foot-in-the-door procedure, the behavior requested initially may be related to the larger favor desired by the requester, but it is not the target behavior itself. . . .

EXPERIMENT 2

Method

Subjects and procedure.   Subjects were 30 male graduate students who resided in dormitory rooms at a large state university and who were contacted in their rooms by a college-age male experimenter posing as a United Way worker.

When subjects answered the experimenter's knock at their doors, the experimenter introduced himself uniformly as follows:

> Hi, my name is _____, and I'm working with the United Way. I'm going around asking people to display United Way posters for us.

At this point, the experimental script differed in accord with the randomly alternated set of procedures designed to obtain performance of the target behavior. The target behavior sought from each subject was the display of a pair of United Way posters.

Control condition.   Control subjects learned from the outset that agreeing to display the posters would require that they procure a "poster packet" at the downstairs dorm desk within an hour of experimental contact. After the standard introduction, the experimenter shuffled through his briefcase and announced:

> I don't have any posters with me now; I must have given my last one to the last person I talked with. But there are packets at the dorm desk downstairs which contain a window poster and a door poster. They'll only be there for the next hour; then they'll be taken to another area. Would you be willing to pick up a packet within the hour and put a poster on your window and one on the outside of your door and leave them up for a week?

Low-ball condition.   Subjects experiencing the low-ball procedures were first asked to display the posters. Those who agreed were then informed that they would have to pick up the posters downstairs within an hour. Thus, after the standard introduction, the experimenter continued, "Would you put up a pair of United Way posters?" If the subject said, "No," he was thanked and the experimenter left; if the subject said, "Yes," the experimenter shuffled through his briefcase and announced:

> I don't have any posters with me now; I must have given my last one to the last person I talked with. But, if you still want to do this, there are packets at the dorm desk downstairs which contain a window poster and a door poster.

The remainder of the script was identical to that of the control condition.

Foot-in-the-door condition.   Subjects in the foot-in-the-door condition initially complied with the request to accept for display a window poster that the experimenter carried with him; they were then asked to perform the more costly target behavior requiring a trip to the downstairs desk within the hour. Thus, after giving the standard introduction, the experimenter continued, "Would you put up a United Way window poster?" All subjects agreed and were provided with a poster. "Thanks. We're also asking people to help by putting up a door poster." The experimenter shuffled through his briefcase and announced:

> I don't have any door posters with me now; I must have given my last one to the last person I talked with. But there are packets at the dorm desk downstairs which contain a door poster.

The remainder of the script was identical to the control condition.

249

Robert B.
Cialdini et al.

Results

A high and approximately equal percentage of verbal compliance occurred across all conditions. With 10 subjects per group, 80% of the subjects in the low-ball condition and 70% of the subjects in the other two conditions agreed to display the posters after being informed of the full cost of so doing. Our major interest, however, concerned performance of the target behavior, which was measured the following day as the percentage of subjects' rooms displaying the posters. It was on this measure of behavioral compliance that the superiority of the low-ball technique asserted itself clearly. We had hypothesized that the greatest performance of the target behavior would occur in the low-ball condition. That expectation was supported by a contrast that pitted behavioral compliance in the low-ball condition(6/10) against that in the combination of the foot-in-the-door (1/10) and control (2/10) conditions; by Fisher exact test, $p < .02$. Further, the superiority of the low-ball treatment maintained itself when only those subjects who verbally complied were considered; that is, 75% (6/8) of verbally compliant subjects in the low-ball condition complied behaviorally, whereas substantially fewer, 28.6% (2/7) and 14.3% (1/7), did so in the control and foot-in-the-door conditions, respectively; by Fisher exact test, $p < .025$. It was also our expectation that the foot-in-the-door condition subjects would show more compliance than the control condition subjects. The difference between those conditions, as tested by a second orthogonal contrast, was clearly nonsignificant and slightly opposite to the predicted direction.

Discussion

The results of Experiment 2 provide evidence of the effectiveness of the low-ball procedure in a novel and naturalistic context. Charitable action, a form of behavior quite unlike the target behaviors to which the tactic is standardly applied, was significantly influenced by the technique in a setting that did not contain (for the subject) the experimental trappings present in Experiment 1. It appears, then, that the low-ball technique has some robustness across target behaviors as well as power in naturalistic situations.

In addition to investigating the generality of the low-ball tactic, a second purpose of Experiment 2 was to determine whether and how it differed from the foot-in-the-door technique. We hypothesized that more performance of the target behavior would occur from the low-ball strategy because it initially induced subjects to decide to enact the target behavior itself rather than a different, though related, behavior. Such a decision was thought to produce a cognitive commitment to the performance of the target behavior that would manifest itself in especially high levels of compliance. Of the two types of compliance measured in the study, it was only in behavioral compliance that the low-ball procedure proved to be clearly superior. The failure of either experimental compliance technique to elicit substantially greater verbal compliance than the control procedure is probably best interpreted as the result of a ceiling effect caused by the very high level of baseline verbal compliance (70%) that occurred in the control condition.

REFERENCES

Carlson, M. D. *How to get your car repaired without getting gypped.* New York: Harrow Books (Harper & Row), 1973.

Consumer Reports, May 1974, *39,* 368.

Freedman, J. L., & Fraser, S. Compliance without pressure: The foot-in-the-door technique. *Journal of Personality and Social Psychology,* 1966, *4,* 195–202.

Orne, M. T. On the social psychology of the psychology experiment: With particular reference to demand characteristics and their implications. *American Psychologist,* 1962, *17,* 776–783.

CHAPTER 11 Group Behavior

11.1 ROBERT B. ZAJONC

Social Facilitation

For many years social psychologists have been interested in the fact that our behavior is sometimes different in front of a group than when we are alone. Sometimes our performance improves when we have an audience, while at other times it deteriorates. In 1965 social psychologist Robert B. Zajonc proposed a motivational drive theory of social facilitation to explain these differences.

Zajonc earned his Ph.D. in psychology in 1955 from the University of Michigan, where he spent most of his professional career. He was a professor of psychology and director of the university's Institute for Social Research until 1992, when he moved to Stanford University. Zajonc has made numerous contributions to social psychology in the fields of social cognition, motivation, and emotion. His theory of social facilitation has generated numerous research studies since it was first published.

This selection is from "Social Facilitation," which was published in *Science* in 1965. Zajonc's theory states that the presence of others causes an increase in arousal, which contributes to an increase in the dominant (most likely) response. What are some applications of this theory? How would you apply this theory to predict whether your behavior would improve or deteriorate in any particular situation?

Key Concept: social facilitation

APA Citation: Zajonc, R. B. (1965). Social facilitation. *Science, 149,* 269–274.

Most textbook definitions of social psychology involve considerations about the influence of man upon man, or, more generally, of individual upon individual. And most of them, explicitly or implicitly, commit the main efforts of social psychology to the problem of how and why the *behavior* of one individual affects the behavior of another. The influences of individuals on each others' behavior which are of interest to social psychologists today take on very complex forms. Often they involve vast networks of interindividual effects, such as one finds in studying the process of group decision-making, competition, or conformity to a group norm. But the fundamental forms of interindividual influence are represented by the oldest experimental paradigm of social psychology: social facilitation. This paradigm, dating back to Triplett's original experiments on pacing and competition, carried out in 1897 (1), examines the consequences upon behavior which derive from the sheer presence of other individuals.

Until the late 1930's, interest in social facilitation was quite active, but with the outbreak of World War II it suddenly died. And it is truly regrettable that it died, because the basic questions about social facilitation—its dynamics and its causes—which are in effect the basic questions of social psychology, were never solved. It is with these questions that this article is concerned. I first examine past results in this nearly completely abandoned area of research and then suggest a general hypothesis which might explain them.

Research in the area of social facilitation may be classified in terms of two experimental paradigms: audience effects and co-action effects. The first experimental paradigm involves the observation of behavior when it occurs in the presence of passive spectators. The second examines behavior when it occurs in the presence of other individuals also engaged in the same activity. We shall consider past literature in these two areas separately.

AUDIENCE EFFECTS

Simple motor responses are particularly sensitive to social facilitation effects. In 1925 Travis (2) obtained such effects in a study in which he used the pursuit-rotor task. In this task the subject is required to follow a small revolving target by means of a stylus which he holds in his hand. If the stylus is even momentarily off target during a revolution, the revolution counts as an error. First each subject was trained for several consecutive days until his performance reached a stable level. One day after the conclusion of the training the subject was called to the laboratory, given five trials alone, and then ten trials in the presence of from four to eight upperclassmen and graduate students. They had been asked by the experimenter to watch the subject quietly and attentively. Travis found a clear improvement in performance when his subjects were confronted with an audience. Their accuracy on the ten trials before an audience was greater than on any ten previous trials, including those on which they had scored highest.

A considerably greater improvement in performance was recently obtained in a somewhat different setting and on a different task (3). Each subject (all were National Guard trainees) was placed in a separate booth. He was seated in front of a panel outfitted with 20 red lamps in a circle. The lamps on this panel light in a clockwise sequence at 12 revolutions per minute. At random intervals one or another light fails to go on in its proper sequence. On the average there are 24 such failures per hour. The subject's task is to signal whenever a light fails to go on. After 20 minutes of intensive training, followed by a short rest, the National Guard trainees monitored the light panels for 135 minutes. Subjects in one group performed their task alone. Subjects in another group were told that from time to time a lieutenant colonel or a master sergeant would visit them in the booth to observe their performance. These visits actually took place about four times during the experimental session. There was no doubt about the results. The accuracy of the supervised subjects was on the average 34 percent higher than the accuracy of the trainees working in isolation, and toward the end of the experimental session the accuracy of the supervised subjects was more than twice as high as that of the subjects working in isolation. Those expecting to be visited by a superior missed, during the last experimental period, 20 percent of the light failures, while those expecting no such visits missed 64 percent of the failures.

Dashiell, who, in the early 1930's, carried out an extensive program of research on social facilitation, also found considerable improvement in performance due to audience effects on such tasks as simple multiplication or word association (4). But, as is the case in many other areas, negative audience effects were also found. In 1933 Pessin asked college students to learn lists of nonsense syllables under two conditions, alone and in the presence of several spectators (5). When confronted with an audience, his subjects required an average of 11.27 trials to learn a seven-item list. When working alone they needed only 9.85 trials. The average number of errors made in the "audience" condition was considerably higher than the number in the "alone" condition. In 1931 Husband found that the presence of spectators interferes with the learning of a finger maze (6), and in 1933 Pessin and Husband (7) confirmed Husband's results. The number of trials which the isolated subjects required for learning the finger maze was 17.1. Subjects confronted with spectators, however, required 19.1 trials. The average number of errors for the isolated subjects was 33.7; the number for those working in the presence of an audience was 40.5.

The results thus far reviewed seem to contradict one another. On a pursuit-rotor task Travis found that the presence of an audience improves performance. The learning of nonsense syllables and maze learning, however, seem to be inhibited by the presence of an audience, as shown by Pessin's experiment. The picture is further complicated by the fact that when Pessin's subjects were asked, several days later, to recall the nonsense syllables they had learned, a reversal was found. The subjects who tried to recall the lists in the presence of spectators did considerably better than those who tried to recall them alone. Why are the learning of nonsense syllables and maze learning inhibited by the presence of spectators? And why, on the other hand, does performance on a pursuit-rotor, word-association, multiplication, or a vigilance task improve in the presence of others?

There is just one, rather subtle, consistency in the above results. It would appear that the emission of well-learned responses is facilitated by the presence of spectators, while the acquisition of new responses is impaired. To put the statement in conventional psychological language, performance is facilitated and learning is impaired by the presence of spectators.

This tentative generalization can be reformulated so that different features of the problem are placed into focus. During the early stages of learning, especially of the type involved in social facilitation studies, the subject's responses are mostly the wrong ones. A person learning a finger maze, or a person learning a list of nonsense syllables, emits more wrong responses than right ones in the early stages of training. Most learning experiments continue until he ceases to make mistakes—until his performance is perfect. It may be said, therefore, that during training it is primarily the wrong responses which are dominant and strong; they are the ones which have the highest probability of occurrence. But after the individual has mastered the task, correct responses necessarily gain ascendency in his task-relevant behavioral repertoire. Now they are the ones which are more probable—in other words, dominant. Our tentative generalization may now be simplified: audience enhances the emission of dominant responses. If the dominant responses are the correct ones, as is the case upon achieving mastery, the presence of an audience will be of benefit to the individual. But if they are mostly wrong, as is the case in the early stages of learning, then these wrong responses will be enhanced in the presence of an audience, and the emission of correct responses will be postponed or prevented.

There is a class of psychological processes which are known to enhance the emission of dominant responses. They are subsumed under the concepts of drive, arousal, and activation (8). If we could show that the presence of an audience has arousal consequences for the subject, we would be a step further along in trying to arrange the results of social-facilitation experiments into a neater package. But let us first consider another set of experimental findings.

CO-ACTION EFFECTS

The experimental paradigm of co-action is somewhat more complex than the paradigm involved in the study of audience effects. Here we observe individuals all simultaneously engaged in the same activity and in full view of each other. One of the clearest effects of such simultaneous action, or co-action, is found in eating behavior. It is well known that animals simply eat more in the presence of others. For instance, Bayer had chickens eat from a pile of wheat to their full satisfaction (9). He waited some time to be absolutely sure that his subject would eat no more, and then brought in a companion chicken who had not eaten for 24 hours. Upon the introduction of the hungry co-actor, the apparently sated chicken ate two-thirds again as much grain as it had already eaten. Recent work by Tolman and Wilson fully substantiates these results (10). In an extensive study of social-facilitation effects among albino rats, Harlow found dramatic increases in eating (11). In one of his experiments, for instance, the rats, shortly after weaning, were matched in pairs for weight. They were then fed alone and in pairs on alternate days. It is clear that considerably more food was consumed by the animals when they were in pairs than when they were fed alone. James (*12*), too, found very clear evidence of increased eating among puppies fed in groups. . . .

The experiments on social facilitation performed by Floyd Allport in 1920 and continued by Dashiell in 1930 (*4, 13*), both of whom used human subjects, are the ones best known. Allport's subjects worked either in separate cubicles or sitting around a common table. When working in isolation they did the various tasks at the same time and were monitored by common time signals. Allport did everything possible to reduce the tendency to compete. The subjects were told that the results of their tests would not be compared and would not be shown to other staff members, and that they themselves should refrain from making any such comparisons.

Among the tasks used were the following: chain word association, vowel cancellation, reversible perspective, multiplication, problem solving, and judgments of odors and weights. The results of Allport's experiments are well known: in all but the problem-solving and judgments test, performance was better in groups than in the "alone" condition. How do these results fit our generalization? Word association, multiplication, the cancellation of vowels, and the reversal of the perceived orientation of an ambiguous figure all involve responses which are well established. They are responses which are either very well learned or under a very strong influence of the stimulus, as in the word-association task or the reversible-perspective test. The problem-solving test consists of disproving arguments of ancient philosophers. In contrast to the other tests, it does not involve well-learned responses. On the contrary, the probability of wrong (that is, logically incorrect) responses on tasks of this sort is rather high; in other words, wrong responses are dominant. Of interest, however, is the finding that while intellectual work suffered in the group situation, sheer output of words was increased. When working together, Allport's subjects tended consistently to write more. Therefore, the generalization proposed in the previous section can again be applied: if the presence of others raises the probability of dominant responses, and if strong (and many) incorrect response tendencies prevail, then the presence of others can only be detrimental to performance. The results of the judgment tests have little bearing on the present argument, since Allport gives no accuracy figures for evaluating performance. The data reported only show that the presence of others was associated with the avoidance of extreme judgments.

In 1928 Travis (*14*), whose work on the pursuit rotor I have already noted, repeated Allport's chain-word-association experiment. In contrast to Allport's results, Travis found that the presence of others decreased performance. The number of associations given by his subjects was greater when they worked in isolation. It is very significant, however, that Travis used stutterers as his subjects. In a way, stuttering is a manifestation of a struggle between conflicting response tendencies, all of which are strong and all of which compete for expression. The stutterer, momentarily hung up in the middle of a sentence, waits for the correct response to reach full ascendancy. He stammers because other competing tendencies are dominant at that moment. It is reasonable to assume that, to the extent that the verbal habits of a stutterer are characterized by conflicting response tendencies, the presence of others, by enhancing each of these response tendencies, simply heightens his conflict. Performance is thus impaired. . . .

THE PRESENCE OF OTHERS AS A SOURCE OF AROUSAL

The results I have discussed thus far lead to one generalization and to one hypothesis. The generalization which organizes these results is that the presence of others, as spectators or as co-actors, enhances the emission of dominant responses. We also know from extensive research literature that arousal, activation, or drive all have as a consequence the enhancement of dominant responses (15). We now need to examine the hypothesis that the presence of others increases the individual's general arousal or drive level.

The evidence which bears on the relationship between the presence of others and arousal is, unfortunately, only indirect. But there is some very suggestive evidence in one area of research. One of the more reliable indicators of arousal and drive is the activity of the endocrine systems in general, and of the adrenal cortex in particular. Adrenocortical functions are extremely sensitive to changes in emotional arousal, and it has been known for some time that organisms subjected to prolonged stress are likely to manifest substantial adrenocortical hypertrophy (16). Recent work (17) has shown that the main biochemical component of the adrenocortical output is hydrocortisone (17-hydroxycorticosterone). Psychiatric patients characterized by anxiety states, for instance, show elevated plasma levels of hydrocortisone (18). . . .

SUMMARY AND CONCLUSION

If one were to draw one practical suggestion from the review of the social-facilitation effects which are summarized in this article he would advise the student to study all alone, preferably in an isolated cubicle, and to arrange to take his examinations in the company of many other students, on stage, and in the presence of a large audience. The results of his examination would be beyond his wildest expectations, provided, of course, he had learned his material quite thoroughly.

I have tried in this article to pull together the early, almost forgotten work on social facilitation, and to explain the seemingly conflicting results. This explanation is, of course, tentative, and it has never been put to a direct experimental test. It is, moreover, not far removed from the one originally proposed by Allport. He theorized (19, p. 261) that "the sights and sounds of others doing the same thing" augment ongoing responses. Allport, however, proposed this effect only for *overt* motor responses, assuming (19, p. 274) that "*intellectual* or *implicit responses* of thought are hampered rather than facilitated" by the presence of others. This latter conclusion was probably suggested to him by the negative results he observed in his research on the effects of co-action on problem solving.

Robert B. Zajonc

REFERENCES

1. N. Triplett, *Amer. J. Psychol.* **9,** 507 (1897).
2. L. E. Travis, *J. Abnormal Soc. Psychol.* **20,** 142 (1925).
3. B. O. Bergum and D. J. Lehr, *J. Appl. Psychol.* **47,** 75 (1963).
4. J. F. Dashiell, *J. Abnormal Soc. Psychol.* **25,** 190 (1930).
5. J. Pessin, *Amer. J. Psychol.* **45,** 263 (1933).
6. R. W. Husband, *J. Genet. Psychol.* **39,** 258 (1931). In this task the blindfolded subject traces a maze with his finger.
7. J. Pessin and R. W. Husband, *J. Abnormal Soc. Psychol.* **28,** 148 (1933).
8. See, for instance, E. Dufy, *Activation and Behavior* (Wiley, New York, 1962); K. W. Spence, *Behavior Theory and Conditioning* (Yale Univ. Press, New Haven, 1956); R. B. Zajonc and B. Nieuwenhuyse, *J. Exp. Psychol.* **67,** 276 (1964).
9. E. Bayer, *Z. Psychol.* **112,** 1 (1929).
10. C. W. Tolman and G. T. Wilson, *Animal Behavior* **13,** 134 (1965).
11. H. F. Harlow, *J. Genet. Psychol.* **43,** 211 (1932).
12. W. T. James, *J. Comp. Physiol. Psychol.* **46,** 427 (1953); *J. Genet. Psychol.* **96,** 123 (1960); W. T. James and D. J. Cannon, *ibid.* **87,** 225 (1956).
13. F. H. Allport, *J. Exp. Psychol.* **3,** 159 (1920).
14. L. E. Travis, *J. Abnormal Soc. Psychol.* **23,** 45 (1928).
15. See K. W. Spence, *Behavior Theory and Conditioning* (Yale Univ. Press, New Haven, 1956).
16. H. Selye, *J. Clin. Endocrin.* **6,** 117 (1946).
17. D. H. Nelson and L. T. Samuels, *ibid.* **12,** 519 (1952).
18. E. L. Bliss, A. A. Sandberg, D. H. Nelson, *J. Clin. Invest.* **32,** 9 (1953); F. Board, H. Persky, D. A. Hamburg, *Psychosom. Med.* **18,** 324 (1956).
19. F. H. Allport, *Social Psychology* (Houghton-Mifflin, Boston, 1924).

11.2 BIBB LATANÉ, KIPLING WILLIAMS, AND STEPHEN HARKINS

Many Hands Make Light the Work

Although groups can often be more effective than individuals working alone, sometimes the members of the group do not work as hard as they do when they are alone. This phenomenon, called social loafing, has been studied extensively by Bibb Latané, Kipling Williams, and Stephen Harkins at Ohio State University.

Latané (b. 1937) earned his degree in social psychology from the University of Minnesota in 1963. He taught at Columbia University, Ohio State University, and the University of North Carolina before accepting his current position at Florida Atlantic University in 1989. Williams (b. 1953) earned his Ph.D. in social psychology from Ohio State University in 1981 and is currently at the University of Toledo. Harkins earned his Ph.D. at the University of Missouri in 1975. He taught at Ohio State University before accepting his current position at Northeastern University.

This selection is from "Many Hands Make Light the Work: The Causes and Consequences of Social Loafing," which was published in the *Journal of Personality and Social Psychology* in 1979. Latané, Williams, and Harkins tested their social impact theory by conducting an experiment that compared the efforts of students as they clapped or cheered either individually or in groups. The results showed a significant decrease in individual effort among the groups. According to Latané and his colleagues, this instance of social loafing occurred because when members of a group perceive themselves as sharing responsibility equally, each individual performs at a reduced rate. As you read this selection, think of other examples of social loafing in everyday life.

Key Concept: social loafing

APA Citation: Latané, B., Williams, K., and Harkins, S. (1979). Many hands make light the work: The causes and consequences of social loafing. *Journal of Personality and Social Psychology, 37*, 822–832.

*T*wo experiments found that when asked to perform the physically exerting tasks of clapping and shouting, people exhibit a sizable decrease in individual effort *when performing in groups as compared to when they perform alone. This decrease, which we call social loafing, is in addition to losses due to faulty coordination of group efforts. Social loafing is discussed in terms of its experimental generality and theoretical importance. The widespread occurrence, the negative consequences for society, and some conditions that can minimize social loafing are also explored.*

There is an old saying that "many hands make light the work." This saying is interesting for two reasons. First, it captures one of the promises of social life—that with social organization people can fulfill their individual goals more easily through collective action. When many hands are available, people often do not have to work as hard as when only a few are present. The saying is interesting in a second, less hopeful way—it seems that when many hands are available, people actually work less hard than they ought to.

Over 50 years ago a German psychologist named Ringelmann did a study that he never managed to get published. In rare proof that unpublished work does not necessarily perish, the results of that study, reported only in summary form in German by Moede (1927), have been cited by Dashiell (1935), Davis (1969), Köhler (1927), and Zajonc (1966) and extensively analyzed by Steiner (1966, 1972) and Ingham, Levinger, Graves, and Peckham (1974). Apparently Ringelmann simply asked German workers to pull as hard as they could on a rope, alone or with one, two, or seven other people, and then he used a strain gauge to measure how hard they pulled in kilograms of pressure.

Rope pulling is, in Steiner's (1972) useful classification of tasks, maximizing, unitary, and additive. In a maximizing task, success depends on how much or how rapidly something is accomplished and presumably on how much effort is expended, as opposed to an optimizing task, in which precision, accuracy, or correctness [is] paramount. A unitary task cannot be divided into separate subtasks—all members work together doing the same thing and no division of labor is possible. In an additive task, group success depends on the *sum* of the individual efforts, rather than on the performance of any subset of members. From these characteristics, we should expect three people pulling together on a rope with perfect efficiency to be able to exert three times as much force as one person can, and eight people to exert eight times as much force.

Ringelmann's results, however, were strikingly different. When pulling one at a time individuals averaged a very respectable 63 kg of pressure. Groups of three people were able to exert a force of 160 kg, only two and a half times the average individual performance, and groups of eight pulled at 248 kg, less than four times the solo rate. Thus the collective group performance, while increasing somewhat with group size, was substantially less than the sum of the individual efforts, with dyads pulling at 93% of the sum of their individual efforts, trios at 85%, and groups of eight at only 49%. In a way somewhat different from how the old saw would have it, many hands apparently made light the work.

The Ringelmann effect is interesting because it seems to violate both common stereotype and social psychological theory. Common stereotype tells us that the sense of team participation leads to increased effort, that group morale and cohesiveness spur individual enthusiasm, that by pulling together groups can achieve any goal, that in unity there is strength. Social psychological theory holds that, at least for simple, well-learned tasks involving dominant responses, the presence of other people, whether as co-workers or spectators, should facilitate performance. It is thus important to find out whether Ringelmann's effect is replicable and whether it can be obtained with other tasks....

EXPERIMENT 1

Clap Your Hands and Shout Out Loud

One of the disadvantages of Ringelmann's rope pulling task is that the equipment and procedures are relatively cumbersome and inefficient. Therefore, we decided to keep our ears open for other tasks that would allow us to replicate the Ringelmann finding conceptually and would provide the basis for extended empirical and theoretical analysis. We chose cheering and clapping, two activities that people commonly do together in social settings and that are maximizing, unitary, and additive. As with rope pulling, output can be measured in simple physical units that make up a ratio scale.

Method

On eight separate occasions, groups of six undergraduate males were recruited from introductory psychology classes at Ohio State University; they were seated in a semicircle, 1 m apart, in a large soundproofed laboratory and told, "We are interested in judgments of how much noise people make in social settings, namely cheering and applause, and how loud they seem to those who hear them. Thus, we want each of you to do two things: (1) Make noises, and (2) judge noises." They were told that on each trial "the experimenter will tell you the trial number, who is to perform and whether you are to cheer (Rah!) or clap. When you are to begin, the experimenter will count backwards from three and raise his hand. Continue until he lowers it. We would like you to clap or cheer for 5 seconds as loud as you can." On each trial, both the performers and the observers were also asked to make magnitude estimates of how much noise had been produced (Stevens, 1966). Since these data are not relevant to our concerns, we will not mention them further.

After some practice at both producing and judging noise, there were 36 trials of yelling and 36 trials of clapping. Within each modality, each person performed twice alone, four times in pairs, four times in groups of four, and six times in groups of six. These frequencies were chosen as a compromise between equating the number of occasions on which we measured people making noise alone or in groups (which would have required more noisemaking in fours and sixes) and equating the number of individual performances contributing to our measurements in the various group sizes (which would have required more noisemaking by individuals and pairs). We also arranged the sequence of performances to space and counterbalance the order of conditions over each block of 36 trials, while making sure that no one had to perform more than twice in a row.

Performances were measured with a General Radio sound-level meter, Model 1565A, using the C scale and the slow time constant, which was placed exactly 4 m away from each performer. The C scale was used so that sounds varying only in frequency or pitch would be recorded as equally loud. Sound-level meters are read in decibel (dB) units, which are intended to approximate the human reaction to sound. For our purposes, however, the appropriate measure is the effort used in generating noise, not how loud it sounds. Therefore, our results are presented in terms of dynes/cm^2, the physical unit of work involved in producing sound pressure.

Because people shouted and clapped in full view and earshot of each other, each person's performance could affect and be affected by the others. For this reason, the group, rather than the individual, was the unit of analysis, and each score was based on the average output per person. Results were analyzed in a $4 \times 2 \times 2$ analysis of variance, with Group Size (1, 2, 4, 6), Response Mode (clapping vs. shouting), and Replications (1, 2) as factors.

Results

Participants seemed to adapt to the task with good humor if not great enthusiasm. Nobody refused to clap or shout, even though a number seemed somewhat embarrassed or shy about making these noises in public. Despite this, they did manage to produce a good deal of noise. Individuals averaged 84 dB (C) clapping and 87 dB cheering, while groups of six clapped at 91 dB and shouted at 95dB (an increment of 6 dB represents a doubling of sound pressure).

As might be expected, the more people clapping or cheering together, the more intense the noise and the more the sound pressure produced. However, it did not grow in proportion to the number of people: The average sound pressure generated *per person* decreased with increasing group size, $F(3, 21) = 41.5$, $p < .001$. People averaged about 3.7 dynes/cm^2 alone, 2.6 in pairs, 1.8 in four-somes, and about 1.5 in groups of six (Figure 1). Put another way, two-person groups performed at only 71% of the sum of their individual capacity, four-person groups at 51%, and six-person groups at 40%. As in pulling ropes, it appears that when it comes to clapping and shouting out loud, many hands do, in fact, make light the work.

People also produced about 60% more sound power when they shouted than when they clapped, $F(1, 7) = 8.79$, $p < .01$, presumably reflecting physical capacity rather than any psychological process. There was no effect due to blocks of trials, indicating that the subjects needed little or no practice and that their performance was not deleteriously affected by fatigue. In addition, there were no interactions among the variables.

Discussion

The results provide a strong replication of Ringelmann's original findings, using a completely different task and in a different historical epoch and culture.

FIGURE 1

Intensity of Noise as a Function of Group Size and Response Mode, Experiment 1

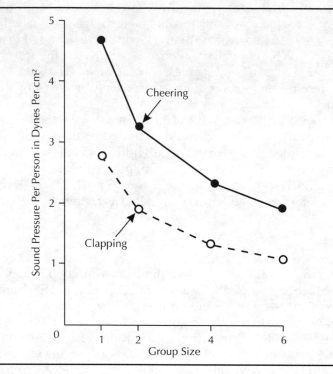

At least when people are making noise as part of a task imposed by someone else, voices raised together do not seem to be raised as much as voices raised alone, and the sound of 12 hands clapping is not even three times as intense as the sound of 2.

Zajonc's (1965) elegant theory of social facilitation suggests that people are aroused by the mere presence of others and are thus likely to work harder (though not necessarily to achieve more) when together. Although social facilitation theory might seem to predict enhanced group performance on a simple task like clapping or shouting, in the present case it would not predict any effect due to group size, since the number of people present was always eight, six participants and two experimenters. Evaluation apprehension theory (Cottrell, 1972) would also not predict any effect as long as it is assumed that coactors and audience members are equally effective in arousing performance anxiety. Therefore, these theories are not inconsistent with our position that an unrelated social process is involved. The results of Experiment 1 also can be taken as support for Latané's (1973) theory of social impact: The impact that the experimenters have on an individual seems to decrease as the number of coperformers increases, leading to an apparent drop in individual performance, a phenomenon we call social loafing. . . .

GENERAL DISCUSSION

The Causes of Social Loafing

The present research shows that groups can inhibit the productivity of individuals so that people reduce their exertions when it comes to shouting and clapping with others. Why does this occur? We suggest three lines of explanation, the first having to do with attribution and equity, the second with submaximal goal setting, and the third with the lessening of the contingency between individual inputs and outcomes.

1. Attribution and Equity. It may be that participants engaged in a faulty attribution process, leading to an attempt to maintain an equitable division of labor. There are at least three aspects of the physics and psychophysics of producing sound that could have led people to believe that the other persons in their group were not working as hard or effectively as themselves. First, individuals judged their own outputs to be louder than those of the others, simply because they were closer to the sound source. Second, even if everyone worked to capacity, sound cancellation would cause group outputs to seem much less than the sum of their individual performances. Finally, the perception of the amount of sound produced in a group should be much less than the actual amount—growing only as the .67 power of the actual amount of sound, according to Stevens's psychophysical power law (1975).

These factors may have led individuals to believe that the other participants were less motivated or less skillful than themselves—in short, were shirkers or incompetents. Thus, differences in the perception of sound production that were essentially the result of physical and psychophysical processes may have been mistakenly attributed to a lack of either skill or motivation on the part of the others, leading individuals to produce less sound in groups because there is no reason to work hard in aid of shirkers or those who are less competent. . . .

2. Submaximal Goal Setting. It may be that despite our instructions, participants redefined the task and adopted a goal, not of making as much noise as possible, but merely of making enough noise or of matching some more or less well-defined standard. Individuals would clearly expect it to be easier to achieve this goal when others are helping, and might work less hard as a consequence. This, of course, would change the nature of noise production from what Steiner (1972) would term a *maximizing* task to an *optimizing* task. A maximizing

263

task makes success a function of how much or how rapidly something is accomplished. For an optimizing task, however, success is a function of how closely the individual or group approximates a predetermined "best" or correct outcome. If participants in our experiments perceived sound production as an optimizing rather than a maximizing task, they might feel the optimal level of sound output could be reached more easily in groups than alone, thereby allowing them to exert less effort....

3. Lessened Contingency Between Input and Outcome. It may be that participants felt that the contingency between their input and the outcome was lessened when performing in groups. Individuals could "hide in the crowd" (Davis, 1969) and avoid the negative consequences of slacking off, or they may have felt "lost in the crowd" and unable to obtain their fair share of the positive consequences for working hard. Since individual scores are unidentifiable when groups perform together, people can receive neither precise credit nor appropriate blame for their performance. Only when performing alone can individual outputs be exactly evaluated and rewarded....

Social Loafing and Social Impact Theory

Each of these three lines of explanation may be described in terms of Latané's (1973) theory of social impact. If a person is the target of social forces, increasing the number of other persons also in the target group should diminish the pressures on each individual because the impact is divided among the group members. In a group performance situation in which pressures to work come from outside the group and individual outputs are not identifiable, this division of impact should lead each individual to work less hard. Thus, whether the subject is dividing up the amount of work he thinks should be performed or whether he is dividing up the amount of reward he expects to earn with his work, he should work less hard in groups....

Social Loafing as a Social Disease

Although some people still think science should be value free, we must confess that we think social loafing can be regarded as a kind of social disease. It is a "disease" in that it has negative consequences for individuals, social institutions, and societies. Social loafing results in a reduction in human efficiency, which leads to lowered profits and lowered benefits for all. It is "social" in that it results from the presence or actions of other people.

The "cure," however, is not to do away with groups, because despite their inefficiency, groups make possible the achievement of many goals that individuals alone could not possibly accomplish. Collective action is a vital aspect of our lives: From time immemorial it has made possible the construction of monuments, but today it is necessary to the provision of even our food and shelter. We think the cure will come from finding ways of channeling social forces so that the group can serve as a means of intensifying individual responsibility rather than diffusing it.

REFERENCES

Cottrell, N. Social facilitation. In C. McClintock (Ed.), *Experimental social psychology*. New York: Holt, Rinehart & Winston, 1972.

Dashiell, J. F. Experimental studies of the influence of social situations on the behavior of individual human adults. In C. Murchison (Ed.), *A handbook of social psychology*. Worcester, Mass.: Clark University Press, 1935.

Davis, J. H. *Group performance*. Reading, Mass.: Addison-Wesley, 1969.

Ingham, A. G., Levinger, G., Graves, J., & Peckham, V. The Ringelmann effect: Studies of group size and group performance. *Journal of Experimental Social Psychology*, 1974, *10*, 371–384.

Köhler, O. Ueber den Gruppenwirkungsgrad der menschlichen Körperarbeit und die Bedingung optimaler Kollektivkroftreaktion. *Industrielle Psychotechnik*, 1927, *4*, 209–226.

Latané, B. *A theory of social impact*. St. Louis, Mo.: Psychonomic Society, 1973.

Moede, W. Die Richtlinien der Leistungs-Psychologie. *Industrielle Psychotechnik*, 1927, *4*, 193–207.

Steiner, I. D. Models for inferring relationships between group size and potential group productivity. *Behavioral Science*, 1966, *11*, 273–283.

Steiner, I. D. *Group process and productivity*. New York: Academic Press, 1972.

Stevens, S. S. A metric for the social consensus. *Science*, 1966, *151*, 530–541.

Stevens, S. S. *Psychophysics: Introduction to its perceptual, neural and social prospects*. New York: Wiley, 1975.

Zajonc, R. B. Social facilitation. *Science*, 1965, *149*, 269–274.

Zajonc, R. B. *Social psychology: An experimental approach*. Belmont, Calif.: Brooks/Cole, 1966.

The Effect of Threat Upon Interpersonal Bargaining

Bargaining is an important aspect of many interpersonal relationships, from marriage partners to national governments. Social psychologists have studied cooperation and competition in laboratory game simulations of bargaining situations. Morton Deutsch and Robert M. Krauss developed the "trucking game" to explore the influence of threat upon interpersonal bargaining.

Deutsch (b. 1920) received his Ph.D. in social psychology from the Massachusetts Institute of Technology in 1948. He held positions at New York University and Bell Telephone Laboratories before accepting his current position as a professor of psychology at Columbia University in 1963. Krauss (b. 1931) earned his Ph.D. in social psychology from New York University in 1964. He is currently a professor of psychology at Columbia University.

This selection is from "The Effect of Threat Upon Interpersonal Bargaining," which was published in 1960 in the *Journal of Abnormal and Social Psychology*. In it, the authors describe a game in which players could cooperate and earn money. However, the experimenters found that when players threatened each other, the majority of their time was spent competing. How might the results of this game apply to bargaining situations? What might be done to reduce conflict and competition and promote cooperation in bargaining situations?

Key Concept: threat and interpersonal bargaining

APA Citation: Deutsch, M., and Krauss, R. M. (1960). The effect of threat upon interpersonal bargaining. *Journal of Abnormal and Social Psychology, 61*, 181–189.

A bargain is defined in *Webster's Unabridged Dictionary* as "an agreement between parties settling what each shall give and receive in a transaction between them"; it is further specified that a bargain is "an agreement or compact viewed as advantageous or the reverse." When the term "agreement" is broadened to include tacit, informal agreements as well as explicit agreements, it is evident that bargains and the processes involved in arriving at bargains ("bargaining") are pervasive characteristics of social life. . . .

Morton Deutsch and Robert M. Krauss

The essential features of a bargaining situation exist when:

1. Both parties perceive that there is the possibility of reaching an agreement in which each party would be better off, or no worse off, than if no agreement were reached.
2. Both parties perceive that there is more than one such agreement that could be reached.
3. Both parties perceive each other to have conflicting preferences or opposed interests with regard to the different agreements that might be reached.

Everyday examples of bargaining include such situations as: the buyer-seller relationship when the price is not fixed, the husband and wife who want to spend an evening out together but have conflicting preferences about where to go, union-management negotiations, drivers who meet at an intersection when there is no clear right of way, disarmament negotiations.

In terms of our prior conceptualization of cooperation and competition (Deutsch, 1949) bargaining is thus a situation in which the participants have mixed motives toward one another: on the one hand, each has interest in cooperating so that they reach an agreement; on the other hand, they have competitive interests concerning the nature of the agreement they reach. In effect, to reach agreement the cooperative interest of the bargainers must be strong enough to overcome their competitive interests. However, agreement is not only contingent upon the *motivational* balances of cooperative to competitive interests but also upon the situational and *cognitive* factors which facilitate or hinder the recognition or invention of a bargaining agreement that reduces the opposition of interest and enhances the mutuality of interest.

These considerations lead to the formulation of two general, closely related propositions about the likelihood that a bargaining agreement will be reached.

1. Bargainers are more likely to reach an agreement, the stronger are their cooperative interests in comparison with their competitive interests.
2. Bargainers are more likely to reach an agreement, the more resources they have available for recognizing or inventing potential bargaining agreements and for communicating to one another once a potential agreement has been recognized or invented.

From these two basic propositions and additional hypotheses concerning conditions that determine the strengths of the cooperative and competitive interests and the amount of available resources, we believe it is possible to explain the ease or difficulty of arriving at a bargaining agreement. We shall not present a full statement of these hypotheses here but turn instead to a description of an experiment that relates to Proposition 1.

The experiment was concerned with the effect of the availability of threat upon bargaining in a two-person experimental bargaining game. Threat is defined as the expression of an intention to do something detrimental to the interests of another. Our experiment was guided by two assumptions about threat:

1. If there is a conflict of interest and one person is able to threaten the other, he will tend to use the threat in an attempt to force the other person to yield. This tendency should be stronger, the more irreconcilable the conflict is perceived to be.

2. If a person uses threat in an attempt to intimidate another, the threatened person (if he considers himself to be of equal or superior status) would feel hostility toward the threatener and tend to respond with counterthreat and/or increased resistance to yielding. We qualify this assumption by stating that the tendency to resist should be greater, the greater the perceived probability and magnitude of detriment to the other and the less the perceived probability and magnitude of detriment to the potential resister from the anticipated resistance to yielding.

The second assumption is based upon the view that when resistance is not seen to be suicidal or useless, to allow oneself to be intimidated, particularly by someone who does not have the right to expect deferential behavior, is to suffer a loss of social face and, hence, of self-esteem; and that the culturally defined way of maintaining self-esteem in the face of attempted intimidation is to engage in a contest for supremacy vis-à-vis the power to intimidate or, minimally, to resist intimidation. Thus, in effect, the use of threat (and if it is available to be used, there will be a tendency to use it) should strengthen the competitive interests of the bargainers in relationship to one another by introducing or enhancing the competitive struggle for self-esteem. Hence, from Proposition 1, it follows that the availability of a means of threat should make it more difficult for the bargainers to reach agreement (providing that the threatened person has some means of resisting the threat). The preceding statement is relevant to the comparison of both of our experimental conditions of threat, bilateral and unilateral (described below), with our experimental condition of nonthreat. We hypothesize that a bargaining agreement is more likely to be achieved when neither party can threaten the other, than when one or both parties can threaten the other.

Consider now the situations of bilateral threat and unilateral threat. For several reasons, a situation of bilateral threat is probably less conducive to agreement than is a condition of unilateral threat. First, the sheer likelihood that a threat will be made is greater when two people rather than one have the means of making the threat. Secondly, once a threat is made in the bilateral case it is likely to evoke counterthreat. Withdrawal of threat in the face of counterthreat probably involves more loss of face (for reasons analogous to those discussed in relation to yielding to intimidation) than does withdrawal of threat in the face of resistance to threat. Finally, in the unilateral case, although the person without the threat potential can resist and not yield to the threat,

METHOD

Procedure

Subjects (Ss) were asked to imagine that they were in charge of a trucking company, carrying merchandise over a road to a destination. For each trip completed they made $.60, minus their operating expenses. Operating expenses were calculated at the rate of one cent per second. So, for example, if it took 37 seconds to complete a particular trip, the player's profit would be $.60 − $.37 or a net profit of $.23 for that particular trip.

Each S was assigned a name, Acme or Bolt. As the "road map" (see Figure 1) indicates, both players start from separate points and go to separate destinations. At one point their paths cross. This is the section of road labeled "one lane road," which is only one lane wide, so that two trucks, heading in opposite directions, could not pass each other. If one backs up, the other can go forward, or both can back up, or both can sit there head-on without moving.

There is another way for each S to reach the destination on the map, labeled the "alternate route." The two players' paths do not cross on this route, but the alternate is 56% longer than the main route. Ss were told that they could expect to lose at least $.10 each time they used the alternate route.

At either end of the one-lane section there is a gate that is under the control of the player to whose starting point it is closest. By closing the gate, one player can prevent the other from traveling over that section of the main route. The use of the gate provides the threat potential in this game. In the bilateral threat potential condition (Two Gates) both players had gates under their control. In a second condition of unilateral threat (One Gate) Acme had control of a gate but Bolt did not. In a third condition (No Gates) neither player controlled a gate.

Ss played the game seated in separate booths placed so that they could not see each other but could see the experimenter (E). Each S had a "control panel" mounted on a 12" × 18" × 12" sloping-front cabinet. The apparatus consisted essentially of a reversible impulse counter that was pulsed by a recycling timer. When the S wanted to move her truck forward she threw a key that closed a circuit pulsing the "add" coil of the impulse counter mounted on her control panel. As the counter cumulated, S was able to determine her "position" by relating the number on her counter to reference numbers that had been written in on her road map. Similarly, when she wished to reverse, she would throw a switch that activated the "subtract" coil of her counter, thus subtracting from the total on the counter each time the timer cycled.

FIGURE 1

Subject's Road Map

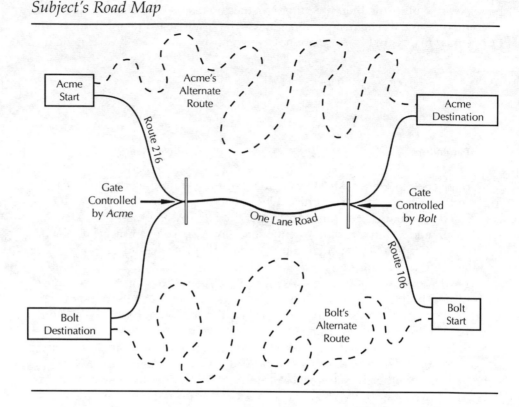

S's counter was connected in parallel to counters on the other S's panel and on E's panel. Thus each player had two counters on her panel, one representing her own position and the other representing the other player's. Provision was made in construction of the apparatus to permit cutting the other player's counter out of the circuit, so that each S knew only the position of her own truck. This was done in the present experiment. Experiments now in progress are studying the effects of knowledge of the other person's position and other aspects of interpersonal communication upon the bargaining process.

The only time one player definitely knew the other player's position was when they had met head-on on the one-way section of road. This was indicated by a traffic light mounted on the panel. When this light was on, neither player could move forward unless the other moved back. The gates were controlled by toggle switches and panel-mounted indicator lights showed, for both Ss, whether each gate was open or closed.

The following "rules of the game" were stated to the Ss:

1. A player who started out on one route and wished to switch to the other route could only do so after first reversing and going back to the start position. Direct transfer from one route to the other was not permitted except at the start position.
2. In the conditions where Ss had gates, they were permitted to close the gates no matter where they were on the main route, so long as they were on the main route (i.e., they were not permitted to close the gate while on the alternate route or after having reached their destinations). However, Ss were permitted to open their gates at any point in the game.

Ss were taken through a number of practice exercises to familiarize them with the game. In the first trial they were made to meet head-on on the one-lane path; Acme was then told to back up until she was just off the one-lane path and Bolt was told to go forward. After Bolt had gone through the one-lane path, Acme was told to go forward. Each continued going forward until each arrived at her destination. The second practice trial was the same as the first except that Bolt rather than Acme backed up after meeting head-on. In the next practice trial, one of the players was made to wait just before the one-way path while the other traversed it and then was allowed to continue. In the next practice trial, one player was made to take the alternate route and the other was made to take the main route. Finally, in the bilateral and unilateral threat conditions the use of the gate was illustrated (by having the player get on the main route, close the gate, and then go back and take the alternate route). The Ss were told explicitly, with emphasis, that they did *not* have to use the gate. Before each trial in the game the gate or gates were in the open position.

The instructions stressed an individualistic motivational orientation. Ss were told to try to earn as much money for themselves as possible and to have no interest in whether the other player made money or lost money. They were given $4.00 in poker chips to represent their working capital and told that after each trial they would be given "money" if they made a profit or that "money" would be taken from them if they lost (i.e., took more than 60 seconds to complete their trip). The profit or loss of each S was announced so that both Ss could hear the announcement after each trial. Each pair of Ss played a total of 20 trials; on all trials they started off together. In other words, each trial presented a repetition of the same bargaining problem. In cases where Ss lost their working capital before the 20 trials were completed, additional chips were given them. Ss were aware that their monetary winnings and losses were to be imaginary and that no money would change hands as a result of the experiment.

Subjects

Sixteen pairs of Ss were used in each of the three experimental conditions. The Ss were female clerical and supervisory personnel of the New Jersey Bell

FIGURE 2

Median Joint Payoff (Acme + Bolt) Over Trials

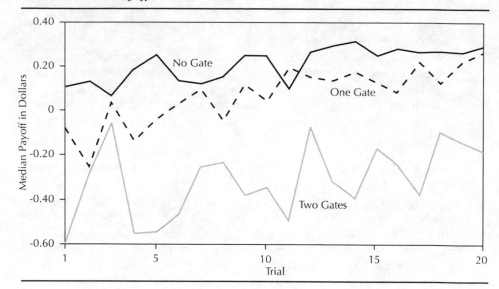

Telephone Company who volunteered to participate during their working day. Their ages ranged from 20 to 39, with a mean of 26.2....

RESULTS

The best single measure of the difficulty experienced by the bargainers in reaching an agreement is the sum of each pair's profits (or losses) on a given trial. The higher the sum of the payoffs to the two players on a given trial, the less time it took them to arrive at a procedure for sharing the one-lane path of the main route. (It was, of course, possible for one or both of the players to decide to take the alternate route so as to avoid a protracted stalemate during the process of bargaining. This, however, always resulted in at least a $.20 smaller joint payoff if only one player took the alternate route, than an optimally arrived at agreement concerning the use of the one-way path.) Figure 2 presents the medians of the summed payoffs (i.e., Acme's plus Bolt's) for all pairs in each of the three experimental conditions over the 20 trials. These striking results indicate that agreement was least difficult to arrive at in the no threat condition, was more difficult to arrive at in the unilateral threat condition, and exceedingly difficult or impossible to arrive at in the bilateral threat condition (see also Table 1).

Examination of Figure 2 suggests that learning occurred during the 20 trials: the summed payoffs for pairs of *S*s tend to improve as the number of trials increases. This suggestion is confirmed by an analysis of variance of

TABLE 1

Mean Payoffs Summated Over the Twenty Trials

Variable	Means				Statistical Comparisons: p values[a]		
	(1) No Threat	(2) Unilateral Threat	(3) Bilateral Threat	Overall	(1) vs. (2)	(1) vs. (3)	(2) vs. (3)
Summed Payoffs (Acme + Bolt)	203.31	-405.88	-875.12	.01	.01	.01	.05
Acme's Payoff	122.44	-118.56	-406.56	.01	.10	.01	.05
Bolt's Payoff	80.88	-287.31	-468.56	.01	.01	.01	.20
Absolute Differences in Payoff (A–B)	125.94	294.75	315.25	.05	.05	.01	ns[a]

[a] Evaluation of the significance of overall variation between conditions is based on an F test with 2 and 45 df. Comparisons between treatments are based on a two-tailed t test.

the slopes for the summed payoffs over the 20 trials for each of the 16 pairs in each of the 3 experimental treatments. The results of this analysis indicate that the slopes are significantly greater than zero for the unilateral threat ($p < .01$) and the no threat ($p < .02$) conditions; for the bilateral threat condition, the slope does not reach statistical significance ($.10 < p < .20$). The data indicate that the pairs in the no threat condition started off at a fairly high level but, even so, showed some improvement over the 20 trials; the pairs in the unilateral threat condition started off low and, having considerable opportunity for improvement, used their opportunity; the pairs in the bilateral threat condition, on the other hand, did not benefit markedly from repeated trials....

DISCUSSION

From our view of bargaining as a situation in which both cooperative and competitive tendencies are present and acting upon the individual, it is relevant to inquire as to the conditions under which a stable agreement of any form develops. However, implicit in most economic models of bargaining (e.g., Stone, 1958; Zeuthen, 1930) is the assumption that the cooperative interests of the bargainers are sufficiently strong to insure that some form of mutually satisfactory agreement will be reached....

In our experimental bargaining situation, the availability of threat clearly made it more difficult for bargainers to reach a mutually profitable agreement. These results, we believe, reflect psychological tendencies that are not confined to our bargaining situation: the tendency to use threat (if the means for threatening is available) in an attempt to force the other person to yield, when the other is seen as obstructing one's path; the tendency to respond with counterthreat or increased resistance to attempts at intimidation. How general are these tendencies? What conditions are likely to elicit them? Answers to these questions are necessary before our results can be generalized to other situations. . . .

SUMMARY

The nature of bargaining situations was discussed. Two general propositions about the conditions affecting the likelihood of a bargaining agreement were presented. The effects of the availability of threat upon interpersonal bargaining were investigated experimentally in a two-person bargaining game. Three experimental conditions were employed: no threat (neither player could threaten the other), unilateral threat (only one of the players had a means of threat available to her), and bilateral threat (both players could threaten each other). The results indicated that the difficulty in reaching an agreement and the amount of (imaginary) money lost, individually as well as collectively, was greatest in the bilateral and next greatest in the unilateral threat condition. Only in the no threat condition did the players make an overall profit. In the unilateral threat condition, the player with the threat capability did better than the player without the threat capability. However, comparing the bilateral and unilateral threat conditions, the results also indicate that when facing a player who had threat capability one was better off *not* having than having the capacity to retaliate in kind.

REFERENCES

Deutsch, M.   A theory of cooperation and competition. *Hum. Relat.*, 1949, **2,** 129–152.

Stone, J. J.   An experiment in bargaining games. *Econometrica*, 1958, **26,** 286–296.

Zeuthen, F.   *Problems of monopoly and economic warfare.* London: Routledge, 1930.

The Groupthink Syndrome

Although many groups can make effective decisions, sometimes their decision-making ability is diminished. Irving L. Janis studied impaired group decision making in a situation called groupthink. Groupthink occurs when the members of a group are so committed to and optimistic about the group that they feel it is invulnerable. The members are therefore so concerned with maintaining consensus that criticism is muted.

Janis (1918–1990) earned his Ph.D. from Columbia University in 1947. He then accepted a position at Yale University, where he stayed until his retirement in 1985. He published many books on the conflict theory model of decision making, including *Crucial Decisions: Leadership in Policymaking and Crisis Management* (Free Press, 1989).

This selection is from chapter 8, "The Groupthink Syndrome," in Janis's book *Groupthink: Psychological Studies of Policy Decisions and Fiascoes*, 2d ed. (Houghton Mifflin, 1982). In it, Janis describes the symptoms and consequences of groupthink. Although it is often examined in the context of political groups, groupthink also occurs in groups in everyday interactions. As you read this selection, think of situations with which you are familiar that might involve groupthink. How can groupthink be prevented?

Key Concept: groupthink

APA Citation: Janis, I. L. (1982). *Groupthink: Psychological studies of policy decisions and fiascoes* (2d ed.). Boston: Houghton Mifflin. [Chapter 8, The groupthink syndrome]

SYMPTOMS OF GROUPTHINK

The first step in developing a theory about the causes and consequences of groupthink is to anchor the concept of groupthink in observables by describing the symptoms to which it refers. Eight main symptoms run through the case studies of historic fiascoes... and are seldom present in the case studies of the nongroupthink decisions.... Each symptom can be identified by a variety of indicators, derived from historical records, observers' accounts of conversations, and participants' memoirs. The eight symptoms of groupthink include group products and processes that reinforce each other, as can be seen most clearly in the case study of the Bay of Pigs invasion plan. The symptoms can be divided into three main types, which are familiar features of many (although not all) cohesive groups observed in research on group dynamics.

Type I: Overestimations of the Group—Its Power and Morality

1. An illusion of invulnerability, shared by most or all the members, which creates excessive optimism and encourages taking extreme risks
2. An unquestioned belief in the group's inherent morality, inclining the members to ignore the ethical or moral consequences of their decisions

Type II: Closed-Mindedness

3. Collective efforts to rationalize in order to discount warnings or other information that might lead the members to reconsider their assumptions before they recommit themselves to their past policy decisions
4. Stereotyped views of enemy leaders as too evil to warrant genuine attempts to negotiate, or as too weak and stupid to counter whatever risky attempts are made to defeat their purposes

Type III: Pressures Toward Uniformity

5. Self-censorship of deviations from the apparent group consensus, reflecting each member's inclination to minimize to himself the importance of his doubts and counterarguments
6. A shared illusion of unanimity concerning judgments conforming to the majority view (partly resulting from self-censorship of deviations, augmented by the false assumption that silence means consent)
7. Direct pressure on any member who expresses strong arguments against any of the group's stereotypes, illusions, or commitments, making clear that this type of dissent is contrary to what is expected of all loyal members
8. The emergence of self-appointed mindguards—members who protect the group from adverse information that might shatter their shared complacency about the effectiveness and morality of their decisions

CONSEQUENCES

When a policy-making group displays most or all of the symptoms in each of the three categories, the members perform their collective tasks ineffectively and are likely to fail to attain their collective objectives as a result of concurrence-seeking. In rare instances, concurrence-seeking may have predominantly positive effects for their members and their enterprises. For example, it may make a crucial contribution to maintaining morale after a defeat and to muddling through a crisis when prospects for a successful outcome look bleak.

But the positive effects are generally outweighed by the poor quality of the group's decision-making. My assumption is that the more frequently a group displays the symptoms, the worse will be the quality of its decisions, on the average. Even when some symptoms are absent, the others may be so pronounced that we can expect all the unfortunate consequences of groupthink.

To be more specific, whenever a policy-making group displays most of the symptoms of groupthink, we can expect to find that the group also displays symptoms of defective decision-making. Seven such symptoms were listed . . . on the basis of prior research on decision-making in government, industry, and other large organizations:

1. Incomplete survey of alternatives
2. Incomplete survey of objectives
3. Failure to examine risks of preferred choice
4. Failure to reappraise initially rejected alternatives
5. Poor information search
6. Selective bias in processing information at hand
7. Failure to work out contingency plans

A study by Philip Tetlock indicates that among the politically relevant consequences is the relatively poor quality of the thinking that goes into the public statements made by national leaders when they announce and try to explain policy decisions that are the products of groupthink. Tetlock did a comparative study of groupthink and nongroupthink decisions, using systematic content analysis techniques to assess the quality of thinking in public speeches made by the President of the United States or the Secretary of State. For the sample of groupthink decisions, he found significantly lower scores on cognitive complexity than for the nongroupthink decisions, indicating more simplistic thinking about the issues.

ANTECEDENT CONDITIONS

In addition to stating the expected observable consequences, an adequate theory of groupthink must also specify the observable *causes*—that is, the antecedent conditions that produce, elicit, or facilitate the occurrence of the syndrome. . . . One major condition . . . has to do with the degree of cohesiveness of the group. We would not expect to find the groupthink syndrome if the members dislike each other and do not value their membership in the group. Any such group that lacks cohesiveness is likely to display symptoms of defective decision-making, especially if the members are engaging in internal warfare. But groupthink is not ever likely to be the cause of their poor decision-making. Only when a group of policy-makers is moderately or highly cohesive can we expect the groupthink syndrome to emerge as the members are working collectively on one or another of their important policy decisions. Even so, the symptoms of groupthink are unlikely to occur to such an extent that they interfere with effective decision-making *unless certain additional antecedent conditions are also present.*

What are those additional conditions? Two of them ... pertain to administrative or structural features of the policy-makers' organization. One condition involves *insulation of the policy-making group,* which provides no opportunity for the members to obtain expert information and critical evaluation from others within the organization. A second feature is *lack of a tradition of impartial leadership.* In the absence of appropriate leadership traditions, the leader of a policy-making group will find it all too easy to use his or her power and prestige to influence the members of the group to approve of the policy alternative he or she prefers instead of encouraging them to engage in open inquiry and critical evaluation. A third administrative or structural factor can also be inferred by comparing the conditions that prevailed during the groupthink decisions ... with those during the nongroupthink decisions ... : *the lack of norms requiring methodical procedures for dealing with the decision-making tasks.*

All three of the administrative or structural conditions can be regarded as factors that facilitate the occurrence of the groupthink syndrome; they involve lack of constraints on collective uncritical thinking. Insofar as they are long-standing features of the organization, each of the three conditions can be ascertained *before* the members of a policy-making group start their deliberations on whatever policy decision is under investigation. I mention this because it is pertinent to the question of whether the groupthink syndrome can be predicted in advance. My answer is that by ascertaining the presence of one or more of the three structural conditions as well as the level of group cohesiveness of the policy-making group (which can also be rated *before* the deliberations begin), such predictions can be made. If the predictions are confirmed in future studies on policy-making groups, we shall be able to conclude that the foregoing-analysis of causal factors that lead to the groupthink syndrome is substantiated by empirical evidence.

HOW WIDESPREAD IS THE GROUPTHINK SYNDROME?

At present we do not know what percentage of all major fiascoes are attributable to groupthink. Some decisions of poor quality that turn out to be fiascoes might be ascribed primarily to mistakes made by just one man, the chief executive. Others arise because of a faulty policy formulated by a group of executives whose decision-making procedures were impaired by errors having little or nothing to do with groupthink. For example, a noncohesive committee may be made up of bickering factions so intent on fighting for political power within the government bureaucracy that the participants have little interest in examining the real issues posed by the foreign policy question they are debating; they may settle for a compromise that fails to take account of adverse effects on people outside their own political arena.

All that can be said from the historical case studies I have analyzed so far is that the groupthink syndrome sometimes plays a major role in producing large-scale fiascoes. In order to estimate how large the percentage might be for various types of decision-making groups, we need investigations of a variety of policy decisions made by groups of executives who have grossly miscalculated the unfavorable consequences of their chosen courses of action. Such investigations should also provide comparative results that are valuable for helping to determine the conditions that promote groupthink.

Irving L. Janis

PART SIX

Helping and Aggression

On the Internet . . .

Sites appropriate to Part Six

This site, from the American Psychological Association, contains an essay that reviews some of the research on television violence and also provides suggestions and resources for parents who wish to moderate television's influence on their children.

http://www.apa.org/pubinfo/violence.html

This American Psychological Association Public Communications Web site contains a report on violence and prosocial behavior entitled "What Makes Kids Care? Teaching Gentleness in a Violent World." This report provides information on how children can be taught to help others.

http://www.apa.org/pubinfo/altruism.html

This is an *ERIC Digest* report entitled "Aggression and Cooperation: Helping Young Children Develop Constructive Strategies." This report contains information on how to help children deal effectively with aggression and develop prosocial attitudes and behaviors.

http://www.kidsource.com/kidsource/
content2/aggression_and_coop.html

The Media Awareness Network site is devoted to media education and to exploring media issues for educators, students, parents, and community members.

http://www.media-awareness.ca/eng/

CHAPTER 12 Prosocial Behavior

12.1 JOHN M. DARLEY AND BIBB LATANÉ

Bystander Intervention in Emergencies: Diffusion of Responsibility

Many social psychologists are interested in discovering the conditions that influence helping behavior, in part because they see a distressingly low rate of helping in emergency situations. John M. Darley and Bibb Latané have found that the larger the crowd of people, the less likely any one of them will help in an emergency. They explain this bystander effect with the concept of "diffusion of responsibility," which says that in larger groups, each person feels less responsibility.

Darley (b. 1938) earned his Ph.D. in social psychology from Harvard University in 1965. He taught at New York University prior to accepting his current position at Princeton University in 1972. Latané (b. 1937) earned his Ph.D. in social psychology from the University of Minnesota in 1963. He taught at Columbia University, Ohio State University, and the University of North Carolina before accepting a position at Florida Atlantic University in 1989. Darley and Latané wrote about their research on helping in their book *The Unresponsive Bystander: Why Doesn't He Help?* (Prentice Hall, 1970).

This selection is from "Bystander Intervention in Emergencies: Diffusion of Responsibility," which was published in the *Journal of Personality and Social Psychology* in 1968. In this study, Darley and Latané simulated an emergency situation and found that the presence of bystanders reduced the likelihood of people helping. As you read this selection, note the careful design of the simulation to replicate real-life circumstances. What do you think you would do if you were a participant in this study?

Key Concept: diffusion of responsibility and helping behavior

APA Citation: Darley, J. M., & Latané, B. (1968). Bystander intervention in emergencies: Diffusion of responsibility. *Journal of Personality and Social Psychology, 8,* 377–383.

*S*s *overheard an epileptic seizure. They believed either that they alone heard the emergency, or that 1 or 4 unseen others were also present. As predicted the presence of other bystanders reduced the individual's feelings of personal responsibility and lowered his speed of reporting (p < .01). In groups of size 3, males reported no faster than females, and females reported no slower when the 1 other bystander was a male rather than a female. In general, personality and background measures were not predictive of helping. Bystander inaction in real-life emergencies is often explained by "apathy," "alienation," and "anomie." This experiment suggests that the explanation may lie more in the bystander's response to other observers than in his indifference to the victim.*

Several years ago, a young woman was stabbed to death in the middle of a street in a residential section of New York City. Although such murders are not entirely routine, the incident received little public attention until several weeks later when the New York Times disclosed another side to the case: at least 38 witnesses had observed the attack—and none had even attempted to intervene. Although the attacker took more than half an hour to kill Kitty Genovese, not one of the 38 people who watched from the safety of their own apartments came out to assist her. Not one even lifted the telephone to call the police (Rosenthal, 1964).

Preachers, professors, and news commentators sought the reasons for such apparently conscienceless and inhumane lack of intervention. Their conclusions ranged from "moral decay," to "dehumanization produced by the urban environment," to "alienation," "anomie," and "existential despair." An analysis of the situation, however, suggests that factors other than apathy and indifference were involved.

A person witnessing an emergency situation, particularly such a frightening and dangerous one as a stabbing, is in conflict. There are obvious humanitarian norms about helping the victim, but there are also rational and irrational fears about what might happen to a person who does intervene (Milgram & Hollander, 1964). "I didn't want to get involved," is a familiar comment, and behind it lies fears of physical harm, public embarrassment, involvement with police procedures, lost work days and jobs, and other unknown dangers.

In certain circumstances, the norms favoring intervention may be weakened, leading bystanders to resolve the conflict in the direction of nonintervention. One of these circumstances may be the presence of other onlookers. For example, in the case above, each observer, by seeing lights and figures in other apartment house windows, knew that others were also watching. However, there was no way to tell how the other observers were reacting. These two facts provide several reasons why any individual may have delayed or failed to help. The responsibility for helping was diffused among the observers; there was also diffusion of any potential blame for not taking action; and finally, it was possible that somebody, unperceived, had already initiated helping action.

When only one bystander is present in an emergency, if help is to come, it must come from him. Although he may choose to ignore it (out of concern for his personal safety, or desires "not to get involved"), any pressure to intervene focuses uniquely on him. When there are several observers present, however, the pressures to intervene do not focus on any one of the observers; instead the responsibility for intervention is shared among all the onlookers and is not unique to any one. As a result, no one helps.

A second possibility is that potential blame may be diffused. However much we may wish to think that an individual's moral behavior is divorced from considerations of personal punishment or reward, there is both theory and evidence to the contrary (Aronfreed, 1964; Miller & Dollard, 1941, Whiting & Child, 1953). It is perfectly reasonable to assume that, under circumstances of group responsibility for a punishable act, the punishment or blame that accrues to any one individual is often slight or nonexistent.

Finally, if others are known to be present, but their behavior cannot be closely observed, any one bystander can assume that one of the other observers is already taking action to end the emergency. Therefore, his own intervention would be only redundant—perhaps harmfully or confusingly so. Thus, given the presence of other onlookers whose behavior cannot be observed, any given bystander can rationalize his own inaction by convincing himself that "somebody else must be doing something."

These considerations lead to the hypothesis that the more bystanders to an emergency, the less likely, or the more slowly, any one bystander will intervene to provide aid. To test this proposition it would be necessary to create a situation in which a realistic "emergency" could plausibly occur. Each subject should also be blocked from communicating with others to prevent his getting information about their behavior during the emergency. Finally, the experimental situation should allow for the assessment of the speed and frequency of the subjects' reaction to the emergency. The experiment reported below attempted to fulfill these conditions.

PROCEDURE

Overview. A college student arrived in the laboratory and was ushered into an individual room from which a communication system would enable him to talk to the other participants. It was explained to him that he was to take part in a discussion about personal problems associated with college life and that the discussion would be held over the intercom system, rather than face-to-face, in order to avoid embarrassment by preserving the anonymity of the subjects. During the course of the discussion, one of the other subjects underwent what appeared to be a very serious nervous seizure similar to epilepsy. During the fit it was impossible for the subject to talk to the other discussants or to find out what, if anything, they were doing abut the emergency. The dependent variable was the speed with which the subjects reported the emergency to the experimenter. The major independent variable was the number of people the subject thought to be in the discussion group.

Subjects. Fifty-nine female and thirteen male students in introductory psychology courses at New York University were contacted to take part in an unspecified experiment as part of a class requirement.

Method. Upon arriving for the experiment, the subject found himself in a long corridor with doors opening off it to several small rooms. An experimental assistant met him, took him to one of the rooms, and seated him at a table. After filling out a background information form, the subject was given a pair of headphones with an attached microphone and was told to listen for instructions.

Over the intercom, the experimenter explained that he was interested in learning about the kinds of personal problems faced by normal college students in a high pressure, urban environment. He said that to avoid possible embarrassment about discussing personal problems with strangers several precautions had been taken. First, subjects would remain anonymous, which was why they had been placed in individual rooms rather than face-to-face. (The actual reason for this was to allow tape recorder simulation of the other subjects and the emergency.) Second, since the discussion might be inhibited by the presence of outside listeners, the experimenter would not listen to the initial discussion, but would get the subject's reactions later, by questionnaire. (The real purpose of this was to remove the obviously responsible experimenter from the scene of the emergency.)

The subjects were told that since the experimenter was not present, it was necessary to impose some organization. Each person would talk in turn, presenting his problems to the group. Next, each person in turn would comment on what the others had said, and finally, there would be a free discussion. A mechanical switching device would regulate this discussion sequence and each subject's microphone would be on for about 2 minutes. While any microphone was on, all other microphones would be off. Only one subject, therefore, could be heard over the network at any given time. The subjects were thus led to realize when they later heard the seizure that only the victim's microphone was on and that there was no way of determining what any of the other witnesses were doing, nor of discussing the event and its possible solution with the others. When these instructions had been given, the discussion began.

In the discussion, the future victim spoke first, saying that he found it difficult to get adjusted to New York City and to his studies. Very hesitantly and with obvious embarrassment, he mentioned that he was prone to seizures, particularly when studying hard or taking exams. The other people, including the real subject, took their turns and discussed similar problems (minus, of course, the proneness to seizures). The naive subject talked last in the series, after the last prerecorded voice was played.

When it was again the victim's turn to talk, he made a few relatively calm comments, and then, growing increasingly louder and incoherent, he continued:

> I-er-um-I think I-I need-er-if-if could-er-er-somebody er-er-er-er-er-er-er give me a little-er-give me a little help here because-er-I-er-I'm-er-er-h-h-having a-a-a real problem-er-right now and I-er-if somebody could help me out it would-it would-er-er s-s-sure be-sure be good... because-er-there-er-er-a cause I-er-uh-I've got a-a one of the-er-sei————er-er-things coming on and-and-and I could really-er-use some help so if somebody would-er-give me a little h-help-uh-er-er-er-er-er c-could somebody-er-er-help-er-uh-uh-uh (choking sounds).... I'm gonna die-er-er-I'm... gonna die-er-help-er-er-seizure-er-[chokes, then quiet].

The experimenter began timing the speed of the real subject's response at the beginning of the victim's speech. Informed judges listening to the tape have estimated that the victim's increasingly louder and more disconnected ramblings clearly represented a breakdown about 70 seconds after the signal for the victim's second speech. The victim's speech was abruptly cut off 125 seconds after this signal, which could be interpreted by the subject as indicating that the time allotted for that speaker had elapsed and the switching circuits had switched away from him. Times reported in the results are measured from the start of the fit.

Group size variable. The major independent variable of the study was the number of other people that the subject believed also heard the fit. By the assistant's comments before the experiment, and also by the number of voices heard to speak in the first round of the group discussion, the subject was led to believe that the discussion group was one of three sizes: either a two-person group (consisting of a person who would later have a fit and the real subject), a three-person group (consisting of the victim, the real subject, and one confederate voice), or a six-person group (consisting of the victim, the real subject, and four confederate voices). All the confederates' voices were tape-recorded.

Variations in group composition. Varying the kind as well as the number of bystanders present at an emergency should also vary the amount of responsibility felt by any single bystander. To test this, several variations of the three-person group were run. In one three-person condition, the taped bystander voice was that of a female, in another a male, and in the third a male who said that he was a premedical student who occasionally worked in the emergency wards at Bellevue hospital.

In the above conditions, the subjects were female college students. In a final condition males drawn from the same introductory psychology subject pool were tested in a three-person female-bystander condition.

Time to help.   The major dependent variable was the time elapsed from the start of the victim's fit until the subject left her experimental cubicle. When the subject left her room, she saw the experimental assistant seated at the end of the hall, and invariably went to the assistant. If 6 minutes elapsed without the subject having emerged from her room, the experiment was terminated.

As soon as the subject reported the emergency, or after 6 minutes had elapsed, the experimental assistant disclosed the true nature of the experiment, and dealt with any emotions aroused in the subject. Finally the subject filled out a questionnaire concerning her thoughts and feelings during the emergency, and completed scales of Machiavellianism, anomie, and authoritarianism (Christie, 1964), a social desirability scale (Crowne & Marlowe, 1964), a social responsibility scale (Daniels & Berkowitz, 1964), and reported vital statistics and socioeconomic data.

RESULTS . . .

Effect of Group Size on Helping

The number of bystanders that the subject perceived to be present had a major effect on the likelihood with which she would report the emergency (Table 1). Eighty-five percent of the subjects who thought they alone knew of the victim's plight reported the seizure before the victim was cut off, only 31% of those who thought four other bystanders were present did so.

Every one of the subjects in the two-person groups, but only 62% of the subjects in the six-person groups, ever reported the emergency. The cumulative distributions of response times for groups of different perceived size indicates that, by any point in time, more subjects from the two-person groups had responded than from the three-person groups, and more from the three-person groups than from the six-person groups.

Ninety-five percent of all the subjects who ever responded did so within the first half of the time available to them. No subject who had not reported within 3 minutes after the fit ever did so. The shape of these distributions suggest that had the experiment been allowed to run for a considerably longer time, few additional subjects would have responded.

Speed of Response

To achieve a more detailed analysis of the results, each subject's time score was transformed into a "speed" score by taking the reciprocal of the response

TABLE 1

Effects of Group Size on Likelihood and Speed of Response

*John M. Darley
and Bibb Latané*

Group Size	N	% responding by end of fit	Time in sec.	Speed score
2 (S & victim)	13	85	52	.87
3 (S, victim, & 1 other)	26	62	93	.72
6 (S, victim, & 4 others)	13	31	166	.51

Note: p value of differences: $\chi^2 = 7.91$, $p < .02$; $F = 8.09$, $p < .01$, for speed scores.

time in seconds and multiplying by 100. The effect of this transformation was to deemphasize differences between longer time scores, thus reducing the contribution to the results of the arbitrary 6-minute limit on scores. A high speed score indicates a fast response.

An analysis of variance indicates that the effect of group size is highly significant ($p < .01$). Duncan multiple-range tests indicate that all but the two- and three-person groups differ significantly from one another ($p < .05$).

Victim's Likelihood of Being Helped

An individual subject is less likely to respond if he thinks that others are present. But what of the victim? Is the inhibition of the response of each individual strong enough to counteract the fact that with five onlookers there are five times as many people available to help? From the data of this experiment, it is possible mathematically to create hypothetical groups with one, two, or five observers. The calculations indicate that the victim is about equally likely to get help from one bystander as from two. The victim is considerably more likely to have gotten help from one or two observers than from five during the first minute of the fit. For instance, by 45 seconds after the start of the fit, the victim's chances of having been helped by the single bystanders were about 50%, compared to none in the five observer condition. After the first minute, the likelihood of getting help from at least one person is high in all three conditions.

Effect of Group Composition on Helping the Victim

Several variations of the three-person group were run. In one pair of variations, the female subject thought the other bystander was either male or female; in another, she thought the other bystander was a premedical student who worked in an emergency ward at Bellevue hospital. As Table 2 shows, the variations in sex and medical competence of the other bystander had no important or detectable affect on speed of response. Subjects responded equally frequently and fast whether the other bystander was female, male, or medically experienced.

Sex of the Subject and Speed of Response

Coping with emergencies is often thought to be the duty of males, especially when females are present, but there was no evidence that this was the case in this study. Male subjects responded to the emergency with almost exactly the same speed as did females (Table 2).

Reasons for Intervention or Nonintervention

After the debriefing at the end of the experiment each subject was given a 15-item checklist and asked to check those thoughts which had "crossed your mind when you heard Subject 1 calling for help." Whatever the condition, each subject checked very few thoughts, and there were no significant differences in number or kind of thoughts in the different experimental groups. The only thoughts checked by more than a few subjects were "I didn't know what to do" (18 out of 65 subjects), "I thought it must be some sort of fake" (20 out of 65), and "I didn't know exactly what was happening" (26 out of 65)....

TABLE 2

Effects of Group Composition on Likelihood and Speed of Response[a]

Group composition	N	% responding by end of fit	Time in sec.	Speed score
Female S, male other	13	62	94	74
Female S, female other	13	62	92	71
Female S, male medic other	5	100	60	77
Male S, female other	13	69	110	68

[a]Three-person group, male victim.

DISCUSSION

Subjects, whether or not they intervened, believed the fit to be genuine and serious. "My God, he's having a fit," many subjects said to themselves (and were overheard via their microphones) at the onset of the fit. Others gasped or simply said "Oh." Several of the male subjects swore. One subject said to herself, "It's just my kind of luck, something has to happen to me!" Several subjects spoke aloud of their confusion about what course of action to take, "Oh God, what should I do?"

When those subjects who intervened stepped out of their rooms, they found the experimental assistant down the hall. With some uncertainty, but without panic, they reported the situation. "Hey, I think Number 1 is very sick. He's having a fit or something." After ostensibly checking on the situation, the experimenter returned to report that "everything is under control." The subjects accepted these assurances with obvious relief.

Subjects who failed to report the emergency showed few signs of the apathy and indifference thought to characterize "unresponsive bystanders." When the experimenter entered her room to terminate the situation, the subject often asked if the victim was "all right." "Is he being taken care of?" "He's all right isn't he?" Many of these subjects showed physical signs of nervousness; they often had trembling hands and sweating palms. If anything, they seemed more emotionally aroused than did the subjects who reported the emergency.

Why, then, didn't they respond? It is our impression that nonintervening subjects had not decided *not* to respond. Rather they were still in a state of indecision and conflict concerning whether to respond or not. The emotional behavior of these nonresponding subjects was a sign of their continuing conflict, a conflict that other subjects resolved by responding.

The fit created a conflict situation of the avoidance-avoidance type. On the one hand, subjects worried about the guilt and shame they would feel if they did not help the person in distress. On the other hand, they were concerned not to make fools of themselves by overreacting, not to ruin the ongoing experiment by leaving their intercom, and not to destroy the anonymous nature of the situation which the experimenter had earlier stressed as important. For subjects in the two-person condition, the obvious distress and his need for help were so important that their conflict was easily resolved. For the subjects who knew there were other bystanders present, the cost of not helping was reduced and the conflict they were in more acute. Caught between the two negative alternatives of letting the victim continue to suffer or the costs of rushing in to help, the nonresponding bystanders vacillated between them rather than choosing not to respond. This distinction may be academic for the victim, since he got no help in either case, but it is an extremely important one for arriving at an understanding of the causes of bystanders' failures to help.

REFERENCES

Aronfreed, J. The origin of self-criticism. *Psychological Review,* 1964, **71,** 193–219.

Christie, R. The prevalence of machiavellian orientations. Paper presented at the meeting of the American Psychological Association, Los Angeles, 1964.

Crowne, D., & Marlowe, D. *The approval motive.* New York: Wiley, 1964.

Daniels, L., & Berkowitz, L. Liking and response to dependency relationships. *Human Relations,* 1963, **16,** 141–148.

Milgram, S., & Hollander, P. Murder they heard. *Nation*, 1964, **198**, 602–604.

Miller, N., & Dollard, J. *Social learning and imitation.* New Haven: Yale University Press, 1941.

Rosenthal, A. M. *Thirty-eight witnesses.* New York: McGraw-Hill, 1964.

Whiting, J. W. M., & Child, I. *Child training and personality.* New Haven: Yale University Press, 1953.

12.2 ROBERT A. BARON

The Sweet Smell of . . . Helping

Discovering how various environmental factors influence helping behavior is an important endeavor. Robert A. Baron has been researching the effects of environmental factors such as temperature and odors on social behavior for many years. The fact that fragrances have long been used to enhance attractiveness and pleasure forms the basis for the research reported in this selection.

Baron (b. 1943) earned his Ph.D. in social psychology from the University of Iowa in 1968. He taught at Purdue University before accepting his present position as a professor of psychology and management at Rensselaer Polytechnic Institute in 1987. Baron has published numerous articles and books, including *Human Aggression,* coauthored by D. R. Richardson (Plenum, 1994).

This selection is from "The Sweet Smell of . . . Helping: Effects of Pleasant Ambient Fragrance on Prosocial Behavior in Shopping Malls," which was published in *Personality and Social Psychology Bulletin* in 1997. In it, Baron describes how he tested the hypothesis that pleasant odors (from bakeries and coffee shops) increases helping behavior (providing change for a dollar). This field study was conducted in a local mall, using natural odors from stores. Notice that fragrance also improved mood in this study, which might in turn lead to more prosocial behavior. Do you think your social behavior is influenced by odors? Might unpleasant odors result in a decrease in helping behavior?

Key Concept: helping behavior

APA Citation: Baron, R. A. (1997). The sweet smell of . . . helping: Effects of pleasant ambient fragrance on prosocial behavior in shopping malls. *Personality and Social Psychology Bulletin, 23,* 498–503.

*I*n a preliminary study, passersby in a large shopping mall were significantly more likely to help a same-sex accomplice (by retrieving a dropped pen or providing change for a dollar) when these helping opportunities took place in the presence of *pleasant ambient odors (e.g., baking cookies, roasting coffee) than in the absence of such odors. Participants also reported significantly higher levels of positive affect in the presence of pleasant odors. In a second study, the order in which passersby were exposed to a helping opportunity and rated their current mood was systematically varied. Results similar to those of the first study were obtained; order of task had no effect on either mood or helping, but helping was significantly greater in the presence of pleasant fragrances than in their absence. In addition, there was some evidence that fragrance-induced increments in helping were mediated by increments in positive affect.*

Human beings have been using pleasant fragrances since the dawn of civilization. For example, when archaeologists excavate the tombs of Egyptian pharaohs—persons who lived thousands of years ago—they often find jars containing traces of fragrant oils (used for anointing one's body) and various forms of incense—substances that, when burned, release pleasant odors. These two major uses of fragrance have continued until the present. Current magazines are filled with ads for perfumes and colognes, and sales of devices for releasing pleasant smells into the air have been rising steadily in recent years (Foderaro, 1988). Indeed, the present author has contributed in a small way to this activity: He has patented a device for enhancing indoor environments through air filtration, noise control, and the release of pleasant fragrances (Edwards, 1995). . . .

Initial research by social psychologists on the effects of pleasant fragrances focused on their use as aids to personal grooming. Such research considered the question of whether individuals could enhance their attractiveness to others through the use of scented products such as perfumes and colognes (Baron, 1981, 1983b, 1986). More recently, researchers have turned their attention to the second use of fragrance noted above; its release into the air as a means of enhancing indoor environments. In this context, pleasant odors are not associated with a specific person; rather, they are used simply to render indoor environments more pleasant. . . .

Previous research . . . suggests one potential mechanism through which ambient fragrance might influence social behavior: by producing mild increments in positive affect. Several findings offer support for this possibility. First, in some recent studies (e.g., Baron & Thomley, 1994), participants exposed to pleasant odors reported higher levels of positive affect than those not exposed to such odors. Similarly, hospital patients exposed to pleasant odors report significantly greater improvements in mood than patients not exposed to such aromas (Dunn et al., 1995). Finally, exposure to pleasant fragrance has been found, in two studies, to increase helping to the same extent as receipt of a small, unexpected gift (Baron & Bronfen, 1994; Baron & Thomley, 1994). Because previous research indicates that receipt of a small gift produces increments in positive affect (cf. Isen, 1987; Spacapan & Oskamp, 1992), these findings suggest, through the method of *converging operations*, that the effects of pleasant odors on social behavior may also stem, at least in part, from fragrance-generated increments in positive affect (Garner, Hake, & Eriksen, 1956)....

The present study was designed to both replicate and extend previous findings concerning the effects of pleasant odors on social behavior and to further investigate the possibility that such effects are mediated, to some degree, by fragrance-induced increments in positive affect. Specifically, it sought to determine whether effects similar to those reported in previous laboratory studies would also be obtained in a field setting and with helping tasks different in nature from those employed in previous investigations. To examine these questions, it was necessary to identify field locations where pleasant odors are present and where individuals can engage in spontaneous acts of helping. Shopping malls appeared to meet these requirements. In large malls, numerous businesses release pleasant odors into the air (e.g., bakeries, coffee-roasters, candle and scent retailers). Moreover, the high volume of shoppers provides ample opportunity to measure several forms of spontaneous helping behavior (cf. Levine, Martinez, Brase, & Sorenson, 1994)....

METHOD

Participants and Design

Participants were 116 passersby in a large shopping mall. The study employed a $2 \times 2 \times 2$ factorial design based on the presence or absence of pleasant odors, gender of passersby, and order (mood measure first, helping opportunity second; helping opportunity first, mood measure second).

Overview. Passersby in a large shopping mall were approached by two accomplices of the same gender as themselves. One of these accomplices asked for change for $1. The second accomplice indicated that he or she was conducting a study of their air quality in the mall and then asked participants whether they smelled anything in the air and, if they did, to rate this odor on a 5-point scale ranging from 1 (*unpleasant*) to 5 (*very pleasant*). The second accomplice also asked participants to rate their current mood, again on a 5-point scale (1 = *very bad*, 5 = *very good*). The order in which these two interactions took place was systematically varied so that half of the participants were first asked for help and then asked to rate the air in the mall and their own mood, whereas for the remaining half, the order of these events was reversed.

Permission to collect data was obtained from the mall director. Permission was granted with one restriction: that accomplices approach only persons of the same gender as themselves. (The mall director was concerned that cross-gender requests for help might be perceived as "pick-up" attempts and would thus be annoying to shoppers.) Specific locations where the study would be conducted were identified so that security guards and store managers could be alerted to the presence of the researchers.

Fragrance.   Prior to the start of the investigation, the author and several other persons (graduate students and a psychologist) visited the mall to identify areas containing and not containing pleasant odors. Locations with pleasant fragrance were near such businesses as Cinnabon (a bakery), Mrs. Field's Cookies (a bakery), and The Coffee Beanery (a coffee-roasting cafe). In contrast, locations without pleasant fragrance were generally located near clothing stores and similar establishments (e.g., Banana Republic, Nine West, and Chess King). Every effort was made to match locations containing fragrance with locations not containing fragrance in terms of volume of pedestrians, mix of nearby stores, lighting, and proximity to mall entrances. Original plans called for conducting the fragrance and no-fragrance conditions in the same locations at times of the day when the businesses in question were, or were not, emitting pleasant odors. However, this proved to be impossible because detectable odors were present near most of the odor-producing businesses at all hours of the day. For this reason, it proved necessary to conduct the fragrance and no-fragrance conditions in different, but closely matched, locations.

Request for help and measures of helping.   The accomplice approached an individual passerby and, showing a $1 bill, asked for change of this bill. Responses to the accomplice's request were scored as *helping* only if the passerby stopped and made change; all other responses (e.g., ignoring the accomplice, indicating verbally that the passerby did not have change) were scored as *no helping*. In all cases, the accomplices approached only passersby of their own gender who were walking toward them alone; passersby who were part of groups were not approached by the accomplices.

The study was conducted in the late morning (11:00 AM to 12:00 noon) and in mid-afternoon (2:00 PM to 4:00 PM) on weekdays. At these times, pedestrian traffic in the mall was moderate, and many passersby were alone rather than in groups....

RESULTS

Helping Behavior

To examine the effects of fragrance condition, task order, and gender on helping, a hierarchical loglinear analysis was conducted on the helping data. In this analysis, three variables—fragrance condition, order, and gender—as well as all two-way and three-way interactions between these variables were examined. This analysis employed a backward elimination procedure ($p = .05$). Results indicated that only removal of the main effect for fragrance condition produced a significant χ^2 for the goodness-of-fit test, $\chi^2(1) = 26.13, p < .001$. Neither removal of order, $\chi^2(1) = 0.18, p > .71$, nor gender, $\chi^2(1) = 0.34, p > .085$, produced significant effects, nor did removal of any of the two-way interactions or the three-way interaction produce significant effects. These findings indicate that a higher proportion of passersby helped the accomplice when pleasant fragrances were present than when they were absent and that this was true for both female and male passersby and occurred regardless of the order in which participants in the study were exposed to the helping request and asked to rate their current moods. The proportion of individuals who helped the accomplice in each condition is shown in Table 1.

Mood

An ANOVA [analysis of variance] in which fragrance, gender of participants, and order were the independent variables was performed on the data for self-reported mood. This analysis yielded one significant effect, that for fragrance condition, $F(1, 114) = 7.95$, $p < .01$. Participants exposed to pleasant fragrance reported higher levels of positive affect ($M = 4.11$) than those not exposed to pleasant fragrance ($M = 3.81$). No other effects in the analysis were significant.

TABLE 1

Percentage of Passersby Who Helped the Accomplice as a Function of Presence of Pleasant Fragrance, Order, and Gender

	No Fragrance		Fragrance	
	Helping First	*Mood First*	*Helping First*	*Mood First*
Males	22.22	25.00	45.45	61.11
Females	16.67	12.50	60.87	59.09

Potential Mediating Role of Positive Affect

To examine the potential mediating role of positive affect (mood) with respect to the effects of pleasant fragrance on helping, procedures recommended by Baron and Kenny (1986) were adopted. These procedures involved a series of regression analyses. In the first, the proposed mediator (self-reported mood) was regressed on the independent variable (fragrance). In the second, the dependent variable (helping) was regressed on the independent variable (fragrance). Finally, in the third, the dependent variable (helping) was regressed on both the independent variable (fragrance) and the mediator (affect). According to Baron and Kenny, there would be evidence of mediation if the following findings emerged: (a) the independent variable affected the mediator in the first equation, (b) the independent variable affected the dependent variable in the second analysis, and (c) the mediator affected the dependent variable in the third equation, whereas the effect of the independent variable was reduced relative to the second analysis.

The results of these analyses indicated that fragrance condition was a significant predictor of mood ($\beta = -.253$, $t = -2.90$, $p < .005$) and was also a significant predictor of helping ($\beta = .119$, $t = 2.13$, $p < .05$). However, when the mediator (mood) was entered into the regression equation along with fragrance condition, fragrance condition was no longer a significant predictor of helping ($\beta = .158$, $t = 1.74$, $p > .08$). In other words, as required by the Baron and Kenny (1986) procedures, the effect of fragrance on the dependent variable was reduced relative to the second equation. Together, these findings offer some support for the suggestion that positive affect (i.e., current mood) mediates the effects of pleasant fragrance on helping. However, once again, this evidence should be interpreted with a degree of caution.

Participants' Awareness of Ambient Fragrance

Among participants in the fragrance condition, 64.4% reported smelling a fragrance. Among those in the no-fragrance condition, 35.6% reported smelling a fragrance, $\chi^2(1) = 4.93$, $p < .03$. Thus it appeared that participants were differentially aware of ambient fragrance in the two conditions....

DISCUSSION

The present findings serve to replicate and extend those reported in previous research (e.g., Baron & Bronfen, 1994; Baron & Thomley, 1994; Warm et al., 1991). As in earlier studies, pleasant odors in the air significantly influenced the behavior of participants. Specifically, passersby were more likely to help the accomplice when pleasant fragrances were present in the air than when they were absent. These findings were obtained in a field setting—a busy shopping mall —with tasks quite different from those employed in previous research. Moreover, they occurred regardless of the order in which participants were exposed to a helping opportunity and rated their current mood. Together, these findings suggest that the effects of pleasant ambient fragrances on behavior may be quite general in scope—that is, they may occur in a wide range of settings.

The present findings also provide additional support, albeit far from conclusive, for the suggestion that the effects of pleasant fragrances on social behavior stem, at least in part, from fragrance-induced increments in positive affect. Support for this suggestion is provided by the results of the regression analyses conducted in accordance with the Baron and Kenny (1986) model for testing mediating effects. These analyses indicated that fragrance condition was a significant predictor of current self-reported mood and a significant predictor of helping. However, this was no longer the case when mood was added to the regression equation. Although these results are consistent with the reasoning of the Baron and Kenny model, they should be interpreted with caution pending the collection of additional data. It should also be emphasized, once again, that there is no intention here of suggesting that affective states are the only potential mediator of pleasant fragrances. On the contrary, recent studies on the behavioral effects of fragrance suggest that other factors, too, may play a role (e.g., Knasko, 1993). Thus further research is clearly needed to obtain full understanding of the mechanisms through which pleasant fragrances influence behavior. What does seem clear from the present and previous findings, however, is that this environmental variable can indeed produce significant effects on some forms of social behavior.

REFERENCES

Baron, R. A. (1981). The role of olfaction in human social behavior: Effects of a pleasant scent on attraction and social perception. *Personality and Social Psychology Bulletin, 7,* 611–617.

Baron, R. A. (1983b). The "sweet smell of success"? The impact of pleasant artificial scents (perfume or cologne) on evaluations of job applications. *Journal of Applied Psychology, 68,* 709–713.

Baron, R. A. (1986). Self-presentation in job interviews: When there can be "too much of a good thing." *Journal of Applied Social Psychology, 16,* 16–28.

Baron, R. A., & Bronfen, M. I. (1994). A whiff of reality: Empirical evidence concerning the effects of pleasant fragrances on work-related behavior. *Journal of Applied Social Psychology, 24,* 1179–1203.

Baron, R. A., & Thomley, J. (1994). A whiff of reality: Positive affect as a potential mediator of the effects of pleasant fragrances on task performance and helping. *Environment and Behavior, 26,* 766–784.

Baron, R. M., & Kenny, D. A. (1986). The mediator-moderator variable distinction in social psychological research: Conceptual, strategic, and statistical considerations. *Journal of Personality and Social Psychology, 51,* 1173–1192.

Dunn, C., Sleep, J., & Collett, D. (1995). Sensing an improvement: An experimental study to evaluate the use of aromatherapy, massage, and periods of rest in an intensive care unit. *Journal of Advanced Nursing, 21,* 34–40.

Edwards, R. (1995). Pleasant aromas chase away those bitter moods. *APA Monitor, 26*(3), 20.

Foderaro, L. W. (1988, February 4). The fragrant house: An expanding market for every mood. *The New York Times,* pp. C1, C10.

Garner, W. R., Hake, H. W., & Eriksen, C. W. (1956). Operationalism and the concept of perception. *Psychological Review, 63,* 149–159.

Isen, A. M. (1987). Positive affect, cognitive processes, and social behavior. In L. Berkowitz (Ed.), *Advances in experimental social psychology* (Vol. 20, pp. 203–253). New York: Academic Press.

Knasko, S. C. (1993). Performance, mood, and health during exposure to intermittent odors. *Archives of Environmental Health, 48,* 305–308.

Levine, R. V., Martinez, T. S., Brase, G., & Sorenson, K. (1994). Helping in 36 U.S. cities. *Journal of Personality and Social Psychology, 67,* 69–82.

Spacapan, S., & Oskamp, S. (Eds.). (1992). *Helping and being helped.* Newbury Park, CA: Sage.

Warm, J. S., December, W. N., & Parasuraman, R. (1991). Effects of olfactory stimulation on performance and stress in a visual sustained attention task. *Journal of the Society of Cosmetic Chemists, 42,* 199–210.

CHAPTER 13 Aggression

13.1 ALBERT BANDURA, DOROTHEA ROSS, AND SHEILA A. ROSS

Imitation of Film-Mediated Aggressive Models

Rising levels of crime and destructive aggression have been studied by psychologists for decades. One ongoing debate has focused on whether or not observation and imitation is a problem with regard to aggression that occurs in the media. Do children imitate the aggressive acts they observe in movies and on television? Through a series of studies, Albert Bandura and his colleagues have begun to answer this question.

Bandura (b. 1925), a leading theorist in observational learning, received his Ph.D. from the University of Iowa in 1952. Shortly afterward, he began his academic career at Stanford University, where he has remained. He has written many books, including *Aggression: A Social Learning Analysis* (Prentice Hall, 1973) and *Social Learning Theory* (Prentice Hall, 1977). Dorothea Ross and Sheila A. Ross both earned a Ph.D. in developmental psychology from Stanford University. Ross and Ross specialized in children's health and cognitive development prior to their retirement.

This selection is from "Imitation of Film-Mediated Aggressive Models," which was published in the *Journal of Abnormal and Social Psychology* in 1963. It details Bandura et al.'s classic study on aggression imitation in standard research article format. Note the care with which the procedure was carried out. An important point for understanding the statistical results is that a probability (p) level less than .05 is significant and indicates a real difference among experimental conditions. Bandura et al.'s findings go against most of the research reported prior to the study, which maintained that film-mediated aggression reduces aggressive drives through a cathartic process.

The research reported in this selection suggests that filmed aggression can facilitate aggression in children. What are the implications of this study for aggression and violence in movies and on television today?

Albert Bandura et al.

Key Concept: observation learning of aggression

APA Citation: Bandura, A., Ross, D., & Ross, S. A. (1963). Imitation of film-mediated aggressive models. *Journal of Abnormal and Social Psychology, 66,* 3–11.

*I*n *a test of the hypothesis that exposure of children to film-mediated aggressive models would increase the probability of Ss' [Subjects—i.e., children] aggression to subsequent frustration, 1 group of experimental Ss observed real-life aggressive models, a 2nd observed these same models portraying aggression on film, while a 3rd group viewed a film depicting an aggressive cartoon character. Following the exposure treatment, Ss were mildly frustrated and tested for the amount of imitative and nonimitative aggression in a different experimental setting. The overall results provide evidence for both the facilitating and the modeling influence of film-mediated aggressive stimulation. In addition, the findings reveal that the effects of such exposure are to some extent a function of the sex of the model, sex of the child, and the reality cues of the model....*

A recent incident (San Francisco Chronicle, 1961) in which a boy was seriously knifed during a re-enactment of a switchblade knife fight the boys had seen the previous evening on a televised rerun of the James Dean movie, *Rebel Without a Cause*, is a dramatic illustration of the possible imitative influence of film stimulation. Indeed, anecdotal data suggest that portrayal of aggression through pictorial media may be more influential in shaping the form aggression will take when a person is instigated on later occasions, than in altering the level of instigation to aggression.

In an earlier experiment (Bandura & Huston, 1961), it was shown that children readily imitated aggressive behavior exhibited by a model in the presence of the model. A succeeding investigation (Bandura, Ross, & Ross, 1961), demonstrated that children exposed to aggressive models generalized aggressive responses to a new setting in which the model was absent. The present study sought to determine the extent to which film-mediated aggressive models may serve as an important source of imitative behavior.

Aggressive models can be ordered on a reality-fictional stimulus dimension with real-life models located at the reality end of the continuum, non-human cartoon characters at the fictional end, and films portraying human models occupying an intermediate position. It was predicted, on the basis of saliency and similarity of cues, that the more remote the model was from reality, the weaker would be the tendency for subjects to imitate the behavior of the model....

To the extent that observation of adults displaying aggression conveys a certain degree of permissiveness for aggressive behavior, it may be assumed that such exposure not only facilitates the learning of new aggressive responses but also weakens competing inhibitory responses in subjects and thereby increases the probability of occurrence of previously learned patterns of aggression. It was predicted, therefore, that subjects who observed aggressive models would display significantly more aggression when subsequently frustrated than subjects who were equally frustrated but who had no prior exposure to models exhibiting aggression.

METHOD

The subjects were 48 boys and 48 girls enrolled in the Stanford University Nursery School. They ranged in age from 35 to 69 months, with a mean age of 52 months.

Two adults, a male and a female, served in the role of models both in the real-life and the human film-aggression condition, and one female experimenter conducted the study for all 96 children.

General Procedure

Subjects were divided into three experimental groups and one control group of 24 subjects each. One group of experimental subjects observed real-life aggressive models, a second group observed these same models portraying aggression on film, while a third group viewed a film depicting an aggressive cartoon character. The experimental groups were further subdivided into male and female subjects so that half the subjects in the two conditions involving human models were exposed to same-sex models, while the remaining subjects viewed models of the opposite sex.

Following the exposure experience, subjects were tested for the amount of imitative and nonimitative aggression in a different experimental setting in the absence of the models.

The control group subjects had no exposure to the aggressive models and were tested only in the generalization situation.

Subjects in the experimental and control groups were matched individually on the basis of ratings of their aggressive behavior in social interactions in the nursery school. The experimenter and a nursery school teacher rated the subjects on four five-point rating scales which measured the extent to which subjects displayed physical aggression, verbal aggression, aggression toward inanimate objects, and aggression inhibition. The latter scale, which dealt with the subjects' tendency to inhibit aggressive reactions in the face of high instigation, provided the measure of aggression anxiety. Seventy-one percent of the subjects were rated independently by both judges so as to permit an assessment of interrater agreement. The reliability of the composite aggression score, estimated by means of the Pearson product-moment correlation, was .80. . . .

*Albert Bandura
et al.*

Subjects in the Real-Life Aggressive condition were brought individually by the experimenter to the experimental room and the model, who was in the hallway outside the room, was invited by the experimenter to come and join in the game. The subject was then escorted to one corner of the room and seated at a small table which contained potato prints, multicolor picture stickers, and colored paper. After demonstrating how the subject could design pictures with the materials provided, the experimenter escorted the model to the opposite corner of the room which contained a small table and chair, a tinker toy set, a mallet, and a 5-foot inflated Bobo doll. The experimenter explained that this was the model's play area and after the model was seated, the experimenter left the experimental room.

The model began the session by assembling the tinker toys but after approximately a minute had elapsed, the model turned to the Bobo doll and spent the remainder of the period aggressing toward it with highly novel responses which are unlikely to be performed by children independently of the observation of the model's behavior. Thus, in addition to punching the Bobo doll, the model exhibited the following distinctive aggressive acts which were to be scored as imitative responses:

The model sat on the Bobo doll and punched it repeatedly in the nose.

The model then raised the Bobo doll and pommeled it on the head with a mallet.

Following the mallet aggression, the model tossed the doll up in the air aggressively and kicked it about the room. This sequence of physically aggressive acts was repeated approximately three times, interspersed with verbally aggressive responses such as, "Sock him in the nose . . . ," "Hit him down . . . ," "Throw him in the air . . . ," "Kick him . . . ," and "Pow."

Subjects in the Human Film-Aggression condition were brought by the experimenter to the semi-darkened experimental room, introduced to the picture materials, and informed that while the subjects worked on potato prints, a movie would be shown on a screen, positioned approximately 6 feet from the subject's table. The movie projector was located in a distant corner of the room and was screened from the subject's view by large wooden panels.

The color movie and a tape recording of the sound track was begun by a male projectionist as soon as the experimenter left the experimental room and was shown for a duration of 10 minutes. The models in the film presentations were the same adult males and females who participated in the Real-Life condition of the experiment. Similarly, the aggressive behavior they portrayed in the film was identical with their real-life performances.

For subjects in the Cartoon Film-Aggression condition, after seating the subject at the table with the picture construction material, the experimenter walked over to a television console approximately 3 feet in front of the subject's table, remarked, "I guess I'll turn on the color TV," and ostensibly tuned in a cartoon program. The experimenter then left the experimental room. The cartoon was shown on a glass lens screen in the television set by means of a rear projection arrangement screened from the subject's view by large panels. . . .

In both film conditions, at the conclusion of the movie the experimenter entered the room and then escorted the subject to the test room.

Aggression Instigation

In order to differentiate clearly the exposure and test situations subjects were tested for the amount of imitative learning in a different experimental room which was set off from the main nursery school building.

The degree to which a child has learned aggressive patterns of behavior through imitation becomes most evident when the child is instigated to aggression on later occasions. Thus, for example, the effects of viewing the movie, *Rebel Without a Cause*, were not evident until the boys were instigated to aggression the following day, at which time they re-enacted the televised switchblade knife fight in considerable detail. For this reason, the children in the experiment, both those in the control group, and those who were exposed to the aggressive models, were mildly frustrated before they were brought to the test room.

Following the exposure experience, the experimenter brought the subject to an anteroom which contained a varied array of highly attractive toys. The experimenter explained that the toys were for the subject to play with, but, as soon as the subject became sufficiently involved with the play material, the experimenter remarked that these were her very best toys, that she did not let just anyone play with them, and that she had decided to reserve these toys for some other children. However, the subject could play with any of the toys in the next room. The experimenter and the subject then entered the adjoining experimental room....

Test for Delayed Imitation

The experimental room contained a variety of toys, some of which could be used in imitative or nonimitative aggression, and others which tended to elicit predominantly nonaggressive forms of behavior. The aggressive toys included a 3-foot Bobo doll, a mallet and peg board, two dart guns, and a tether ball with a face painted on it which hung from the ceiling. The nonaggressive toys, on the other hand, included a tea set, crayons and coloring paper, a ball, two dolls, three bears, cars and trucks, and plastic farm animals....

The subject spent 20 minutes in the experimental room during which time his behavior was rated in terms of predetermined response categories by judges who observed the session through a one-way mirror in an adjoining observation room. The 20-minute session was divided in 5-second intervals by means of an electric interval timer, thus yielding a total number of 240 response units for each subject....

Albert Bandura
et al.

TABLE 1

Mean Aggression Scores for Subgroups of Experimental and Control Subjects

Response category	Real-life aggressive		Human film aggressive		Cartoon film aggressive	Control group
	F Model	M Model	F Model	M Model		
Total aggression						
Girls	65.8	57.3	87.0	79.5	80.9	36.4
Boys	76.8	131.8	114.5	85.0	117.2	72.2
Imitative aggression						
Girls	19.2	9.2	10.0	8.0	7.8	1.8
Boys	18.4	38.4	34.3	13.3	16.2	3.9
Mallet aggression						
Girls	17.2	18.7	49.2	19.5	36.8	13.1
Boys	15.5	28.8	20.5	16.3	12.5	13.5
Sits on Bobo doll[a]						
Girls	10.4	5.6	10.3	4.5	15.3	3.3
Boys	1.3	0.7	7.7	0.0	5.6	0.6
Nonimitative aggression						
Girls	27.6	24.9	24.0	34.3	27.5	17.8
Boys	35.5	48.6	46.8	31.8	71.8	40.4
Aggressive gun play						
Girls	1.8	4.5	3.8	17.6	8.8	3.7
Boys	7.3	15.9	12.8	23.7	16.6	14.3

[a] This response category was not included in the total aggression score.

RESULTS

The mean imitative and nonimitative aggression scores for subjects in the various experimental and control groups are presented in Table 1.

Since the distributions of scores departed from normality and the assumption of homogeneity of variance could not be made for most of the measures, the Freidman two-way analysis of variance by ranks was employed for testing the significance of the obtained differences.

Total Aggression

The mean total aggression scores for subjects in the real-life, human film, cartoon film, and the control groups are 83, 92, 99, and 54 respectively. The results of the analysis of variance performed on these scores reveal that the main effect of treatment conditions is significant ($Xr^2 = p < .05$), confirming the prediction that exposure of subjects to aggressive models increases the probability that subjects will respond aggressively when instigated on later occasions. Further analyses of pairs of scores by means of the Wilcoxon matched-pairs signed-ranks test show that subjects who viewed the real-life models and the film-mediated models do not differ from each other in total aggressiveness but all three experimental groups expressed significantly more aggressive behavior than the control subjects. . . .

Influence of Sex of Model and Sex of Child

In order to determine the influence of sex of model and sex of child on the expression of imitative and nonimitative aggression, the data from the experimental groups were combined and the significance of the differences between groups was assessed by t tests for uncorrelated means. In statistical comparisons involving relatively skewed distributions of scores the Mann-Whitney U test was employed.

Sex of subjects had a highly significant effect on both the learning and the performance of aggression. Boys, in relation to girls, exhibited significantly more total aggression ($t = 2.69$, $p < .01$), more imitative aggression ($t = 2.82$, $p < .005$), more aggressive gun play ($z = 3.38$, $p < .001$), and more nonimitative aggressive behavior ($t = 2.98$, $p < .005$). Girls, on the other hand, were more inclined than boys to sit on the Bobo doll but refrained from punching it ($z = 3.47$, $p < .001$).

The analyses also disclosed some influences of the sex of the model. Subjects exposed to the male model, as compared to the female model, expressed significantly more aggressive gun play ($z = 2.83$, $p < .005$). The most marked differences in aggressive gun play ($U = 9.5$, $p < .001$), however, were found between girls exposed to the female model ($M = 2.9$) and males who observed the male model ($M = 19.8$). Although the overall model difference in partially imitative behavior, Sits on Bobo, was not significant, Sex × Model subgroup comparisons yielded some interesting results. Boys who observed the aggressive female model, for example, were more likely to sit on the Bobo doll without punching it than boys who viewed the male model ($U = 33$, $p < .05$). Girls reproduced the nonaggressive component of the male model's aggressive pattern of behavior (i.e., sat on the doll without punching it) with considerably higher frequency than did boys who observed the same model ($U = 21.5$, $p < .02$). The highest incidence of partially imitative responses was yielded by the group of girls who viewed the aggressive female model ($M = 10.4$), and the lowest values by the boys who were exposed to the male model ($M = 0.3$). This difference was significant beyond the .05 significance level. These findings, along with the sex of child and sex of model differences reported in the preceding sections, provide further support for the view that the influence of models in promoting social learning is determined, in part, by the sex appropriateness of the model's behavior (Bandura et al., 1961). . . .

DISCUSSION

The results of the present study provide strong evidence that exposure to filmed aggression heightens aggressive reactions in children. Subjects who viewed the aggressive human and cartoon models on film exhibited nearly twice as much aggression than did subjects in the control group who were not exposed to the aggressive film content. . . .

Filmed aggression, not only facilitated the expression of aggression, but also effectively shaped the form of the subjects' aggressive behavior. The finding that children modeled their behavior to some extent after the film characters suggests that pictorial mass media, particularly television, may serve as an important source of social behavior. In fact, a possible generalization of responses originally learned in the television situation to the experimental film may account for the significantly greater amount of aggressive gun play displayed by subjects in the film condition as compared to subjects in the real-life and control groups. It is unfortunate that the qualitative features of the gun behavior were not scored since subjects in the film condition, unlike those in the other two groups, developed interesting elaborations in gun play (for example, stalking the imaginary opponent, quick drawing, and rapid firing), characteristic of the Western gun fighter.

REFERENCES

Bandura, A., & Huston, Aletha C. Identification as a process of incidental learning. *J. abnorm. soc. Psychol.*, 1961, **63,** 311–318.

Bandura, A., Ross, Dorothea, & Ross, Sheila A. Transmission of aggression through imitation of aggressive models. *J. abnorm. soc. Psychol.*, 1961, **63,** 575–582.

San Francisco Chronicle. "James Dean" knifing in South City. *San Francisco Chron.*, March 1, 1961, 6.

Psychological Processes Promoting the Relation Between Exposure to Media Violence and Aggressive Behavior by the Viewer

Social psychologists have been concerned about the effects of media violence on aggression for many years. Research in this area is difficult to conduct, and the research results are often difficult to interpret. L. Rowell Huesmann has developed a model to explain the relationship between exposure to media violence and increased aggressive behavior.

Huesmann (b. 1943) earned his Ph.D. in psychology and information science from Carnegie Mellon University in 1969. He taught at Yale University and the University of Illinois at Chicago prior to accepting his current position at the University of Michigan Institute for Social Research in 1992. His research has focused on the study of aggression.

The current selection is from "Psychological Processes Promoting the Relation Between Exposure to Media Violence and Aggressive Behavior by the Viewer," which was published in the *Journal of Social Issues* in 1986. In it, Huesmann presents a developmental theory suggesting that children learn aggressive scripts by observing media violence. He argues that these aggressive scripts are carried into adulthood. As you read this selection, note the variables that influence the learning of aggressive behavior. Can you think of any other variables that affect aggression? How might destructive aggression in society be controlled?

Key Concept: media violence and aggression

APA Citation: Huesmann, L. R. (1986). Psychological processes promoting the relation between exposure to media violence and aggressive behavior by the viewer. *Journal of Social Issues, 42,* 125–139. (Abridged)

*L. Rowell
Huesmann*

*T*he question of whether media violence "causes" people to behave more violently has been a major topic of concern to psychologists, communication scientists, and policy makers for well over 15 years. And it was a topic of concern to at least a few scientists more than 50 years ago when movies first became widely distributed. By now, an enormous body of research has emerged, much of which is summarized in this issue. It is implausible to believe at this point that any single new study is going to change the balance much. Those who believe media violence has little or no effect on either children's or adults' violent behavior are unlikely to be convinced by one more study with positive results. Those who believe media violence plays a significant role in increasing at least some children's or adults' antisocial behavior are unlikely to be influenced greatly by one more study with negative results.

Almost all researchers would agree that more aggressive children generally watch more television and prefer more violent television. This appears to be true of children in societies with rigidly controlled media and little media violence as of children in free societies with substantial media violence. It also is as true today of girls in the United States as of boys. In fact, the relation disappears only when children are denied individual choice about what is viewed and subjected to strong group norms about how to react to what is viewed—e.g., among kibbutz children—(Huesmann & Eron, 1986). Most readers would also agree that the behavior of adults and children immediately after viewing a violent scene is more likely to be violent than at other times. The disagreements revolve around *why* these relations obtain, *whether* these relations are large enough to be of concern, and *whether* the so-called violent behaviors represent significant antisocial threats.

One reason why these controversies have persisted is that many researchers have taken too simplistic a view of the possible reasons for the relations. Instead of attempting to explain the relations as the outcomes of psychological processes, many have taken a shallower sociological or statistical perspective, and have simply asked whether it is more plausible that aggressive behavior is a linear function of television habits or that television habits are a linear function of aggressive behavior. In fact, both may be true. The most important question is not which comes first, the television habit or the aggressive habit; the main question is through what psychological processes do these two behaviors become related and stay related.

In this article, I present a model for explaining why increased exposure to media violence in childhood is related both to increased childhood aggressiveness and to increased aggressiveness in adulthood. The model emphasizes the role of the subject's cognitions in determining how the subject processes information observed in the media. It draws heavily on recent thinking in cognitive social psychology. However, it is not asserted that the model encompasses all the possible psychological processes through which exposure to media violence and aggressive behavior become related. Nor is it asserted that the "most important" determinants of aggressive behavior are all represented in the model. Rather, the model provides an explanation, consistent with observed data and established cognitive social theory, of how certain psychological processes contribute to a cyclical process in which exposure to media violence and aggressive behavior mutually engender each other....

LEARNING AGGRESSIVE BEHAVIOR FROM VIOLENCE VIEWING

How does a child's exposure to media violence promote aggressive behavior by the child? A number of different theories have been proposed over the past two decades, all of which hypothesize a learning process (Huesmann, 1982). The theories have differed in terms of exactly what is learned—specific behaviors, cue-behavior connections, attitudes, or arousal patterns. In all cases, though, exposure to media violence is seen as increasing the chances that a child will respond to frustration and victimization with aggression. The transformation of the child's initial aggressive behavior into habitual aggressive behavior, of course, may depend as much on the responses of the child's environment to the aggression, the continuance of the precipitating factors, and the convergence of other casual factors, as on the exposure to the media violence.

In the remainder of this article I attempt to describe in more detail the developmental process by which exposure to media violence, aggressive behavior, and other factors interact to produce an habitual style of aggressive responding in a child. I focus on the cognitive, social, and emotional changes rather than on the physiological changes that exposure to violence seems to engender, not because the physiological changes are less important, but because my own research has not touched on them. Let me begin by outlining the information-processing perspective on social behavior that underlies the proposed model.

The Control of Social Behavior

Social behavior is controlled to a great extent by "programs" for behavior that have been learned during a person's early development. These programs can be described as cognitive *scripts* that are stored in a person's memory, and are used as guides for behavior and social problem solving. These scripts must be encoded and stored in memory in much the same way as are programs and strategies for intellectual behavior. By *encoding* I mean the "formation of a representation of an external stimulus in the memory system" (Kintsch, 1977, p. 485). The scripts may be closely associated with specific cues in the encoding context or they may be abstractions unconnected to specific cues. To encode a particular script, a child must attend to it. Thus, scripts with particularly salient cues for the child are more likely to be encoded. To maintain the script in memory, the child would probably need to rehearse it from time to time. The more elaborative, ruminative type of rehearsal characteristic of children's fantasizing is likely to generate greater connectedness for the script, thereby increasing its accessibility in memory. Also, through such elaborative rehearsal the child may abstract higher order scripts representing more general strategies for behavior than the ones initially stored. In order for a script to influence future behavior, it not only must be encoded and maintained in memory, but it also must be retrieved and utilized when the child faces a social problem. The same laws for recall would apply here as apply for verbal material. Thus, for example, a script is much more likely to be utilized if the same specific cues are present in the environment at retrieval time as were present at encoding time.

Within this framework, an habitually aggressive child is one who regularly retrieves and employs scripts for social behavior that emphasize aggressive responding. But why does this child retrieve mostly aggressive scripts? In some situations it may be that the cues present in the environment trigger the recall only of aggressive scripts. However, the regular retrieval and use of aggressive scripts would also suggest that more aggressive scripts were stored in memory.

The Learning of Aggressive Scripts

One possibility is that the child has tried various social strategies and only the aggressive ones have resulted in positive reinforcement. These strategies, therefore, have been rehearsed most and are the most readily accessible. Certainly, if a specific aggressive response is reinforced, the script that suggested that response is more likely to be retrieved and to be employed in the future. Furthermore, the effect of the reinforcement may generalize to scripts that are abstractions of the specific script promoting a generalized disinhibition of aggression. The boy who solves a social problem successfully by hitting will be more likely in the future not just to hit, but to kick, punch, or push. Nevertheless, it is difficult to believe the complex scripts for social behavior that children rapidly acquire are the results of random emission and selective reinforcement. The laboratory evidence—see Geen & Thomas (1986) and Rule & Ferguson (1986)—suggests that, on the contrary, scripts for social behavior are often encoded from patterns of behaviors observed in others. Just as a boy may encode a motor program for throwing a football from observing others throw, a boy may encode a script for hitting those who victimize him from observing others hit those who victimize them.

According to this model, children are constantly observing others, encoding what seems salient, and integrating these observations into encoded scripts for behavior. Not every aggressive behavior they observe is encoded or stimulates the encoding of an aggressive script. Not every aggressive script is retained or remains accessible for long. The more initially salient an observed aggressive scene is to the child, and the more the child ruminates upon, fantasizes about, and rehearses the observed scene, the more likely it is that an aggressive script based on that scene is recalled and followed in a social problem-solving situation. The more the aggressive scene is consistent with the scripts for behavior that the child has already acquired, the more easily it is integrated into memory. The more the aggressive scene is perceived as realistic and the more the child can identify with an aggressive actor in the scene, the more salient the scene seems to the child. The child constructs scripts for behavior that have subjective utility as potential strategies for social problem solving. Aggressive acts perceived as unreal and performed by actors with whom the child cannot identify do not fulfill this requirement.

The likelihood that a child will access a script for specific aggressive behaviors is certainly dependent on how many relevant cues are present in the environment at recall time. Theoretically, the most important cues are characteristics of the environment (even seemingly irrelevant ones) that are identical to those present when the script was encoded. However, other cues for general aggressive behavior (e.g., guns) may also trigger the recall of specific scripts for aggressive behavior even if they were not associated with the scene at encoding. Finally, a generalized disinhibition of aggression could occur when a child forms a general aggressive behavior script on the basis of his or her observation of numerous scenes of specific aggressive behaviors. If the aggressive script becomes associated with successful social problem solving, new aggressive behaviors may emerge that are unrelated to the original observed behaviors.

Cumulative and Immediate Effects of Violent Scenes

… [T]he majority of laboratory and field studies indicate that a child's viewing of media violence is both correlated with aggressive behavior and a precursor of increased aggressive behavior. The script model explains this correlation primarily as the outcome of a cumulative learning process in which the child's observation of violence eventually leads to the child employing more aggressive scripts for behavior. In accord with such a cumulative model, most longitudinal field data seem to indicate that the relation between earlier violence viewing and later aggression becomes larger as the lag between measurement periods increases (Eron, Huesmann, Lefkowitz, & Walder, 1972; Huesmann, Lagerspetz, & Eron, 1984; Milavsky, Kessler, Stipp, & Rubins, 1982).

Whereas media violence seems to exert its cumulative long-term effect on children by providing examples of aggressive scripts, it also seems to exert short-term effects on adults and children by cueing the retrieval of already-learned aggressive scripts. Though they both increase aggressiveness, the two effects are quite different psychologically. One represents an acquisition process, the other, a retrieval process. The same intervening variable might play quite different roles in the two processes. For example, one would expect younger children to be more susceptible to acquiring new aggressive scripts while older children would have a greater repertoire of aggressive scripts that might be triggered by a nonspecific cue. In fact, the highest correlations between habitual violence viewing and habitual aggression do seem to be obtained for children under 11 years, but immediate aggression in response to media violence has been displayed even by adults.

Intervening Variables in the Link Between Violence Viewing and Aggression

Thus far I have avoided the question of which comes first, the violence viewing or the aggression. The reason is that, within the framework of the proposed information-processing model for the acquisition, maintenance, and retrieval of scripts, the distinction is unimportant. As described above, media violence both provides examples of new aggressive scripts to be acquired, and cues the use of existing specific or general aggressive scripts. Aggressive behavior is increased as a result. But, of course, the aggressive behavior has consequences. One of the major consequences of a child's behaving aggressively is that the child becomes more likely to see new scenes of violence both in the media and in his or her environment. Other consequences stem from the response of the child's environment to aggression and from the effects of aggression on a number of intervening variables linked to both television viewing and aggression. Five such variables seem to play particularly important roles in maintaining the television viewing–aggression relation. These variables are the child's intellectual achievement, the child's social popularity, the child's identification with television characters, the child's belief in the realism of the violence shown on television, and the child's fantasizing about aggression.

Intellectual achievement. Children who have poorer academic skills behave more aggressively, watch television more regularly, watch more television violence, and believe violent programs tell about life as it really is (Huesmann & Eron, 1986). This is true in most Western countries, particularly for boys but also for girls. If one controls statistically for intellectual achievement, the relation between television viewing and aggression usually is still significant but diminished. Poor intellectual achievement contributes to the association between violence viewing and aggression, but it does not fully account for it.

Why is low intellectual achievement related to aggression? At a young age (e.g., under eight), intellectual failures may frustrate a child and stimulate aggression. However, recent research (Huesmann, Eron, & Yarmel, 1986) has shown that from age 8 to adulthood, aggressiveness seems to interfere with intellectual achievement much more than intellectual failures stimulate aggression. Perhaps aggressiveness interferes with the social interactions with teachers and peers that a child needs in order to develop his or her academic potential.

Why is slow intellectual achievement related to heightened television violence viewing? Heightened television viewing in general may interfere with intellectual achievement; Lefkowitz, Eron, Walder, and Huesmann (1977) reported such a longitudinal effect over 10 years. However, it may also be that children who cannot obtain gratification from success in school turn to heroic television shows to obtain vicariously the successes they miss in school. As the lower achieving children also perceive television violence as more like life "really is," they may be more likely to encode the violent scenes as scripts for future behavior.

Social popularity. A second intervening variable that seems important in maintaining the reciprocal relation between television viewing and aggression is popularity. In most societies, more aggressive children are substantially less popular with their peers (Huesmann & Eron, 1986). This is particularly true in societies emphasizing the importance of prosocial cooperative behavior, e.g., kibbutz societies (Huesmann & Bachrach, 1985). Longitudinal regression analyses, however, suggest that the relation between unpopularity and aggression is bidirectional, at least in the United States (Huesmann et al., 1984); not only do more aggressive children become less popular, but less popular children seem to become more aggressive. In addition, less popular children view more television and see more violence on television. In this case, the relation is mostly unidirectional. TV viewing per se is not predictive over time of lower popularity.

Identification with television characters.　　Children who identify more with television characters, (e.g., by perceiving themselves as like television characters) are more likely to be influenced by the aggressive scripts they observe (Huesmann et al., 1984). This is particularly true for boys, for whom the longitudinal effects of violence viewing are clearly enhanced when they identify with aggressive characters (Huesmann et al., 1984). At the same time, more aggressive children tend to identify more with more aggressive television characters, and those who identify more with television characters tend to watch more television. Thus, aggression, violence viewing, and identification with television characters are all intercorrelated and all influence each other.

Belief in the realism of television violence.　　Since the earliest investigations of television violence, the realism of the violence has been hypothesized to be an important intervening variable (Feshbach, 1972). For a script to be encoded and maintained through rehearsal, it must be salient to the child. A violent action that a child perceives to be totally unrealistic is unlikely to receive the attention necessary to be encoded and maintained. In fact, children's belief in the realism of television violence is positively related to both their own aggression and the amount of television violence they watch. As with identification with television characters, the relation between violence viewing and aggression is exacerbated for children who believe the violence is representative of real life (Huesmann et al., 1984).

Fantasizing about aggression.　　Although some have suggested that aggressive fantasizing might decrease the chances of aggressive behavior in a child through a cathartic process, the script model would suggest otherwise. The retrieval and rehearsal of an aggressive script through fantasy would strengthen the encoding of the script and increase the likelihood that it would be retrieved. Particularly elaborate fantasies might even generate new scripts in memory. In fact, children's self-reports of aggressive fantasy are positively correlated with both their aggression and their television viewing (Huesmann & Eron, 1986). More aggressive children fantasize more about aggression, and children who watch more television fantasize more about both heroic and aggressive acts. The children who report the most heroic and aggressive fantasies are those who watch a lot of television, see a lot of violence, believe the violence is realistic, and identify with television characters.

Reciprocal Processes Promoting the Television Violence–Aggression Relation

Taken together, these relations suggest a reciprocal process through which aggression and violence viewing perpetuate themselves and each other. Children who are heavy viewers of television violence regularly observe characters behaving aggressively in order to solve interpersonal problems. To the extent that the children (particularly boys) identify with the aggressive characters, the children may encode in memory the aggressive solutions they observe. I have hypothesized that social behavior is controlled to a great extent by cognitive scripts, schemas, and strategies that the child observes, encodes into memory, and uses as a guide for behavior. The child constantly exposed to violence is more likely to develop and maintain cognitive scripts emphasizing aggressive solutions to social problems. These violent scenes may also stimulate aggressive fantasies in which the encoded aggressive scripts are rehearsed, making them more likely to be recalled and utilized in the future. If the aggressive behaviors are emitted in the appropriate situations, the aggressive behaviors may be reinforced with desirable outcomes, making their future occurrence more likely. However, as the aggression becomes habitual, it must eventually interfere with both social and academic success. The more aggressive child becomes the less popular child and the poorer academic achiever in school. These academic and social failures may become frustrators instigating more aggressive responses. In addition, however, children who are less successful in school and less popular become the more regular television viewers. Perhaps they can obtain the satisfactions vicariously from television that they are denied in school and in their social life. They may also be better able to justify their own previous aggression after seeing more aggression in the media.

These less popular, less intellectually able children watch more television violence, identify more with television characters, and believe the violence they observe on television reflects real life. All these conditions promote the learning of new aggressive schemas from television and the reinforcement of old ones. Since these children's intellectual capacities are more limited, the easy aggressive solutions they observe may be incorporated more readily into their behavioral repertoires. Heavy television viewing isolates them from their peers and gives them less time to work toward academic success. The violence they see on television may reassure them that their own behavior is appropriate or may teach them new coercive techniques, which they then attempt to use in their interactions with others. Thus, they behave more aggressively, which in turn makes them even less popular and drives them back to television. The cycle continues with aggression, academic failure, social failure, violence viewing, and fantasizing about aggression mutually facilitating each other....

L. Rowell Huesmann

SUMMARY

A developmental theory is presented to account for the linkage between increased exposure to media violence and increased aggressive behavior. It is argued that the effect of media violence on individual differences in aggression is primarily the result of a cumulative learning process during childhood. Aggressive scripts for behavior itself stimulates the observation of media violence. In both childhood and adulthood, certain cues in the media may trigger the activation of aggressive scripts acquired in any manner and thus stimulate aggressive behavior. A number of intervening variables may mitigate or exacerbate these reciprocal effects. However, if undampened, this cumulative learning process can build enduring schemas for aggressive behavior that persist into adulthood.

REFERENCES

Eron, L. D., Huesmann, L. R., Lefkowitz, M. M., & Walder, L. O. (1972). Does television violence cause aggression? *American Psychologist, 27,* 253–263.

Feshbach, S. (1972). Reality and fantasy in filmed violence. In J. P. Muray, E. A. Rubinstein, & G. A. Comstock (Eds.), *Television and social behavior: Television and social learning* (pp. 318–345). Washington, D. C.: U.S. Government Printing Office.

Huesmann, L. R. (1982). Television violence and aggressive behavior. In D. Pearl, L. Bouthilet, & J. Lazar (Eds.), *Television and behavior: Ten years of programs and implications for the 80's* (pp. 126–137). Washington, D.C.: U.S. Government Printing Office.

Huesmann, L. R., & Bachrach, R. S. (1985). *Differing reactions to television in kibbutz and city children.* Paper presented at meetings of American Psychological Association, Los Angeles, CA.

Huesmann, L. R., & Eron, L. D. (Eds.) (1986). *Television and the aggressive child: A cross-national comparison.* Hillsdale, NJ: Lawrence Erlbaum Associates.

Huesmann, L. R., Eron, L. D., Lefkowitz, M. M., & Walder, L. O. (1984). The stability of aggression over time and generations. *Developmental Psychology, 20,* 1120–1134.

Geen, R. G., & Thomas, S. L. (1986). The immediate effects of media violence and behavior. *Journal of Social Issues, 42,*(3), 7–27.

Huesmann, L. R., Eron, L. D., & Yarmel, P. (1986). Intellectual functioning and aggression. *Journal of Personality and Social Psychology, 50.*

Huesmann, L. R., Lagerspetz, K., & Eron, L. D. (1984). Intervening variables in the TV violence-aggression relation: Evidence from two countries. *Developmental Psychology, 20,* 746–775.

Kintsch, W. (1977). *Memory and cognition.* New York: Wiley.

Lefkowitz, M. M., Eron, L. D., Walder, L. O., & Huesmann, L. R. (1977) *Growing up to be violent: A longitudinal study of the development of aggression.* New York: Pergamon.

Milavsky, J. R., Kessler, R., Stipp, H., & Rubens, W. (1982). *Television and aggression: The results of a panel study.* New York: Academic Press.

Rule, B. G., & Ferguson, T. J. (1986). The effects of media violence on attitudes, emotions, and cognitions. *Journal of Social Issues, 42*(3), 29–50.

Some Lessons to Be Drawn

Aggression has been studied by social psychologists for many years. Defining aggression, studying it, and trying to control destructive violence have been controversial pursuits in social psychology. Leonard Berkowitz, who has spent over 30 years studying aggressive behavior, is a pioneer in the area of aggression.

Berkowitz (b. 1926) earned his Ph.D. in social psychology from the University of Michigan in 1951. He has been a professor of psychology at the University of Wisconsin–Madison since 1955. Berkowitz has written hundreds of articles and books, including the influential book *Aggression: A Social-Psychological Analysis* (McGraw-Hill, 1962).

This selection is from chapter 14, "In Conclusion: Some Lessons to Be Drawn," of Berkowitz's book *Aggression: Its Causes, Consequences, and Control* (McGraw-Hill, 1993). Writing in an objective yet conversational style, the author reviews the types and causes of aggression and offers some thoughts on how to control destructive aggression. He explains why people develop aggressive tendencies and how we might reduce some of the negative effects of aggression. As you read this selection, develop your own hypotheses explaining the causes and consequences of aggression in our everyday lives.

Key Concept: aggression

APA Citation: Berkowitz, L. (1993). *Aggression: Its causes, consequences, and control.* New York: McGraw-Hill. [Chapter 14: In conclusion: Some lessons to be drawn.]

DIFFERENT KINDS OF AGGRESSION: INSTRUMENTAL AND EMOTIONAL

One of my major themes is that there is more than one kind of aggression. Attempts to hurt or destroy other people do not all arise in the same manner and are not all governed by the same biological and psychological processes, though all aggression is aimed at the deliberate injury of another person. Investigators who study the processes involved in aggression don't always agree in detail about what the main types of aggression are.

There is, however, good reason to distinguish between instrumental and affective or emotional aggression. Assaults which are carried out in the hope of gaining a noninjurious objective such as money, social status, enhanced

317

self-identity, or the elimination of an unpleasant situation are very different in many ways from attacks which are prompted by intense emotional arousal. It's important to understand both types of aggression, since both contribute to unhappiness and distress in social relationships and tear at the social fabric. Nevertheless, at the risk of seeming to deemphasize instrumental aggression, my focus in this [selection] is on the sort of violence which is driven by strong feelings.

Many social scientists fail to recognize the difference between instrumental aggression and emotional aggression. Quite often this happens in part because their particular theories of behavior give little weight to the relatively involuntary and automatic aspects of emotional conduct. Some students of human behavior unquestioningly assume, along with Sigmund Freud and other psychodynamic theorists, that all behavior is motivated. For them, every action, or at least every act of social significance, is carried out with an aim in mind. Aggressors must want to do more than inflict pain or destruction. Social scientists who espouse this position believe their primary task is to uncover the hidden purposes that spur people to assault others. They seek to learn what else is involved besides the infliction of pain or destruction—what the attackers "really" want to accomplish.

Other investigators phrase their reasoning in other words, but their underlying assumptions are very similar. They prefer to say that behavior is mainly brought about by incentives, the rewards that are anticipated for performing a given set of responses. From this perspective, a child who strikes her sister, a husband who batters his wife, and a robber who kills his victim all act as they do because they believe that their behavior will benefit them in some way. These researchers want to determine what incentives govern aggression, and learn how these expected benefits operate.

My guess is that the failure to recognize the often impulsive and unthinking nature of emotional aggression has another cause in addition to their adherence to a specific psychological theory, whether Freudian, behavioral, or cognitive. Many social scientists look for a hidden purpose behind all aggressive behavior because they want to believe that humans are rational much of the time—not that all actions are necessarily based on intelligent decisions but that they have meaning from the actors' viewpoints. For these social scientists, to deny the existence of an underlying motive for aggression would be to unduly demean the aggressors and perhaps all humankind. Surely, they tell themselves, people must be more than unthinking robots or even animals. Even a murderer, no matter how callous or brutal, must have thought about what he was doing and why, and must have carried out his assault for a reason that made sense to him.

As I see it, however, to insist upon the basic rationality of all significant human conduct is to be blind to the marvelously complex and diversified nature of human behavior. Our thoughts and calculations, the cost-benefit analyses we carry out, do regulate our actions much of the time—but not always. We can also be highly emotional at times—carried away by the feelings and emotional impulses of the moment. We are multifaceted, "many-splendored" things, and to deny our emotionality is to deny part of our humanity.

Now that I have taken this stance, I have to make my beliefs about how emotional aggression operates very clear.

In distinguishing between instrumental and emotional aggression, I am not saying that emotional-driven assaults have no purpose. They do have a goal: the victim's injury (or in more extreme instances, destruction). My contention is that harm or destruction is a major objective in emotional aggression even when other aims can also be identified. Laboratory subjects who have just been insulted by "another student" may well want to comply with the experimenter's instructions when they give the other student electric shocks. In addition, however, having been provoked, they want to hurt the other student. Similarly, an enraged wife who shoots her abusive husband may want to make him stop beating her, but she also wants to do him severe harm.

I believe also that the strength of an emotional assault is largely determined by the intensity of the aggressor's internal agitation; as I have suggested, inner stimulation impels the attack, often in a relatively unthoughtful manner. An infuriated wife doesn't calculate long-term costs and benefits. She knows only that she wants to hurt (or maybe even kill) her tormentor, and as she lashes out at him, her actions are spurred by her strong internal arousal.

This doesn't mean that all emotional attacks are necessarily completely unrestrained. Inhibitions can block an impelled assault to some degree, at least partly because of strong prior learning that aggression is wrong and/or may bring punishment. A mother who is furious with her daughter for disobeying her may readily shout at the girl and may even slap her. However, very few adults kick their children or hit them with clubs. Most people's inhibitions against aggression are activated to some extent even when they are furious, and the inhibitions keep them from doing serious injury. The more strongly aroused a person is, of course, the weaker the activation of these relatively automatic blocks will be and also the less effective the inhibitions will be. By the same token, the stronger the person's usual restraints against aggression, the less likely it is that any degree of arousal will cause her or him to lash out in an uncontrolled outburst of violence. I will say more about self-restraints later in this [selection].

IS VIOLENCE INEVITABLE?

It would be difficult, and probably even impossible, to eliminate violence altogether from social life. This is not because human beings are inherently evil and possess a built-in drive to kill and destroy. There is clear and compelling evidence that the aggressive instinct posited by Sigmund Freud, Konrad Lorenz, and other theorists actually does not exist. Rather, it's better to say that some level of violence may always be a part of human life, for at least two reasons: first, because it's all too easy for people to learn that aggression pays, some of the time; and second, because—if I'm right about negative affect as a preprogrammed spur to emotional aggression—no one can hope to avoid all distress and unhappiness.

We're apt to employ aggressive tactics to further our ends to the degree that we've seen aggression work. What's surprising is not the general proposition that we can learn to use aggression instrumentally but the sometimes subtle ways in which people find out that it can pay to assault others. For example, many of us learned as we were growing up that we could sometimes successfully stop others from bothering us by attacking them. Our parents may have admonished or disciplined us for hitting siblings who were annoying us, but every once in a while we still saw that our aggression had accomplished its purpose—that it had terminated the annoyance, at least for a brief time. Thus we found that aggression does occasionally pay off by eliminating or at least lessening a disturbing state of affairs. In addition, emotionally aroused aggressors are also rewarded by their victims' pain and distress. A brother who is angry with his sister will be gratified simply by seeing her cry after he hits her. As if this weren't enough, think of how often adults reinforce their offsprings aggression by letting the children have their own way when they shout and scream or otherwise show their anger.

In the cases I've been citing, the aggressors' own actions are rewarded, but rewards can strengthen aggressive tendencies even when we see them being given to someone else. . . . [W]e can learn to regard aggression favorably simply by watching aggressors get what they want when they threaten, insult, or hit other people. Unless there are countervailing influences, we may come to think that we too might profit by behaving aggressively.

All this means, then, is that we can see aggression pay off in many different ways. Favorable outcomes, whether we obtain them for ourselves or see others get them, can heighten the chances that we will attack someone in the future, either verbally or physically, when an appropriate opportunity arises, at least if our inhibitions are low.

Don't forget, though, that aggression isn't only carried out in hope of an external benefit. It can also be stimulated by negative feelings. In this connection, recall the many kinds of unpleasant situations that can give rise to anger, hostility, and even violence if the circumstances are conducive—for example, situations in which people experience frustrations, economic stresses, unpleasantly high temperatures, atmospheric pollution, foul odors, and depressing or sad events. Though a person's thoughts can modify or even change the anger/aggression emotional state initially produced by negative affect, such emotion-altering, higher-order thinking doesn't always occur. We can be so carried away by intense unpleasant sensations or by a compelling situation that we don't stop to think about all the available information. We may be especially likely to ignore possible reasons for our bad feelings, and we may not even try to think about the most appropriate ways of behaving in the particular situation. As a consequence, our negative affect can lead to impulsive acts of hostility and aggression. In short, though we can regulate and change the way our negative experiences influence our actions if we think carefully enough, we don't always do the necessary thinking.

Priming effects can also promote aggression. Hostile ideas can come to mind and aggressive inclinations can be generated, for a brief time anyway, when people merely see or hear something that has an aggressive meaning. A wide variety of objects and incidents (including guns and knives, the sight and sound of people fighting, news stories about violent crimes, athletic contests interpreted as aggressive encounters, and war reports) may have such a meaning and may thus prime short-lived hostile thoughts and aggressive impulses.

With so many and such varied factors promoting aggression, is it really going to be possible to eliminate violence from contemporary society?

THE DETERMINANTS AS RISK FACTORS

While I believe that it's virtually impossible to escape or eliminate all the factors that can give rise to aggression, I am not saying that these influences are necessarily always very strong nor that each of them always operates to generate open violence. Consider the role of poverty in the production of violent crimes. There's pretty good evidence that economic deprivation can contribute to spouse battering, child abuse, and homicides. Despite this evidence, political conservatives who oppose social welfare programs have long denied that poverty breeds crime. In a recent example, the Archbishop of Canterbury aroused the ire of the Conservative party in Great Britain when he attributed a serious riot in a northern English city to the high level of unemployment and economic hardship in the community. A prominent Conservative politician dismissed the Archbishop's interpretation altogether by noting that churchgoing poor people were less apt to riot or steal than were equally impoverished people who did not attend church. This meant, he insisted, that it was moral decay rather than poverty that led to crime and violence.

Most social scientists would say the politician was being simplistic and had thought only in absolutist, yes-or-no terms. No serious researcher really believes that economic deprivations in themselves inevitably and always produce lawbreaking. Rather, in line with the position I've taken . . . , it's better to say that poverty is a risk factor, a condition which heightens the *likelihood* of antisocial actions but does not necessarily always produce this behavior. Analogously, cigarette smoking doesn't always lead to lung cancer and heart disease, but frequent smokers are nonetheless at risk for developing these disorders.

This is the perspective that should be taken in considering all the conditions that can promote violence. People aren't always incited to attack others when they experience disappointments or see weapons. Very few moviegoers become assaultive after watching violent films. People who are exposed to unpleasantly hot weather don't always go on rampages and loot and burn the stores in their neighborhoods. A great many poor persons don't break laws. Yet, as . . . research . . . demonstrates, each of these factors increases the chance of aggression. The probability that any one of these factors alone will produce a violent outburst in a given situation is low. Several conditions clearly have to be present if these influences are to give rise to an open attack on an available target in a given situation, much as any one cigarette smoker won't develop lung cancer unless he or she has the appropriate predispositions and bodily conditions. Nevertheless, it's important to know about the individual risk factors, because each raises the likelihood of an undesirable outcome.

Moreover, although the increased probability of violence as a result of each risk factor may be small, a significant number of people may be affected when the population is large enough. In an area the size of a city, a state, or a nation, the poorer residents considered as a whole are more likely to break the law and assault each other than are their economically better off fellow citizens. Similarly, while there's only a small chance that any one person in a movie or TV audience will punch someone in the nose after watching a violent scene, millions of viewers may see the scene, and thus there may be several hundred more acts of violence in the country than otherwise would have occurred. Law enforcement authorities could not confiscate all the millions of handguns that abound in the United States even if they wanted to, but the ready availability of so many weapons undoubtedly means that each year hundreds of people are killed in the United States who otherwise would not have died.

In general, then, it's advisable to think probabilistically about the conditions that can foster aggressive behavior. Indeed, society could benefit from a probabilistic perspective in many different domains of life, including business and commerce, the natural sciences, engineering, education, politics, and the social sciences. To make the best possible decision in any of these areas, it is necessary to consider the odds that a certain event will or will not take place and, on the basis of the available knowledge and information, to estimate the chance (whether it's great, moderate, or small) that the event will actually occur. Even then, the resulting estimate will be only a probability statement—not a certainty. Just so, ... research ... allows us to make reasonably good estimates, or probability statements, about what conditions foster aggression.

CONTROLLING VIOLENCE

Though it's unlikely that humankind will ever abolish all violence from the face of the earth, we could take some steps to lessen the chances that people will attack or be nasty to others. Obviously, one such step would be to reduce the number of aggression-priming stimuli. Equally obviously, however, this would be difficult in a free society. Aside from the complex constitutional issues, this step would be controversial on a social level. Quite a few persons enjoy violent movies, and a good number think that they can protect themselves from dangerous intruders by having revolvers in their homes. However, the United States would do well to weigh these possible social benefits against the costs of allowing so many violent scenes to be shown on the nation's TV and movie screens, as well as against the costs of permitting the unrestrained sale of firearms in many areas of the country. Is the pleasure that some people derive from seeing actors shoot, stab, kick, punch, and kill each other really worth the hundreds of "extra" violent incidents, some of them very serious or fatal, which occur in the nation? Does the illusory feeling of safety (or the sense of power and virility) which some people gain from owning handguns really count for more than the many hundreds of lives that are taken every year by these firearms? Policymakers and citizens alike should face these questions instead of avoiding them, and then decide.

Even if society does nothing to reduce the amount of violence shown in the movies, on television, and on the printed page, the impact of these depictions could be weakened.... [T]he effect which the sight of people being beastly to each other will have on the audience members depends to a considerable extent on what they think of the witnessed aggression. Parents, educators, other authority figures, and the media could help to shape viewers' attitudes toward the events shown on the screen. At the very least, they should remind children, and the public in general, that aggression is socially undesirable even when the movie hero beats up the bad guys.

Steps could also be taken to reduce the aggression-inciting effects of unpleasant occurrences. Even if human beings are genetically disposed to become angry and inclined toward aggression when they have negative feelings, they can learn not to behave aggressively after the unpleasant events that caused the feelings. Here too, parents and educators can play active parts. They can teach their charges that aggression doesn't pay and that it is possible to cope with life's difficulties in a constructive and nonaggressive manner. People should also learn that they don't have to "release" their supposedly pent-up aggressive impulses by engaging in real or fantasy aggression and that, in the long run anyway, fighting is more apt to heighten than to reduce the likelihood of further conflict.

My emphasis on avoiding aggression and aggression-priming events doesn't mean that I am recommending that we pretend that all's right with the world. I'm not calling for a denial of the existence of conflict and unhappiness. Instead, ... while I believe that people make trouble for themselves by brooding about their hardships and/or the wrongs they think they've suffered, I also believe that a person who has had a serious disagreement with someone else, or who has met with a tragedy or a serious disappointment, would do well to tell the significant individuals in his or her life about the unpleasant event and about the accompanying feelings. In general, I favor more communication —not less. However, communication should not be accompanied by ranting and raving and should involve the transmission of information rather than the overt expression of hostility and hatred.

To take a broader view, the procedures I recommend generally call for a mixture of cognitive changes and heightened inhibitions, or self-restraints, which play a major role in the reduction of aggression.

It's my impression that mental health specialists who are interested in the control of aggression haven't always given sufficient attention to the importance of inhibitory mechanisms.... A number of important theorists have emphasized the psychological processes that help to instigate aggression but have neglected the processes involved in restraining this behavior. This neglect is unfortunate, particularly because a relatively few persons account for the greatest proportion of the serious acts of violence which occur in society. Many of these highly assaultive individuals are defective in self-control. They may be disposed to see threats in the world around them, and they're also all too likely to attribute malevolence to others who have thwarted them. But they are often also unable to restrain their emotional impulses so that they frequently lash out in temper, even when there's a good chance that their aggression will be punished.

What should be done with extremely violent persons?... The threat of punishment doesn't seem to be very effective in deterring them from violent crimes, partly because they believe (with some justification) that the odds are good that they will get away with their misdeeds, but also because of their emotional reactivity. Even the possibility of the ultimate punishment, execution, doesn't hold them back for very long, according to the available evidence. Nor are extremely violent people good prospects for rehabilitation. Recent research suggests that certain psychological interventions can benefit at least some adolescent delinquents, but there is no good reason to think that such interventions will work with very antisocial, highly assaultive adults. In my view, the U.S. criminal justice system typically sends too many people to prison for too long and for too many different kinds of offenses. Still, imprisonment may be the only answer for extremely violent individuals. Social scientists' understanding of what has caused them to act as they do doesn't mean that society should tolerate their highly antisocial conduct.

PART SEVEN

Applications of Social Psychology

On the Internet . . .

Sites appropriate to Part Seven

The Population and Environmental Psychology Web site provides information on environmental psychology, including a list of environmental links and information about issues on the environment.

```
http://web.uvic.ca/~apadiv34/index.html
```

The Noise Pollution Clearinghouse site provides extensive resources on noise, including information on hearing loss, legal issues, and an understanding of the effects of noise on behavior.

```
http://www.nonoise.org
```

The Health Psychology Web site facilitates collaboration among psychologists and health care professionals interested in psychological and behavioral aspects of physical and mental health.

```
http://www.health-psych.org
```

CHAPTER 14 Environment and Health Psychology

14.1 ROBERT SOMMER AND FRANKLIN D. BECKER

Territorial Defense and the Good Neighbor

Environmental psychologists are interested in discovering how the environment influences human behavior. We tend to surround ourselves with a bubble of personal space that we claim as our own. Robert Sommer and Franklin D. Becker are interested in how people mark their space to prevent others from getting too close. They suggest that learning how people use markers to identify territorial space can help us to become better neighbors.

Sommer (b. 1929) earned his Ph.D. in psychology from Kansas University in 1956. He has taught at the University of California–Davis since 1963. Sommer is the author of 11 books, including *Personal Space* and *The Mind's Eye*. Becker (b. 1946) earned his Ph.D. in environmental psychology at the University of California–Davis in 1972. He is currently a professor of design and environmental analysis at Cornell University. Becker is the author of *Housing Messages* (Van Nostrand Reinhold, 1977).

This selection is from "Territorial Defense and the Good Neighbor," which was published in *Journal of Personality and Social Psychology* in 1969. In it, Sommer and Becker describe a series of experiments they designed to investigate the effect of territorial marking on social interaction. Notice how the various types of markers helped to prevent the invasion of personal space, and note the reactions of neighbors. How do we learn to interpret territorial markers in our society? How prevalent is this behavior in everyday life?

Key Concept: territorial defense

APA Citation: Sommer, R., & Becker, F. D. (1969). Territorial defense and the good neighbor. *Journal of Personality and Social Psychology, 11,* 85–92.

A series of experimental studies was designed to explore how people mark out and defend space in public areas. The use of space is affected by instructions to defend actively the area or retreat, by room density, and by the location of walls, doors, and other physical barriers. Under light population pressure, most markers are capable of reserving space in a public area, but more personal markers have the greatest effect. As room density increases, the effect of the marker is seen in delaying occupancy of the area and in holding onto a smaller subarea within the larger space. Neighbors play an important part in legitimizing a system of space ownership.

... In a previous study, the reactions to staged spatial invasions were investigated (Felipe & Sommer, 1966). There was no single reaction to a person coming too close; some people averted their heads and placed an elbow between themselves and the intruder, others treated him as a nonperson, while still others left the area when he came too close. The range of defensive gestures, postures, and acts suggested that a systematic study of defensive procedures would contribute materially to our knowledge of human spatial behavior. Following the tradition of ecological research, the studies would be undertaken in naturally occurring environments....

EXPERIMENTAL STUDIES

Most territories are marked and bounded in some clear way. In the animal kingdom, markers may be auditory (bird song), olfactory (glandular secretions by deer), or visual (bear-claw marks on a tree). Since humans rely almost exclusively on visual markers, the authors decided to test the strength of various markers ranging from the physical presence of a person to impersonal artifacts.

Study 1

The first study took place in a popular soda fountain on campus. The soda fountain was located in a converted office building which still contained a number of small rooms. Patrons would obtain their refreshments at a central counter and then repair to one of the smaller rooms to eat and chat informally. Prior to the study, the authors had been struck by the sight of students walking up and down the corridor looking for an empty room. One of the small rooms which contained three square tables, each surrounded by four chairs, was used for the study. A 20-year-old girl who appeared to be studying stationed herself at a table facing the door. On other occasions during the same hours she stationed herself down the hall so she could observe who entered the experimental room. A session took place only when the room was unoccupied at the outset.

If an all-or-none criterion of room occupancy is applied, the experimenter's defense was not very successful. During only 1 of the 10 experimental sessions was she able to keep the entire room to herself. The average length of time before the room was occupied during the experimental sessions was 5.8 minutes compared to 2.6 minutes during the control sessions, but the difference was not statistically reliable. Although the experimenter was unable to keep the room to herself, she was able to protect the table at which she studied. The remaining three seats were occupied only once during the experimental sessions compared to 13 occupancies during the control sessions ($p < .01$). It seems clear that territorial defense in a public area is not an all-or-none affair. The defender's presence may be seen in a delay in occupancy rather than an absence of invaders and in the avoidance of a subarea within the larger area.

Study 2

The next study took place in a more traditional open-plan soda fountain and, instead of the physical presence of the experimenter, three sorts of objects were used as territorial markers—a sandwich wrapped in cellophane, a sweater draped over a chair, and two paperback books stacked on the table. In each case the experimenter located two adjacent empty tables and arbitrarily placed a marker on one with the other as a control. Seating himself some distance away, he was able to record the duration of time before each table was occupied. The sessions all took place at moderate room density. There were 8 sessions with a sandwich marker, 13 with a sweater, and 20 with the books.

The authors were interested in whether a marker would reserve an entire table as well as the marked chair. The answer for all of the markers was affirmed. The unmarked control tables were occupied significantly sooner than were the marked tables, and the difference was significant for each of the three markers. In fact, in all 41 sessions the control table was occupied sooner or at the same time as the marked table. In only three of the sessions did anyone sit at the marked *chair*. All three were occupied by males.... It is also interesting to examine the occupancy patterns at the two sorts of tables. The marked tables were eventually occupied by 34 lone individuals and 4 groups of 2 persons, while the unmarked tables were occupied by 18 lone individuals and 20 groups. It can be noted that a group of 2 or 3 could easily be accommodated at a marked table even assuming that the marker represented one person, yet virtually all the groups sat at unmarked tables. It is clear that the markers were able to (*a*) protect the particular chair almost totally, (*b*) delay occupancy of the entire table, and (*c*) divert groups away from the table.

Study 3

A similar study using books and newspapers as markers was undertaken in a dormitory study hall at a time of very light room density. Virtually all the markers proved effective in reserving the marked chair. The only exceptions were two sessions when the school paper which had been used as a marker was treated as litter and pushed aside. After more than 30 individual sessions where virtually all the markers were respected, the authors decided to move the experiments to the main university library where room density was much heavier. It seemed clear that at low densities almost any marker is effective. One qualification is that the object must be perceived as a marker and not as something discarded and unwanted by its former owner. Certain forms of litter such as old newspapers or magazines may, indeed, attract people to a given location.

The locus of study was switched to the periodical room in the university library where room density was high and pressure for seats was great. This room contained rectangular six-chair tables, three chairs to a side. The experimenter arrived at one of the six seats at a designated table at 6:50 P.M., deposited a marker, and then departed to another table at 7:00 P.M. to view any occupancy at the marked position by a student seeking space. During each session, a similarly situated empty chair which was unmarked was used as the control. There were 25 experimental sessions, each lasting 2 hours. The markers included two notebooks and a textbook, four library journals piled in a neat stack, four library journals randomly scattered on the table, a sports jacket draped over the chair, and a sports jacket draped over the chair in addition to the notebooks on the table.

If one compares the average time before occupancy of the marked and the control chairs, it is apparent that all markers were effective. Seventeen of the 25 marked chairs remained vacant the entire 2-hour period, while *all* control chairs were occupied. The average interval before the control chairs were occupied was 20 minutes. Some of the markers were more potent than others. Only one student occupied a chair that was marked either by a sports jacket or a notebook-and-text. Chairs marked by the neatly-piled journals were occupied three of the five sessions, while chairs marked by the randomly placed journals were occupied all five sessions, even though the interval in each case exceeded that of the control chairs. It is clear that the personal markers, such as the sports jacket and notebooks, were able to keep away intruders entirely, while the impersonal library-owned markers (journals) could only delay occupancy of the marked chairs....

Study 4

Since the role of the neighbor seemed an important aspect of a property-ownership system, the authors decided to investigate it experimentally. The first of such studies involved two experimenters and a person sitting alongside an empty chair. One experimenter seated himself next to a stranger (the neighbor) for 15 minutes and then departed, leaving behind an open book and an open notebook upon the table as territorial markers. After a fixed interval, the second experimenter, in the role of a student looking for a chair, came and inquired about the marked space nonverbally. The nonverbal questioning was a pantomime which included catching the neighbor's eye, pulling out the chair slightly, hesitating, looking at the place markers and at the neighbor, and then back at the markers. The authors had very little experience with such non-verbal cues, but expected that the neighbor's reactions might include verbal defenses ("That seat is taken") and nonverbal defenses (moving the books to re-inforce the marker). The independent variable was the length of time between the departure of the first experimenter and the arrival of the second—which was either a 5- or a 20-minute interval. Some sessions had to be terminated when the neighbor departed before the second experimenter arrived on the scene.

Overall the results were discouraging. In only 6 of the 55 trials did the neighbor respond to the nonverbal gestures of the second experimenter in what could be described as a space-defending manner, such as a statement that the seat was taken. Five of the six defensive acts occurred when the experimenter had been away 5 minutes, compared to only one defensive act when he had been away 20 minutes, but considering that there were 55 trials the difference was unimpressive.

Study 5

The authors decided to make another attempt to see if the neighbor could be involved in property defense on a spontaneous basis—that is, if he would defend marked space without being questioned directly. Unlike in the preceding study, the "owner" attempted to establish a relationship with the neighbor prior to the "owner's" departure. There were two phases of the study; when it seemed that the first approach was not leading anywhere, another approach was used. The markers were a neat stack of three paperback books left on the table in front of a chair. The sessions took place at six-chair tables where there was at least 1 empty seat between the marker and the neighbor. The first ex-perimenter entered the room and found the location meeting the experimental requirements (a person sitting at the end chair of a six-person table with two empty chairs alongside him—O–O–S). The experimenter (a girl) sat down on the same side of the table but one seat away (E–O–S). There were 13 trials in each of the following conditions: (*a*) The experimenter sat 5 minutes and then departed from the table, leaving her books neatly stacked on the table. During this time she did not interact with her neighbor. (*b*) Similar to Condition *a*, the experimenter sat for 5 minutes except that during the 5-minute wait, the ex-perimenter asked the neighbor "Excuse me, could you tell me what time it is?" (*c*) Similar to Condition *a*, the experimenter sat for 5 minutes except that dur-ing the 5-minute wait the experimenter engaged the neighbor in conversation four times and, while leaving and placing the stack of three paperback books on the table, declared, "See you later." Fifteen minutes later, the second experimenter (a male) entered the room, walked directly to the marked chair, pushed the books directly ahead of him, and sat down at the table.

The results were again discouraging. In none of the 39 trials involving Conditions *a, b,* and *c* did the neighbor inform the intruder that the seat was taken. The authors therefore decided to strengthen the conditions by having the "owner" return and directly confront the intruder. Seven of such trials were added to Condition *a,* six to Condition *b,* and 6 to Condition *c,* making 19 trials in all when the "owner" came back and told the intruder "You are sitting in my chair." Each time she hesitated about 30 seconds to see if the neighbor would intervene, and then she picked up her books and departed. There was no verbal response from the neighbor in any of the 19 sessions. The most that occurred would be a frown or a look of surprise on the part of the neighbor, or some nonverbal communication with someone else at the table. Stated simply, despite a flagrant usurpation of a marked space, all neighbors chose to remain uninvolved. It became clear that if one wanted to study the neighbor's role in such an informal regulatory system one would have to question him directly as to whether the seat was occupied.

Study 6

The next study employed two experimenters, a male and a female, and the same three paperback books as markers. Two different girls were used as experimenters, and the sessions occurred in two different, nearby college libraries. The experimental situation involved six-chair tables where the first experimenter (female) sat down at the same side of a table with a subject, leaving an empty chair between them (E–O–S). The goal of the study was to learn whether a greater amount of interaction between the former occupant and the neighbor would increase the neighbor's likelihood of defending the chair. Unlike in the previous study, the neighbor was questioned directly as to whether the seat was taken. There were three different instructional sets, and these took place according to a prearranged random order. In 14 trials, the first experimenter sat at the chair for 5 minutes without saying anything, deposited the marker (three paperback books), and left. Fourteen other sessions were similar except that at some time during her 5-minute stay, the first experimenter asked the neighbor for the time. Ten other sessions were similar except that the experimenter engaged the neighbor in conversation as to where to get a Coke, what was happening on campus, and other minor matters. Fifteen minutes after the first experimenter departed, the second experimenter (a male) entered the room, walked over to the marked chair, and asked the neighbor "Excuse me, is there anyone sitting here?"

The results differ markedly from those in the previous study. A total of 22 out of the 38 neighbors defended the seat when questioned directly on the matter. The typical defense response was "Yes, there is" or "There is a girl who left those books."[1] However the amount of contact between the first experimenter and the neighbor made little difference in defensive behavior. When there had been no contact, or minimal contact, between the first experimenter and neighbor, the seat was protected 58% of the time, while the use of several items of conversation between the experimenter and her neighbor raised the percentage of defensive responses only to 66%. The difference between conditions is small and statistically unreliable; what is impressive is the great increase in defensive behavior when the neighbor was questioned directly. Two other parameters of the situation are (a) the time that the first experimenter remained in the seat before depositing her marker, and (b) the length of time that the first experimenter was out of room before the second experimenter approached the marked chair.

Study 7

The final study employed two experimenters, both males, and the same three paperback books. The sessions took place at six-chair tables in the library, where the first experimenter again sat down on the same side of the table with a subject, leaving an empty chair between them (E–O–S). He remained either 5 minutes or 20 minutes, depending upon the experimental condition, and then departed, leaving on the table a neat stack of three paperback books. After a designated interval of either 15 or 60 minutes, the second experimenter entered the room and asked the neighbor whether the (marked) chair was taken. The second experimenter recorded the neighbor's reply verbatim just as soon as he was able to sit down somewhere. Since both experimenters were males, it was decided to use only male neighbors in the experiment.

The independent variables were (a) the length of time the first experimenter had been seated before he left his marker and departed and (b) the length of time the first experimenter was absent before the neighbor was questioned by the second experimenter. Some sessions were unusable since the neighbor departed before the designated time and could not be interviewed. Most of the unusable sessions occurred when the experimenter had been absent for 60 minutes. The sessions took place at times of light-to-moderate room density.

Although the design had not called for comparison of marked and unmarked chairs, it is noteworthy that the markers were effective in keeping people away. Not one of the 64 marked chairs was ever occupied. Regarding the inclination of the neighbor to defend the marked space when questioned by the second experimenter, a content analysis of the neighbor's responses to the query "Is this seat taken?" into defense and nondefense categories revealed that 44 neighbors defended the marked space by indicating that it was taken, while 20 failed to do so either by pleading ignorance or by stating that the chair was empty. The response to a direct question stands in contrast to the lack of involvement when neighbors were approached nonverbally. The length of time that the first experimenter had originally occupied the chair (his tenure period) had no effect on the willingness of the neighbor to defend the chair. However, the length of time that the previous owner was away—either 15 or 60 minutes—had a significant effect. When the former owner had been absent 15 minutes, 80% of the neighbors defended the space compared to 54% defending it when the former owner had been away a full hour ($p < .05$)....

DISCUSSION

The present article represents a small beginning toward understanding how markers reserve space and receive their legitimacy from people in the area (neighbors) and potential intruders. Psychologists have paid little attention to boundary markers in social interaction, perhaps because such markers were regarded as physical objects relegated to the cultural system (the province of the anthropologist) rather than an interpersonal system which is the true province of the social psychologist. Generally it is the geographers and lawyers who are most concerned with boundaries and markers. Since the present studies took place in public spaces, we are dealing more with norms and customs than with legal statutes. Stated another way, the situations involve an interpersonal system where sanctions are enforced by the individuals immediately present. . . .

People are now spending an increasing portion of their time in public or institutional spaces, including theaters, airport lobbies, buses, schools, and hospitals, where the use of personal belongings to mark out temporary territories is a common phenomenon. The study of territories, temporary as well as enduring ones, deserves study by psychologists. There is some danger that such work will lose much of its force if some semantic clarity is not obtained. While the ethologist's definition of a territory as "any defended area" has considerable heuristic value, there is no need to assume that the mechanisms underlying human and animal behavior are identical. The paucity of data about human territorial behavior makes it most reasonable to assume that the mechanisms are analogous rather than homologous.

In conclusion, the present series of studies suggests that further investigation of spatial markers is feasible and warranted. The physical environment has for too long been considered the background variable in psychological research. The time is past when we can have theories of man that do not take into account his surroundings. Boundary markers not only define what belongs to a person and what belongs to his neighbor, but also who he is and what it means to be a neighbor in a complex society.

NOTES

1. The neighbor's replies to the intruder's question were scored separately by two coders as indicating defense of the space ("Yes, that seat is taken") or nondefense ("No, it isn't taken" or "I don't know"). There was 100% agreement between the two raters in scoring the replies into defense or nondefense categories.

REFERENCES

Felipe, N., & Sommer, R. Invasions of personal space. *Social Problems*, 1966, **14**, 206–214.

Environmental Noise Level as a Determinant of Helping Behavior

Having to cope with noise is a consequence of living in modern society. Popular opinion is that noise, or unwanted sound, is detrimental to pro-social behavior. However, psychology is an empirical science, and research is therefore needed to understand the effects of environmental noise on behavior. Kenneth E. Mathews, Jr., and Lance Kirkpatrick Canon conducted an experimental study on environmental noise level and helping behavior. Mathews was with the Law and Justice Planning Office in Seattle, Washington, and Canon was a professor of psychology at the University of New Hampshire when their research was published.

This selection is from "Environmental Noise Level as a Determinant of Helping Behavior," which was published in *Journal of Personality and Social Psychology* in 1975. In it, Mathews and Kirkpatrick present two studies that were designed to test the hypothesis that environmental noise leads to a decrease in helping behavior. In both a laboratory experiment and a field study, they tested whether participants would be more likely to help pick up another student's dropped books under low or high noise conditions. As you read this selection, notice the attention that was given to details to make the conditions as natural as possible. Do you think the people being tested were aware of the noise levels during the experiments? To what extent do you think people are influenced by their environment?

Key Concept: environment and helping behavior

APA Citation: Mathews, K. E., Jr., & Canon, L. K. (1975). Environmental noise level as a determinant of helping behavior. *Journal of Personality and Social Psychology, 32,* 571–577.

*T*he results of research dealing with the effects of noise on intrapersonal behavior suggest a variety of possible consequences for interpersonal functioning. The effects *of various levels of noise on simple helping behavior were explored in a laboratory and a field setting for a total of 132 subjects. In both experiments, subjects exposed to 85–db. white noise were less likely than those in lower noise conditions to offer assistance to a person in need. The results were interpreted on the basis of prior research suggesting that noise-produced arousal leads to a restriction in attention deployment or cue utilization. Alternative accounts in terms of the effect of noise on mood and on drive level were also considered.*

The effect of noise on intrapersonal behavior has long been of interest to general experimental and physiological psychologists, and the publication in recent years of a number of volumes on this topic (e.g., Broadbent, 1971; Kryter, 1970; Welch & Welch, 1970) attests to the significance that these issues are currently accorded. Public concern over "noise pollution," congressional legislation dealing with permissible noise exposure levels in industrial settings, and work such as that of Cameron, Robertson, and Zaks (1972), suggesting that noise may be associated with the incidence of chronic and acute illness, provide further impetus for research of this sort. Investigations of the interpersonal impact of ambient noise, however, are much less in evidence, though Glass and Singer (1972) have provided a nice bridge between these two complementary focuses, and there has been work on the relationship between noise and conformity (Dustin, 1968), aggression (Geen & O'Neal, 1969; Geen & Powers, 1971), and verbal disinhibition (Holmes & Holzman, 1966).

Earlier research by the authors on the psychosocial effects of ambient noise level has provided indirect support for the hypothesis that high noise levels may lead to lessened attention to the incidental social cues that structure and guide significant aspects of interpersonal behavior. Since an individual's interpretation of some situation as one in which helping behavior is appropriate might well be based on such cues and would seem to be a necessary antecedent to assisting behaviors, the present study explored the effects of various levels of ambient noise on the likelihood of helping in a very simple situation....

One implication of this effect for interpersonal processes is that with noisy environments, individuals may become less aware of relatively subtle cues produced in interpersonal interactions that more clearly define other's meanings, intentions, and behavior. In addition, this approach suggests that the course of ongoing behavior and/or interaction would be less flexible and less likely to change to a new direction, since individuals would be less attentive to events that are not directly related to ongoing activities. This implies that persons may become relatively more single-minded in their actions, and in a situation that involves another in need of assistance, less likely to interrupt present activities to perform helping acts....

To test these implications, two studies were conducted in which subjects were presented with an opportunity to assist another person in a simple, non-emergency situation under various levels of ambient noise. Since the primary interest concerned the effects of noise rather than the complex concept of altruism, the circumstances involved a very uncomplicated and basic helping paradigm: The parties had no prior history of interaction, engaged in only the briefest of contacts with no expectation of further involvement with one another, and were alone at the time of the contrived incident. The laboratory experiment involved a book-dropping episode and three intensities of noise, while the field study used a similar occasion for helping and two noise levels. An additional manipulation in the latter study was designed to produce two levels of incidental cues indicating the degree to which the accomplice was in need of assistance.

The attention-restriction position would predict a decrease in the tendency to help with an increase in noise level. Further, an interaction between noise level and the effect of the cues-for-helping manipulation would be expected. That is, presence of these cues should be associated with a higher likelihood of assistance giving in the low-noise conditions but not in the high-noise setting.

337

Kenneth E. Mathews, Jr., and Lance Kirkpatrick Canon

EXPERIMENT 1: LABORATORY

Method

Procedure. Fifty-two male subjects reported for an experiment on interpersonal perception. They were met at the door to the laboratory by the experimenter who indicated that they would have to wait for a few minutes before beginning the study. They were directed to a waiting room where they found another male "subject" (a confederate of the experimenter) seated in one of the two available chairs reading an article in one of the several journals he held in his lap. The confederate was in the chair farthest from the door to the room, and thus the subject took the seat just adjacent to that door. After only a moment, the experimenter reappeared in the doorway and called the confederate to take his turn in the experiment. As he arose, he awkwardly clasped to his chest the two books, five journals, and miscellaneous papers that had been in his lap, and as he crossed in front of the subject, the papers and journals slipped from his grasp and scattered on the floor. He moved without hesitation to recover the dropped materials that were spread over at least a 3 square foot (.9 m^2) area and proceeded out of the room.

The dependent variable in the study was the presence or absence of helping behavior on the part of the subject in front of whom the materials had been dropped. A helping response was recorded only if the subject actually rose and assisted the confederate in retrieving the dropped materials.

The independent variable was the ambient noise level in the room during the period of the study. Three conditions were employed: (a) no artificially induced noise was present, and the natural level was 48 db. (C) ±5 db. (C)—no noise; (b) a white noise generator was used to produce an ambient level of broadband, white noise at 65 db. (C)—low noise; (c) a broadband, white noise level of 85 db. (C) was maintained—high noise.

No explanation was given for the presence of the white noise, and its source was not immediately apparent, as the speakers employed were hidden

from view behind a curtained area adjacent to the subject and the confederate. . . .

RESULTS

A one-way analysis of variance and linear trend analysis were performed on the
dichotomous data (help vs. not help; see Edwards, 1972, pp. 124–125, regarding
the robustness of the F test when using binomial data).

The results of the analysis of variance indicated a marginally significant
difference between mean helping rates for the three noise levels, $F(2, 49) = 2.878$,
$.05 < p < .10$. However, when the results were tested for a linear trend (see
Myers, 1972, pp. 386–388, for coefficient determination for unequal-n treatment
intervals), there was a significant linear relation between increased noise levels
(as measured in decibels) and decreased helping, linear $F(1, 49) = 6.63, p < .025$.
(See Table 1.)

TABLE 1

Subjects' Helping in the Laboratory Experiment

Helping behavior	Noise level		
	Ambient[a]	Low[b]	High[c]
Yes	13	10	7
No	5	5	12
% helping	72.2	66.7	36.8

[a]48 db.
[b]65 db.
[c]85 db.

EXPERIMENT 2: FIELD STUDY

A second experiment was conducted in a field setting in which nonreactive
measures could be obtained and that might provide convergent corroboration
of the data that resulted from the laboratory study. In addition, this study was
designed to test the effect of noise level upon cue utilization. This provided an
opportunity both to replicate the findings of the laboratory study and to obtain
data that would permit clearer determination of the value of the explanation in
terms of reduced cue utilization. The absence or presence of a cue designed to
indicate the degree of legitimacy of the confederate's need for assistance was
manipulated by having the confederate wear a full-length arm cast for half of
the staged incidents.

*Kenneth E.
Mathews, Jr.,
and Lance
Kirkpatrick
Canon*

Procedure.　The responses of 80 male subjects to an opportunity to render assistance to another male in a natural setting were observed. The locale was a curving, tree-lined, low-traffic-density street in a student apartment residential area. Three persons were involved in carrying out the study: An observer was hidden in a recessed stairwell across the street from the scene of the incident, which was staged by the other two accomplices. The observer had a clear view of the street from approximately 60 yards (54 m) above and below the incident site, and his duties were to give a "ready" signal when an appropriate subject was approaching, to give a "go" signal when that subject reached a point 12 feet (3.6 m) from the incident site, and to record the subject's response to the contrived situation. An appropriate subject was defined as any male walking alone, that is, one who was neither preceded nor followed by another person for a distance of 30 yards (27 m).

A second confederate was positioned with his back facing the sidewalk and leaning over inside the open rear door of a parked four-door automobile. The incident was staged in front of a house with a large lawn flanked by an apartment building on one side and a hedge on the other. Both the apartment building and the hedge continued from each side of the house up to the sidewalk. Because of the slight curve of the street and the presence of a series of trees in the planting strip between street and sidewalk, an approaching pedestrian's view of the confederate's activities was partially blocked. He could be seen bending over with his upper torso extending into the car, but a clear view of just what he was doing was not available. The confederate busied himself at arranging some books that were stacked high in a 24 × 6 × 12 inch (.6 × 1.5 × .3 m) cardboard box that was seated atop another similar sized box. On the signal from the observer indicating that the subject had reached a point 12 feet (3.6 m) from him, the confederate picked up the boxes from the rear seat of the car, withdrew from its doorway, turned, and began walking toward the house in the background. He did nothing to acknowledge the presence of the approaching subject, who was by this time approximately 6 feet (1.3 m) from the confederate as he crossed the sidewalk. At this point, two of the books delicately balanced atop the overflowing box spilled out, and as the confederate made a move to save them, several more fell, scattering over a wide area on the half of the sidewalk nearest the house. He paused for a brief moment, apparently puzzled over the dilemma in which he now found himself; that is, in order to retrieve the lost books, he would obviously have to go to the trouble of putting down somewhere the two apparently heavy boxes in his arms. At no time did he glance toward the subject or in any way indicate that he wished assistance. Following that brief pause, he either stopped and picked up the displaced books or, if the subject assisted him or asked if he could be of assistance, thanked him for his help and proceeded toward the house.

The third assistant was stationed in the yard of the adjacent house apparently worrying over a balky gasoline-engined reel-power lawn mower. He was kneeling next to the mower, intently examining the throttle mechanism with his back to the sidewalk and the activity going on there. At no time did he shift his attention from his work and appeared to be quite unaware of the presence of others and the book-dropping incident. His position was 25 feet (7.5 m) from the point of the drop and approximately 8 feet (2.4 m) to the right of the other confederate's direct path to the house.

In the low-noise condition the lawn mower was inoperative, and the average ambient noise level was roughly 50 db. (C). To create a high-noise condition, the lawn mower was running with its muffler removed, creating a noise level at the point of the drop of approximately 87 db. (C).

To manipulate cues indicating the legitimacy of the confederate's need for assistance, in one condition the confederate wore a cast on his right arm that extended from his wrist to his shoulder with a right angle bend at the elbow. In the other condition, of course, he was not so encumbered. . . .

RESULTS

A 2×2 (Noise $\times$ Cues) factorial analysis of variance performed on the dichotomous data (help or not help) resulted in highly significant results. As in the laboratory experiment, increased noise produced a significant decrease in helping in that although 50% of the subjects helped in the ambient-noise condition, only 12.5% helped in the high-noise condition, $F(1, 76) = 20.00$, $p < .001$. (See Table 2.)

The cue-for-helping manipulation was also significant in that only 15% of the subjects helped the confederate when he was not wearing an arm cast, while 47.5% of the subjects provided assistance to the confederate when he was wearing the cast, $F(1, 76) = 15.03$, $p < .001$.

TABLE 2

Subjects' Helping in the Field Experiment

	Helping behavior		
Condition	Yes	No	% helping
No cast			
Ambient noise[a]	4	16	20
High noise[b]	2	18	10
Cast			
Ambient noise[a]	16	4	80
High noise[b]	3	17	15

[a]50 db.
[b]87 db.

The Noise $\times$ Cue interaction was also highly significant as the presence or absence of the cast on the confederate's arm was highly influential in determining the likelihood of helping under ambient noise conditions (80% of the subjects helped the confederate wearing the cast, while only 20% of the subjects helped the confederate not wearing the cast), whereas the effect of differential cues was nonsignificant for the high-noise condition (15% helping the confederate with the cast, 10% helping the confederate without the cast), $F(1, 76) = 10.70, p < .005$.

GENERAL DISCUSSION

The basic findings of these two investigators are consistent and straightforward. With increasing ambient noise levels, the likelihood of simple helping behavior decreases. An interaction was present in that the physical characteristics of the confederate, which provided visual cues regarding the legitimacy and degree of his need for assistance, influenced the likelihood of his being helped in the low- but not in the high-noise conditions of the field study.

These results are consistent with the notion that high levels of ambient noise produce attenuation of attention to peripheral cues, that is, those not related to central, ongoing activities and concerns. This tendency for perceptual "filtering to be more extensive and evidence to be considered almost entirely from one source rather than any other" (Broadbent, 1971, p. 16) with noise-induced arousal may well have general social implications, since one of its consequences may be, as Zimbardo (1969b) has suggested, that individuals may orient toward others in a less personal and individual fashion. The presence of high levels of noise and the attendant attention restriction would be expected to curtail the directive influence on behavior that the cues presented by another person and his or her characteristics would have in the absence of high-intensity noise.

REFERENCES

Broadbent, D. E. *Decision and stress.* New York: Academic Press, 1971.

Cameron, P., Robertson, D., & Zaks, J. Sound pollution, noise pollution, and health: Community parameters. *Journal of Applied Psychology*, 1972, *56*, 67–74.

Dustin, D. S. Crowd noise and conformity. *Psychology Reports*, 1968, *23*, 425–426.

Edwards, A. L. *Experimental design in psychological research* (4th ed.). New York: Holt, 1972.

Geen, R. G., & O'Neal, E. C. Activation of cue-elicited aggression by general arousal. *Journal of Personality and Social Psychology*, 1969, *11*, 289–292.

Geen, R. G., & Powers, P. C. Shock and noise as instigating stimuli in human aggression. *Psychological Reports*, 1971, *28*, 983–985.

Glass, D. C., & Singer, J. E. *Urban stress: Experiments on noise and social stressors.* New York: Academic Press, 1972.

Holmes, C., & Holzman, P. S. Effect of white noise on disinhibition of verbal expression. *Perceptual and Motor Skills*, 1966, *23*, 1039–1042.

Kryter, K. D. *The effects of noise on man.* New York: Academic Press, 1970.

Myers, J. L. *Fundamentals of experimental design* (2nd ed.). Boston: Allyn & Bacon, 1972.

Welch, B. L., & Welch, A. S. *Physiological effects of noise.* New York: Plenum Press, 1970.

Zimbardo, P. G. The human choice: Individuation, reason, and order versus deindividuation, impulse, and chaos. In W. J. Arnold & D. Levine (Eds.), *Nebraska Symposium on Motivation.* Lincoln: University of Nebraska Press, 1969. (b)

14.3 SHELLEY E. TAYLOR

Adjustment to Threatening Events: A Theory of Cognitive Adaptation

Health psychologists focus on topics such as the promotion of health, the role of psychological factors in illness, the management of stress, and the improvement of health care. Psychologist Shelley E. Taylor has been a leader in studying how people adapt to events that threaten their health.

Taylor (b. 1946) earned her Ph.D. in social psychology from Yale University in 1972. She taught at Harvard University before accepting her current position as a professor of psychology at the University of California at Los Angeles in 1979. She has written several books, including *Health Psychology* (McGraw-Hill, 1991).

This selection is from "Adjustment to Threatening Events: A Theory of Cognitive Adaptation," which was published in *American Psychologist* in 1983. Taylor's theory suggests that adjustment to threatening events (such as cancer) focuses on three processes: searching for meaning, regaining mastery, and restoring self-esteem. As you read this selection, think about how you adapt to health problems. What other social psychological processes are involved in a person's adaptation to health-related threats?

Key Concept: cognitive adaptation theory in health psychology

APA Citation: Taylor, S. E. (1983). Adjustment to threatening events: A theory of cognitive adaptation. *American Psychologist, 38,* 1161–1173.

One of the most impressive qualities of the human psyche is its ability to withstand severe personal tragedy successfully. Despite serious setbacks such as personal illness or the death of a family member, the majority of people facing such blows achieve a quality of life or level of happiness equivalent to or even exceeding their prior level of satisfaction. Not everyone readjusts, of course (Silver & Wortman, 1980), but most do, and furthermore they do so substantially on their own. That is, typically people do not seek professional help in dealing with personal problems. They use their social networks and individual resources, and their apparent cure rate, if self-reports of satisfaction are to be trusted, is impressive even by professional standards (Gurin, Veroff, & Feld, 1960; Wills, 1982).

These self-curing abilities are a formidable resource, and our recent work with cancer patients, cardiac patients, rape victims, and other individuals facing life-threatening events has explored them. The consequence of these investigations is a theory of cognitive adaptation. I will argue that when an individual has experienced a personally threatening event, the readjustment process focuses around three themes: a search for meaning in the experience, an attempt to regain mastery over the event in particular and over one's life more generally, and an effort to enhance one's self-esteem—to feel good about oneself again despite the personal setback....

The following analysis draws heavily on the responses of 78 women with breast cancer and many of their family members whom Rosemary Lichtman, Joanne Wood, and I have intensively interviewed during the past two years (Taylor, Lichtman, & Wood, 1982). Some of the these women have good prognoses, others do not. Some have achieved a high quality of life following their illness (although it may have taken them several years to do so), others have not. But virtually all of them have shown some attempt to resolve the three issues of meaning, mastery, and self-enhancement....

THE SEARCH FOR MEANING

The search for meaning involves the need to understand why a crisis occurred and what its impact has been. One of the ways in which meaning is addressed is through causal attributions. Attribution theory (Heider, 1958; Kelley, 1967) maintains that following a threatening or dramatic event, people will make attributions so as to understand, predict, and control their environment (Wong & Weiner, 1981). By understanding the cause of an event, one may also begin to understand the significance of the event and what it symbolizes about one's life. In the case of cancer, of course, no one knows the true cause or causes. There are a number of known causes, such as heredity, diet, or specific carcinogens, but a search for the cause of cancer on the part of a patient would seem to be a fruitless endeavor.

Nonetheless, cancer patients do try to understand why they developed cancer. Ninety-five percent of our respondents offered some explanation for why their cancer occurred. In an effort to have some comparison group against which to judge this rate, we also asked the spouses of these patients whether they had any theory about the cause of their partner's cancer. One would also expect spouses' rates of making attributions to be inflated, relative to an uninvolved person, since they, like the patients, have been strongly affected by the cancer experience. Nonetheless, their rate of making causal attributions was significantly less (63%), suggesting that the need for an explanation was more insistent among the patients themselves.

Does any particular form of the attributional explanation meet the search for meaning better than others? This question can be partially addressed by looking at the specific content of the cancer patients' explanations and then relating those explanations to overall psychological adjustment. The largest number (41%) attributed their cancer either to general stress or to a particular type of stress. When a particular stressor was mentioned, it was often either an ongoing problematic marriage or a recent divorce. Thirty-two percent of the sample attributed their cancer to some particular carcinogen, including ingested substances such as birth control pills, DES, or primarin (which is an estrogen replenisher prescribed for menopausal women) or to environmental carcinogens such as having lived near a chemical dump, a nuclear testing site, or a copper mine. Twenty-six percent of the women attributed their cancer to hereditary factors. Another 17% attributed it to diet (usually to a diet high in protein and fat and low in vegetables), and 10% blamed some blow to the breast such as an automobile accident, a fall, or in one case, being hit in the breast by a frisbee. (The numbers exceed 100% because a number of people had multiple theories.) It is noteworthy that with the exception of heredity, all of these causes are either past, rather than ongoing events, or they are events over which one currently has some control, such as stress or diet. This fact anticipates a point to be made shortly—that meaning and mastery may often be intertwined.

When one relates these specific attributions to overall psychological adjustment to the cancer, no single attribution stands out as more functional than any other. All are uncorrelated with adjustment. It would be premature to conclude from this information that these attributional explanations are functionally interchangeable. However, the high frequency of making attributions, coupled with the fact that no specific attribution produces better adjustment, suggests that causal meaning itself is the goal of the attributional search rather than the specific form through which it is realized.

The search for meaning involves not only understanding why the event occurred, but what its implications for one's life are now. Slightly over half of our respondents reported that the cancer experience had caused them to reappraise their lives. Here is one example from a 61-year-old woman:

> You can take a picture of what someone has done, but when you frame it, it becomes significant. I feel as if I were for the first time really conscious. My life is framed in a certain amount of time. I always knew it. But I can see it, and it's made better by the knowledge. . . .

To summarize, the attempt to find meaning in the cancer experience takes at least two forms: a causal analysis that provides an answer to the question of why it happened and a rethinking of one's attitudes and priorities to restructure one's life along more satisfying lines, changes that are prompted by and attributed to the cancer.

GAINING A SENSE OF MASTERY

A sudden threatening event like cancer can easily undermine one's sense of control over one's body and one's life generally (e.g., Leventhal, 1975). Accordingly, a second theme of the adjustment process is gaining a feeling of control over the threatening event so as to manage it or keep it from occurring again. This theme of mastery is exemplified by beliefs about personal control.

Many cancer patients seem to solve the issue of mastery by believing that they personally can keep the cancer from coming back. Two thirds of the patients we interviewed believed they had at least some control over the course of or recurrence of their cancer, and 37% believed they had a lot of control. Some of the remaining one third believed that although they personally had no control over the cancer, it could be controlled by the doctor or by continued treatments. Hence, belief in direct control of the cancer is quite strong. Again, using the significant others as a comparison population, belief in both the patient's ability to control the cancer and the physician's ability to control the cancer are less strong, suggesting that mastery needs are greater among patients. Significantly, both the belief that one can control one's own cancer and the belief that the physician or treatments can control it are strongly associated with overall positive adjustment, and both together are even better.

Many of the patients' efforts at control were mental. One of the most common manifestations was a belief that a positive attitude would keep the cancer from coming back:

> I believe that if you're a positive person, your attitude has a lot to do with it. I definitely feel I will never get it again.

> My mental attitude, I think, is the biggest control over it I have. I want to feel there is something I can do, that there is some way I can control it.

> I think that if you feel you are in control of it, you can control it up to a point. I absolutely refuse to have any more cancer.

A substantial number attempted to control their cancer by using specific techniques of psychological control. These techniques included meditation, imaging, self-hypnosis, positive thinking, or a combination of factors. Many had read the Simonton and Simonton (1975) work suggesting that people can control their own cancers using these kinds of methods, and they saw no harm in trying them on their own; a number had great faith in them. . . .

Although many patients have regained a sense of mastery by thinking about their cancer differently, others adopt direct behavioral efforts to keep the cancer from coming back. In a number of cases, patients made changes in their lives that both enabled them to reduce the likelihood of recurrence (they believed) and gave them something to control now. For some, these were dietary changes; a full 49% of our sample had changed their diet since the cancer bout, usually in the direction of adding fresh fruit and vegetables and cutting down on red meats and fats. For others, eliminating the medications they had taken like birth control pills or estrogen replenishers fulfilled the same function. . . .

Attempting to control the side effects of one's treatments represents another effort at mastery. For example, 92% of the patients who received chemotherapy did something to control its side effects. For slightly under half, this involved simply medications or sleep, but the remaining half used a combination of mental efforts at control. These included imaging, self-hypnosis, distraction, and meditation. Similar efforts were made to control the less debilitating but still unpleasant side effects of radiation therapy. For example, one woman who was undergoing radiation therapy would imagine that there was a protective shield keeping her body from being burned by the radiation. Another woman imaged her chemotherapy as powerful cannons which blasted away pieces of the dragon, cancer. One 61-year-old woman simply focused her attention on healing with the instruction to her body, "Body, cut this... out."

A sense of mastery, then, can be achieved by believing that one can control the cancer by taking active steps that are perceived as directly controlling the cancer or by assuming control over related aspects of one's cancer, such as treatment. This belief in mastery and its relationship to adjustment ties in with a large body of literature indicating that manipulated feelings of control enhance coping with short-term aversive events (Averill, 1973; see Thompson, 1981, for a... review). The cancer patients' experiences suggest that self-generated feelings of control over a chronic condition can achieve the same beneficial effects.

THE PROCESS OF SELF-ENHANCEMENT

The third theme identified in our patients' adjustment process was an effort to enhance the self and restore self-esteem. Researchers exploring a range of threatening events from the death of one's child (Chodoff, Friedman, & Hamburg, 1964) to going on welfare (Briar, 1966) have documented the toll such events can take on self-regard. Even when the events can be legitimately attributed to external forces beyond the individual's control, there is often a precipitous drop in self-esteem. After experiencing such a drop, however, many individuals then initiate cognitive efforts to pull themselves back out of their low self-regard.

In some cases, esteem-enhancing cognitions are quite direct. During our interviews, we asked our respondents to describe any changes that had occurred in their lives since the cancer incident. To digress momentarily, I think people are always curious about how others change their lives when they have had a life-threatening experience. Popular images would have patients changing jobs, changing spouses, moving, or squandering all their money on a series of self-indulgent adventures. In fact, these major changes are fairly rare, and when they do occur, they are associated with unsuccessful overall adjustment. Frequently, a couple will have one "binge" such as taking a cruise or buying a Cadillac, but otherwise there are typically few overt dramatic changes. After people reported the changes they had experienced in their lives since cancer, we asked them to indicate whether those changes were positive or negative. Only 17% reported *any* negative changes in their lives. Fifty-three percent reported only positive changes; the remainder reported no changes. We also asked our patients to rate their emotional adjustment before any signs of cancer, at various points during the cancer bout, and at the time of the interview. Not only did patients see themselves as generally well adjusted at the time of the interview and as better adjusted than they were during the cancer bout, they also saw themselves as better adjusted than before they had any signs of cancer! When you consider that these women usually had had disfiguring surgery, had often had painful follow-up care, and had been seriously frightened and lived under the shadow of possible recurrence, this is a remarkable ability to construe personal benefit from potential tragedy.

Some of the most intriguing illusions that contribute to self-enhancement are generated by social comparisons (Festinger, 1954; Latané, 1966; Suls & Miller, 1977). Drawing on some provocative suggestions by Wortman and Dunkel-Schetter (1979) concerning cancer patients' needs for social comparison, we hypothesized that if we could identify the women's objects of comparison we could predict who would perceive themselves as coping well or badly. The media highlight people who are models of good adjustment to crises. With respect to breast cancer, women such as Betty Ford, Shirley Temple Black, or Marvella Bayh come to mind. We reasoned that such models might demoralize normal women by making them feel they were not doing well by comparison (Taylor & Levin, 1976). In contrast, comparisons with average women who might be experiencing a number of more negative reactions to cancer should yield more favorable self-evaluations. An alternative prediction derived from Festinger's (1954) social comparison theory (Wheeler, 1966) is that people will compare themselves with someone doing slightly better than they are—in other words, make upward comparisons in order to learn how to cope more effectively.

What we found conformed neither to our analysis nor to the upward comparison prediction (Wood, Taylor, & Lichtman, 1982). Instead, virtually all the women we interviewed thought they were doing as well as or somewhat better than other women coping with the same crisis. Only two said they were doing somewhat worse. If we had an unusually well-adjusted sample, of course, these perceptions could be veridical, but we know from other information that this was not true. These results suggest that these women are making downward comparisons, comparing themselves with women who were as fortunate or less fortunate than they. These results tie in with a more general body of literature recently brought together by Wills (1981) indicating that when faced with threat, individuals will usually make self-enhancing comparisons in an apparent effort to bolster self-esteem. Downward comparisons, then, would seem to be a fairly robust method of self-protection against threat.

In some cases, these downward comparisons were drawn explicitly. For example, one woman took great glee from the fact that her Reach to Recovery volunteer (the woman sent in by the American Cancer Society to serve as a model of good adjustment) seemed to be more poorly adjusted than she was.

Despite some direct comparisons, however, many of the social comparisons seem to be made against hypothetical women.... It seems, then, that the need to come out of the comparison process appearing better off drives the process itself; the process does not determine the outcome. If a comparison person who makes one appear well adjusted is not available from personal experience, such a person may be manufactured.

Choice of comparison target is not the only way that social comparison processes can operate to enhance self-esteem. One must also consider the dimensions selected for evaluation. Conceivably, one could select a dimension that would make one appear more advantaged than others or one could select a dimension for evaluation that would put one at a disadvantage....

In our study, several women with lumpectomies compared themselves favorably to women with mastectomies; no woman with a mastectomy ever evaluated herself against a woman with a lumpectomy. Older women considered themselves better off than younger women; no younger woman expressed the wish that she had been older. Married women pitied the single woman; no single woman pointed out that it would have been easier if she'd been married. The women who were the worst off consoled themselves with the fact that they were not dying or were not in pain. The amount of self-enhancement in these dimensional comparisons is striking. Not only choice of comparison target, then, but also choice of comparison dimension is important for restoring self-enhancement in the face of threat. The issue of dimension selection in social comparisons is one that has been almost entirely ignored in the social comparison literature. This would seem to be an important oversight, particularly for research that examines social comparisons made under threat (Taylor, Wood, & Lichtman, in press).

The fact that social comparison processes can be used to enhance oneself is important, because it meshes social psychological processes with clinically significant outcomes. However, these social comparisons appear to serve important functions other than just self-enhancement. Several researchers (e.g., Fazio, 1979; Singer, 1966) have made a distinction between social comparisons that are made to validate one's self-impression versus social comparisons that are drawn to construct self-impressions. The results just described can be construed as efforts to validate a favorable self-image. However, one can also see evidence of constructive social comparisons among the respondents. Specifically, some of the comparisons involved instances in which women selected as comparison objects other women who were worse off physically (such as women with nodal involvement, women with metastatic cancer, or women with double mastectomies) but who were coping very well. Such comparisons are self-enhancing, but they are also instructive and motivating. That is, the fact that women worse off are coping well seems to inspire the person drawing the comparison to try to do as well and to pattern her own behavior after the comparison person. These comparisons are particularly important because self-enhancement, and indeed cognitive illusion generally, is often written off as defensive and dysfunctional. Instead, these illusions may have multiple functions. In addition to self-enhancement, they can instill motivation and provide information, as these downward comparisons apparently did for some of our respondents (see Brickman & Bulman, 1977). . . .

What, then, can be learned from the analysis of cancer patients' comparative processes? These women made downward comparisons instead of upward ones, and appear to have selected their comparison persons to enhance their self-esteem rather than letting their self-esteem be determined by who was available for comparison. If other appropriate persons were not readily available for comparison, they manufactured a norm that other women were worse off than they were. The dimensions singled out for comparison were ones on which they appeared better, rather than worse, off. Physically disadvantaged but successful copers also were selected as models. One, then, has the best of both worlds: The comparisons enable one to feel better about oneself, but one does not lose the advantage of having a successful model on which to pattern one's efforts at adjustment. . . .

CONCLUSION

. . . As a theoretical and empirical venture, cognitive adaptation theory is still in its infancy. It suggests a general strategy for studying adaptation to threatening events by focusing on multiple cognitively adaptive efforts simultaneously, rather than upon the adaptive value of particular cognitions in isolation. It also takes a stand against laboratory-based examinations of reactions to threat that fail to acknowledge the relation of particular cognitions to overriding goals or values. More specifically, the theory points to some directions for beginning research. Systematically documenting the themes of meaning, mastery, and self-enhancement in adjustment to threatening events other than cancer is an important empirical step. In this context, it is encouraging to note that evidence for each of the three themes—meaning (Chodoff et al., 1964; Frankl, 1963; Mechanic, 1977; Visotsky et al., 1961; Weisman & Worden, 1975), mastery (Bulman & Wortman, 1977; Janoff-Bulman, 1979; Rothbaum et al., 1982), and self-enhancement (Pearlin & Schooler, 1978; Wills, 1981)—has already been reported by investigators exploring misfortunes as varied as economic difficulty, marital problems, rape, and physical illness other than cancer. A second beginning line of research stems from the different predictions that cognitive adaptation theory generates for reactions to disconfirmation of cognitions, as compared with reactance or learned helplessness theory. The theory suggests, for example, that in field settings where people have multiple response options at their disposal, they will turn their frustrated efforts at control, understanding, or self-enhancement to tasks on which they are more likely to be successful. . . .

My biologist acquaintances frequently note that the more they know about the human body, the more, not less, miraculous it seems. The recuperative powers of the mind merit similar awe. The process of cognitive adaptation to threat, though often time-consuming and not always successful, nonetheless restores many people to their prior level of functioning and inspires others to find new meaning in their lives. For this reason, cognitive adaptation occupies a special place in the roster of human capabilities.

*Shelley E.
Taylor*

REFERENCES

Averill, J. R. Personal control over aversive stimuli and its relationship to stress. *Psychological Bulletin*, 1973, *80*, 286–303.

Briar, S. Welfare from below: Recipient's views of the public welfare system. *California Law Review*, 1966, *54*, 370–385.

Brickman, P., & Bulman, R. J. Pleasure and pain in social comparison. In J. M. Suls & R. L. Miller (Eds.), *Social comparison processes: Theoretical and empirical perspectives.* Washington, D.C.: Hemisphere, 1977.

Bulman, R. J., & Wortman, C. B. Attributions of blame and coping in the "real world": Severe accident victims react to their lot. *Journal of Personality and Social Psychology,* 1977, *35*, 351–363.

Chodoff, P., Friedman, P. B., & Hamburg, D. A. Stress, defenses and coping behavior: Observations in parents of children with malignant disease. *American Journal of Psychiatry*, 1964, *120*, 743–749.

Fazio, R. H. Motives for social comparison: The construction-validation distinction. *Journal of Personality and Social Psychology*, 1979, *37*, 1683–1698.

Festinger, L. A theory of social comparison processes. *Human Relations*, 1954, *7*, 117–140.

Frankl, V. E. *Man's search for meaning.* New York: Washington Square Press, 1963.

Gurin, G., Veroff, J., & Feld, S. *Americans view their mental health.* New York: Basic Books, 1960.

Heider, F. *The psychology of interpersonal relations.* New York: Wiley, 1958.

Janoff-Bulman, R. Characterological versus behavioral self-blame: Inquiries into depression and rape. *Journal of Personality and Social Psychology*, 1979, *37*, 1798–1809.

Kelley, H. H. Attribution theory in social psychology. In D. Levine (Ed.), *Nebraska Symposium on Motivation* (Vol. 15). Lincoln: University of Nebraska Press, 1967.

Latané, B. Studies in social comparison: Introduction and overview. *Journal of Experimental Social Psychology*, 1966, *Supplement 1*, 1–5.

Leventhal, H. The consequences of depersonalization during illness and treatment. In J. Howard & A. Strauss (Eds.), *Humanizing health care.* New York: Wiley, 1975.

Mechanic, D. Illness behavior, social adaptation, and the management of illness. *Journal of Nervous and Mental Disease*, 1977, *165*, 79–87.

Perlin, L. I., & Schooler, C. The structure of coping. *Journal of Health and Social Behavior,* 1978, *19*, 2–21.

Rothbaum, F., Weisz, J. R., & Snyder, S. S. Changing the world and changing the self: A two-process model of perceived control. *Journal of Personality and Social Psychology,* 1982, *42*, 5–37.

Silver, R. L., & Wortman, C. B. Coping with undesirable life events. In J. Garber & M. E. P. Seligman (Eds.), *Human helplessness: Theory and applications.* New York: Academic Press, 1980.

Simonton, O. C., & Simonton, S. Belief systems and management of the emotional aspects of malignancy. *Journal of Transpersonal Psychology*, 1975, *7*, 29–48.

Singer, J. E. Social comparison: Progress and issues. *Journal of Experimental Social Psychology*, 1966, *Supplement 1*, 103–110.

Suls, J. M., & Miller, R. L. M. *Social comparison processes: Theoretical and empirical perspectives*. New York: Wiley, 1977.

Taylor, S. E., & Levin, S. *The psychological impact of breast cancer: Theory and practice*. San Francisco: West Coast Cancer Foundation, 1976.

Taylor, S. E., Lichtman, R. R., & Wood, J. V. *Adjustment to breast cancer: Physical, sociodemographic, and psychological predictors*, Manuscript submitted for publication, 1982.

Taylor, S. E., Wood, J. V., & Lichtman, R. R. It could be worse: Selective evaluation as a response to victimization. *Journal of Social Issues*, in press.

Thompson, S. C. Will it hurt less if I can control it? A complex answer to a simple question. *Psychological Bulletin*, 1981, *90*, 89–101.

Visotsky, H. M., Hamburg, D. A., Goss, M. E., & Lebovits, B. Z. Coping behavior under extreme stress. *Archives of General Psychiatry*, 1961, *5*, 423–448.

Weisman, A. D., & Worden, J. W. Psychological analysis of cancer deaths. *Omega*, 1975, *6*, 61–75.

Wheeler, L. Motivation as a determinant of upward comparison. *Journal of Experimental Social Psychology*, 1966, *Supplement 1*, 27–31.

Wills, T. A. Downward comparison principles in social psychology. *Psychological Bulletin*, 1981, *90*, 245–271.

Wills, T. A. Social comparison and help-seeking. In B. M. DePaulo, A. Nadler, & J. D. Fisher (Eds.), *New directions in helping: Vol. 2. Help-seeking*. New York: Academic Press, 1982.

Wong, P. T. P., & Weiner, B. When people ask "why" questions, and the heuristics of attributional search. *Journal of Personality and Social Psychology*, 1981, *40*, 650–663.

Wortman, C. B., & Dunkel-Schetter, C. Interpersonal relationships and cancer: A theoretical analysis. *Journal of Social Issues*, 1979, *35*, 120–155.

Wood, J. V., Taylor, S. E., & Lichtman, R. R. *Social comparison processes in adjustment to cancer*. Manuscript submitted for publication, 1982.

ACKNOWLEDGMENTS

1.1 From *Social Psychology* (pp. 3–4, 10–13) by F. H. Allport, 1924. New York: Houghton Mifflin Company. References omitted.

1.2 From "The Rise and Fall of Deception in Social Psychology and Personality Research, 1921–1994" by S. D. Nicks, J. H. Korn, and T. Mainieri, 1997, *Ethics & Behavior, 7*, pp. 69–71, 73–77. Copyright © 1997 by Lawrence Erlbaum Associates, Inc. Reprinted by permission.

1.3 Excerpted from "A Glance Back at a Quarter Century of Social Psychology" by E. Berscheid, 1992, *Journal of Personality and Social Psychology, 63*, pp. 525, 527–533. Copyright © 1992 by The American Psychological Association. Reprinted by permission.

2.1 From "The Warm-Cold Variable in First Impressions of Persons" by H. H. Kelley, 1950, *Journal of Personality, 18*, pp. 431–439. Copyright © 1950 by Blackwell Publishers Ltd. Reprinted by permission.

2.2 From "A Theory of Social Comparison Processes" by L. Festinger, 1954, *Human Relations, 7*, pp. 117–120, 124–125, 129–130, 135–136, 138–140. Copyright © 1954 by Plenum Publishing Corporation. Reprinted by permission. Notes omitted.

2.3 From "Toward a Self-Evaluation Maintenance Model of Social Behavior" by A. Tesser, 1988. In *Advances in Experimental Social Psychology, vol. 21* (pp. 181–185, 188–195, 222–227) ed. by L. Berkowitz. San Diego, CA: Academic Press, Inc. Copyright © 1988 by Academic Press, Inc. Reprinted by permission.

3.1 From "Self-Efficacy: Toward a Unifying Theory of Behavioral Change" by A. Bandura, 1977, *Psychological Review, 84*, pp. 193–195, 200, 202, 213–215. Copyright © 1977 by The American Psychological Association. Reprinted by permission.

3.2 From "The Social Self: On Being the Same and Different at the Same Time" by M. B. Brewer, 1991, *Personality and Social Psychology Bulletin, 17*, pp. 475–482. Copyright © 1991 by The Society for Personality and Social Psychology, Inc. Reprinted by permission of Sage Publications, Inc. Notes omitted.

3.3 From "The Self and Social Behavior in Differing Cultural Contexts" by H. C. Triandis, 1989, *Psychological Review, 96*, pp. 508–511, 517–520. Copyright © 1989 by The American Psychological Association. Reprinted by permission.

4.1 From "The Measurement of Psychological Androgyny" by S. L. Bem, 1974, *Journal of Consulting and Clinical Psychology, 42*, pp. 155–159, 161–162. Copyright © 1974 by The American Psychological Association. Reprinted by permission.

4.2 From "Sex Differences in Conformity: Status and Gender Role Interpretations" by A. H. Eagly and C. Chrvala, 1986, *Psychology of Women Quarterly, 10*, pp. 203–219. Copyright © 1986 by The American Psychological Association. Reprinted by permission of Cambridge University Press. Notes omitted.

4.3 Edited from "Individualistic and Collectivistic Perspectives on Gender and the Cultural Context of Love and Intimacy" by K. K. Dion and K. L. Dion, 1993, *Journal of Social Issues, 49*, pp. 53–60, 67–69. Copyright © 1993 by The Society for the Psychological Study of Social Issues. Reprinted by permission of Blackwell Publishers Ltd.

5.1 From "Attitude–Behavior Relations: A Theoretical Analysis and Review of Empirical Research" by I. Ajzen and M. Fishbein, 1977, *Psychological Bulletin, 84*, pp. 889–891, 913–914, 916. Copyright © 1977 by The American Psychological Association. Reprinted by permission. Notes omitted.

5.2   From "Attitudes vs. Actions" by R. T. LaPiere, 1934, *Social Forces, 13*, pp. 230–234, 237. Copyright © 1934 by The University of North Carolina. Reprinted by permission of *Social Forces*. Notes omitted.

6.1   From "Cognitive Consequences of Forced Compliance" by L. Festinger and J. M. Carlsmith, 1959, *Journal of Abnormal and Social Psychology, 58*, pp. 203–208, 210. Notes omitted.

6.2   From "The Effects of Involvement on Responses to Argument Quantity and Quality: Central and Peripheral Routes to Persuasion" by R. E. Petty and J. T. Cacioppo, 1984, *Journal of Personality and Social Psychology, 46*, pp. 69–72, 77–81. Copyright © 1984 by The American Psychological Association. Reprinted by permission. Notes omitted.

6.3   From "Persuasion and Culture: Advertising Appeals in Individualistic and Collectivistic Societies" by S. Han and S. Shavitt, 1994, *Journal of Experimental Social Psychology, 30*, pp. 326–334, 342–343, 346–350. Copyright © 1994 by Academic Press, Inc. Reprinted by permission. Notes omitted.

7.1   From *The Nature of Prejudice* (pp. 6–9, 13–15) by G. W. Allport, 1954. Reading, MA: Addison-Wesley. Copyright © 1954, 1958, renewed 1979, by Addison-Wesley Publishing Company, Inc. Reprinted by permission of Perseus Books Publishers, a member of Perseus Books, LLC. Notes and references omitted.

7.2   From "Superordinate Goals in the Reduction of Intergroup Conflict" by M. Sherif, 1958, *The American Journal of Sociology, 63*, pp. 349–350, 352–356. Copyright © 1958 by University of Chicago Press. Reprinted by permission. Notes omitted.

7.3   From "Affirmative Action, Unintentional Racial Biases, and Intergroup Relations" by J. F. Dovidio and S. L. Gaertner, 1996, *Journal of Social Issues, 52*, pp. 51, 53-60, 71-75. Copyright © 1996 by The Society for the Psychological Study of Social Issues. Reprinted by permission of Blackwell Publishers Ltd.

8.1   From "What Is Beautiful Is Good" by K. Dion, E. Berscheid, and E. Walster, 1972, *Journal of Personality and Social Psychology, 24*, pp. 286–290. Copyright © 1972 by The American Psychological Association. Reprinted by permission. Some notes omitted.

8.2   From "The Strategies of Human Mating" by D. M. Buss, 1994, *American Scientist, 82*, pp. 238–242, 249. Copyright © 1994 by *American Scientist*. Reprinted by permission. Bibliography omitted.

8.3   From "Measuring the Physical in Physical Attractiveness: Quasi-Experiments on the Sociobiology of Female Facial Beauty" by M. R. Cunningham, 1986, *Journal of Personality and Social Psychology, 50*, pp. 925–927, 929–930, 934–935. Copyright © 1986 by The American Psychological Association. Reprinted by permission. Notes omitted.

8.4   From "Some Evidence for Heightened Sexual Attraction Under Conditions of High Anxiety" by D. G. Dutton and A. P. Aron, 1974, *Journal of Personality and Social Psychology, 30*, pp. 510–513, 516–517. Copyright © 1974 by The American Psychological Association. Reprinted by permission. Notes omitted.

9.1   From *The Triangle of Love: Intimacy, Passion, Commitment* (pp. 37–48, 51–61) by R. J. Sternberg, 1988. New York: Basic Books. Copyright © 1988 by Basic Books, Inc. Reprinted by permission of Robert J. Sternberg.

9.2   From " 'I Love You More Today Than Yesterday': Romantic Partners' Perceptions of Changes in Love and Related Affect Over Time" by S. Sprecher, 1999, *Journal of Personality and Social Psychology, 76*, pp. 46–53. Copyright © 1999 by The American Psychological Association. Reprinted by permission. Notes omitted.

9.3   From "Romantic Love Conceptualized as an Attachment Process" by C. Hazan and P. Shaver, 1987, *Journal of Personality and Social Psychology, 52*, pp. 511–515, 521, 523–524. Copyright © 1987 by The American Psychological Association. Reprinted by permission.

10.1 From "Behavioral Study of Obedience" by S. Milgram, 1963, *Journal of Abnormal and Social Psychology, 67*, pp. 371–378. Copyright © 1963 by Stanley Milgram. Reprinted by permission of Alexandra Milgram, literary executor.

10.2 From "Compliance Without Pressure: The Foot-in-the-Door Technique" by J. L. Freedman and S. C. Fraser, 1966, *Journal of Personality and Social Psychology, 4*, pp. 195–198, 202. Copyright © 1966 by The American Psychological Association. Reprinted by permission.

10.3 From "Low-Ball Procedure for Producing Compliance: Commitment Then Cost" by R. B. Cialdini, R. Bassett, J. T. Cacioppo, and J. A. Miller, 1978, *Journal of Personality and Social Psychology, 36*, pp. 463–468. Copyright © 1978 by The American Psychological Association. Reprinted by permission. Notes omitted.

11.1 From "Social Facilitation" by R. B. Zajonc, 1965, *Science, 149*, pp. 269–274. Copyright © 1965 by The American Association for the Advancement of Science. Reprinted by permission.

11.2 From "Many Hands Make Light the Work: The Causes and Consequences of Social Loafing" by B. Latané, K. Williams, and S. Harkins, 1979, *Journal of Personality and Social Psychology, 37*, pp. 822–825, 829–832. Copyright © 1979 by The American Psychological Association. Reprinted by permission.

11.3 From "The Effect of Threat Upon Interpersonal Bargaining" by M. Deutsch and R. M. Krauss, 1960, *Journal of Abnormal and Social Psychology, 61*, pp. 181–189. Notes omitted.

11.4 From *Groupthink: Psychological Studies of Policy Decisions and Fiascoes*, 2d ed. (pp. 174–178) by I. L. Janis, 1982. Boston: Houghton Mifflin Company. Copyright © 1982 by Houghton Mifflin Company. Reprinted by permission. Notes omitted.

12.1 From "Bystander Intervention in Emergencies: Diffusion of Responsibility" by J. M. Darley and B. Latané, 1968, *Journal of Personality and Social Psychology, 8*, pp. 377–383. Copyright © 1968 by The American Psychological Association. Reprinted by permission.

12.2 From "The Sweet Smell of . . . Helping: Effects of Pleasant Ambient Fragrance on Prosocial Behavior in Shopping Malls" by R. A. Baron, 1997, *Personality and Social Psychology Bulletin, 23*, pp. 498–503. Copyright © 1997 by The Society for Personality and Social Psychology, Inc. Reprinted by permission of Sage Publications, Inc.

13.1 From "Imitation of Film-Mediated Aggressive Models" by A. Bandura, D. Ross, and S. A. Ross, 1963, *Journal of Abnormal and Social Psychology, 66*, pp. 3–11. Copyright © 1963 by The American Psychological Association. Reprinted by permission.

13.2 Abridged from "Psychological Processes Promoting the Relation Between Exposure to Media Violence and Aggressive Behavior by the Viewer" by L. R. Huesmann, 1986, *Journal of Social Issues, 42*, pp. 125–126, 130–136, 138–139. Copyright © 1986 by The Society for the Psychological Study of Social Issues. Reprinted by permission of Blackwell Publishers Ltd.

13.3 From *Aggression: Its Causes, Consequences, and Control* (pp. 428–436) by L. Berkowitz, 1993. New York: McGraw-Hill. Copyright © 1993 by McGraw-Hill, Inc. Reprinted by permission of The McGraw-Hill Companies.

356

Acknowledgments

14.1 From "Territorial Defense and the Good Neighbor" by R. Sommer and F. D. Becker, 1969, *Journal of Personality and Social Psychology, 11,* pp. 85, 87–92. Copyright © 1969 by The American Psychological Association. Reprinted by permission.

14.2 From "Environmental Noise Level as a Determinant of Helping Behavior" by K. E. Mathews, Jr., and L. K. Canon, 1975, *Journal of Personality and Social Psychology, 32,* pp. 571–577. Copyright © 1975 by The American Psychological Association. Reprinted by permission. Notes omitted.

14.3 From "Adjustment to Threatening Events: A Theory of Cognitive Adaptation" by S. E. Taylor, 1983, *American Psychologist, 38,* pp. 1161–1166, 1171–1173. Copyright © 1983 by The American Psychological Association. Reprinted by permission. Notes omitted.

Index